All the names you'll find here were given to people born in the USA between 1880 and 2023.

For this book, we've decided to present the most popular names of recent years. 5,000 names for girls and 5,000 names for boys.

Each name is accompanied by statistics and details of its origin and meaning, enabling you to better understand the essence of each name.

At the beginning of the book, you'll also find popularity rankings for names by origin.

All statistics are provided by the US government.

We sincerely hope that this book will help you find the right name for you.

TABLE OF CONTENTS

The most popular names of recent years.

Girl	1880 to 2023	2013 to 2023	2023	Boy	1880 to 2023	2013 to 2023	2023
OLIVIA	538,805	200,189	15,270	LIAM	315,184	214,306	20,802
EMMA	749,903	197,079	13,527	NOAH	488,429	207,547	18,995
SOPHIA	414,202	166,195	11,944	WILLIAM	4,178,180	155,309	10,598
AVA	327,483	156,114	9,682	JAMES	5,226,569	147,588	11,670
ISABELLA	395,255	154,524	10,808	ELIJAH	357,932	144,726	11,452
CHARLOTTE	427,311	135,158	12,596	BENJAMIN	807,016	141,273	10,172
AMELIA	255,502	125,256	12,311	OLIVER	239,415	140,978	14,741
ABIGAIL	402,659	105,287	5,661	MASON	329,640	138,920	7,237
EVELYN	621,387	104,917	9,082	LUCAS	309,990	131,859	10,842
HARPER	124,787	103,921	7,769	ETHAN	471,166	131,099	7,763
EMILY	884,942	101,528	6,154	MICHAEL	4,410,095	130,902	8,383
ELIZABETH	1,674,865	92,034	6,566	ALEXANDER	721,180	130,641	7,875
SOFIA	170,293	89,751	7,641	DANIEL	1,966,009	124,515	8,356
AVERY	159,008	86,206	5,859	LOGAN	376,005	119,548	6,686
MADISON	410,184	84,247	5,160	HENRY	745,172	115,192	10,941
CHLOE	241,654	77,747	5,960	AIDEN	246,290	115,024	6,675
CAMILA	109,596	75,574	7,565	JACKSON	283,583	113,264	7,284
SCARLETT	100,055	74,614	6,288	MATTHEW	1,639,789	112,569	7,190
GRACE	524,649	71,605	4,886	DAVID	3,662,190	107,960	7,354
ARIA	83,503	71,032	5,996	JOSEPH	2,654,627	107,871	7,237
VICTORIA	519,519	70,196	4,434	SAMUEL	803,262	106,787	7,973
LAYLA	118,366	69,264	5,678	SEBASTIAN	200,747	103,186	8,865
LILY	176,745	67,144	6,146	JAYDEN	244,036	101,865	5,627
PENELOPE	97,434	66,616	6,041	JOHN	5,166,241	101,633	7,750
HANNAH	457,525	61,729	4,102	OWEN	230,786	99,861	7,985
NORA	180,557	60,999	5,994	GABRIEL	382,625	97,151	6,745
ELEANOR	321,822	60,925	6,739	JACK	739,609	97,123	8,683
LILLIAN	467,088	60,880	3,927	LUKE	308,925	96,751	7,217
RILEY	132,790	60,781	4,617	CARTER	194,432	96,150	5,847
ZOE	151,810	58,732	5,160	LEVI	195,590	95,832	9,347

The most popular names since 1880.

Girl	1880 to 2023	2013 to 2023	2023
MARY	4,136,872	25,989	2,062
ELIZABETH	1,674,865	92,034	6,566
JENNIFER	1,470,608	10,981	583
LINDA	1,454,476	4,290	321
BARBARA	1,436,052	3,355	305
MARGARET	1,259,974	23,554	2,070
DOROTHY	1,110,746	5,666	658
SARAH	1,092,927	40,983	2,749
JESSICA	1,049,745	12,655	545
HELEN	1,022,786	8,317	768
NANCY	1,003,860	3,489	279
LISA	966,683	3,436	313
EMILY	884,942	101,528	6,154
SANDRA	875,083	3,148	233
ASHLEY	855,746	28,345	2,174
KIMBERLY	844,065	21,885	1,329
RUTH	832,503	14,237	1,594
MICHELLE	815,059	14,034	763
AMANDA	789,367	9,430	629
MELISSA	758,550	12,126	742
REBECCA	754,124	15,340	977
EMMA	749,903	197,079	13,527
STEPHANIE	744,014	12,010	654
DEBORAH	742,174	3,551	264
SHARON	722,645	2,610	173
KATHLEEN	713,209	3,421	246
CYNTHIA	710,869	4,900	306
SHIRLEY	686,089	1,722	137
VIRGINIA	651,766	6,209	535
KATHERINE	647,473	29,366	1,697

Boy	1880 to 2023	2013 to 2023	2023
JAMES	5,226,569	147,588	11,670
JOHN	5,166,241	101,633	7,750
ROBERT	4,841,968	57,808	3,807
MICHAEL	4,410,095	130,902	8,383
WILLIAM	4,178,180	155,309	10,598
DAVID	3,662,190	107,960	7,354
JOSEPH	2,654,627	107,871	7,237
RICHARD	2,574,402	24,226	1,638
CHARLES	2,423,009	72,515	5,395
THOMAS	2,344,940	75,291	6,598
CHRISTOPHER	2,059,620	85,647	5,171
DANIEL	1,966,009	124,515	8,356
MATTHEW	1,639,789	112,569	7,190
GEORGE	1,481,487	32,257	2,689
ANTHONY	1,475,541	95,702	6,237
DONALD	1,413,982	6,152	414
PAUL	1,395,583	18,319	1,351
ANDREW	1,320,002	86,421	4,781
EDWARD	1,300,350	24,245	1,723
STEVEN	1,290,496	22,915	1,387
JOSHUA	1,238,699	86,000	5,035
TIMOTHY	1,080,635	25,912	1,733
JEFFREY	978,431	10,976	617
RYAN	956,600	75,016	4,020
NICHOLAS	919,811	55,575	3,242
FRANK	914,732	9,106	646
STEPHEN	863,003	13,235	892
JONATHAN	862,870	66,542	4,066
BENJAMIN	807,016	141,273	10,172
SAMUEL	803,262	106,787	7,973

The most popular Native American names of recent years.

Girl	1880 to 2023	2013 to 2023	2023	Boy	1880 to 2023	2013 to 2023	2023
DAKOTA	39,241	13,661	1,183	KODA	5,457	4,217	771
NAYELI	22,526	8,489	929	TAKODA	1,689	565	45
CHEYENNE	70,116	7,434	354	KAWHI	369	369	23
YARITZA	8,312	2,534	183	COYOTE	127	104	19
TALLULAH	3,475	2,219	338	DYAMI	360	96	6
WINONA	12,099	1,380	305	CHEVEYO	157	89	0
SHYANNE	9,362	1,058	46	PECOS	46	30	0
SEQUOIA	3,764	845	80	NASHOBA	55	29	0
KAMIAH	1,694	797	41	DACODA	544	26	0
DENALI	1,624	785	75	SITKA	25	25	9
KATERI	2,460	518	41	WAKINYAN	39	21	9
ENOLA	2,983	330	70	AKICITA	11	11	0
TOPANGA	734	303	45	COCHISE	76	10	0
TENNESSEE	938	296	21	CHAYANNE	394	8	0
CHEROKEE	2,553	289	16	TECUMSEH	64	8	0
CATORI	321	195	27	WAKIYAN	7	7	0
CHENOA	1,713	148	7	QUANAH	192	6	0
HALONA	359	114	9	SAKONI	5	5	5
SHASTA	4,304	114	8	MOJAVE	5	5	0
TULSA	133	112	38	DAKOATA	25	0	0
CHYENNE	1,372	56	5	DECOTA	36	0	0
NAKOMA	83	46	0	DAYKOTA	6	0	0
AQUINNAH	107	32	0	OSCEOLA	61	0	0
SHANDIIN	162	25	0				
SHENANDOAH	342	22	0				
MANHATTAN	79	21	0				
POCAHONTAS	217	15	0				
WYOMING	23	12	7				
DKOTA	12	12	0				
NEBRASKA	42	10	5				

The most popular Hawaiian names of recent years.

Girl	1880 to 2023	2013 to 2023	2023	Boy	1880 to 2023	2013 to 2023	2023
LEILANI	49,255	27,973	3,543	KAI	62,078	39,280	4,946
ALANI	15,238	11,115	1,647	KEKOA	1,938	694	65
KEHLANI	10,506	10,506	1,854	MAKOA	1,095	677	125
KAILANI	10,404	8,341	1,315	KAIMANA	943	401	43
NOELANI	3,423	1,214	124	KANOA	818	293	43
ANUHEA	483	259	16	IKAIKA	1,018	266	23
HANALEI	252	167	15	KAWIKA	1,190	211	18
MIALANI	207	157	38	KAINALU	632	198	19
KAIULANI	435	146	12	KAHIAU	229	127	8
KAHEALANI	447	141	18	KEOKI	503	69	9
LILINOE	209	135	14	KANALOA	88	64	11
NOHEALANI	258	122	15	AUKAI	85	44	5
NEYLANI	109	109	46	KEAWE	136	42	11
LEILAHNI	108	103	26	KAPONO	197	38	5
MILILANI	123	103	8	KAIKANE	37	37	0
KHLANI	88	88	21	KAIKEA	59	35	0
MELEANA	270	85	5	KAHEKILI	43	26	0
TAIMANE	174	84	12	KAMAEHU	35	23	0
KAMALANI	286	79	12	HAAHEO	21	16	5
HEALANI	80	74	7	POOKELA	76	15	0
LILIKOI	70	46	0	KEALOHA	46	14	7
KEHAULANI	331	43	7	LOPAKA	134	10	0
LEIALOHA	102	42	5	KOAMALU	15	6	0
LANIAKEA	41	41	6	KEAHILANI	6	6	0
KAMAILE	210	41	0	KAIMIPONO	12	6	0
LOKELANI	135	34	5	ELIJAHKAI	5	5	0
OKALANI	39	33	6	KAIALEXANDER	5	5	0
KEALOHILANI	115	32	7	KAMAKANA	17	5	0
HOKULANI	122	32	5	KALAHIKIOLA	5	5	0
KEIHLANI	30	30	9	KAWAIOLA	5	0	0

The most popular English names of recent years

Girl	1880 to 2023	2013 to 2023	2023	Boy	1880 to 2023	2013 to 2023	2023
EVELYN	621,387	104,917	9,082	WILLIAM	4,178,180	155,309	10,598
AVERY	159,008	86,206	5,859	MASON	329,640	138,920	7,237
RILEY	132,790	60,781	4,617	JACKSON	283,583	113,264	7,284
VIOLET	170,954	56,252	6,342	JACK	739,609	97,123	8,683
HAZEL	289,743	53,216	6,154	CARTER	194,432	96,150	5,847
AUDREY	299,916	49,951	3,032	WYATT	195,253	94,069	6,237
WILLOW	55,552	41,868	4,727	GRAYSON	116,866	83,008	6,449
HAILEY	176,200	40,684	2,776	HUDSON	97,639	71,254	7,935
SERENITY	72,844	39,106	2,548	LINCOLN	95,565	69,261	4,842
IVY	72,183	37,536	5,036	HUNTER	256,506	67,785	3,110
EVERLY	37,616	36,634	3,159	LANDON	180,362	66,736	3,637
PIPER	58,861	35,324	2,066	COLTON	144,882	58,353	3,696
PEYTON	84,806	35,170	1,953	EASTON	72,847	53,433	3,637
ASHLEY	855,746	28,345	2,174	AUSTIN	431,550	52,771	3,475
FAITH	145,256	27,502	1,256	BRAYDEN	133,014	50,325	2,274
KIMBERLY	844,065	21,885	1,329	PARKER	123,801	49,118	3,792
SYDNEY	176,305	20,959	1,001	JAXSON	63,932	47,122	2,556
DAISY	152,365	20,877	2,412	CHASE	177,027	42,970	2,378
LAUREN	473,898	20,800	898	WESLEY	236,936	40,723	4,539
SUMMER	87,231	19,010	1,960	JAMESON	56,181	40,060	3,471
LONDYN	25,408	18,434	1,131	EVERETT	127,614	39,335	3,808
PAIGE	145,008	17,936	860	SAWYER	60,092	39,061	2,833
EVERLEIGH	17,414	16,847	1,920	WESTON	65,710	38,853	4,356
PRESLEY	29,030	16,804	1,517	BRYSON	78,282	38,688	2,434
KENDALL	64,599	16,786	978	BRANDON	767,558	38,566	1,654
EMERSYN	18,206	16,066	1,930	RYDER	61,154	38,490	2,822
MARLEY	30,968	15,391	1,104	BENTLEY	56,509	37,850	1,906
BLAKELY	17,253	14,834	1,854	HARRISON	93,076	35,447	3,060
DESTINY	150,625	14,547	704	WAYLON	44,700	33,202	4,881
EMBER	18,480	14,151	1,696	KINGSTON	42,497	32,579	2,511

The most popular French names of recent years.

Girl	1880 to 2023	2013 to 2023	2023	Boy	1880 to 2023	2013 to 2023	2023
CHARLOTTE	427,311	135,158	12,596	BEAU	55,698	30,274	4,090
AVERY	159,008	86,206	5,859	CORBIN	39,860	14,073	675
SCARLETT	100,055	74,614	6,288	TRAVIS	306,901	12,562	840
ELEANOR	321,822	60,925	6,739	HARVEY	125,067	8,030	1,022
CLAIRE	205,074	47,073	3,195	ROYCE	31,865	7,460	694
BRIELLE	45,698	28,702	2,064	DAX	11,076	6,496	519
JOCELYN	111,431	19,525	885	FORREST	51,977	5,845	737
REMI	18,831	16,343	2,170	TRIPP	7,798	5,395	671
NOELLE	41,484	14,743	1,451	CURTIS	260,052	4,653	255
JACQUELINE	425,018	10,235	560	LANCE	105,265	4,297	298
MADELEINE	44,330	9,969	688	JERMAINE	41,780	2,625	140
MALLORY	57,444	7,464	713	MAISON	4,266	2,587	160
ESME	8,965	6,894	944	LEROY	200,410	2,577	266
ANGELIQUE	29,740	4,231	254	BELLAMY	2,242	2,242	347
SYLVIE	6,473	4,113	725	DOMINIQUE	23,310	2,114	139
ESTELLE	55,421	3,790	395	GUY	90,414	1,552	111
MAVIS	21,939	3,624	501	JARVIS	17,595	1,300	91
DIOR	4,780	3,616	384	KORBEN	2,195	1,096	57
ELODIE	4,731	3,240	380	AMAURI	2,018	1,044	89
LANDRY	5,360	3,152	212	JACQUES	9,591	754	54
DESIREE	83,192	3,143	196	CROIX	1,068	700	55
SOLEIL	4,432	2,054	263	ARAMIS	2,178	543	47
ANNETTE	168,963	2,029	164	BEAUDEN	546	508	100
BERNADETTE	54,536	1,752	185	CHAUNCEY	9,619	508	30
MARGAUX	3,703	1,746	195	PERRIN	1,516	431	36
CHEVELLE	3,567	1,629	109	BEAUREGARD	555	346	42
NICOLETTE	16,912	1,458	108	PERCIVAL	1,260	334	63
YVETTE	63,788	1,402	111	ETIENNE	1,565	301	21
ODETTE	3,739	1,251	181	AVENIR	397	299	36
JAQUELINE	15,371	1,219	67	BLEU	300	272	55

The most popular Germanic names of recent years.

Girl	1880 to 2023	2013 to 2023	2023	Boy	1880 to 2023	2013 to 2023	2023
EMMA	749,903	197,079	13,527	HENRY	745,172	115,192	10,941
AMELIA	255,502	125,256	12,311	CHARLES	2,423,009	72,515	5,395
ALICE	581,028	37,784	3,336	ROBERT	4,841,968	57,808	3,807
ADELINE	73,177	31,320	3,074	LUIS	287,626	36,015	2,760
EMERY	37,399	29,260	3,104	CARLOS	301,917	32,626	2,546
ADALYNN	30,635	26,333	2,148	RICHARD	2,574,402	24,226	1,638
ELOISE	64,984	20,469	2,916	DEREK	236,496	15,966	1,238
GISELLE	48,498	12,918	887	LOUIS	403,535	14,576	1,474
ADELAIDE	32,773	12,369	1,103	RAYMOND	778,062	12,725	900
ANNALISE	15,709	8,181	719	JEFFREY	978,431	10,976	617
MATILDA	35,650	6,884	706	FRANK	914,732	9,106	646
LORELAI	8,531	5,723	650	OTTO	37,427	7,928	1,191
AUBRIE	14,805	5,651	231	HUGO	35,835	7,900	765
ZELDA	16,026	4,452	401	ENRIQUE	60,157	6,951	515
LINDA	1,454,476	4,290	321	ALBERT	490,910	6,712	481
ERIKA	125,225	3,511	237	GERARDO	54,127	6,549	486
EMMELINE	5,582	3,491	275	FREDERICK	264,569	6,518	595
FRIDA	8,164	3,383	209	RODRIGO	26,496	6,369	606
LANDRY	5,360	3,152	212	GUSTAVO	39,461	5,356	430
BELINDA	72,733	1,872	122	CONRAD	37,851	5,298	547
MARLIE	4,254	1,871	132	RICKY	222,572	4,401	269
BERNADETTE	54,536	1,752	185	BRUNO	18,140	4,199	373
ELOUISE	10,783	1,729	272	CARL	504,402	3,842	232
ANNELIESE	5,595	1,630	101	JEFFERY	230,276	2,940	153
ADALIE	2,218	1,576	160	REGINALD	111,224	2,771	192
GERALDINE	211,174	1,481	131	ALFONSO	40,984	2,762	224
WILHELMINA	12,840	1,314	139	KAISER	3,300	2,497	335
GRETCHEN	53,723	1,255	64	GILBERT	129,860	2,094	175
AUBREIGH	1,464	918	37	RODOLFO	33,523	1,932	129
LORALEI	1,688	796	52	FREDDY	26,521	1,805	157

The most popular Greek names of recent years.

Girl	1880 to 2023	2013 to 2023	2023
SOPHIA	414,202	166,195	11,944
SOFIA	170,293	89,751	7,641
CHLOE	241,654	77,747	5,960
PENELOPE	97,434	66,616	6,041
NORA	180,557	60,999	5,994
ZOE	151,810	58,732	5,160
GENESIS	86,155	43,504	3,651
ARIANA	115,541	42,523	2,716
ELENA	98,543	39,438	4,261
MELANIE	258,286	31,828	2,114
KATHERINE	647,473	29,366	1,697
ALEXANDRA	242,713	26,530	1,467
ATHENA	47,792	26,310	2,984
ALYSSA	313,099	24,601	927
IRIS	94,640	22,754	2,921
ANASTASIA	53,403	18,300	1,725
CALLIE	66,706	17,893	1,646
VANESSA	259,845	16,173	1,010
TESSA	53,887	13,869	960
EVANGELINE	33,002	13,482	1,407
PHOEBE	40,104	12,897	1,580
ELAINA	29,775	12,783	1,147
MELISSA	758,550	12,126	742
STEPHANIE	744,014	12,010	654
PARIS	32,510	10,554	618
DAPHNE	40,861	9,975	1,257
HELEN	1,022,786	8,317	768
KATHRYN	454,622	8,216	427
CHRISTINA	478,938	7,786	401
OPHELIA	23,343	7,770	1,166

Boy	1880 to 2023	2013 to 2023	2023
ALEXANDER	721,180	130,641	7,875
SEBASTIAN	200,747	103,186	8,865
ANDREW	1,320,002	86,421	4,781
CHRISTOPHER	2,059,620	85,647	5,171
THEODORE	291,668	75,731	11,041
ELIAS	112,664	57,886	6,980
NICHOLAS	919,811	55,575	3,242
DAMIAN	103,420	38,404	3,281
GEORGE	1,481,487	32,257	2,689
ALEX	282,866	28,120	1,806
JUDE	49,264	27,363	2,258
TIMOTHY	1,080,635	25,912	1,733
STEVEN	1,290,496	22,915	1,387
NICOLAS	97,504	22,216	1,886
XANDER	37,238	22,166	1,700
PETER	585,713	20,126	1,738
THEO	27,717	20,108	4,122
LEON	177,451	18,472	2,447
ATLAS	18,019	16,724	3,197
JORGE	137,191	16,328	1,221
KYRIE	15,646	14,838	1,474
PHOENIX	22,268	13,873	1,243
STEPHEN	863,003	13,235	892
ADONIS	18,388	12,200	2,093
HECTOR	107,064	11,340	828
ORION	21,020	10,722	861
TROY	215,166	10,352	662
NICO	17,522	10,338	1,462
DAMON	67,538	7,955	742
PHILIP	342,860	7,656	605

The most popular Italian names of recent years.

Girl	1880 to 2023	2013 to 2023	2023	Boy	1880 to 2023	2013 to 2023	2023
ARIA	83,503	71,032	5,996	GIOVANNI	83,403	32,492	2,911
GIANNA	98,496	50,905	6,129	ANTONIO	258,813	26,836	2,018
BELLA	79,007	41,844	2,540	LORENZO	79,603	24,649	2,810
SIENNA	35,085	17,619	1,989	EMILIANO	35,983	21,958	2,778
KIARA	54,409	11,122	1,302	ROMEO	24,519	10,464	1,123
BIANCA	76,277	8,786	659	SERGIO	80,347	10,402	782
FRANCESCA	33,346	8,084	820	ARMANI	14,042	7,499	822
GIULIANA	11,489	5,866	301	ALONZO	44,759	6,297	548
ALESSIA	8,112	5,817	1,021	SANTINO	11,768	6,103	752
ANTONELLA	8,143	5,648	1,092	ERNESTO	44,154	3,654	271
CAPRI	5,353	3,067	518	ALDO	17,257	3,612	238
AMERICA	13,293	2,141	97	JOVANNI	6,446	2,468	258
CHIARA	5,477	1,722	200	DEANGELO	12,082	1,968	136
SERAFINA	3,271	1,532	147	GIANLUCA	3,576	1,861	187
GIULIA	3,388	1,530	202	MASSIMO	3,504	1,617	288
MIABELLA	1,894	1,199	69	MONTE	22,905	1,211	120
ROSABELLA	1,116	825	58	GIUSEPPE	6,134	1,169	112
ALLEGRA	4,655	642	54	VITO	14,829	993	106
FIORELLA	1,484	622	54	GIORGIO	2,008	783	77
GIANELLA	964	545	98	FEDERICO	8,801	727	71
ROSETTA	28,062	481	37	STEFANO	3,036	599	69
VITTORIA	1,503	478	66	MICHELA-NGELO	1,263	586	44
ILARIA	688	425	52	PIETRO	2,346	386	41
FRANCHESCA	4,352	357	34	GIACOMO	1,810	345	37
BELLADONNA	410	232	20	DONATELLO	428	344	46
NICOLINA	1,773	216	15	MICHAEL-ANGELO	1,377	331	18
GUILIANA	515	203	12	LEOVANNI	333	316	52
GIANNINA	462	166	31	VALENTE	1,873	309	30
MICHELINA	2,156	153	20	ENRICO	4,715	281	22
VENEZIA	393	148	20	GIANMARCO	801	239	16

The most popular Irish names of recent years.

Girl	1880 to 2023	2013 to 2023	2023	Boy	1880 to 2023	2013 to 2023	2023
KENNEDY	87,810	42,052	3,069	LIAM	315,184	214,306	20,802
SLOANE	20,642	15,861	1,890	AIDEN	246,290	115,024	6,675
MAEVE	23,330	15,555	3,046	RYAN	956,600	75,016	4,020
ALAYNA	33,656	14,685	978	CONNOR	229,695	60,051	2,855
DELANEY	42,712	13,503	1,283	DECLAN	53,177	38,274	2,799
MCKENNA	42,712	13,281	940	DONOVAN	60,459	10,901	649
RAEGAN	23,936	12,254	729	KEEGAN	37,569	10,587	441
KIARA	54,409	11,122	1,302	RORY	32,465	10,506	1,442
KEIRA	32,860	10,553	519	DESMOND	38,287	10,288	789
CASSIDY	59,626	10,372	616	SHANE	191,658	9,769	525
RYLIE	21,978	9,236	544	GRADY	50,732	9,250	800
COLLINS	8,251	7,650	1,269	SHAWN	305,679	8,654	436
KELLY	473,327	5,699	362	SULLIVAN	13,529	8,479	914
MONROE	6,070	5,248	571	FINNEGAN	11,811	7,956	608
BRIDGET	91,582	4,941	375	CASEY	114,482	6,956	1,050
EILEEN	188,659	4,580	444	BRENDAN	91,386	6,115	261
KATHLEEN	713,209	3,421	246	DILLON	64,686	5,850	334
BREANNA	82,186	3,166	119	BRADEN	45,891	5,566	187
SAOIRSE	3,596	2,866	270	BRENNAN	32,821	5,172	212
CAITLIN	111,944	2,806	80	BODIE	6,349	4,260	822
SHAYLA	30,701	2,706	130	NEIL	104,299	4,215	302
MURPHY	3,249	2,440	582	BRAYAN	15,831	3,909	282
AISLINN	5,240	2,381	163	KYLIAN	2,606	2,550	948
SHEA	12,163	2,352	246	DWAYNE	76,491	2,378	140
IRELAND	6,155	2,211	100	COLEMAN	17,297	2,305	176
DARCY	22,833	2,205	245	BROGAN	4,094	1,209	57
KALEIGH	16,122	1,923	78	FINNICK	1,201	1,192	157
SHEILA	238,606	1,307	101	KEYON	5,780	1,064	76
KACIE	12,566	1,216	89	NOLEN	3,329	830	52
AOIFE	2,007	1,080	88	NIALL	1,885	796	88

The most popular Portuguese names of recent years.

Girl	1880 to 2023	2013 to 2023	2023
MANUELA	10,871	825	72
MARIAFE-RNANDA	1,122	331	22
BRAZIL	601	326	33
MARIAED-UARDA	252	88	7
EVORA	301	66	11
ANACRISTINA	229	10	0
MARIAVITORIA	5	5	5
MARGARIDA	27	0	0
MARIADE-LOURDES	17	0	0
BENVINDA	5	0	0
ARMELINDA	17	0	0
DEOLINDA	243	0	0
ALMERINDA	35	0	0
MADEIRA	27	0	0
ANABEATRIZ	12	0	0

Boy	1880 to 2023	2013 to 2023	2023
MIGUEL	186,938	25,294	1,883
THIAGO	24,047	22,668	4,505
FRANCISCO	139,992	14,737	1,121
RICARDO	144,736	12,539	873
PEDRO	92,587	8,952	753
VICENTE	21,010	3,777	441
ALVARO	16,696	3,031	369
RAMIRO	25,547	2,260	171
NEYMAR	2,782	2,235	87
TIAGO	2,854	1,692	212
SANTHIAGO	465	440	64
CARLITO	1,314	365	13
JOSEMANUEL	1,266	258	12
TAVARES	2,950	211	9
EDERSON	187	161	40
JOAOPEDRO	225	80	6
HERMINIO	1,414	64	7
LUISFERNANDO	306	47	0
JORGELUIS	401	36	0
JOAOLUCAS	35	35	7
JOSIMAR	97	30	0
PEDROHE-NRIQUE	114	23	5
JOAOMIGUEL	17	17	7
MONTERIO	316	15	0
LOBO	14	14	0
JOAOGABRIEL	16	10	5
JOAOVICTOR	127	6	0
AFONSO	10	5	0
EPITACIO	11	0	0
CABRAL	5	0	0

The most popular Spanish names of recent years.

Girl	1880 to 2023	2013 to 2023	2023
XIMENA	36,208	24,737	1,809
ESMERALDA	49,842	9,120	904
ALONDRA	41,359	8,247	577
ALORA	8,887	5,585	1,488
REYNA	17,596	5,102	520
XIOMARA	10,851	4,432	761
GUADALUPE	66,483	4,283	246
DULCE	19,509	4,140	360
TERESA	415,423	4,130	320
ESTRELLA	15,834	4,023	424
PALOMA	10,146	3,284	262
ESPERANZA	20,403	2,892	258
ARACELI	19,509	2,782	348
MERCEDES	45,896	2,467	157
MIREYA	9,503	2,022	196
CIELO	4,073	1,830	309
YESENIA	39,223	1,727	132
LITZY	7,044	1,652	113
MILAGROS	10,148	1,648	168
AZUL	4,195	1,581	169
VALENCIA	11,892	1,523	179
MARIBEL	24,618	1,516	141
LETICIA	42,746	1,495	124
LUCERO	7,463	1,485	149
MONTANA	8,334	1,465	174
ESTEFANIA	6,859	1,353	112
SOLANA	2,433	1,300	283
GRACIELA	16,100	1,261	94
ROSALINDA	15,459	1,113	104
MARIAJOSE	2,403	1,110	79

Boy	1880 to 2023	2013 to 2023	2023
MATEO	104,179	83,698	11,229
SANTIAGO	88,788	49,426	6,328
JUAN	360,602	33,284	2,526
DIEGO	121,245	33,024	2,734
CARLOS	301,917	32,626	2,546
ANTONIO	258,813	26,836	2,018
MIGUEL	186,938	25,294	1,883
ALEJANDRO	142,747	22,913	1,825
THIAGO	24,047	22,668	4,505
EMILIANO	35,983	21,958	2,778
JORGE	137,191	16,328	1,221
FRANCISCO	139,992	14,737	1,121
ARLO	19,288	14,305	2,297
CRISTIAN	67,923	12,931	1,024
RICARDO	144,736	12,539	873
FERNANDO	101,353	12,505	967
CRUZ	28,633	11,940	1,012
JOAQUIN	33,646	11,129	997
SERGIO	80,347	10,402	782
LEONEL	25,031	9,721	1,070
PEDRO	92,587	8,952	753
ESTEBAN	34,222	7,943	698
ENRIQUE	60,157	6,951	515
GERARDO	54,127	6,549	486
ALONZO	44,759	6,297	548
JAIME	70,590	6,167	490
GUSTAVO	39,461	5,356	430
SALVADOR	48,892	4,419	378
VICENTE	21,010	3,777	441
SANTANA	7,179	3,725	401

The most popular African names of recent years.

Girl	1880 to 2023	2013 to 2023	2023	Boy	1880 to 2023	2013 to 2023	2023
ZENDAYA	3,387	3,241	328	ZAIRE	8,204	4,585	654
JHENE	1,435	1,385	213	JAKARI	4,418	2,450	398
FATOUMATA	2,319	926	103	TRAYVON	3,357	754	45
AMINATA	2,161	868	68	JAHEIM	3,958	748	61
MALAIKA	2,498	694	72	MAMADOU	1,723	673	62
XOLANI	618	587	176	SHAQUILLE	5,698	525	28
NUBIA	2,344	532	61	OUSMANE	641	305	46
FATOU	1,111	393	44	SEKOU	1,059	268	22
AISSATOU	871	358	53	TYRIQUE	1,892	231	23
OUMOU	690	341	20	ABOUBACAR	431	196	25
FANTA	1,103	295	30	SHAQUAN	2,110	158	12
KADIATOU	544	235	25	ASKARI	258	148	18
KEYSHA	1,905	218	26	SIMBA	145	125	28
ZYIAH	234	150	16	MOROCCO	134	120	14
XOLA	156	144	26	AMAZI	109	109	58
NDEYE	475	135	20	ALIEU	216	102	11
SOKHNA	273	130	17	MAHAMADOU	380	101	8
AFRICA	1,029	113	12	BABACAR	207	88	5
RAMATOULAYE	185	85	5	TYKEEM	378	88	5
SALIMATA	177	82	0	SHOMARI	1,114	82	0
SEYNABOU	189	79	9	CHEICK	190	80	10
SAFIATOU	131	72	9	EBRIMA	248	66	0
NIGERIA	805	67	0	ALIOUNE	170	63	5
NYOTA	83	64	13	SALIOU	129	59	5
DJENEBA	150	58	8	NKOSI	367	59	0
ROKHAYA	128	46	7	ELHADJI	163	58	6
NZINGA	325	46	0	SAFAREE	52	52	6
DJUNA	375	41	6	JADEVEON	51	51	0
MAZURI	39	39	24	SIAIRE	44	44	17
AMAHLE	37	37	17	ALASSANE	137	41	7

The most popular Arabic names of recent years.

Girl	1880 to 2023	2013 to 2023	2023
LAYLA	118,366	69,264	5,678
AALIYAH	104,561	44,676	2,845
ALAIA	12,923	12,504	2,300
FATIMA	37,028	10,620	893
SAMARA	20,796	9,296	1,190
NADIA	45,413	8,986	622
NYLAH	12,443	8,446	804
AISHA	25,116	6,721	809
MARYAM	12,165	6,439	738
AMIRAH	9,570	5,145	669
ZAHRA	8,271	4,848	543
ZANIYAH	6,770	3,841	382
YAMILETH	6,104	3,217	292
ZAINAB	6,668	3,181	306
JAIDA	9,550	2,279	73
DIYA	4,836	2,043	119
KHADIJA	4,780	2,007	201
NAHLA	3,109	1,842	81
YUNA	2,560	1,722	198
ALEIGHA	4,738	1,693	68
AYESHA	6,372	1,683	161
YUSRA	2,340	1,527	201
NAIMA	4,575	1,491	101
ALAIYAH	1,836	1,392	175
HAFSA	2,303	1,248	151
YASMEEN	5,960	1,147	98
RANIA	2,969	994	78
NOUR	2,630	987	106
SAIRA	3,467	952	89
SUMAYA	1,999	923	75

Boy	1880 to 2023	2013 to 2023	2023
AMIR	48,765	29,562	3,620
MUHAMMAD	19,030	10,701	1,237
KHALIL	23,348	9,650	979
ZAYN	10,304	9,596	1,413
MALIK	48,119	9,386	831
IBRAHIM	16,041	8,097	774
MOHAMED	18,236	6,731	542
AHMED	16,501	5,374	419
HAMZA	9,450	4,793	523
KAREEM	17,368	4,076	441
ABDULLAH	8,725	3,756	330
HASSAN	11,419	3,457	388
YOUSEF	6,323	3,162	297
MUSA	4,884	3,121	414
JAMAL	32,886	3,085	211
MUSTAFA	6,727	2,617	263
IDRIS	4,290	2,471	319
ZAHIR	4,073	2,460	344
IMRAN	4,088	2,165	241
KABIR	3,128	2,154	213
RASHAD	16,056	2,018	108
HAKEEM	6,020	1,900	176
RAHEEM	8,259	1,777	157
NAZIR	3,512	1,717	209
JAHMIR	3,012	1,706	302
SYED	5,759	1,568	144
TAHJ	3,697	1,565	140
OSMAN	3,493	1,549	221
ISMAIL	3,655	1,525	132
YASIR	2,889	1,466	162

The most popular Persian names of recent years.

Girl	1880 to 2023	2013 to 2023	2023	Boy	1880 to 2023	2013 to 2023	2023
ARIANA	115,541	42,523	2,716	ARSALAN	585	321	73
JASMINE	255,544	24,999	1,585	MEHTAB	244	205	30
DAYANA	14,584	5,896	627	DASTAN	309	192	10
SORAYA	6,205	2,261	212	DARIOUS	1,544	173	12
YAZMIN	9,101	1,615	128	SHAHZAIN	180	164	24
AZARI	1,376	1,120	413	KEYVON	654	161	14
ARIYANA	3,334	1,036	62	OMID	771	161	14
RUHI	1,137	795	78	DARYAN	544	160	15
SITARA	662	407	75	XERXES	268	152	16
NAZLI	307	209	27	SARTAJ	232	145	11
MAHSA	278	205	35	FARAZ	647	108	12
ANAHITA	466	196	15	KAVEH	403	97	13
PERSIA	775	179	7	FARZAD	140	55	0
NAZANIN	214	143	22	NICKAN	58	53	0
SHIRIN	774	143	10	AFRAZ	76	47	10
DELARA	173	139	28	MUHAMMA-DJON	44	44	12
YASNA	128	123	27	KOUROSH	180	41	0
ELHAM	330	118	15	ERFAN	39	39	5
SETAYESH	106	96	23	SHEHBAAZ	38	38	7
SETAREH	225	96	0	BEHRUZ	34	34	0
NASREEN	371	89	11	ASHKAN	231	32	5
FARYAL	144	74	5	SHEHZAD	65	31	17
BANEEN	144	69	6	ARSHAWN	113	30	0
FARZONA	68	68	0	ALIREZA	233	30	0
YASEMIN	442	64	7	DARIUSH	144	28	8
YALDA	108	57	13	SAEID	33	28	7
MAHROSH	74	50	0	JAHONGIR	33	28	0
KHEUMANI	41	41	26	ROSTAM	24	24	14
MEHNAZ	41	36	6	SOHRAB	85	22	5
AZADEH	170	36	5	SARFARAZ	21	21	0

The most popular Asian names of recent years.

Girl	1880 to 2023	2013 to 2023	2023	Boy	1880 to 2023	2013 to 2023	2023
MAYA	115,577	43,903	4,067	BODHI	11,856	10,215	1,117
ANAYA	16,290	8,406	784	KOBE	21,128	7,871	753
ANIKA	16,216	4,794	284	KASEN	10,233	6,876	497
OPAL	72,090	4,108	624	RONIN	9,043	6,747	638
TORI	36,799	3,504	202	ARJUN	11,070	6,031	469
KAIYA	8,009	3,171	351	VIHAAN	5,123	4,119	280
INDIE	3,497	3,168	514	REYANSH	2,838	2,527	142
AADHYA	2,931	2,713	255	DHRUV	4,079	1,952	189
SAANVI	4,394	2,678	267	RISHI	4,741	1,644	228
KARMA	7,314	2,267	197	JIRAIYA	1,792	1,636	357
RITA	284,112	1,991	164	ATHARV	1,974	1,630	222
PRISHA	2,660	1,771	170	ADITYA	5,247	1,447	78
SHANAYA	2,961	1,759	128	KAIZEN	1,534	1,408	486
YUNA	2,560	1,722	198	KANAN	1,427	1,199	197
PRIYA	6,352	1,645	124	SIDDHARTH	3,204	1,199	64
ANANYA	3,878	1,542	69	PRANAV	4,106	1,166	65
SHREYA	4,905	1,331	72	NIKHIL	5,307	1,016	44
AKSHARA	1,829	1,262	69	SHAURYA	1,463	996	87
ANJALI	5,681	1,219	73	AGASTYA	1,149	957	159
KIYOMI	1,641	1,057	186	AYANSH	914	897	95
INDIANA	1,922	985	97	SHIVANSH	946	877	122
NIRVANA	1,471	918	99	SHIV	2,008	843	90
SAHASRA	1,587	894	61	KRISHIV	929	750	162
EMORI	1,109	890	135	DEVANSH	861	708	67
AHANA	1,154	870	72	ABHIRAM	1,214	678	53
AARADHYA	874	836	64	ADVAITH	985	677	56
SURY	1,349	834	83	KRISHNA	2,258	671	53
AASHVI	871	789	136	SHLOK	971	631	47
AMBAR	2,794	701	92	VEDANT	1,182	614	80
SWARA	872	697	44	HIRO	798	601	60

Our predictions for 2025.

#	Girl name		#	Boy name
1	OLIVIA		1	LIAM
2	EMMA		2	NOAH
3	CHARLOTTE		3	OLIVER
4	AMELIA		4	JAMES
5	SOPHIA		5	ELIJAH
6	ISABELLA		6	MATEO
7	AVA		7	THEODORE
8	EVELYN		8	HENRY
9	HARPER		9	LUCAS
10	SOFIA		10	WILLIAM
11	CAMILA		11	BENJAMIN
12	ELEANOR		12	LEVI
13	ELIZABETH		13	SEBASTIAN
14	VIOLET		14	JACK
15	SCARLETT		15	EZRA
16	EMILY		16	MICHAEL
17	HAZEL		17	DANIEL
18	LILY		18	OWEN
19	GIANNA		19	SAMUEL
20	AURORA		20	HUDSON
21	PENELOPE		21	ALEXANDER
22	ARIA		22	ASHER
23	NORA		23	ETHAN
24	CHLOE		24	JOHN
25	AVERY		25	DAVID
26	LAYLA		26	JACKSON
27	ABIGAIL		27	MASON
28	ISLA		28	JOSEPH
29	MADISON		29	LUKE
30	ZOE		30	MATTHEW

1,000 most popular names for girls.

AADHYA Means "the first power" or "the primeval power" and it originates from Sanskrit, a classical language of India.

AALIYAH Means "exalted" or "noble" and originates from Arabic.

AARADHYA Means "worshiped" or "one who is adored" and has Sanskrit origins.

AASHVI Indian origin and means "blessed and victorious."

ABIGAIL Means "my father's joy" and originates from Hebrew.

ABIGALE Means "my father is joyful" and it originates from the Hebrew name Avigayil.

ACACIA Means "thorny tree" and has origins in Greek and Hebrew.

ADALEIGH English origin and means "noble pasture."

ADALIE The first name Adalie is of German origin and means "noble."

ADALYNN Means "noble beauty" and originated as a combination of the Germanic element "adal" meaning noble, and "lynn" a variant of "lin" meaning beautiful.

ADAMARIS Means "beautiful" or "lovely" and it has Latin origins.

ADARA Means "noble" or "virgin" and has Hebrew origins.

ADDISYN Modern and variant spelling of the name Addison, derived from a surname meaning "son/descendant of Adam" in English origin.

ADDYSON Means "son of Adam" and originated from the English surname Addison.

ADELAIDE Means "noble and kind" and has Germanic origins.

ADELINE Means "noble" or "nobility" and originates from Germany.

ADHARA Means "virgin" or "pure" and originates from the Arabic language.

ADILENE Feminine given name of uncertain origin, possibly a variation of the name Adeline or a combination of Ada and the suffix -lene.

ADLEY Unisex name of English origin, meaning "one who is just and honorable."

ADORE Means "to love and admire greatly" and has origins in Latin.

AERIS Means "air" or "goddess of the air" and originates from the Latin word "aer" meaning "air."

AFTON Means "from the aftershine" and has English and Scottish origins.

AGATHA Means "good" or "kind" and originates from the Greek name "Agathe."

AGNES Means "pure" or "chaste" and originated from the Greek name "Hagne," derived from the hagnos, meaning "pure, holy, or chaste."

AHANA Means "first rays of the sun" and originates from the Sanskrit language.

AHUVA Means "beloved" in Hebrew and has an origin in the Jewish religion.

AINARA Means "swallow; bird" and it is of Basque origin.

AINHOA Basque feminine name originating from the town of Ainhoa in France, meaning "swift."

AISHA Means "alive" or "living" and originates from Arabic.

AISLINN Means "vision" or "dream" and originated from Irish Gaelic.

AITANA Means "glory" or "radiance" and originates from the Basque language.

AIYLA Ayla is a feminine given name of Hebrew origin meaning "oak tree" or "halo of light."

AKSHARA Means "imperishable" or "indestructible" and has its origin in Sanskrit.

ALAHNI The first name Alahni is an invented name of uncertain origin and meaning.

ALAIA Means "joyful" or "exalted" and has Arabic origins.

ALAIYAH Arabic origin and means "exalted" or "sublime."

ALANI Means "orange tree" or "serenity" and has Hawaiian and Polynesian origins.

ALASKA Means "great land" and originates from the Aleut word "alaxsxaq."

ALAURA Modern American feminine given name derived from the combining of the names Alana and Laura, meaning "harmony" or "peaceful beauty."

ALAYNA	Means "fair one" and has origins in various cultures, including English, Irish, and Scottish.
ALEIDA	Means "noble, majestic" and has Dutch and Spanish origins.
ALEIGHA	Modern variation of the name Aaliyah, derived from Arabic origins meaning "exalted, noble."
ALEKSANDRA	The first name Aleksandra, of Slavic origin, means "defender of mankind."
ALESSIA	Means "defender" or "defender of mankind" and has Italian origin.
ALETHEA	Means "truth" in Greek and has origins in Greek mythology as well as being a variant of the name Aletheia, which was the Greek personification of truth.
ALEXANDRA	Means "defender of mankind" and originates from Greek origins.
ALEXIS	Means "defender" or "helper" and originates from Ancient Greece.
ALICE	Means "noble" or "of noble kind" and is of Old French and Germanic origin.
ALISHA	Feminine given name of Arabic origin meaning "noble" or "protected by God."
ALITZEL	The meaning and origin of the first name Alitzel is "noble princess" and it originated from the indigenous Nahuatl language in Mexico.
ALLEGRA	Means "joyful" and has Italian origins.
ALLISON	Means "noble kind" or "son of Alice" and is of English and Scottish origin.
ALMA	Means "soul" or "kind-hearted" and has Latin origins.
ALONDRA	Means "lark" in Spanish and it originated from ancient Greek.
ALORA	Means "my dream" or "my dream come true" and has uncertain origins, possibly stemming from various sources including the Spanish name Alondra meaning "lark" or a combination of names like Alice and Laura.
ALTHEA	Means "healer" or "wholesome" and is of Greek origin.
ALYSSA	Means "noble" or "rational" and it is of Greek origin.
ALYVIA	Means "olive tree" and has English origin.
AMAIRA	Arabic origin and means "princess" or "commander."
AMANDA	Means "lovable" or "worthy of love" and originates from Latin.
AMARIANA	The name Amariana originated from the combination of the names Amara and Ariana, and it means "eternally beautiful."
AMARYLLIS	Means "sparkling" or "to sparkle" and originates from Greek mythology, associated with a shepherdess who loved a shepherd named Alteo.
AMBAR	Means "sky" or "amber" and is of Arabic and Sanskrit origin.
AMELIA	Means "work" or "industrious" in Latin, and it originated from the Germanic name Amalia.
AMERICA	The meaning of the first name America is derived from the Latin word "Americus" meaning "ruler of the home," and it originated as a feminine form of the name Amerigo, which was famously associated with Italian explorer Amerigo Vespucci, who explored the
AMETHYST	Means "a violet variety of quartz" and has its origin in Greek mythology.
AMINATA	The first name Aminata is of African origin and means "trustworthy" or "faithful".
AMIRAH	Means "princess" or "noblewoman" and originates from Arabic.
AMOURA	Arabic origin and means "beloved" or "loved one."
ANAHI	The name Anahi originates from the indigenous Guarani people of South America and means "beautiful soul."
ANAIS	Means "grace" or "favor" and originated from ancient Greek.
ANAISHA	The first name Anaisha is of American origin and it means "special, unique, or one of a kind."
ANALIAH	Hebrew origin, meaning "God has answered" or "grace" and it is predominantly used in the United States.
ANALIYAH	Modern feminine name of Hebrew origin, meaning "grace of God" or "answered prayer."
ANANYA	Means "unique, matchless" and originates from the Sanskrit language in India.
ANASOFIA	Means "gracious wisdom" and originates from the combination of the names Ana and Sofia, which both have Hebrew and Greek origins.
ANASTASIA	Means "resurrection" and originates from ancient Greek.
ANAYA	Female name of Indian origin meaning "caring, compassion, kindness."
ANDROMEDA	Means "ruler of men" and originates from Greek mythology, referring to the princess who was saved from a sea monster by the hero Perseus.

ANGELINA The first name Angelina originated from the Latin name Angelus, meaning "angel" or "messenger of God," and it is commonly used in various cultures worldwide.

ANGELIQUE Means "angelic" and it has its origins in French.

ANGIE Means "messenger" and originates from the Greek name Angelos.

ANIKA Means "grace" or "favor" in several cultures, and it originated from various origins including Hebrew, Indian, and Dutch.

ANIYLAH The name Aniyah is of Hebrew origin and means "caring" or "compassionate."

ANJALI Means "divine offering" in Sanskrit and is of Indian origin.

ANNABELLE English origin and means "loving and graceful," often associated with beauty and elegance.

ANNABETH Feminine given name of English origin, derived from the combination of the names Anna and Beth, meaning "gracious meadow or house of grace."

ANNALISE Means "graceful" or "favor" and originated from Germany or Scandinavia.

ANNAMARIE Italian and German origin, meaning "grace" or "favor" in Latin, and combines the names Anna and Marie.

ANNELIESE Means "grace" or "favor" and has German origins.

ANNETTE Means "grace" and it originates from French and Hebrew.

ANNISTON Means "town by the stream" and has English origins.

ANSLEIGH English origin and means "meadow of the noble ones" or "clearing of the nobles".

ANTOINETTE Means "priceless" or "of inestimable worth" and it is of French origin.

ANTONELLA Means "priceless" and originates from Italian.

ANYA The name Anya, meaning "grace" or "favor," originated from ancient Russia and is a diminutive form of Anna or Anne.

AOIFE Traditional Irish name meaning "beautiful" or "radiant," originating from Irish mythology.

APRIL Means "to open" or "beginning" and has its origin from the Latin word "aprilis," referring to the month of April in the Roman calendar, symbolizing the start of spring.

ARABELLA Feminine given name of Latin origin, meaning "yielding to prayer" or "beautiful altar."

ARACELI Means "altar of the sky" and is of Spanish origin.

ARANTZA Basque feminine name meaning "thornbush" or "thorny shrub," derived from the Basque word "arantza."

ARANZA The name Aranza originated in Mexico and means "altar of grace" or "altar of flowers."

ARIA Italian origin, means "air" or "melody" and is also associated with a musical piece characterized by a vocal solo.

ARIADNE Means "most holy" and it originates from Greek mythology, specifically from the story of Theseus and the Minotaur.

ARIANA Means "most holy" or "very holy" and has Persian and Greek origins.

ARIELLA Means "lioness of God" and originates from Hebrew.

ARISBETH The name Arisbeth originated as a combination of the names Aris and Beth, and it means "gift of God" or "pledged to God."

ARIYANA Means "noble" or "holy" and is of Persian origin.

ARIZONA Means "small spring" or "place of the small spring" and originates from the native American Navajo language.

ARLETH Means "pledge" and derives from the English language.

ARTEMIS Means "goddess of the hunt" and it originates from Greek mythology.

ARWEN Means "noble maiden" and originates from the Elvish language created by J.R.R. Tolkien in his fantasy works such as "The Lord of the Rings."

ASHANTI Means "people of Ashanti" and originates from the Akan ethnic group in Ghana.

ASHLEIGH Means "meadow of ash trees" and originated from an English surname derived from a place name.

ASHLEY Old English origin, means "meadow of ash trees" and is traditionally a gender-neutral name, now more commonly used for girls.

ASHLYN Modern English name of uncertain origin, possibly derived from Ashley and Lynn and may mean "ash tree lake" or "dream".

ASPEN Means "from the tree" and is of American origin.

ASTRID Means "divinely beautiful" and originates from Old Norse.

ATHENA Means "goddess of wisdom and war" and originates from Greek mythology.

AUBREIGH Means "ruler of elves" and it is a variant of the name Aubrey, which originated from the Germanic name Alberich.

AUBRIE Means "noble ruler," and it is derived from the Germanic name Alberich.

AUBRIELLE The name Aubrielle originates from the combination of the names Aubrey and Gabrielle, and it means "noble strength."

AUDREY Means "noble strength" and originates from Old English.

AUDRIANA Means "noble strength" and it is a feminine form of the name Adrian, originating from Latin.

AUDRINA Means "noble strength" and is of Old English origin.

AURELIA Means "golden" and it originates from Latin.

AURORA Means "dawn" and originates from the Latin word "aurora" which also means "dawn" or "morning light."

AUTUMN Means "season of harvest" and it originates from the Latin word "autumnus."

AVA The name "Ava" meaning "life" or "like a bird" originated as a variant of Eve in the Middle Ages.

AVALON The name Avalon originates from Arthurian legend and means "island of apples" or "island of paradise."

AVEAH Modern invented name with no specific meaning or origin, often chosen as a variation of the name Ava.

AVERY Means "ruler of elves" and has both English and French origins.

AVONLEA Feminine first name of Irish origin meaning "meadow of the river" or "river island."

AVYANNA Modern American name derived from the combination of the names Ava and Yanna, and it has no specific meaning.

AYALA Hebrew origin and means "doe" or "female deer".

AYESHA Means "alive" or "she who lives" in Arabic and originates from Islamic tradition, specifically from the wife of the Prophet Muhammad.

AYLIN Turkish origin and it means "moon halo" or "halo around the moon".

AYVAH Means "life" and it has Hebrew origins.

AZALEA Means "dry" or "flower" in Greek and is derived from a type of flower called Azalea, which is native to Asia and North America.

AZARI Persian origin, means "royal" or "powerful."

AZARIAH Means "Yahweh has helped" and has Hebrew origins.

AZARIYAH Means "Yahweh has helped" and has Hebrew origins.

AZENETH Spanish variant of the Greek name Asenath, meaning "belonging to the goddess Neith" and it is of biblical origin.

AZUL Means "blue" in Spanish and it is of Spanish and Portuguese origin.

BAILA Hebrew name meaning "dance" or "rejoice," commonly used in Jewish communities.

BAILEIGH Variant spelling of the name Bailey, which originated from an English surname meaning "bailiff" or "steward."

BARBARA Means "foreign" or "strange" and originated from Greek.

BATSHEVA Means "daughter of Sheba" and originates from Hebrew.

BAYLIE Means "bailiff" or "steward" and originated from the Middle English word "bai(l)i(e)" derived from the Old French word "bailif."

BEATRICE Means "bringer of happiness" and originates from Latin.

BELINDA Means "beautiful serpent" and it originated from Italian/Portuguese forms of the Germanic name, Betlinde.

BELLA Means "beautiful" and it is of Italian and Latin origin.

BELLAROSE Means "beautiful rose" and likely originated as a combination or variation of the names Bella and Rose.

BERENICE Means "bearer of victory" and it originates from ancient Greek.

BERKELEY The name Berkeley originates from Old English and means "birch wood or meadow of birch trees."

BERKLEY Means "from the birch tree meadow" and has English origins.

BERNADETTE Means "brave as a bear" and it originated from Germanic or Old French.

BERNICE	Means "victory bringer" and originates from Greek and biblical sources.
BETHANY	Means "house of figs" and originated from the Hebrew language.
BETHEL	Means "house of God" and originates from Hebrew.
BETSY	The name Betsy is an English diminutive form of Elizabeth, meaning 'God is abundance' or 'pledged to God', and it originated from Hebrew.
BEXLEY	Means "from the clearing of box trees" and it originated from the English surname Bexley, derived from a place name in Kent, England.
BIANCA	The name Bianca originated from Italian and means "white" or "pure."
BIRDIE	Means "little bird" and has origins in English and Scottish.
BLAKELEIGH	The first name Blakeleigh is of English origin and means "meadow of dark-haired ones."
BLAKELY	Unisex name of English origin, meaning "dark wood or dark clearing" and became popular as a given name in the late 20th century.
BLAYKE	Means "dark-haired" and it is a modern variant of the English name Blake.
BLESSING	Means "a divine gift or favor" and originates from English-speaking countries.
BLOSSOM	Means "flower or blooming" and originated from Old English.
BLYTHE	Means "cheerful" or "carefree" and originated from an English surname derived from Old English blīðe, meaning "happy" or "joyous."
BRACHA	Hebrew origin, means "blessing" or "one who brings blessings."
BRAILYNN	Modern American invention, likely combining the elements Bray and Lynn, and does not have a widely recognized meaning.
BRAYLEIGH	The name Brayleigh originated as a phonetic variation of the English name Brayden and means "broad meadow" or "dweller near the broad meadow."
BREANNA	Means "noble" or "strong" and originates from the Irish name Brianna, derived from the masculine name Brian.
BRELYNN	American origin and means "strong and beautiful" or "beautiful raven."
BRIDGET	Means "exalted one" and originates from the Irish and Gaelic language.
BRIELLE	Means "God is my strength" and is of French origin.
BRIGHTON	Means "bright town" and has English origins.
BRIGITTE	Means "exalted, divine" and originates from the Celtic name Brigid, which was associated with the goddess of fire in Irish mythology.
BRILEE	Means "strong-willed" and has American roots.
BRISEIDA	The first name Briseida originates from Greek mythology and means "daughter of Briseus," referring to the daughter of a Trojan prince who was captured by Achilles during the Trojan War.
BRISTOL	Means "meeting place by the bridge" and originated from Old English.
BRITNEY	The first name Britney is of English origin and means "from Britain" or "someone who comes from England."
BRITTANY	Means "from the region of Brittany" and it originates from the Celtic language.
BROOKELYNN	The meaning of the first name Brookelynn is "dweller near the brook" and it is a modern invented name composed of the elements "brook" and "-lynn".
BROOKLYN	Means "broken land" and it originated as a surname referencing the borough of Brooklyn in New York City.
BRYNLEE	Means "hill with brooks" and originates from Welsh and English roots.
BRYNLEIGH	Modern feminine name of American origin, derived from the combination of Bryn and Leigh, meaning "hill" and "meadow."
CADENCE	Means "rhythm" or "flow" and has Latin origins.
CAITLIN	Means "pure" and it originated from the Irish Gaelic name Cáitlín, a variant of Catherine or Katherine.
CALISTA	Means "most beautiful" and is of Greek origin.
CALLIE	Feminine given name of Greek origin meaning "beautiful" or "most beautiful".
CALLIOPE	Means "beautiful voice" and originates from Greek mythology, where Calliope was the Muse of epic poetry and eloquence.
CAMBRIA	The name Cambria originates from Wales and means "place of the Celtic warriors."
CAMILA	Means "attendant at a religious ceremony" and originates from the Latin language.
CAMPBELL	Means "crooked mouth" and has a Scottish origin.

CAMRYN	The first name Camryn is of Scottish origin and means "bent nose" or "crooked river."
CANDACE	Means "queen mother" in ancient Ethiopian language and originated from the title given to the female rulers of the ancient Kingdom of Kush.
CAPRI	The first name Capri originates from the Italian word "capra" meaning "goat" and symbolizes a sense of vitality, curiosity, and adventure.
CARMEN	Latin origin and means "song" or "poem", it became popular due to the famous 1875 opera "Carmen" composed by Georges Bizet.
CAROLINE	Means "free woman" and originates from the feminine form of the Latin name Carolus, which means "man".
CARRINGTON	Means "settlement of Carr's people" and it is of English origin.
CASSANDRA	Greek name meaning "shining upon men" and it originates from Greek mythology.
CASSIDY	The first name Cassidy, of Irish origin, means "clever" or "curly-haired."
CATALEYA	The first name Cataleya has Latin origins and means "orchid".
CATALINA	Means "pure" or "immaculate" and has its origin in the Late Greek name Aikaterine.
CATTLEYA	The first name Cattleya originated from the Cattleya orchid, symbolizing femininity, beauty, and refined elegance.
CECILIA	Means "blind" or "dim-sighted" and originates from the Latin name "Caecilia", derived from the Roman family name "Caecilius".
CELESTE	Means "heavenly" or "celestial" and it originated from Latin.
CELINE	French origin, means "heavenly" or "moon" and is derived from the Latin name Caelina.
CHARISMA	Means "compelling attractiveness or charm" and originates from the Greek word "charis" meaning grace, kindness, or favor.
CHARITY	Means the virtue of giving assistance to those in need, and it originated from the English word derived from the Latin "caritas" meaning "charity, love, affection."
CHARLEIGH	Modern variation of the name Charlie, originally derived from the masculine given name Charles of Germanic origin meaning "free man."
CHARLESTON	English origin and means "from Charles's town" or "manly and free."
CHARLIE	Means "free man" and is of English origin.
CHARLOTTE	Means "free man" and has origin from the feminine form of the male name Charles in French.
CHAYA	Means "life" and originates from the Hebrew language.
CHELSEA	Means "chalk landing place" and originated from Old English.
CHERISH	Means to hold dear, treasure, or care for affectionately, and it originated from the English vocabulary word "cherish" which entered the baby name lexicon in the late 20th century.
CHESNEY	Means "oak grove" and its origin is English.
CHEVELLE	Means "horse, mare" and originated from the French language.
CHEYENNE	Native American origin, means "people of a different speech" and is associated with the Cheyenne tribe.
CHIARA	Means "bright" or "clear" and has Italian origin.
CHLOE	Means "young green shoot" and has Greek origins.
CHRISTINA	Means "follower of Christ" and originates from the Greek name "Christinos" or "Christina."
CHRISTY	Diminutive form of the name Christina, derived from the Greek name "Christos" meaning "anointed one" or "follower of Christ."
CHYNA	Means "China" and originates from the English term for the country.
CIELO	Means "sky" in Spanish and has its origin in the Latin word "caelum."
CIERRA	Means "mountain range" or "dark-haired" and originates from the Spanish language.
CINDY	Diminutive form of the name Cynthia, meaning "moon goddess," and it originated from Ancient Greek mythology.
CLAIRE	Means "clear" or "bright" and originates from the French language.
CLARA	Means "clear, bright" and originates from the Latin language.
CLARISSA	Means "bright, clear" and its origin is Latin.
CLAUDIA	Means "lame" or "disabled" and has originated from the Roman Empire.
CLEMENTINE	Means "merciful" or "gentle" and originated from the Latin name Clemens.
CLEO	Greek origin and means "glory" or "fame."
CLOE	The name Cloe, derived from the Greek name Chloe, means "blooming" or "green shoot" and has biblical origins.

CLOVER Means "lucky" or "fortunate" and originates from the English language.

COLBIE English origin, means "victorious person" or "dark-haired" and is often used as a gender-neutral name.

COLETTE Means "victorious" or "people of victory" and it originated from France and is derived from the name Nicholas.

COLLINS Collins means "son of Colin" and is of Irish origin.

CONSTANCE Latin origin, means "steadfast" or "constant" and is derived from the Latin word "constantia."

CORALINE Means "coral" or "little coral" and it is derived from the Latin word "corallium."

CORDELIA Means "daughter of the sea" and has Celtic origins.

CORINNE Means "maiden" or "maiden-like" and originated from the Greek name Korinna.

COURTNEY Unisex name of English origin, meaning "from the courts" or "court attendant."

CRIMSON Means a deep shade of red and originated as a word used to describe the color of certain fabrics or dyes.

CRISTINA Means "a Christian" and is of Latin origin.

CRYSTAL Means "clear, brilliant like a crystal" and originates from the English language.

CYNTHIA Means "moon goddess" and has Greek origins.

DAENERYS Means "stormborn" and it originated as a fictional name created by author George R.R. Martin in his book series "A Song of Ice and Fire," popularized by the television series "Game of Thrones."

DAFNE Means "laurel" or "victory" and originated from Greek mythology, specifically from the story of Daphne, who was transformed into a laurel tree.

DAHLIA The first name Dahlia has a Hebrew origin and means "flower."

DAISY Means "day's eye" and originates from the English word for the flower.

DAKOTA Means "friend" or "ally" and has Sioux Native American origins.

DALETT The name "Dalett" does not have a widely recognized meaning or origin, as it appears to be a very rare or unique name.

DALEYZA The name Daleyza originated in the United States and means "skilled and determined."

DANICA Means "morning star" and has Slavic and Croatian origins.

DAPHNE Means "laurel tree" and has Greek origins.

DARCY The first name Darcy is of French and Irish origin, meaning "dark-haired one" or "from Arcy."

DARLENE Means "tenderly loved" and originates from the English language.

DAYANA Feminine given name of Persian and Arabic origin, meaning "radiant" or "shining".

DAYANARA Means "heavenly, divine" and originated from Spanish and Greek languages.

DEASIA African-American origin, and it means "devoted or dedicated to God."

DEBORAH Means "bee" and originated from Hebrew.

DEJA French origin and it means "already, previously" symbolizing a sense of familiarity or a feeling that something has already happened before.

DELAINEY Means "from the alder grove" and is of Old English origin.

DELANEY The meaning of the first name Delaney is "from the alder grove" and it has Irish origins.

DELIA Means "from Delos" and originates from the Greek mythological name of the island Delos, the birthplace of the goddess Artemis and her twin brother Apollo.

DELILAH Means "delicate, weak" and derives from Hebrew origins.

DENALI Means "the great one" and its origin is Native American, specifically from the Athabaskan language.

DESIREE Means "longed for" or "desired" and originates from French.

DESTINY Means "fate" or "the predetermined course of events" and is of English origin.

DIAMOND Means "a precious gemstone" and originated as a given name in the United States during the 20th century, influenced by the popularity of the gemstone as a symbol of rarity and beauty.

DIOR French origin, means "golden" or "gift of God".

DIVINE Means "of or related to a deity" and originates from Latin.

DIXIE The name Dixie refers to the Southern United States, specifically the region below the Mason-Dixon Line, and it originated as a nickname for the word "ten-dollar bill" which featured the French word "dix" meaning ten.

DIYA	The first name "Diya" is of Arabic origin and means "light" or "brightness."
DOLORES	Means "sorrows" or "suffering" and originates from Spanish.
DOROTHY	Means "gift of God" and has English origins.
DREAM	Means an imaginative or aspirational state, and its origin is derived from the English word dream.
DULCE	Means "sweet" in Spanish and originates from Latin.
EBONY	English origin and means "deeply dark wood; dark beauty."
ECHO	Means "reverberating sound" and has its origin in Greek mythology, referring to a nymph condemned to repeat the words of others as a punishment.
EDITH	Means "prosperous in war" and originates from Old English.
EGYPT	The name EGYPT has its origins in ancient Egypt and it refers to the country located in northeastern Africa with a rich history and cultural heritage.
EILEEN	Means "bright, shining one" and has Irish Gaelic origins.
EIZA	Spanish-originated name meaning "pledged to God."
ELAINA	Greek origin, means "bright, shining light" and it is derived from the name Elaine.
ELEANOR	Means "bright, shining one" and it originated from the Old French name Alienor, formed from the combination of elements "alain" (meaning "other") and "ais" (meaning "to speak").
ELENA	Means "bright, shining light" and has origins in various cultures, including Greek, Spanish, Italian, and Slavic.
ELINOR	Means "light" and it originated from the Greek name "Helenē" meaning "torch" or "bright light."
ELISE	French female given name meaning "pledged to God", derived from the Hebrew name Elizabeth.
ELISHEVA	Hebrew origin and it means "God is my oath" or "God is my satisfaction".
ELIYANAH	Means "God has answered" and it has Hebrew origins.
ELIZABETH	Means "God is my oath" and originates from Hebrew.
ELLAMAE	Combination of the names Ella and Mae, and it originated from English and Hebrew roots; it means "beautiful pearl" or "goddess of the sea."
ELLINGTON	Surname-derived given name meaning "son of Ellis" and has English roots.
ELODIE	French feminine name derived from the Provençal dialect form of "Alodia," which was the name of a saint in the 9th century.
ELOISE	Means "healthy" or "wide" and originated from the Germanic elements "heil" (meaning "healthy") and "wide" (meaning "wide" or "wide ruling").
ELOUISE	Means "renowned warrior" and has Germanic origins.
ELOWYN	Means "elf-friend" and originated from a combination of the Welsh name element "el-" meaning "kind, friendly" and the Old English word "wyn" meaning "friend."
ELSIE	Diminutive form of the name Elizabeth that originates from Scotland and means "pledged to God."
ELVIRA	The name Elvira originates from the Spanish and Portuguese languages, meaning "truth" or "truly inspired."
ELYANA	Means "God has answered" and has Hebrew origins.
ELYSIA	Means "blissful" or "heavenly" and it originates from Greek mythology, specifically from Elysium, a paradise in the afterlife for heroes.
ELYZA	Hebrew origin and means "God is my oath."
EMBER	The name Ember originated from the English word for a glowing piece of coal or wood, and it symbolizes warmth, passion, and energy.
EMBERLEIGH	Modern invented name, likely derived from the word "ember" which means a small piece of burning coal or wood, combined with the suffix "-leigh" to create a unique and trendy name.
EMBERLY	Means "sparkling and fiery" and is a modern invented name derived from the word "ember."
EMERALD	Means "a green gemstone" and originated from the Latin word "smaragdus," which translates to "green gem."

EMERSYN Modern gender-neutral name derived from the English surname Emerson, meaning "son of Emery."

EMERY Means "industrious leader" and originates from the Germanic elements "amal" meaning "work" and "ric" meaning "ruler."

EMILY Means "industrious" and is derived from the Latin name Aemilia, which means "rival."

EMMA Means "whole" or "universal" and originates from the Germanic word "ermen" meaning "whole" or "universal."

EMMALEE Means "industrious, striving" and it is a modern variant of the names Emma and Emily.

EMMALEIGH Means "work" or "rival" and is derived from the combination of the names Emma and Leigh.

EMMAROSE Means "universal beauty" and is of English origin.

EMMELINE Means "hardworking" and originates from the Germanic name Amelina, ultimately derived from the Germanic element "amal" meaning "work."

EMMYLOU Means "hardworking maiden" and originated from English and Germanic roots.

EMORI The first name Emori likely originated from the Japanese language and means "blessing" or "abundant beauty".

EMPRESS Means a female ruler of supreme power or authority, and its origin is derived from the English word "empress" which is ultimately derived from the Latin word "imperatrix."

EMRYN Welsh origin and means "peaceful, holy place" or "river with metallic strength."

ENSLEY English origin and means "one who belongs to the town near the springs."

EOWYN Means "horse joy" or "horse lover" and it originates from Old English, inspired by the character Eowyn in J.R.R. Tolkien's "The Lord of the Rings" series.

ERIKA Means "ruler" or "eternal ruler" and is of Scandinavian and German origin.

ERYN Means "peace" and it is of Welsh origin.

ESHAAL Means "fragrance of a flower" and it originates from the Persian language.

ESME French name meaning "beloved" or "esteemed," derived from the Old French word "esmer."

ESMERALDA Means "emerald" in Spanish and originated from the Greek word "smeraldo" which also means "emerald."

ESPERANZA Means "hope" and originates from the Spanish language.

ESSENCE Means "the fundamental nature or quality of something or someone" and has its origins in the English language.

ESTEFANIA Spanish feminine given name meaning "crown" or "garland" and has origins in ancient Greece.

ESTELLE Means "star" and has its origin in the Old French language.

ESTHER Means "star" and it originates from Hebrew.

ESTRELLA "Estrella" is a Spanish name that means "star" and originates from the Latin word "stella."

ESTY The meaning of the first name Esty is "star" and it is of Yiddish origin.

ETERNITY Means infinite or everlasting and has origins in the English language.

EUNICE Means "good victory" and originates from ancient Greece.

EVALUNA Means "beautiful moon" and has Latin and Spanish origins.

EVANGELINE Means "bearer of good news" and originated from Greek and Latin sources.

EVE Means "life" and originates from Hebrew biblical accounts, as it is the name of the first woman according to the Book of Genesis.

EVELYN Means "desired" or "wished for" and it has English origins.

EVERLEIGH The name Everleigh originated as a combination of the English names "Ever" meaning always, and "Leigh" meaning meadow; it means "forever meadow."

EVERLY Modern English name derived from the surname Everley, meaning "boar clearing" or "wild boar clearing," originating from Old English roots.

EVIANNA Evianne is a modern invented name of unknown origin, possibly created as a variation of the name Yvonne or a combination of "Eva" and "Anne," with no specific meaning attached.

EVOLET Fictional origin, popularized by the 2008 film "10,000 BC," and its meaning is not known.

FABIOLA Feminine given name of Latin origin that means "bean grower" or "bean farmer".

FAIGY Hebrew name of Yiddish origin meaning "bird".

FAITH	Means "complete trust and belief" and was derived from the English word faith, ultimately originating from the Old English word "fæith."
FATIMA	Means "captivating" in Arabic and has its origins in Islamic tradition as the name of the Prophet Muhammad's daughter.
FATOUMATA	Means "youngest daughter" in the Malinke language and it originated from West Africa, particularly in Guinea and Mali.
FELICITY	Means "happiness" or "good fortune" and is of English origin.
FERN	Means "fern plant" and originates from the Old English word "fearn" or Old High German "farn," referring to a type of green, leafy plant.
FINLEIGH	Scottish and Irish origin and means "fair hero" or "white warrior".
FIORELLA	Means "little flower" in Italian and it is derived from the Italian word "fiore," which means "flower."
FLORENCE	Means "flourishing" and has Latin and English origins.
FRANCES	Means "free" or "from France," and it originated from the Latin name Franciscus.
FRANCESCA	Francesca is an Italian name meaning "free" or "from France" and it originated from the Latin name Franciscus.
FRANCINE	Means "free" or "from France" and has French origins.
FRANKIE	Diminutive form of the name Frank, which originates from the Germanic name "Franciscus" meaning "free man."
FREYA	Means "lady" or "noblewoman" and originates from Old Norse mythology, where Freya was the goddess of love, beauty, and fertility.
FRIDA	Means "peaceful" and it originates from Germanic and Scandinavian languages.
GABBY	Shortened form of the name Gabrielle or Gabriel, of Hebrew origin, meaning "God is my strength."
GALILEA	Feminine Spanish name meaning "to sing" or "to rejoice," derived from the Hebrew word "gilah" and the Latin word "gallus."
GENESIS	Means "beginning" or "origin" and is of Greek origin, derived from the biblical term referring to the creation of the world.
GENEVA	Latin origin, means "juniper tree" and is derived from the name of a city in Switzerland.
GENEVIEVE	Means "woman of the race" and originated from France.
GEORGIANA	English origin and means "farmer" or "earthworker."
GEORGINA	Georgina, meaning "farmer" or "earthworker," originated from the masculine name George and is of Greek origin.
GERALDINE	Feminine given name of English origin, meaning "ruler with the spear," derived from the Germanic elements 'ger' (spear) and 'wald' (rule).
GIANELLA	Means "God is gracious" and it originates from Italian and Spanish.
GIANNA	Female given name of Italian origin, meaning "God is gracious" or "Gift from God".
GIAVANNA	The name Giavanna originates from Italy and means "God is gracious."
GIGI	Means "earth worker" and has French and Italian origins.
GINGER	Means "reddish-orange spice" and originated as a nickname for people with red hair or a spicy personality.
GISELLE	Means "pledge, oath" and originated from the Germanic language.
GITTY	Hebrew name meaning "good" or "fortunate" and is often used as a diminutive form of the name Gittel or Gitel.
GIULIA	Italian origin and it means "youthful" or "downy-bearded."
GIULIANA	Means "youthful" and originates from Italian.
GIULIETTA	Means "youthful" or "youthful downy-bearded" and it originates from Italy.
GLORIA	Means "glory" or "renown" and originates from Latin.
GOLDIE	Means "golden" and originates from the English language.
GRACE	Means "elegance, charm, and divine favor" and is derived from the Latin word "gratia".
GRACELYNN	Modern American name that combines the elements of Grace, meaning "elegance" or "divine favor," and Lynn, a surname-turned-given-name derived from Welsh origins, collectively portraying a combination of grace and strength.

GRACIELA   Feminine Spanish name meaning "grace" or "charm," deriving from the Latin name Gratia.

GRECIA   Means "Greece" in Spanish and Italian, and it is derived from the Latin word "Graecia," referring to the country in Southern Europe.

GRETA   Means "pearl" and it originates from the Old Norse language.

GRETCHEN   Means "pearl" and its origin is German.

GUADALUPE   The first name Guadalupe originated in Spanish and means "river of the wolf."

GUINEVERE   Arthurian legend, means "white shadow" and originates from Welsh mythology.

GWENDOLYN   Means "white ring" or "fair bow" and is of Welsh origin.

GWENYTH   Means "fortunate" or "blessed" in Welsh, and it has Welsh origins.

GWYNETH   Means "blessed" or "happy" and has Welsh origins.

HADASSAH   Means "myrtle tree" and is of Hebrew origin.

HADLEIGH   Means "heathery clearing" and has English origins.

HAFSA   Means "young lioness" in Arabic, and it originates from Islamic culture, as it was borne by one of the wives of the Islamic prophet Muhammad.

HAILEY   Means "heroine" or "field of hay" and it originated from the Old English surname and place name Hailey or Hawley.

HAILIE   Means "heroine" and it originated as a variant of the name Hailey, which is derived from the Old English word "hæg."

HAIZLEY   Means "meadow of the hares" and is of English origin.

HALIMA   Means "gentle, mild-mannered" in Arabic and it originated from Islamic tradition.

HALO   Means "divine aura" or "circle of light" and it originates from the English language.

HANNAH   Means "grace" or "favour," and it originated from the Hebrew name ◻ ◻ ◻ ◻ (Ḥannah) which appears in the Old Testament of the Bible.

HARBOR   Means "a safe place for ships" and its origin can be traced back to the English language.

HARLOW   Means "hill with a grove of trees" and originates from Old English.

HARMONY   Means "agreement, concord, and pleasant combination" and originates from the English word harmony, derived from the Latin word "harmonia" meaning "order, agreement."

HARPER   The name Harper originated as a surname in England, meaning "harp player," and later became a popular given name for both boys and girls.

HARTLEY   Means "stag meadow" and is of Old English origin.

HATTIE   Diminutive form of the name Harriet, meaning "ruler of the household," and it originated as a nickname in the United States during the 19th century.

HAVEN   Haven is an English name that means "a safe place or shelter" and conveys the idea of protection and security.

HAYVEN   American origin, means "a sanctuary or place of refuge."

HAZEL   Means "hazel tree" and originates from the Old English word "hæsel."

HEATHER   Feminine name of English origin, derived from the name of a flowering plant, symbolizing beauty and solitude.

HEAVEN   The name Heaven refers to a concept of the afterlife in various religious beliefs and has been adapted as a given name with uncertain origin but likely influenced by the English word for paradise.

HEAVENLY   Means divine or celestial and originated as a modern English name derived from the word "heaven."

HEIRESS   Means a female inheritor of wealth or social status, and its origin is derived from the English language.

HELEN   Means "bright, shining one" and originates from Greek mythology, specifically from the character Helen of Troy who was known for her beauty.

HENLEY   The name Henley originated from Old English and it means "high meadow."

HENNESSY   Means "descendant of Aonghus" and it originated as an Irish surname which was derived from the given name Aonghus, meaning "one choice".

HENRIETTA   Means "ruler of the home" and originated from the Germanic name Heinrich.

HERMIONE   Means "messenger" and has Greek origins.

HIBA   Feminine given name of Arabic origin meaning "gift" or "bestowal."

HILLARY   Means "cheerful" or "joyful" and originates from Old English.

HOLLAND   The first name Holland originated as a surname derived from the Old English word "hāland," meaning "land on the hill" or "hollow land."

HONESTY	Means integrity and truthfulness; it originated from the English vocabulary word honesty, derived from Old French "honesté" meaning "honor, virtue."
HONEY	The first name Honey, of English origin, symbolizes sweetness and affection.
HUDA	Means "guidance" or "rightly guided" in Arabic, and it is of Arabic origin.
HUNTLEIGH	English origin and means "meadow of hunters" or "one who resides near the hunter's meadow."
ILIANA	Means "bright" or "shining" and has Greek origins.
IMANI	Imani means "faith" in Swahili and has its origin in East Africa.
IMOGEN	Means "beloved child" and originates from the Celtic language.
INDIANA	Means "land of the Indians" and is derived from the name of the US state, which was named after the Indiana Territory, itself named to honor the Native American tribes who originally inhabited the region.
INDIE	The name Indie, typically short for Indiana or Indigo, means "independent" and originated as a nickname or alternative form of these names.
INES	Means "pure" and it originated from the Greek name Agnes.
INGRID	Means "beautiful, beloved warrior" and originates from the Old Norse language.
IRELAND	Means "land of the Irish" and originated from the country of Ireland.
IRIS	Means "rainbow" and has its origin in Greek mythology, derived from the Greek word "eir□ nē,"meaning "peace."
IRMA	Means "noble, whole" and originates from Germanic and Old Norse languages.
ISABELLA	Means "pledged to God" and originates from Hebrew and Italian.
ISADORA	Means "gift of Isis" and its origin is Greek and Egyptian.
ISELA	Spanish origin and means "Consecrated to God."
ISLA	Scottish origin and means "island."
ITALY	The first name "Italy" does not have a widely recognized meaning or origin, as it is typically used as a geographical name referring to the country in Southern Europe.
ITZAYANA	The first name Itzayana is of Aztec origin and means "black obsidian."
ITZEL	Means "rainbow lady" and originates from the Mayan culture.
IVANNA	Means "God is gracious" and it has Slavic origins.
IVORY	Means "white, pure" and originates from the English vocabulary word for the hard, creamy-white substance derived from the tusks and teeth of animals such as elephants and used in making ornaments and other items.
IVY	Means "climbing plant" and originates from the English word for a type of evergreen vine.
IZABELLE	Feminine given name derived from the name Isabelle, which originated from the Hebrew name Elisheba, meaning "God is my oath."
JACKELINE	Feminine given name of English origin, derived from the masculine name Jack meaning "God is gracious" combined with the suffix "-line" often used to create feminine forms of names.
JACKIE	Diminutive of the given name Jack or Jacqueline and originated as a pet form of the name John or Jacqueline in English-speaking countries.
JACKLYN	Means "God is gracious" and is a variant of the name Jacqueline, which originated from the French name Jacques or Jacob.
JACQUELINE	Means "supplanter" and has French origins.
JAHZARA	Means "blessed princess" and has Hebrew and Swahili origins.
JAIDA	Modern American name of uncertain origin and meaning, possibly derived from the name Jade or influenced by the Arabic name Jaida/Jada, meaning "valley."
JANAE	Means "God has answered" and it is of American origin.
JANELLE	Feminine given name that originated from the combination of the names Jane and Elle, and it means "God is gracious" or "gift from God."
JANICE	Feminine given name derived from the name Jane or Janet, originating from Hebrew meaning "God is gracious."
JANYLA	The first name JANYLA is of modern origin and its meaning is uncertain.
JAQUELINE	Means "supplanter" and it originates from the French name Jacques, ultimately derived from the Hebrew name Ya'aqov (Jacob).

JASLENE   Means "jasmine flower" and has Indian origins.

JASMINE   Persian origin, means "fragrant flower" and symbolizes grace, elegance, and sensuality.

JAYCIE   The meaning of the first name Jaycie is "rejoice" and it is a modern American variant of the name Jacey or Jacie.

JAYLANI   American origin and means "mighty warrior" or "gift of God."

JAZIYAH   The first name Jaziyah is of Arabic origin and means "one who will be rewarded."

JAZLYN   Means "beautiful; the combination of the names Jasmine and Lynn" and has a modern origin.

JEANETTE   Means "God is gracious," and it is of French origin.

JENNIFER   Means "white wave" and originated from the Cornish form of Guinevere, a legendary Queen of King Arthur's court.

JERSEY   The first name Jersey is of English origin and means "island of grass or deer park."

JESSALYN   The name Jessalyn, which is of English origin, means "God beholds" or "fair and beautiful."

JESSICA   Means "God beholds" and it originates from Hebrew.

JEWEL   Means "precious stone" or "gem" and has English origin.

JHENE   Modern feminine name of uncertain origin, possibly of West African or Celtic origin.

JOCELYN   Means "member of the Gauts" and has English and French origins.

JOELLA   Means "Jehovah is God" and is of Hebrew origin.

JOHANNA   Feminine given name of Hebrew origin meaning "gift from God."

JOSEFINA   Means "God will add" and has Spanish and Portuguese origins.

JOSEPHINE   Means "God will increase" and it originates from the Hebrew name Yosef meaning "God shall add" combined with the feminine suffix –ine.

JOSETTE   Feminine given name of French origin, meaning "may Jehovah add" or "God will increase".

JOURNEE   Means "daytime journey" and it has an English origin.

JOVIE   Modern English name derived from the word "jovial," meaning cheerful or good-natured.

JUANITA   Means "God is gracious" and originates from the Spanish language.

JUBILEE   Means "a time of celebration or rejoicing" and originates from the Hebrew word "yobel," referring to a trumpet blast signifying the start of a special event or year of remission.

JUDITH   Hebrew origin, means "woman of Judea" or "he will be praised."

JULIETTE   Means "youthful" or "downy-bearded" and derived from the Latin name Julius and its feminine form Julia.

JULISSA   Means "youthful" or "downy-haired" and originated from a combination of the names Julia and Melissa.

JUNIPER   Means "youthful" or "evergreen shrub" and originated from the Latin word "juniperus."

JUNO   Means "queen of the heavens" in Latin, and it originates from Roman mythology, where Juno was the queen of the gods and the goddess of marriage and childbirth.

JUPITER   Means "supreme god" and originates from Roman mythology, derived from the Latin word "Iuppiter."

KACIE   Irish origin and means "alert; vigilant."

KAILANI   Means "sea and sky" and originates from the Hawaiian language.

KAITLYN   Means "pure" and originated as a variation of the name Catherine or Caitlin.

KAIYA   Means "forgiveness" and it has Hawaiian and Japanese origins.

KALEIGH   Modern American variant of the Irish name Kayleigh, derived from the combination of the names Kay and Lee, meaning "pure and slender" or "keeper of the keys."

KALINA   The name Kalina has Polish and Slavic roots and it means "viburnum tree" or "flowering shrub."

KAMBREE   Means "crooked nose, arched bridge" and it originated from American usage as a modern variation of the name Cambria.

KAMIAH   Means "desirable" or "unique" and originates from the Native American Nez Perce tribe.

KAMILLE   Means "perfect" or "unblemished" and has origins in French, German, and Danish.

KAMIYAH   American origin and means "a unique or special gift from God."

KAORI   Means "fragrance" in Japanese, and it is derived from the combination of the kanji characters ☐ (ka) meaning "fragrance" and ☐ (ori) meaning "weave" or "fabric."

KARMA Means "action" or "fate" and originates from Sanskrit.

KAROLINA Means "free woman" and originates from the feminine form of the Latin name Carolus, meaning "manly" or "strong".

KARSYN Modern variation of the name Carson, originally derived from an Irish surname meaning "son of Carr," referring to someone who dwelled near a rocky place or a marsh.

KATELYN American origin and means "pure" or "pure beauty".

KATERINA Means "pure" or "clear" and it is of Greek origin.

KATHERINE The name Katherine, derived from the Greek name Aikaterinē, means "pure" or "clear" and has origins in Greek mythology.

KATHLEEN Means "pure" or "innocent" and is of Irish origin.

KATHRYN Means "pure" and is of Greek origin.

KATHY Diminutive form of Katherine, derived from the Greek name Aikaterinē, meaning "pure" or "clear," and it became popular in the English-speaking world during the 20th century.

KATRINA Feminine given name of Greek origin meaning "pure," derived from the name Katherine.

KAYDENCE American origin and means "rhythm" or "musicality."

KAYLEE Modern and feminine name of American origin, likely derived from the combination of the names Kay and Lee.

KAYLEIGH Means "slender, pure" and is of Irish origin.

KAYLENE Means "slender" or "narrow" and it is of American origin.

KAYLIANA Means "pure" or "beloved" and it has origins in both Italian and Hawaiian cultures.

KEHLANI Means "sea and sky" in Hawaiian and it originated from Hawaiian and Polynesian cultures.

KEILANY Modern feminine name of uncertain origin, possibly derived from Gaelic or Arabic origins.

KEIRA Means "dark-haired" or "black-haired" and is of Irish and Gaelic origin.

KELLY Means "warrior" or "bright-headed" and originates from the Irish surname Ó Ceallaigh.

KELSEY The first name Kelsey is of English origin and means "from Cenel's island," referring to someone from a place called Kells or Kelsey in Lincolnshire, England.

KENDALL Means "valley of the River Kent" and originates from Old English.

KENDRA Means "wise ruler" and originates from the English language.

KENLEIGH Means "from the royal meadow" and has English origins.

KENNADI Means "descendant of Cennétig" and originates from Scotland and Ireland.

KENNEDY Means "descendant of Cinnéidigh" and originates from the Irish surname Ó Cinnéidigh, derived from the Gaelic word "cinnidh" which means "ugly head".

KENSINGTON The first name Kensington is of English origin and means "from the town of Cynsige's people."

KENZIE Variant of the Scottish surname McKenzie and it means "son of the fair one" or "born of fire."

KENZLEIGH Modern American name that is a variant of the name Kenley, meaning "brave warrior" or "from the royal meadow."

KERRIGAN Means "son of Fergan," and it is of Irish origin.

KEYLA Means "crown of laurels" and it is derived from the Spanish and Portuguese name Kayla.

KEZIAH Means "cassia tree" and originates from Hebrew.

KHADIJA Means "premature baby" or "the early one" in Arabic and it originates from Islamic tradition, specifically from the name of prophet Muhammad's first wife.

KHALANI The name Khalani originated from Arabic and means "eternal, everlasting."

KHALEESI Means "queen" or "ruler" and originated from the fictional Dothraki language in George R.R. Martin's book series "A Song of Ice and Fire" and its TV adaptation "Game of

KHALIYAH Arabic origin meaning "queenly" or "royalty."

KIARA Means "dark-haired" or "black" and has Italian and Irish origins.

KIERSTEN Feminine given name of Scandinavian origin meaning "follower of Christ".

KIMBER The first name Kimber is an English name of Old English origin, meaning "from the royal fortress meadow."

KIMBERLY Means "from the meadow of the royal fortress" and originated from Old English.

KIMORA Means "ruler" or "noble one" and originated from the Swahili language.

KINSEY The first name Kinsey is of English origin and means "royal victory."

KINSLEIGH English origin and means "a royal meadow or field."

KINSLEY Means "king's meadow" and originated as a surname in medieval England.

KIRA Means "sparkling" or "beam of light" and it originates from multiple cultures, including Russia, Japan, and Africa.

KIRSTEN Means "follower of Christ" and originates from the Scandinavian and Germanic cultures.

KIYOMI Means "pure beauty" in Japanese and is typically given to females.

KOLLYNS The first name Kollyns is of American origin and is a modern variation of the name Collins, derived from a surname meaning "son of Colin" or "young wolf cub."

KRISTEN Means "follower of Christ" and originated from the Scandinavian variant of the name Christian.

KYAH Australian Aboriginal origin, meaning "forgiving" or "explorer."

KYNLEE Modern American name that combines the sounds and spellings of traditional English names, Kinsley and Kaylee, to create a unique and contemporary name for girls.

KYNNEDI Modern variant of the name Kennedy, derived from an Irish surname meaning "misshapen head."

KYNZLEE Modern American name, most likely a variant of the name Kinley, and has no widely acknowledged meaning.

LAIKYN The meaning and origin of the first name Laikyn is that it is a modern American name derived from the surname "Larkin," meaning "fierce" or "fierce land."

LAINEY Diminutive form of the Irish surname Ó Leathlobhair meaning "half-leper," which was derived from the Gaelic word "leath" (half) and "lobhar" (leper).

LAKELYNN Modern American name composed of the elements "Lake" and "Lynn," possibly chosen for its pleasant and nature-inspired sound.

LAKYN Modern variant of the name Lakin, which originated as a variation of the English surname Lakin/Lakey meaning "son of Lake/Luke."

LANDRY Means "ruler" and originated from a French surname related to the Germanic name Landric.

LANEY The first name Laney is of English origin and is derived from the surnames Lane or Delaney, meaning "path" or "from the alder grove."

LARAMIE Native American origin, meaning "tear of a cheek" or "clear, limpid water".

LARKIN English origin and means "fierce, warlike."

LAUREN Means "from the place of the laurel trees" and originated from the English surname derived from the Latin word "laurus."

LAURIE Means "from Laurentum" and it originates from the English and Scottish surnames derived from the male given name Lawrence.

LAVENDER The name Lavender originated from the English language and refers to the fragrant and vibrant purple-colored flowering plant.

LAVINIA Means "woman from the ancient city of Lavinium" and is of Latin origin.

LAYKEN The first name Layken is of American origin and its meaning is currently unknown.

LAYLA Means "night" or "dark beauty" and has Arabic origins.

LAYNIE The first name Laynie, of English origin, means "gracious" or "dweller near the path".

LEAH Means "weary" or "delicate" and has Hebrew origins.

LEGACY Means an inheritance or something handed down, and it originated from the English language.

LEIA Means "weary" or "tired" and is of Hebrew origin.

LEIANA Means "heavenly child" and originates from the Hawaiian language.

LEIGHTON The name Leighton originated from an English surname and means "from the town by the meadow."

LEILANI Means "heavenly flower" or "royal child" in Hawaiian, and it originates from the Hawaiian language and culture.

LEONIE Means "lioness" or "brave like a lion" and originated from the Latin name "Leo" meaning "lion."

LEONORA Means "light" or "torch" and is of Spanish, Italian, and German origin.

LESLIE Means "garden of holly" and originated from Scottish and Gaelic backgrounds.

LETICIA The name Leticia, derived from the Latin word "laetitia," means joy or happiness and has Spanish origin.

LIBERTY Means "freedom" and is of American origin.

LILITH Means "night creature" or "belonging to the night" and originates from ancient Mesopotamian mythology.

LILLIAN The feminine given name Lillian means "lily" and originated from the Latin word "lilium."

LILY Means "pure" or "flower" and is derived from the Latin word "lilium."

LINDA Means "beautiful" in Spanish and Portuguese, and it originated from the German word "lind" meaning "gentle, soft".

LINDSEY Means "island of linden trees" and it originates from an Old English surname derived from the place name Lindsey in Lincolnshire, England.

LISA Means "pledged to God" and originates from Hebrew as a short form of Elizabeth.

LITZY Means "keeper of secrets" and has Spanish origin.

LIYANA Swahili origin and means "softness" or "tenderness."

LIZBETH Diminutive form of Elizabeth, originating from Hebrew, and it means "God is my oath" or "God's promise".

LIZETH Means "God is my oath" and it is of Hebrew origin.

LIZZIE Diminutive form of the name Elizabeth, originating from Hebrew, meaning "God's promise" or "my God is abundance."

LONDYN Means "from London" and originates from the English language.

LORALEI Means "alluring enchantress" and originates from German folklore, specifically from the tale of a maiden who lured sailors to their doom with her bewitching beauty and song.

LORELAI Means "siren" or "alluring" and originated from German folklore, specifically from the legend of Lorelei, a mythological water nymph associated with the Rhine River.

LORRAINE Means "from Lorraine," derived from the region in northeastern France.

LOTTIE The first name Lottie originally derived from the name Charlotte and means "free man" or "petite".

LOTUS Means "symbol of purity and enlightenment" and originates from both Greek and Hindu mythology.

LOURDES Means "lady of Lourdes" and originates from the town of Lourdes in southwestern France, where the Virgin Mary is believed to have appeared to a young girl named Bernadette Soubirous in 1858.

LOVE The first name "Love" derives from the Old English word "lufu," which means deep affection or strong feeling of attraction.

LOVELY Means pleasant or lovable, and its origin is derived from the English language.

LUCERO Means "morning star" and originates from the Spanish language.

LUCIA Means "light" in Latin and has origins in Ancient Roman times.

LUCIANA Means "light" or "illumination" and originated from the Latin name Lucianus, derived from the Latin word "lux" meaning "light".

LUCINDA Portuguese origin and means "light" or "illumination."

LUELLA Means "famous warrior" and it is of English origin.

LULU German origin and means "famous warrior."

LUPITA Spanish origin and is a diminutive form of Guadalupe, meaning "Our Lady of Guadalupe" and is commonly used as a given name in Mexico.

LYDIA Means "woman from Lydia" and originates from the ancient region of Lydia in Anatolia, now modern-day Turkey.

LYNETTE Welsh origin and it means "pretty one" or "idolized".

LYRA Means "lyre" and it has Greek origins.

LYRICA Greek origin and means "beautiful song."

MABEL Means "lovable" and originates from the Latin name Amabilis, which means "lovable, dear."

MABRY Means "wealthy ruling" and has origins in English and Scottish surnames.

MACKENNA Means "son of Ken" and has Gaelic and Scottish origins.

MACKENZIE Means "son of the fair one" and originated as a Scottish surname.

MADELEINE Means "woman of Magdala" and has French origins.

MADELYN Means "woman from Magdala" and has Hebrew and English origins.

MADISON Means "son of Matthew" and originated as a surname in 18th-century England.

MAEVE Means "she who intoxicates" and it originates from Irish mythology.

MAGALY Means "pearl" and has Spanish and Greek origins.

MAGDALENA Means "from Magdala" and has its origin in the Hebrew biblical name Migdal-Eden, meaning "tower of strength."

MAGGIE English origin and it is a diminutive form of the name Margaret, meaning "pearl" or "child of light."

MAGNOLIA Latin origin, means "flower" and represents beauty, grace, and dignity.

MAHOGANY The first name Mahogany is of English origin and means "a rich, reddish-brown colored tropical hardwood tree."

MAISIE The name Maisie, meaning "pearl," is of Scottish origin and is derived from the name Margaret.

MAITE Means "lovable" or "beloved" and originates from the Basque region of Spain.

MAJESTY Means grandeur or greatness, and its origin can be traced back to the English language.

MAKAYLA Modern variation of the name Michaela, derived from the Hebrew name Michael meaning "who is like God."

MAKIYAH Modern variant of the feminine name MaKayla, likely derived from the combination of the names Ma and Kayla.

MALAIKA Means "angel" in Swahili and originates from Eastern Africa.

MALAYAH The name "Malayah" is a modern and feminine variant of the name "Malaya," originating from the Tagalog language of the Philippines, meaning "free" or "independent."

MALAYSIA The name "Malaysia" originates from the country of the same name in Southeast Asia and means "land of the Malays."

MALINDA Means "sweet and gentle" and it originated from the combination of the names Mal and Linda, which are both derived from Germanic origins.

MALKA Means "queen" or "royalty" in Hebrew, and it originates from Jewish tradition.

MALLORY Means "unfortunate or unlucky" and originates from Old French.

MANHA The first name Manha is of Arabic origin and means "gift of God" or "blessing."

MANUELA Means "God is with us" and it is of Spanish and Portuguese origin.

MARBELLA The first name Marbella is of Spanish origin and means "beautiful sea."

MARCELINE The first name Marceline originates from the Latin name Marcellus, meaning "young warrior," and it is derived from the Roman god of war, Mars.

MARGARET Means "pearl" and has Latin origins.

MARGAUX Means "pearl" and originated from the French variant of the name Margaret.

MARGOT Means "pearl" and it originates from the Greek name Margarites.

MARGUERITE Means "daisy" and is of French origin.

MARIAH Variant of the name Maria, which is of Hebrew origin and means "bitter" or "wished for child."

MARIAJOSE Compound name of Spanish origin, formed by combining the names Maria and Jose, and it is commonly used as a combination of the Virgin Mary and Saint Joseph.

MARIBEL Combination of the names Maria and Isabel and originated in the Spanish language.

MARIELLE Means "beloved" or "bright one" and it is of French origin.

MARIGOLD Means "golden flower" and has English origins.

MARILYN Means "beautiful lake" and originated as a combination of the names Mary and Lynn.

MARINA Means "from the sea" and has Latin origins.

MARJORIE Means "pearl" and it originated from the French name Marguerite, derived from the Latin word "margarita" meaning "pearl."

MARLEIGH English origin, means "pleasant meadow" or "marshy meadow."

MARLEY The name Marley originated from an English surname and means "pleasant wood" or "meadow near the lake."

MARLIE Feminine given name of German origin, meaning "strong-willed" or "famous in battle."

MARY Means "bitter" or "beloved" and originates from the Hebrew name Miryam, borne from the New Testament in reference to the mother of Jesus Christ.

MARYAM Means "beloved" or "sea of bitterness" in Arabic and it originates from the Hebrew name Miriam.

MARYJANE	Compound name derived from the combination of the names Mary and Jane, and it typically conveys a blend of the traditional and contemporary aspects associated with both names.
MATILDA	Means "strength in battle" and is of Germanic origin.
MAVIS	Means "songbird" or "song thrush" and is of Old French origin.
MAXINE	Means "the greatest" and it originates from the Latin name Maximus.
MAYA	The name Maya originates from multiple cultures and means "illusion" in Sanskrit, "water" in Hebrew, and "goddess of spring" in Greek mythology.
MAYZIE	Modern and creative variation of the name Daisy, often derived from the English word for the flower.
MAZIKEEN	Means "one who instills confusion" and originates from Hebrew mythology and Jewish folklore.
MCKENNA	Means "son of Cionaodh" and has Irish and Gaelic origins.
MCKENZIE	Means "son of the fair one" and has Scottish Gaelic origins.
MCKINLEY	Means "son of the fair-haired warrior" and has Scottish-Gaelic origins.
MEADOW	Means a grassy field or meadow and originated as an English surname before becoming a nature-inspired given name.
MEARA	Irish origin and means "bitter" or "pearl."
MEGHAN	Means "pearl" and it originates from the Welsh name "Megan" or the Greek name "Meghanē."
MELANIE	Greek origin, means "black, dark" and it was derived from the Greek word "melaina."
MELISSA	Means "honeybee" and originates from Greek mythology.
MELODY	Means "a sequence of pleasing musical notes" and comes from the English language.
MERCEDES	Means "mercies" and has Spanish origins, often associated with the Virgin Mary of Mercies.
MERCY	Means "compassion, forgiveness, and kindness" and originates from the Latin word "merces" meaning "reward" or "mercy, compassion".
MEREDITH	Means "great ruler" and originated from a Welsh surname.
MERRITT	Means "worthy" or "deserving" and it originated as a surname derived from Old English, referring to someone who was meritorious or deserving.
MIABELLA	Means "my beautiful" and it is a combination of the names Mia and Bella, of Italian and Latin origin respectively.
MIAH	Variant of the name Maia, originating from Greek mythology and meaning "great" or "mother."
MIAMOR	Means "my love" in Spanish and is a modern and unique name choice.
MICHELLE	Means "who is like God" and originates from the Hebrew name Michael.
MILAGROS	Means "miracles" in Spanish, and it has its origin in the Spanish-speaking countries.
MILANIA	The name Milania originates from Italy and means "gracious" or "beloved."
MILDRED	Means "gentle strength" and is of Old English origin.
MILLICENT	Means "strong worker" and originated from Old English.
MILLIE	Diminutive form of the name Millicent/Mildred, with origins in Old English/Germanic, meaning "gentle strength" or "strong in work".
MINERVA	Latin name meaning "wisdom" and is derived from the Roman goddess of wisdom and strategic warfare.
MIRABEL	Means "wondrous beauty" and has Latin origins.
MIRACLE	Means "extraordinary event or phenomenon" and it originated from the English language.
MIRANDA	Means "admirable" or "worthy of admiration" and originates from Latin.
MIREYA	Means "admirable" or "wonderful" and it originated from Spanish and Portuguese languages.
MIRIAM	Hebrew name meaning "wished-for child" or "bitterness," commonly originating from the Old Testament figure, the sister of Moses and Aaron.
MISHKA	Means "bear cub" and has Russian and Slavic origins.
MOANA	Means "ocean" in Polynesian and originates from the Maori language.
MOIRA	The first name Moira originated from Greek mythology and means "fate" or "destiny."

MOLLY	Means "bitter" and originated as a diminutive form of Mary in Ireland.
MONICA	Means "advisor" or "counselor" and originates from the Latin name "Monica," which was derived from Latin word "monere" meaning "to advise" or "to warn."
MONIQUE	Means "advisor" and originated from the Latin name Monica.
MONROE	Means "mouth of the River Roe" and has Scottish and Irish origins.
MONSERRAT	The first name Monserrat originated from the Catalan region in Spain and it means "mountain."
MONTANA	Means "mountainous" and originated from the Spanish word "montaña" which translates to "mountain."
MONTSERRAT	Means "serrated mountain" and originates from the Catalan language.
MORGAN	Means "sea-born" and it originates from Wales.
MURPHY	The first name Murphy has an Irish origin and means "sea warrior."
MYKA	Variant of the name Micah, of Hebrew origin, meaning "who is like God?".
NADIA	Means "hope" or "delicate" and it originates from Russian, Slavic, and Arabic languages.
NAHLA	Means "a drink of water" and primarily originates from Arabic.
NAHOMI	Hebrew origin and means "comforter" or "pleasantness."
NAIMA	Means "peaceful" or "tranquil" and originates from Arabic/Islamic culture.
NAIROBI	The first name Nairobi has Swahili origins and means "cool water" or "meeting place."
NANCY	Means "grace" or "favor" and originated from the medieval diminutive of the name Ann/Anne.
NAOMI	Means "pleasant" or "beautiful" and has Hebrew origins.
NATALEIGH	Modern variation of Natalie, derived from the Latin natalis meaning "birth" or "Christmas" originally used to signify someone born on Christmas day.
NATALIE	Means "birth or Christmas" and has Latin origins.
NATALYA	Means "born on Christmas Day" and is of Slavic origin.
NATASHA	Russian origin and means "birthday of the Lord" or "born on Christmas Day".
NATHALIA	The name Nathalia, derived from the name Natalia, originated from Latin and means "of or born on Christmas Day."
NAVY	The name "Navy" originated as a word referring to the water-based branch of a country's armed forces, and as a given name it likely conveys attributes of strength, bravery, and determination.
NAYELI	Means "I love you" or "I love." It has its origin in the Zapotec Native American language.
NAZARETH	Means "from Nazareth" and has its origins in the biblical town of Nazareth in the region of Galilee.
NECHAMA	Means "comfort" or "consolation" in Hebrew and is of Jewish origin.
NELLIE	Means "bright, shining one" and is a diminutive form of the name Helen, which has Greek origins.
NERIAH	Means "lamp of God" and originates from Hebrew.
NEVAEH	Means "heaven" spelled backward and was created in the United States during the late 20th century.
NEVEAH	Modern American name derived from "heaven" spelled backward, symbolizing a contemporary trend of unique and unconventional baby names.
NICOLETTE	Means "victorious people" and has French and Greek origins.
NIHIRA	Means "rare" or "unique" and has origins in the Sanskrit language.
NIKKI	Diminutive form of the name Nicole, which originated from the Greek name Nikolaos, meaning "victory of the people."
NIRVANA	Means "a state of perfect happiness and peace" and is of Sanskrit origin.
NOELANI	Hawaiian name meaning "heavenly mist" or "beautiful one from heaven."
NOELLE	Means "Christmas" in French and it is derived from the Latin word "natalis" which means "birth."
NOEMI	Hebrew origin and means "pleasantness" or "delightful."
NORA	Means "honor" or "light" and is derived from the Arabic name "Nur" or the Greek name "Eleanor."
NOUR	Means "light" in Arabic and is of Arabic origin.
NOVALEE	Means "new meadow" and is a combination of the Latin word "nova" meaning new and the Old English word "lee" meaning meadow.

NOVALEIGH Modern feminine name of American origin, combining the prefix "Nova" meaning "new" and the suffix "-leigh" meaning "meadow," symbolizing a new beginning or fresh start in life.

NOVELLA Means "new" or "novel" and originates from the Latin word "novellus" which means "new, young, fresh."

NYLAH Means "winner or achiever" and has Arabic and Swahili origins.

OAKLEIGH Means "meadow of oak trees" and has English origins.

OAKLEY Means "oak grove" and is of English origin.

OAKLYNN Means "oak tree near the waterfall" and is of English origin.

OCTAVIA Means "eighth" and originates from Latin.

OCTOBER Means "eighth month" and originates from the Latin word "october," referring to the eighth month in the ancient Roman calendar.

ODESSA Means "long journey" and originates from the ancient Greek city of Odessos, located in modern-day Bulgaria.

ODETTE Means "wealthy" or "prosperous" and originates from French.

OFELIA The name Ofelia originated from Greek mythology and it means "helpful" or "help from God."

OLGA Means "holy" or "sacred" and it originated from Old Norse and Slavic languages.

OLIVIA Means "olive tree" and is of Latin origin.

OLYMPIA Means "from Mount Olympus" and has Greek origins.

OPAL Means "precious gemstone" and originates from the Sanskrit word "upala."

OPHELIA Means "helpful serpent" or "serpent of wisdom," and its origin is Greek.

PAIGE The first name Paige, derived from the English word for a servant attending to an English Lord, has a meaning related to service and originated as a surname.

PAISLEIGH Means "from the meadow" and is a variant spelling of the name Paisley, which originates from a Scottish surname.

PAISLEY Scottish origin, refers to a pattern of intricate and colorful design commonly associated with textiles.

PAITYN The first name Paityn is of American origin and means "noble" or "small rock".

PALMER English origin, means "pilgrim" or "bearer of palm leaves."

PALOMA Means "dove" in Spanish and its origin can be traced back to Latin.

PAMELA Means "all sweetness" and it originates from the Greek name "Pamēla" meaning "all honey".

PARIS Means "from Paris, France" and originates from Greek mythology, as Paris was the prince of Troy who started the Trojan War by abducting Helen, the wife of Menelaus.

PATIENCE Means the ability to persevere calmly and originiates from the English vocabulary word "patience."

PAULETTE Means "small" or "humble" and it originated from the French feminine form of Paul.

PAULINA Feminine form of Paul, meaning "small" or "humble" derived from the Latin name Paulinus, popularized by early Christian saints.

PAYTEN Means "from the town of Pagus" and originates from Old English.

PEARL Means a precious gem formed within a mollusk, and it originated from the English vocabulary word for the same.

PENELOPE Means "weaver" and originates from Greek mythology where Penelope was the faithful wife of Odysseus.

PENNY Means "small coin" and originates from the English language.

PERLA Means "pearl" in Spanish and originates from the Latin word "perla" which also means "pearl".

PERSEPHONE Means "bringer of destruction" and originates from Greek mythology as the daughter of Zeus and Demeter, who was abducted by Hades and becomes the queen of the underworld.

PETRA Means "rock" and has Hebrew origins.

PEYTON English origin, means "from the warrior's town" or "from the peaceful town."

PHILOMENA The name Philomena originates from Greek mythology and means "lover of strength" or "friend of strength."

PHOEBE Means "bright" or "shining" and has Greek origins.

PIPER Means "flute player" and originated as a surname derived from the English word "pipe" referring to a musical instrument.

POLINA Russian origin and it means "small" or "humble".

POPPY The name Poppy originated as a flower name but has gained popularity as a given name, symbolizing remembrance and vibrant beauty.

PRECIOUS Means highly valued or beloved, and it originates from the English language.

PRESLEIGH Modern and feminine variant of the English surname "Presley," derived from a place name meaning "priest's meadow" in Old English.

PRESLEY English origin and means "priest's meadow."

PRESLIE The first name Preslie is of Scottish origin and means "dweller at the brushwood meadow."

PRIMROSE The first name Primrose, of English origin, means "first rose" or "first flower" signifying purity and delicacy.

PRISCILLA Means "ancient" or "venerable" and originated from the Latin name Priscilla, derived from the Roman family name Prisius.

PRISHA Indian origin, means "beloved" or "cherished one."

PRIYA Means "beloved" in Sanskrit and it originates from India.

PROMISE Means a commitment or assurance, and it originates from English vocabulary word referring to a pledge or vow.

PRUDENCE Means "caution, wisdom" and originated from the Latin word "prudentia."

QUINLEY Means "descendant of Cunaigh" and has Irish origins.

QUINN Means "descendant of Conn" and originates from Ireland or Scotland.

RACHEL Means "ewe" or "lamb" and originated from Hebrew.

RAEGAN Means "little king" or "wise ruler" and has Irish and Gaelic origins.

RAELEIGH Means "field of deer" and is of English origin.

RAELYNN Means "queen" and has American origins.

RAHAF Means "beautiful or delicate like a gazelle" and originates from Arabic cultures.

RAHMA Arabic origin and means "mercy" or "compassion."

RAIZY Diminutive form of the Hebrew name Raizel, meaning "rose" or "my secret" and it is of Yiddish origin.

RANIA Means "queen" and it has Arabic origins.

RAQUEL Means "ewe" and has Old Testament origins, derived from the biblical name Rachel.

REAGAN Means "little king" and originated from Ireland.

REBECCA Means "captivating" and it originated from the Hebrew word Rebekah, found in the Bible.

REESE Means "ardor" or "fiery warrior" and originates from Wales.

REGINA Means "queen" in Latin and it originates from ancient Rome.

REMEDY Means a solution or cure and it derives from the English vocabulary word referring to a means of alleviating or resolving something.

REMI French origin and means "oarsman" or "rower."

RENATA Means "reborn" or "born again" in Latin, and it originated from the Latin word "renatus."

RENESMEE The first name Renesmee originated from the character of the same name in the Twilight book series by Stephenie Meyer, and it has no specific meaning outside of the fictional context.

REYNA Means "queen" in Spanish and has origins in Latin.

RHIANNON Means "great queen" and it originates from Welsh mythology.

RILEY English origin and means "courageous" or "valiant."

RIPLEY Means "meadow near the river" and is of Old English origin.

RITA Means "pearl" and it originates from Sanskrit.

RIVERLYNN Means "graceful river" and originated as a combination of the names River and Lynn.

RIVKA Means "to bind" or "to tie" in Hebrew and it originates from the biblical figure of Rebecca in the Old Testament.

ROSABELLA Italian origin, means "beautiful rose" and combines the elements "rosa" meaning rose and "bella" meaning beautiful.

ROSALEIGH English origin and it means "beautiful rose meadow," combining the elements of "rose" and "leigh."

ROSALIE	Means "rose" or "beautiful flower" and originated from the Latin name Rosalia, derived from the word "rosa" meaning "rose."
ROSALINDA	Means "beautiful rose" and has Spanish origins.
ROSARIO	Means "rosary" in Spanish and it has origins in Latin America and Spain.
ROSELYN	The meaning of the first name Roselyn is "beautiful rose," and it originates from the combination of the names Rose and Lynn.
ROSEMARY	Means "dew of the sea" and is of Latin origin.
ROSIE	English origin, means "rose" or "shining with fame" and is often used as a diminutive form of the name Rosemary or Rose.
ROSLYN	Means "pretty rose" and has Scottish and English origins.
ROYALTY	Means a person of royal or noble descent and it originates from the English language.
RUBY	Means "red gemstone" and originated from the Latin word "rubeus."
RUHI	Means "spiritual" or "divine" and has Arabic and Persian origins.
RUTH	Means "compassionate friend" and originates from the Hebrew language.
RUTHIE	Diminutive of the Hebrew name Ruth, meaning "companion" or "friend," and it has been in use as a given name since the late 19th century.
RYLEI	Variant spelling of the name Riley, of Irish origin, which means "courageous" or "valiant".
RYLEIGH	Modern feminine variant of the Irish surname Riley, derived from the Old Irish name Raghailleach, meaning "valiant" or "courageous."
RYLIE	Means "courageous" or "valiant warrior" and can be of Irish or English origin.
RYLYNN	Modern American name of combination origin, derived from the names Ryan and Lynn, typically given to girls.
SAANVI	Indian origin and means "one who is holy or highly intelligent."
SABINA	Means "sabine woman" and originates from Latin.
SABRINA	Means "river Severn" and originated from Celtic mythology.
SADIE	Means "princess" or "mercy" and has Hebrew and English origins.
SAGE	Means "wise" or "one who possesses wisdom" and originated from the English word for a type of herb associated with wisdom and healing.
SAHASRA	Means "thousand" in Sanskrit and originates from Indian languages.
SAIRA	Means "princess" and it originates from Arabic.
SAKURA	Japanese name which means "cherry blossom" and symbolizes the beauty and fleeting nature of life.
SALLY	Means "princess" and originated as a diminutive form of Sarah or Salome.
SALOME	The biblical name Salome means "peaceful" and it originates from Hebrew and Greek origin.
SAMANTHA	Means "listener" or "heard by God" and it originated from the Aramaic language.
SAMARA	The name Samara has Hebrew and Arabic origins, meaning "protected by God" or "successful" in Hebrew, and "she who guards" or "watchful" in Arabic.
SANDRA	Means "defender of mankind" and it originates from the Greek name Alexandra.
SAOIRSE	Means "freedom" in Irish Gaelic, and it originates from Ireland.
SAPPHIRE	Sapphire, derived from the precious gemstone, signifies wisdom, protection, and loyalty, and has its origins in Ancient Greek.
SARAH	The name Sarah originated from the Hebrew language and carries the meaning of "princess" or "noblewoman."
SARIYAH	The name "Sariyah" is a feminine Hebrew name meaning "princess" or "noblewoman."
SAVANNAH	Means "flat tropical grassland" and originates from the Taino tribe in the Caribbean.
SAYLOR	The name "Saylor" originated as a gender-neutral English name meaning "mariner" or "one who sails."
SCARLETT	Means "bright red" and originates from the English language, derived from the Old French term "escarlate."
SCOTLYN	Means "combination of Scott, meaning 'from Scotland,' and the suffix -lyn denoting a feminine name" and has no specific origin.
SCOTTIE	Diminutive form of the name Scott, meaning "from Scotland," and it originated as a surname.

SEDONA	Means "a place of red rocks" and originates from the city of Sedona in Arizona, USA, known for its beautiful red sandstone formations.
SELINA	Feminine given name of Greek origin meaning "moon" or "goddess of the moon".
SEQUOIA	Means "giant redwood tree" and originates from the language of the Cherokee, a Native American tribe.
SERAFINA	Feminine given name of Italian origin meaning "ardent" or "fiery."
SERAPHINA	Means "fiery ones" or "burning ones" and has its origin in Hebrew.
SERENA	Means "peaceful" and it originates from Latin.
SERENITY	The name Serenity originates from the English word for calm and peacefulness, implying a sense of tranquility and harmony.
SEVYN	Means "seven" and is a modern variant spelling of the English word.
SHAINDY	Means "beautiful" or "admirable" and is of Hebrew origin.
SHANAYA	Indian origin and it means "beautiful."
SHARON	Means "a fertile plain" and originates from the Hebrew language.
SHAYLA	Irish origin, meaning "from the fairy palace" or "from the gaelic word for gracious".
SHEA	Means "admirable" or "hawk-like" and originates from the Irish surname Ó Séaghdha, meaning "descendant of Séaghdha."
SHEILA	Means "blind" or "heavenly" and originated from the Irish name Síle, a variant of Cecilia or derived from Hebrew name Shulamit.
SHELBY	The first name Shelby originated as an English surname meaning "willow farm" or "from the hillside town."
SHERLYN	The meaning of the first name Sherlyn is "bright hill" and it is of English origin.
SHILOH	Unisex Hebrew name meaning "peaceful" or "tranquil," derived from the Hebrew word shalom.
SHIRLEY	Means "bright meadow" and it originated as a combination of two Old English words, "scīr" which means "bright" and "lēah" which means "meadow".
SHOSHANA	Means "lily" or "rose" in Hebrew, and it originates from the Hebrew language and Jewish culture.
SHREYA	Indian origin, means "auspicious" or "fortunate."
SHYANNE	Modern variant of the name Cheyenne, which originated from the Native American Cheyenne tribe and means "people of the alien speech."
SIDRA	Means "like a star" and it originates from Arabic.
SIENNA	Feminine given name of Italian origin, meaning "reddish-brown" or "orange" inspired by the color and the Tuscan city of Siena.
SILVIA	Means "from the forest" and it originates from Latin.
SINAI	Means "a mountain of divine revelation" and it originates from Hebrew.
SIOBHAN	Means "God is gracious" and originates from the Irish language.
SKYE	Means "island in the sky" and it originated as the name of a Scottish island.
SKYLAR	Means "scholar" or "eternal life" and originated from the Dutch surname Schuyler.
SKYLYNN	The first name Skylynn likely originated as a blend of the words "sky" (referring to the celestial atmosphere) and "lynn" (derived from a Welsh or English name meaning "lake" or "waterfall"), and is of American origin.
SLOANE	Means "warrior" and it originated as an Irish or Gaelic surname before becoming a popular given name.
SNOW	Means "white, pure" and originates from the English language.
SOFIA	Means "wisdom" and originates from Greek.
SOLANA	Spanish name meaning "sunshine" or "east wind" and is of Latin origin.
SOLEIL	Means "sun" in French and it originated from the French language.
SOPHIA	Means "wisdom" and is of Greek origin.
SORAYA	Means "princess" or "star" and has Persian origins.
SPARROW	Means "a small bird" and originates from the Old English word "sperwe."
STACY	Means "resurrection" and originated from Greek and English backgrounds.
STARLA	Modern American name that originated from the combination of the English word "star" and the name suffix "-la," meaning "little star."

STELLA Means "star" and it originated from Latin.

STEPHANIE Feminine given name of Greek origin, meaning "crown" or "garland", often given to honor the concept of royalty or victory.

STEVIE The name Stevie originated as a diminutive form of the name Stephen or Stephanie, meaning "crown" or "garland," and it became popular as a gender-neutral given name in the 20th century.

STORMI Means "stormy" or "tempestuous" and is of American origin.

SUMAYA Means "determined" or "one who is gracious" and its origin can be traced back to Arabic/Islamic culture.

SUMMER Means "the warmest season of the year" and originated as a given name in the English language.

SUNDAY Means "day of the sun" and originated from the English vocabulary word referring to the day of the week.

SUNNIE Means "sunny" or "bright" and originated as a modern nickname or variant of the English word "sunny."

SUNSHINE Means warmth, brightness, and happiness, with its origin derived from the English vocabulary word referring to the radiance and warmth of the sun.

SURY Sanskrit origin and it means "sun" or "sun god."

SUSANNA Means "lily" or "graceful lily" and has Biblical origins, originating from the Hebrew name Shoshana.

SUTTON Unisex English name meaning "south settlement," derived from Old English and Old Norse origins.

SUZANNE Means "lily" or "graceful lily" and has French origins.

SWARA Indian origin and means "musical note" or "sound" in Sanskrit.

SWAYZE Irish origin and means "adventurous" or "free-spirited."

SYBIL The first name "Sybil" is of Greek origin and it means "prophetess or oracle."

SYDNEY The name Sydney originated from an English surname derived from the Old English words "sīdan" meaning "wide" and "īeġ" meaning "island," with the meaning "wide island."

SYLVIE Means "from the forest" and it is a French variation of the Latin name Silvia.

SYMPHONY Means "harmonious musical composition" and it originated from the English word for a large-scale orchestral arrangement of music.

TABITHA Means "gazelle" and originates from the Aramaic language.

TALIA Means "dew from heaven" and has Hebrew origins.

TALLULAH Feminine name of Native American origin meaning "leaping water" or "running water."

TARAJI Means "hope" or "faith" and it is of Swahili origin.

TASNEEM Means "a spring in paradise" and originates from Arabic.

TATIANA Means "fairy queen" or "princess" and has Russian and Latin origins.

TAYLYNN Modern invented name with no specific meaning or origin, likely a combination of the names Taylor and Lynn.

TAYTUM Means "brave and happy" and originates from the English language.

TEIGAN The first name Teigan, of Greek origin, means "beautiful" or "fair."

TEMPERANCE Means "moderation or self-restraint" and has its origin in the English language.

TENZIN Means "upholder of teachings" and originates from Tibetan culture.

TERESA Feminine given name of Spanish origin meaning "harvester/reaper" or "summer", ultimately derived from the Greek word for "huntress".

TESSA Short form of the name Theresa, of Greek origin, meaning "to harvest" or "reaper".

THALIA Means "blooming" or "to blossom" and originates from Greek mythology, being the name of one of the nine muses, the protector of comedy and idyllic poetry.

THEADORA Female given name of Greek origin meaning "gift of God".

THERESA Means "harvester" and originated from Greek and Latin variations of the name Therasia.

TIFFANY Means "manifestation of God" and has origins in medieval English and Greek.

TIRZAH Means "delight" and it originates from biblical Hebrew.

TORI Means "bird" and originates from the Japanese language.

TOVA Means "good" or "beautiful" in Hebrew and originates from the biblical name Tovah/Tov, derived from the Hebrew word "tov" meaning "good."

TRACY	Means "warlike" and originated from an English surname derived from the Norman French word "trasse" meaning "to hunt."
TREASURE	Means "valuable possessions" and originates from the English vocabulary word.
TRINITY	Means "threefold" and originates from the Latin word "trinitas," referring to the Christian concept of the Holy Trinity representing the Father, the Son, and the Holy Spirit.
TRULY	Means "genuine" or "sincere" and is of English origin.
UNIQUE	Means "one of a kind" and originates from the English language.
VADA	Means "knowledge" or "wise" and it originated from the Arabic language.
VALENCIA	The first name Valencia, of Spanish origin, means "brave" or "strong."
VALENTINA	The first name Valentina originates from Latin and means "strong and healthy."
VALERIE	Female given name of French origin meaning "strength" or "bravery."
VALKYRIE	Means "chooser of the slain" and originates from Old Norse mythology, referring to powerful female figures who selected warriors to be taken to the afterlife.
VANELLOPE	Means "butterfly" and is of American origin.
VANESSA	Greek origin and means "butterfly" or "essence of a butterfly", originally popularized by Jonathan Swift in his poem "Cadenus and Vanessa" as a pen name for Esther
VAYDA	Means "life" or "to live" and it is of Turkish origin.
VENUS	Means "goddess of love" and originates from Roman mythology.
VERA	Means "faith" or "truth" and comes from the Russian and Slavic languages.
VERONICA	Means "true image" and has Latin origins.
VESPER	Means "evening star" and has Latin origins.
VIANNEY	Means "lively" and originates from the French and Latin languages.
VICTORIA	Means "victory" and originates from the Latin language.
VIOLET	Feminine given name of English origin that represents the flower associated with modesty, faithfulness, and virtue.
VIRGINIA	Means "pure, maiden" and it originates from the ancient Roman name Virginius, derived from the Latin word virgo.
VIVIAN	Means "full of life" and has its origins in Latin.
WAVERLY	The meaning and origin of the first name Waverly is "from the field of quivering aspens" and it is of English origin.
WEDNESDAY	The meaning of the first name Wednesday is "the day of the week named after the Norse god Odin," and it originates from Middle English and Old English.
WENDY	Means "friend" and was first coined by J.M. Barrie for the character Wendy Darling in his play "Peter Pan" (1904).
WHITLEY	Whitley is an English name meaning "white clearing" and is derived from a surname referring to someone who lived near a white or clear field.
WILHELMINA	Means "resolute protection" and originated from Germany.
WILLOW	English origin, means "a slender and graceful tree or shrub with narrow leaves."
WINIFRED	Welsh origin, means "blessed peacemaking" or "friend of peace."
WINONA	Means "firstborn daughter" and originates from the Dakota Sioux tribe of Native Americans.
WINRY	English origin and its meaning is "blessed and strong."
WINSLOW	Winslow is an English surname turned first name that means "hill with a meadow."
WINTER	Means "the season of winter" and has origins in English and Germanic languages.
WREN	Means "small bird" and originates from Old English.
WRENLEIGH	The first name Wrenleigh likely originated from the blending of the English word "wren," referring to a small songbird, and the suffix "-leigh," which means "meadow or clearing" in Old English, conveying a name meaning "meadow of wrens."
WRENLEY	Means "from the wren meadow" and has originated from English surnames derived from the Old English word "wrenlēah."
XENA	Mythological and unique name of Greek origin, meaning "hospitality" or "welcoming" in ancient Greek culture.
XIMENA	Spanish feminine name, derived from the masculine name Simón, meaning "one who hears."

XIOMARA	Means "ready for battle" and is of Spanish origin.
XITLALI	Means "star" or "luminous" and originates from the Nahuatl language spoken by the Aztecs in ancient Mexico.
XOCHITL	Means "flower" in Nahuatl and originates from the indigenous cultures of Mesoamerica, particularly the Aztec civilization.
XOLANI	Means "peace" or "forgiveness" and has its origin in Zulu and Ndebele cultures in South Africa.
YAHAIRA	Means "to shine" and it originated from the Hebrew name Yaira.
YAMILETH	Means "beautiful one" and originates from Hebrew and Arabic.
YARELI	Means "water lady" or "daughter of the sea," and it is of Native American origin.
YARETZI	Means "you will always be loved" and originates from the Nahuatl language spoken by the indigenous people of Mexico.
YARITZA	The first name Yaritza is of Native American origin and holds the meaning "small butterfly."
YASMEEN	Means "jasmine flower" and it originates from Arabic.
YATZIRI	Female name of Nahuatl origin meaning "new growth" or "blooming flower".
YAZMIN	Means "jasmine flower" and originates from Arabic and Persian cultures.
YESENIA	Means 'palm tree' and it originated in the Spanish language.
YOCHEVED	Means "God's glory" and it has Hebrew origins.
YOSELIN	Means "God sees" and originates from Hebrew.
YUNA	Means "moon" and originates from various cultures such as Korean, Japanese, and Arabic.
YUSRA	Yusra is an Arabic name meaning "wealth" or "ease" and is derived from the Qur'an.
YVETTE	The name Yvette originated from the French version of the name Yvonne, meaning "yew wood" or "archer" and has roots in Old Germanic and Old French languages.
YVONNE	Means "yew wood" and it originates from France.
ZAHRA	Means "bright, shining" and it originates from Arabic.
ZAINAB	Arabic origin, means "beautiful and fragrant flower" and is often used as a name for girls in Muslim communities.
ZAMORA	Means "olive tree" and it is of Spanish origin.
ZANIYAH	Feminine given name of Arabic origin meaning "beautiful and graceful."
ZELDA	Means "gray battle" and originates from the German language.
ZEMIRA	The first name Zemira is of Hebrew origin and means "song."
ZENDAYA	Means "to give thanks" and it has African origins.
ZEYNEP	The first name Zeynep is of Turkish origin and means "precious beauty" or "adorned with beauty."
ZHAVIA	The first name Zhavia has no widely accepted meaning or origin as it is a unique and unusual name.
ZHURI	Means "beautiful" or "lovely" and it originates from the Bantu language of the Ndau people in Zimbabwe and Mozambique.
ZINNIA	Flower-inspired name of Latin origin, symbolizing beauty and remembrance.
ZIPPORAH	Means "bird" in Hebrew and has biblical origins as the name of the wife of Moses in the Old Testament.
ZIVA	Means "radiance" or "brightness" and has Hebrew origins.
ZOE	Greek origin and means "life" or "alive".
ZULEMA	Feminine given name of Arabic origin meaning "full of beauty and grace."
ZULEYKA	The first name Zuleyka is of Arabic origin and means "beautiful."
ZURI	Means "beautiful" in Swahili and originates from the East African region, particularly Tanzania and Kenya.

4,000 more names for girls.

AADHINI The meaning of the first name AADHINI is "First Power" and its origin is Sanskrit.

AADHYAR EDDY The first name AADHYAREDDY is of Indian origin and it means "noble and powerful ruler".

AADRITI The first name AADRITI is of Indian origin and means "one who is worshipped or respected."

AARUSHI Means "first ray of the sun" and originates from Sanskrit.

AASHRITHA Means "one who seeks shelter or refuge" and has Indian origins.

ABEEHA Arabic origin and it means "one who is intelligent and quick-witted."

ABERDEEN Means "mouth of the river Dee" and originates from the Scottish city of Aberdeen.

ABIGAIL GRACE Means "my father is joyful" and is a combination of the Hebrew name Abigail and the English name Grace.

ABIMBOLA Yoruba name meaning "born wealthy" or "born into wealth", commonly given to children in Nigeria.

ABLESSYN Modern and unique variation of the name Abilene, likely inspired by the biblical city mentioned in the Book of Genesis.

ABSALAT The first name Absalat has a meaning of "devotion" and its origin can be traced back to Persian and Arabic languages.

ABUK South Sudanese female name of Dinka origin, meaning "born during the rainy season."

ABYSSINIA Means "land of the Ethiopians" and is of Ethiopian origin.

ACHSAH Means "anklet" or "adorned" in Hebrew, and it has biblical origins.

ADAEZE Means "princess" and it originates from the Igbo language of Nigeria.

ADALAYA Modern, feminine given name of uncertain origin with no widely recognized specific meaning.

ADALEINE Variation of the name Adeline, derived from the Germanic elements "adel" meaning "noble" and "lind" meaning "soft, tender."

ADALETH The first name Adaleth originates from Germanic roots and means "noble and gentle."

ADALIENE Unknown origin and meaning.

ADANELY Modern invented name likely derived from the biblical name "Adonai" meaning "my lord" or "master" in Hebrew.

ADAOLISA Nigerian name meaning "princess of a noble father" or "daughter of a nobleman."

ADAORA Means "daughter of all" in Igbo language, derived from Nigerian origin.

ADDILEE Modern invented American name derived from combining the names Addison and Lee, typically used as a feminine given name.

ADELANI Means "royal" and it has African Yoruba origins.

ADELAYDA Means "noble" or "exalted" and it has uncertain origins.

ADELENA Means "noble" or "noble and tender" and has Germanic origins.

ADELHEID Means "noble, kind" and originated from Germanic roots.

ADELITA Means "noble" or "noble one" and originates from Spanish and Portuguese languages.

ADEOLA Means "crown of wealth" and originates from the Yoruba language of Nigeria.

ADERINSOLA Means "the crown of wealth" and originates from Yoruba, a language and ethnic group in Nigeria.

ADESUWA Means "royalty is due" and originates from the Edo people in Nigeria.

ADHITHI Hindu name of Indian origin meaning "guest" or "visitor".

ADIBA Means "cultured, learned" and is of Arabic origin.

ADITRI Means "the highest honor" and has its origin in Sanskrit.

ADLIH The name ADLIH does not have a known meaning or origin as it appears to be an uncommon or invented name.

ADMIRE   Means "to regard with approval or respect" and originates from the Shona language in Zimbabwe.

ADRINA   The first name Adrina is of uncertain origin and meaning, but it is believed to have Germanic roots and may have variations in spelling and pronunciation in different

ADWOA   Means "born on Monday" and originates from the Akan people of Ghana.

AELIANA   Means "sun" or "sunlight" and has Latin origins.

AELITA   Means "sun" or "morning star" and is of Greek origin.

AEMILIA   Means "rival" or "emulating" and originated from the Latin name Aemilius.

AERILYN   Feminine given name of American origin, meaning "ocean fairies."

AESIRA   Means "goddess of the dawn" and has Scandinavian origins.

AFFINITY   Means a natural liking or connection, and its origin is English.

AFIFA   Means "virtuous" or "chaste" in Arabic, originating from the Islamic tradition.

AFOMIA   The first name Afomia is of Ethiopian origin and its meaning is "given."

AFRICA   Means "pleasant" or "sunny" and it is of Latin origin.

AGAPE   Means "unconditional love" and originated from Greek.

AHILANY   The first name Ahilany has a possible origin in Sanskrit and it means "graceful, beautiful sunrise."

AHINARA   Means "beautiful flower" and has origins in the Native American culture.

AHINOA   Basque name meaning "only daughter" or "unique" and originates from the Basque Country in Spain.

AHLAM   Means "dreams" in Arabic and it is of Arabic origin.

AHLAYAH   The name Ahlayah has an uncertain origin and its meaning is unknown.

AHLORA   Modern invented name that does not have a widely recognized meaning or origin.

AHMEIRA   Arabic origin, meaning "princess" or "leader".

AHMINA   The first name Ahmina is of uncertain origin and meaning.

AHMIRACLE   The name "Ahmiracle" is a modern American name that likely derives from combining "Ah" meaning divine or sacred and "miracle" suggesting an extraordinary event or phenomenon.

AHMYA   Uncertain origin and meaning, but it is most commonly used in the United States.

AHNESTY   Means "truthfulness" and it is a modern variant of the word "honesty" combined with the name "Annie."

AHNYLA   Modern and invented name with no clearly defined meaning or origin, commonly used as a feminine given name.

AHONESTI   Means "honest" and it originates from the English language.

AHRIYAH   Means "lioness" and has Hebrew origins.

AHSOKA   Means "she who is not alone" and originated from the Star Wars franchise.

AHTZIRI   Means "graceful" or "beautiful" and originates from the Nahuatl language spoken by indigenous people in Mexico.

AHZURI   Unique Swahili name meaning "calm, peaceful, serene."

AIDALY   Uncertain origin and meaning.

AIKO   Means "love child" and originates from Japanese.

AILEANA   Means "beauty, grace" and it is of Scottish origin.

AILED   Spanish female name meaning "noble, kind-hearted," originating from the Old French word "Ailie" derived from the Germanic name "Adalheidis."

AILISH   Means "noble" or "consecrated to God" and has origins in Ireland.

AIMSLEY   The first name Aimsley likely originated as a variant spelling of the English surname Ainsley, meaning "meadow near the River Ayr" or "an oak clearing."

AINHARA   The first name Ainhara is of Basque origin and means "graceful beauty."

AINOHA   The first name Ainoha has Basque origins and is thought to mean "only daughter."

AINSLIE   The first name Ainslie originated from Scotland and means "one who comes from Ainslie's field."

AIRAREDDY   Indian origin and means "son of the wind."

AISHANI   Means "goddess Durga" and originates from Hindu mythology.

AISHWARYA   Indian origin and it means "wealth, prosperity, and beauty."

AISOSA   African origin and it means "God's gift" or "God's blessing" in the Edo language of Nigeria.

AISSATOU	Means "born on Saturday" and has African origin.
AITIANA	The first name Aitiana likely has Spanish origins and its meaning is currently unknown or less common.
AIXA	Feminine given name of Arabic origin, often associated with Islamic culture, meaning "peaceful" or "alive".
AIZEL	Hebrew origin and means "noble."
AIZLYNN	Combined origins, derived from the Old English word "aesc" meaning "ash tree" and the Welsh word "llyn" meaning "lake," symbolizing strength and harmony.
AJOURNEY	The first name AJOURNEY has an English origin and it means "a path or passage taken towards a specific destination or goal."
AJREAM	The first name AJREAM does not have a widely recognized meaning or origin as it appears to be a unique or invented name.
AJUNI	The first name Ajuni has no widely recognized meaning or origin.
AJWA	Arabic origin and means "fragrant tree"; it is commonly given to girls.
AKANE	The name Akane has the meaning "deep red" and originates from Japanese.
AKANKSHA	Feminine Indian name of Sanskrit origin meaning "desire" or "wish."
AKEELAH	The first name Akeelah has African origins and means "intelligent" or "wise."
AKIKO	Means "bright" or "sparkling" in Japanese, and it originates from the Japanese language and culture.
AKOSUA	Female given name of Akan origin from Ghana, meaning "born on a Sunday."
ALABAMA	Means "thicket clearers" and is of Native American origin.
ALAIYNA	American origin and means "beautiful, peaceful, serene."
ALANOUD	Means "delicate" or "fragile" and is of Arabic origin.
ALAYASIA	The name Alayasia originated from the combination of the names Aaliyah and Asia and holds no specific meaning.
ALAYSHA	Modern invented name with an uncertain origin and meaning, possibly influenced by various cultures and languages.
ALAYTHIA	The first name Alaythia is of uncertain origin and meaning.
ALAYZIA	American origin and its meaning is uncertain as it is a modern and unique name.
ALAZNE	Basque feminine name meaning "miracle" or "miraculous," originating from the Basque region of Spain.
ALBANY	Means "from Alba" and originates from Scottish Gaelic.
ALEANA	Means "noble" or "gracious" and originates from the Greek name Alina.
ALEGACI	The name Alegaci does not have a commonly recognized meaning or origin, suggesting that it may be a rare or unique name.
ALEJANDRINA	Means "defender of men" and it is of Spanish origin.
ALESANA	Hawaiian origin and means "path" or "road".
ALESSANDRIA	Means "defender of mankind" and originated from the Italian form of Alexandria, a Greek name derived from the city of Alexandria in Egypt.
ALEXIANNA	Means "defender of mankind" and has a Greek origin.
ALEXZAN DRIA	Modern variation of Alexandria, derived from the Greek name Alexandros meaning "defender of men."
ALEYSSA	Means "noble" or "of noble kind" and is of Greek origin.
ALHELI	The first name "Alheli" is of Arabic origin and is derived from the word "al-hurriya" meaning "freedom" or "liberty."
ALIANI	Modern American name of uncertain origin, possibly a variant of the name Eliana, derived from the Hebrew name □ □ □ □ □ □ (Eliyahu) meaning "my God is Yahweh".
ALICENT	Modern English name derived from the Latin name "Alixentia," which means noble and gracious.
ALICIANA	The meaning of the first name Aliciana is not clear as it does not have a widely recognized origin or meaning.
ALIVIYAH	Variant spelling of the name Olivia, which originated from the Latin word "oliva" meaning "olive."
ALIZAE	The first name Alizae originated from the combination of the names Ali and Zaynab, and it means "exalted, beautiful, and graceful."

ALIZETTE	Means "noble" or "of noble descent" and is believed to have originated from French or Hebrew language.
ALLURE	Means captivating or attracting, and its origin is derived from the English language.
ALMIRA	Means "princess" and has origins in Arabic and Spanish.
ALPHONSINE	The first name Alphonsine is of Germanic origin and means "noble" or "ready for battle."
ALVINA	The first name Alvina is of German origin and means "noble friend."
ALYESKA	Means "great land" and has Alaska Native origins.
ALYONA	Variant of the Russian name Alena, meaning "bright, shining" and its origin is Russian or Czech.
ALYSSANDRA	English origin and means "defender of mankind".
ALYXANDRIA	Means "defender of mankind" and has its origins in Greek.
ALZAHRA	Means "the shining one" and originates from Arabic culture, referencing the title given to the Prophet Muhammad's daughter Fatimah.
AMAHLE	Means "beautiful" or "goodness" in Zulu and is of South African origin.
AMAIRANI	The name Amaiairani is of Nahuatl origin and means "a worthy sacrifice" in indigenous Mexican culture.
AMALTHEA	Means "tender goddess" and originates from Greek mythology, referring to the foster mother of Zeus.
AMANDINE	Means "lovable" or "worthy of love" and originates from the Latin name "Amandus."
AMANITA	Means "beloved" and has origins in various cultures, including Greek and Latin.
AMARACHI	Means "God's grace" and is of Igbo origin in Nigeria.
AMARACH UKWU	Means "God's grace" and it originates from the Igbo language of Nigeria.
AMARIGRACE	Modern American name combining "Amar" meaning "immortal" and "Grace" meaning "elegance," reflecting a fusion of timeless beauty and grace.
AMARISSA	The first name Amarissa originated from Greek and it means "promised to God" or "loved by God."
AMARIYANA	Means "a beautiful blend of two cultures" and its origin is a modern American invention that combines the names Amara and Yana.
AMARYAH	Means "gift from God" and originates from Hebrew.
AMATULLAH	Means "female servant of Allah" and it originates from Arabic.
AMAYALEE	The meaning and origin of the first name Amayalee are uncertain as it appears to be a unique or uncommon name without a widely known etymology.
AMAZING	The meaning and origin of the first name Amazing are unknown as it is not a traditional or commonly-used name.
AMBERLEE	Modern American name composed of the gemstone "amber" and the suffix "-lee," meaning "amber meadow" or "meadow of amber."
AMBIKA	The name Ambika originated from Sanskrit and means "mother or goddess, divine."
AMEENAH	Means "trustworthy" or "honest" and originates from Arabic.
AMEILA	The first name Amelïa is a unique creation that does not have a widely recognized meaning or origin.
AMELIAJAMES	The first name AmeliaJames was likely created by combining the names Amelia and James, possibly as a unique or hybrid name.
AMELIAMARIE	Combination of the names Amelia, meaning "industrious" in Latin, and Marie, a variation of Mary which means "beloved" in Hebrew.
AMELIANA	Feminine given name of Latin origin, meaning "rival" or "emulating" and can be considered as a variation of the name Amelia.
AMELIAROSE	Means "a combination of the names Amelia and Rose" and has originated from English and Latin origins.
AMELIYAH	Means "work of the Lord" and is a variant of the name Amalia derived from Germanic and Hebrew origins.
AMEYALI	Means "noble and peaceful" and originates from the Nahuatl language of the indigenous peoples of Mexico.

AMICIA   Means "friendship" and has Latin origins.

AMIDALA   Means "beautiful flower" and it originates from the Star Wars franchise, specifically from the character Queen Padmé Amidala.

AMIERA   Means "princess" and has Arabic origins.

AMIRIYAH   Feminine Arabic name meaning "royal" or "princess," originating from the Arabic word "amir" which means prince or commander.

AMOGHA   Means "unfailing" or "infallible" and has its origin in Sanskrit.

AMOREENA   Feminine given name of Italian origin meaning "beloved," derived from the Italian word "amore" which means love.

AMORETTE   Means "little love" and it has French origins.

AMORIAH   Feminine given name of Hebrew origin, meaning "love of God."

AMRAH   The meaning and origin of the first name Amrah is Arabic and it means "virgin."

AMRITA   Means "immortality" and originates from Sanskrit.

AMRUTHA   Means "immortal" or "nectar" in Sanskrit and has Indian origins.

AMULYA   Means "invaluable" or "priceless" and it originates from Sanskrit, an ancient Indian language.

AMUNET   Means "hidden one" and has origins in ancient Egyptian mythology.

AMYLEE   Means "beloved wind" and is of French origin.

AMYRIE   The first name Amyrie is of uncertain origin and meaning as it does not have clear historical or cultural roots.

ANACLARA   Compound name of Portuguese origin, derived from the names Ana, meaning "grace" or "favor," and Clara, meaning "clear" or "bright," representing someone who possesses grace and clarity.

ANAGHA   Means "sinless" or "pure" in Sanskrit, and it originates from Hindu mythology and traditional Indian culture.

ANAHITA   Means "goddess of fertility, water, and wisdom" and originates from ancient Persian mythology.

ANAHLIA   American origin and it does not have a specific meaning.

ANAISABEL   Compound name of French and Spanish origin, meaning "gracious and beautiful" (Ana) combined with "God is my oath" (Isabel).

ANAJULIA   The first name Anajulia originated from a combination of Ana, meaning "grace" or "favor" in Hebrew, and Julia, derived from the Latin name Julius, meaning "youthful" or "downy-bearded."

ANALAURA   Combination of two feminine names, Ana originating from Hebrew meaning "grace" and Laura originating from Latin meaning "laurel," symbolizing victory and honor.

ANALEIA   The meaning and origin of the first name Analeia is uncertain and there are no specific records available.

ANALUCIA   Spanish origin and means "graceful light".

ANALUISA   Combination of the Spanish names Ana and Luisa, meaning "gracious and renowned warrior" or "graceful warrior."

ANAMIKA   Means "nameless" or "without a name" in Sanskrit and it is of Indian origin.

ANANDI   Means "blissful" or "full of happiness" and originates from Sanskrit, an ancient Indo-Aryan language.

ANAPAULA   Means "gracious, small" and has Portuguese origins.

ANASOPHIA   Means "graceful wisdom" and it is a combination of the names Ana (of Hebrew origin meaning "grace") and Sophia (of Greek origin meaning "wisdom").

ANASTAISA   The name Anastasia means "resurrection" and has Greek and Russian origins.

ANASTAZJA   Means "resurrection" or "rebirth," and it is of Greek origin.

ANASTYN   Modern variation of the name Anastasia, derived from the Greek word "anastasis" meaning "resurrection" or "rebirth".

ANAVEAH   Modern invention and does not have a widely recognized meaning or origin.

ANAVICTORIA   The name Anavictoria combines the Hebrew name Ana, meaning "grace" or "favor," with the Latin name Victoria, meaning "victory," resulting in a name associated with grace and victoriousness.

ANAYALIZ Modern and unique name of uncertain origin, possibly a combination of the names Ana and Liza.

ANAYANSI Indigenous origins and means "everlasting and honest" in the Guarani language.

ANBERLIN The first name Anberlin does not have a clear meaning and appears to be derived from a Christian rock band name.

ANDILYN Modern, invented name with no known meaning or origin.

ANDRAYA Means "strong and brave" and is of Greek origin.

ANDREINA Feminine given name of Italian origin, derived from the name Andrea, meaning "manly" or "brave."

ANEESAH Means "close friend" or "intimate companion" and has Arabic origins.

ANEIRA Feminine given name of Welsh origin meaning "golden" or "splendid."

ANELIZ Feminine given name of uncertain origin and meaning.

ANEMONE The first name Anemone originates from the Greek language and means "windflower."

ANGELES Means "angels" in Spanish and has its origin in religious belief.

ANGELIKI Means "angel" and its origin is Greek.

ANGELMARIE Means "angelic Marie" and originates from the combination of the names Angel and Marie.

ANIAYA The meaning and origin of the first name ANIAYA is unknown.

ANISE The name ANISE refers to a plant with aromatic seeds, and it is of Greek origin.

ANJANA Means "merciful" and it has its origin in Sanskrit.

ANJELICA Variant of Angelica, derived from the Latin word "angelicus," meaning "angelic" or "of the angels," and it is of Greek origin.

ANJOLAO LUWA Means "wealth is of God" in Yoruba and is of Nigerian origin.

ANNACLAIRE The name Annaclaire combines the names Anna and Claire, and its meaning is a combination of "grace" (Anna) and "clear" or "bright" (Claire).

ANNAELISE Combination of two traditional names, Anna and Elise, and portrays a charming and graceful personality.

ANNAKATE "Annakate" is a modern combination of the names Anna and Kate, likely created as a unique and fusion name for girls.

ANNAKAT HERINE Compound name of Anna, originating from Hebrew meaning "grace" or "favor," and Katherine, originating from Greek meaning "pure" or "innocent."

ANNALYSIA Modern variant of the name Annalise, which is derived from the combination of the names Anna (meaning "grace") and Elizabeth (meaning "my God is an oath").

ANNAPURNA Means "Goddess of Food and Nourishment" in Sanskrit and originates from Hindu mythology.

ANNIEMAE The first name Annimae means "graceful" or "favor, grace of God" and is derived from the combination of the names Ann and Mae.

ANOKHI ANOKHI is an Indian feminine name meaning "unique" or "unparalleled," originating from Sanskrit.

ANORI Means "light" or "radiance" and has a Maori origin.

ANOUK Feminine Dutch name meaning "grace," derived from the French name Anne.

ANOUSHKA Means "favor, grace" and it originates from the Russian diminutive form of the name Anna.

ANOVA ANOVA is not a first name but rather an acronym for "Analysis of Variance," a statistical method used to analyze differences between groups, originating in the field of statistics in the early 20th century.

ANSHIKA Means "partial or beautiful moon" and originates from the Hindi language in India.

ANTHONELLA Means "beyond praise" and it is a feminine variant of the name Anthony.

ANTIGONE Means "against birth" or "against generation" and it has Greek origins derived from the mythological character in Greek tragedy.

ANTIONETTE Means "beyond praise," and it is an English variant of the French name Antoinette, which is the feminine form of Antoine, derived from the Latin name Antonius.

ANTONETTE	Means "priceless" and has Latin and French origins.
ANTONIETTA	The first name Antonietta originates from Italian and means "priceless" or "beyond value."
ANUHEA	Means "cool fragrance" in Hawaiian and has Polynesian origins.
ANUM	Arabic origin and means "blessing" or "gift from God."
ANUOLUWA	Means "God's mercy" and originates from the Yoruba culture in Nigeria.
ANUOLUW APO	Means "God's mercy is abundant" and originates from the Yoruba language in Nigeria.
ANUSHKA	Means "grace" or "favor" and is of Russian origin, derived from the name Anna.
ANUSHREE	Means "one who shines like the morning sun" and it originates from Sanskrit, an ancient Indo-Aryan language.
APHRODITE	The first name Aphrodite derives from Greek mythology and refers to the goddess of love, beauty, and desire.
APOLLONIA	Means "belonging to Apollo" and has Greek origins.
APPHIA	The name Apphia likely derives from the Greek word "apphia," meaning "affection" or "friendship," and has biblical origins.
AQUA	Means "water" in Latin.
AQUETZALI	Nahuatl name of Aztec origin meaning "precious water."
ARADHANA	Indian origin and means "worship" or "devotion" in Hindi.
ARADIA	Means "holy one" or "daughter of the moon" and originates from Italian folklore and the book "Aradia, or the Gospel of the Witches" by Charles Leland.
ARAINA	The meaning and origin of the first name Araina is derived from the combination of the names "Ara" meaning "brings rain" and "Ina" meaning "queen," resulting in "queen who brings rain" or "ruling rain."
ARAMINTA	Means "defender" and has English origins.
ARAOLUWA	Means "wonder of God" and originates from the Yoruba-speaking people of Nigeria and West Africa.
ARAYLA	Modern invented name with no specific origin, often used as a feminine given name.
ARCADIA	Means "idyllic place or utopia" and has its origins in Greek mythology, specifically in the region of Arcadia in ancient Greece.
ARCELIA	The first name Arcelia originated in Spanish and it means "altar of heaven" or "treasure".
ARELYS	The name Arelis means "golden" and it is of English and Latin origin.
ARETHA	Means "excellence" or "virtue" and it originates from the Greek word "arete."
AREVIK	Arevik is an Armenian given name derived from the word "arev" meaning "sun," symbolizing warmth, vitality, and brightness.
ARHAREDDY	The meaning and origin of the first name Arhareddy are unknown.
ARIABELLA	Combination of the names Ariana and Isabella, and it originated from combining different elements of various cultures and languages.
ARIALYNN	American origin and it means "lioness of God" or "a noble strength."
ARIANELLY	Means "holy one" and has no known origin or meaning; it is a modern name created by combining various elements.
ARIAUNA	Means "noble, graceful" and originated from the combination of the names Aria and Shauna.
ARIAYL	The name Ariayl does not have a distinct meaning or origin as it does not appear to be a name of any known language or culture.
ARILENA	Means "peaceful and lionlike" and has an origin in Greek.
ARIROSE	English origin and it means "a beautiful rose."
ARITZIA	Basque feminine name, meaning "oak tree" or "from the oak tree," derived from the Basque word "haritz" meaning oak, often used to symbolize strength and resilience.
ARIYEL	Means "lion of God" and has Hebrew origins.
ARLENYS	The first name Arlenys is of Spanish origin and it means "prominent, noble, or honorable."
ARLOWE	Means "fort on the hill" and has English origins.
ARMIYAH	Means "gift from God" and has Hebrew origins.
AROARA	The first name Aroara has no widely recognized meaning or origin as it appears to be a unique and uncommon name.

ARPI	Unisex Armenian name derived from the Persian word "arpi" meaning "sunbeam" or "ray of sunlight."
ARRIETTY	Variant of the name Harriet, derived from the Germanic name "Heimrich", meaning "ruler of the household."
ARTEMISIA	Female given name of Greek origin, derived from the Greek goddess Artemis, and it means "gift of Artemis" or "safe and healthy."
ARVAEYAH	The meaning and origin of the first name Arvaeyah are uncertain and might be of unique or uncommon origin.
ARYIAH	Modern and unique name of uncertain origin, possibly derived from the Hebrew name Arya meaning "lioness" or the Sanskrit word Aria meaning "noble."
ARZOIE	Feminine name of Persian origin, meaning "wish" or "desire".
ARZOYI	The first name Arzoyi has an Armenian origin and its meaning is unknown.
ASEDA	Ghanaian name meaning "thanks" or "gratitude".
ASENATH	Means "gift of the Egyptian goddess Neith" and it has origins in Hebrew and Egyptian cultures.
ASHELYNN	Modern feminine name derived from the combination of "Ashley" and "Lynn," often associated with the United States.
ASHERAH	Means "she who walks at night" or "she who treads on the sea" and originates from ancient Semitic cultures, specifically Canaanite and Hebrew.
ASHIYA	Japanese origin and means "foot of a reed."
ASHYLA	The first name Ashyla does not have a widely recognized meaning or origin.
ASLY	Modern American name that could be a variant of the name Ashley and may have originated as a feminine form of the Old English name Asher, meaning "happy" or
ASMAHAN	Asmahan is an Arabic name meaning "highest, most exalted" and it is of Arabic origin.
ASSATA	Means "she who struggles" and is of Swahili origin.
ASSETOU	Means "she who is born on Saturday" and has its origin in the West African region, particularly in Mali and Senegal.
ASTORIA	Means "hawk" or "star" in Greek and originated as a feminine form of the name Astor.
ASTRAEA	Means "star" or "goddess of justice" and originates from Greek mythology.
ASTREA	Means "star" and has its origin in Greek mythology, as Astrea was the goddess of justice and innocence.
ASUNA	Means "tomorrow" in Japanese and is derived from the Japanese words "asu" meaning "tomorrow" and "na" meaning "name" or "beauty".
ATENEA	Means "goddess of wisdom" and it has its origins in Greek mythology, specifically referring to the goddess Athena.
ATHALIAH	Means "Yahweh is exalted" and originates from the Hebrew language.
ATHENAROSE	The name AthenaRose originated from Greek mythology and signifies a combination of wisdom (Athena) and beauty (Rose).
ATINA	Means "firm, determined" and it has Persian origins.
ATLANTIS	Means "mythical island" and it originated from Greek mythology as a legendary lost continent.
ATLEIGH	Means "from the meadow" and has English origins.
ATZI	The meaning and origin of the first name Atzi are unknown as it does not have a widely recognized origin or meaning.
AUBREANNA	Feminine name of American origin, likely derived from the combination of the names Aubrey and Brianna, and it means "noble and strong."
AUBREI	Gender-neutral variant of the name Aubrey, derived from the Germanic name Alberic, meaning "ruler of elves."
AUBRYN	Means "ruler of the elves" and is of English origin.
AUBURN	Means "reddish-brown color" and originates from the English language.
AUDREYA NNA	Modern and feminine name of American origin, which likely combines elements of the names Audrey and Anna.
AUDRIELLA	The name Audriella combines the names Audrey and Gabriella, meaning "noble strength" and "God is my strength," and has no specific origin as it is a modern invented name.

AUNESTI	The meaning and origin of the first name Aunesti is uncertain as it does not have commonly known origins or definitions.
AUNIKA	Modern variation of the feminine name Annika, derived from the Hebrew name Hannah meaning "grace" or "favor" and originally popularized in Scandinavia.
AUNISTY	The name Aunisty does not have a widely recognized meaning or origin as it appears to be a unique or rare name with no known specific historical or cultural background.
AUNYSTEE	There is no information available about the meaning or origin of the first name AUNYSTEE as it does not appear to have any known origin or usage.
AUNYX	Unknown origin and meaning.
AURAYA	The name "Auraya" does not have a widely recognized meaning or origin as it is a relatively rare and unique name.
AURORAROSE	Means "dawn rose" and has Latin and English origins.
AUSET	Means "throne" and originates from ancient Egyptian mythology, as Auset was the goddess of fertility, healing, and wisdom.
AUTUMNROSE	Means a combination of the seasons "Autumn" and "Rose," conveying a sense of beauty and transformation, with its origin likely being a modern English amalgamation of nature-inspired names.
AUZARIA	Unique and modern name of uncertain origin.
AVACYN	Means "protector" or "guardian" and originates from the fictional world of the collectible trading card game, Magic: The Gathering.
AVAEAH	The first name Avaeh means "like a tiny, delicate bird" and is of uncertain origin.
AVAEYA	The name AVAEYA does not have a widely recognized meaning or origin as it appears to be unique and may have been created or derived from other names or words.
AVAGRACE	Means "beautiful grace" and originated as a combination of the names Ava and Grace.
AVAMAE	Modern invented name with no known meaning or origin.
AVANGELINA	Means "bearer of good news" and it is derived from the Greek name Evangeline.
AVANTI	The name Avanti originates from Sanskrit and means "forward" or "ahead" in English.
AVANTIKA	Means "princess of Ujjain" and originates from ancient Hindu mythology and culture.
AVAREE	Modern feminine name of uncertain origin and meaning.
AVAROSE	Means "graceful flower" and possibly has origins in both the Old English name Ava and the Latin name Rosa.
AVEIYAH	Modern invented name with no specific origin, sometimes used as a variation of the name Avaya.
AVELINA	Spanish origin and means "desired or longed for."
AVENLY	American origin, means "heavenly" or "from the river Aven."
AVEREIGH	Averiegh is a modern, unique variation of the name Averie, of English origin meaning "ruler of the elves."
AVERIANA	Feminine name of uncertain origin and meaning.
AVERLEY	The name Averley originated from Old English, meaning "meadow of the boar."
AVEYAH	Modern feminine name of Hebrew origin, meaning "my father is God" or "my father is Yahweh".
AVIANNE	Modern invented name likely derived from the word "avian," meaning bird, and the suffix "anne" which is of French origin and means gracious or favor.
AVIELLE	Hebrew origin, means "my father is God" or "God is my father."
AVIENDHA	Fictional name of uncertain meaning and origin, originating from the Wheel of Time fantasy book series by Robert Jordan.
AVIGAYIL	The first name Avigail means "father's joy" and has Hebrew origins.
AVILA	Feminine given name of Spanish origin meaning "from a village or town."
AVIONNA	Modern American feminine name of unknown origin, possibly a variant of the name "Aviana," meaning "bird-like" or "like a bird."
AVISHKA	Feminine given name of Sanskrit origin meaning "grand, majestic" or "ruler, queen."
AVLEEN	Feminine Indian name meaning "one who is devoted and absorbed in God" and is derived from the Punjabi language.
AVNEET	Punjabi name of Indian origin, derived from the combination of the Sanskrit elements "avni" meaning "earth" or "stone" and "neet" meaning "morality" or "the embodied soul," suggesting a person with a down-to-earth and morally virtuous nature.

AVNOOR	The first name Avnoor is of Punjabi origin and means "one who is blessed with peace and enlightenment."
AYAME	Means "iris" in Japanese, and it is of Japanese origin.
AYANFEO LUWA	Means "joy becomes mine" in Yoruba and is of Nigerian origin.
AYELET	The Hebrew name Ayelet means "gazelle" and is of biblical origin.
AYEZA	Arabic origin, means "respected" or "honored."
AYLANIE	The first name Aylaníe, of unknown origin, is believed to be a modern and unique name with no widely accepted meaning.
AYMARA	Means "sacred and beloved" and it originates from the Aymara people, an indigenous group found in the Andes region of South America.
AYNAZ	Means "beautiful fairy" in Persian and is of Iranian origin.
AYNUR	Turkish origin and means "radiant moon" or "enlightened."
AYRABELLA	Unknown origin, likely means "beautiful melody" or "beautiful voice."
AYSHE	Turkish origin and it means "alive" or "she who lives."
AYSIA	The first name Aysia is of uncertain origin and meaning, possibly derived from the name Asia, referring to the continent.
AYTHANA	Hebrew origin and means "gift of God."
AYZAL	Kazakh origin and means "moon gift" or "moonlight."
AZADEH	Means "freedom" and originates from Persian/Iranian culture.
AZAHARA	Means "blooming flower" and originates from Arabic.
AZAHRI	Masculine Arabic name meaning "blossoming" or "flourishing," originating from the Arabic root word "zahr" which means flower.
AZAILAH	Modern, unique name of Hebrew origin that means "God is my strength."
AZALEYAH	Hebrew origin and means "God has spared; God's helper."
AZAYLEA	The first name Azaylea is of American origin and means "a variant spelling of Azalea, a type of flowering shrub."
AZAYLIE	Modern invented name with no known origin or meaning.
AZEALIA	The first name Azealia is of uncertain origin and meaning.
AZELIE	French name of uncertain origin, with a likely meaning of "noble" or "noble maiden."
AZHARI	Means "radiant" or "illuminated" and has Arabic origins.
AZIZAH	Feminine Arabic name meaning "beloved" or "honored," originating from the Arabic word "azza," which connotes strength and power.
AZMARIAH	Hebrew origin and means "Yahweh has helped or supported."
AZUCENA	Feminine given name of Spanish origin, meaning "lily" or "madonna lily."
AZYRA	Feminine name of uncertain origin and meaning.
BABYGIRL	The first name "Babygirl" is a term of endearment often used to refer to a young girl or a loved one, and its origin is derived from English as a descriptive term for a young woman or the youngest daughter.
BAHATI	The name Bahati originated in Swahili and means "luck" or "fortune".
BALBINA	Means "stammerer" and originates from Latin.
BANEEN	Means "intelligent" or "wise" and it is of Persian origin.
BARBIE	Diminutive of Barbara and originated in English-speaking countries, derived from the Greek name Barbaros, meaning "foreigner" or "stranger."
BAREERAH	Muslim name of Arabic origin, meaning "pious, righteous, and pleasing to the eye."
BARKAT	Muslim Arabic name meaning "blessing" or "abundance," usually given to a child as a sign of good fortune and prosperity.
BASYA	Hebrew origin and means "daughter of God" or "God's daughter."
BATHSHEBA	Means "daughter of the oath" and has Hebrew origins.
BATOOL	Means "devoted worshipper" and originates from Arabic culture.
BAYOLETH	The meaning and origin of the first name Bayoleth are currently unknown.
BEAUTIFUL	The first name "Beautiful" likely originated as a modern English name, derived from the English word meaning attractive or pleasing to the senses.
BEAUTY	Means attractiveness or loveliness and is derived from the English word beauty itself.
BELIEVE	Means to have confidence and trust in something, and it is derived from the English word "believe" which comes from the Old English word "belyfan."

BELIZE The first name "Belize" has no widely recognized meaning or origin as it is primarily used as a geographical name for a country in Central America.

BELKIS Unknown origin, means "peerless beauty" and is often associated with the Queen of Sheba in biblical and Islamic traditions.

BELLADONNA Means "beautiful woman" and is derived from Italian, where "bella" means beautiful and "donna" means woman.

BELLAGRACE The first name Bellagrace originated as a combination of the Italian word "bella," meaning beautiful, and the English word "grace," suggesting elegance and charm.

BELLATRIX Means "female warrior" and originates from Latin.

BELLISSIMA Means "very beautiful" and originates from the Italian language.

BELOVED Means cherished or dearly loved, and it has usage in multiple cultures and languages.

BENTLEIGH Modern American variant of the English surname Bentley, meaning "clearing covered with bent grass," derived from Old English.

BERGEN Means "from the mountains" and originates from the Old Norse language and Scandinavian culture.

BERKLEIGH English origin and it means "from the birch tree meadow."

BERKLIE The meaning of the first name Berklie is "from the birch tree meadow", and its origin is a variant of the English name Berkeley.

BERLYN Means "from Berlin" and has German origins.

BERNADINE German origin and it means "bold as a bear."

BERTHA German origin, means "bright" or "famous."

BERTIE Diminutive form of the name Bert or Berta, and it originated as a nickname for names starting with "Bert" in English-speaking countries.

BETANIA Means "house of affliction" and originates from Aramaic and Hebrew.

BETHESDA Bethesda means "house of mercy" in Hebrew, and it is most commonly associated with a pool in Jerusalem believed to have healing powers in the Bible.

BETHLEHEM The first name Bethlehem, of Hebrew origin, means "house of bread" or "place of bread" and is traditionally associated with the biblical birthplace of Jesus Christ.

BETHSAIDA Means "house of fishing" and has roots in biblical Hebrew.

BETSABE Means "daughter of the oath" and it originates from Hebrew.

BETSAIDA Means "house of fishing" or "place of fishing" in Hebrew and it originates from the biblical city mentioned in the New Testament.

BETSELOT Means "daughter of Selot/Selod" and has Hebrew origin.

BETTINA Means "God is my oath" and it is of Italian origin.

BETZABETH The name Betzabeth originated as a combination of the Hebrew name "Elizabeth" meaning "God is my oath" and the Spanish name "Betsabe" meaning "woman of beauty."

BEULAH The name Beulah derives from Hebrew and means "married" or "to marry," often symbolizing a biblical land of peace and prosperity.

BEVERLEY Means "dweller near the beaver stream" and has English origins.

BEXLEIGH The first name Bexleigh is of modern origin and its meaning is unclear.

BEXLIE The first name Bexlie is of English origin and its meaning is "a field full of beans."

BEYZA Means "white as egg" in Turkish and it originates from the Turkish language.

BHAVYA Means "auspicious" or "splendid" and originates from Sanskrit.

BHUMI Means "earth" and has its origin in Sanskrit.

BIBI Arabic origin, means "lady" or "miss" and is often used as a nickname or a term of endearment.

BIBIANA Means "alive, full of life" and originates from the Latin name Bibianus, derived from the ancient Roman family name Vibius.

BIBIHAWA Muslim girl's name that means "sweet smile" in Arabic.

BIJOU French name meaning "jewel" or "gem," often used as a term of endearment; it became a popular given name in the late 19th century.

BINAH Hebrew origin and means "understanding" or "intelligence."

BINTA Means "young girl" in Arabic and is of African origin.

BISMA Means "polite" or "well-mannered" and has origins in the Arabic language.

BITHIAH Means "daughter of Yahweh" and it has Hebrew origin.

BIXBY The first name Bixby originated as a surname derived from Old Norse and Old English elements meaning "axe" and "village," and it refers to someone who hails from Bixby or a place associated with axes.

BLAIKLEE The first name Blaiklee is of American origin and has a modern, unique sound.

BLAKLEIGH Modern English feminine name, likely a variant of the name Blake or derived from the color black, with the addition of the ending "-leigh" which has Old English origins.

BLAKLEY Means "dark meadow" and has English origins.

BLAYKLEIGH Modern and unique variation of the name Blake, likely derived from English surnames and associated with qualities like strength and dark complexion.

BLESSENCE Means "blessing" and its origin is unclear.

BLIMA Yiddish origin and means "flower" or "blossom".

BOBBIJO Feminine name of American origin, created by combining the names Bobbi and Jo.

BONITA Means "beautiful" in Spanish and Portuguese and it originates from those languages.

BRAEYA Modern variant of the name Brayden, originating from English and Irish origins.

BRALEIGH Modern American name of uncertain origin, likely a combination or variation of existing names.

BRAYLEI The first name Braylei is of American origin and it means "brave and spirited."

BRAYLIE The first name Braylie is of American origin and it means "beautiful and courageous."

BRAZIL Portuguese origin and means "red ember" or "burning coal."

BREALYNN The meaning and origin of the first name BREALYNN is a modern American name created by combining Brayden and Lynn.

BREASIA The name Breasia likely originated in modern times and its exact meaning is unclear.

BRECKLYN Means "from the hilly land" and has an American origin.

BREIDY The first name Breidy has a Hispanic or Latino origin and means "exalted, revered."

BREINDY The first name "Breindy" is of Yiddish origin, meaning "blessed" or "happy."

BRENDALYN Modern American feminine name created by combining the names Brenda and Lynn.

BRESLIN Irish origin and means "speckled" or "freckled".

BREXLEIGH Modern American invented name, likely derived from the combination of the prefix "Brex" and the suffix "leigh," with no specific meaning or origin.

BREXLEY Unknown origin and meaning.

BRIANNY The first name Brianny is of American origin and it is likely a modern variation or combination of the names Brian and Brianna, often used for girls.

BRIARROSE Means "a thorny, rose-like plant" and originates from the combination of the words "briar" and "rose," often associated with the fairy tale "Sleeping Beauty."

BRIENNA Means "strong, virtuous" and it is believed to be a modern variation of the name Brianna, which originated from Ireland.

BRIGHTLY Means "shining, full of brightness" and has an English origin.

BRILLIANCE The meaning of the first name Brilliance is "exceptional intelligence or brightness," and its origin is derived from the English word brilliance, meaning great brightness or shine.

BRINKLEY The first name Brinkley is of Old English origin and means "meadow on the hilly slope."

BRINLYN American origin and it means "beacon on the hill" or "hill with water".

BRISIA The first name Brisia is of Spanish origin and means "one who comes from Brescia."

BRISTYN Modern variant derived from the Old Norse word "brjóstin," meaning "broken, shattered," and it is of English origin.

BRITAIN Means "from Britain" and is of English origin.

BRITHANY Uncertain origin and meaning, possibly derived from the name Brittany or a variation of the name Bethany.

BRITHNEY The first name "Brithney" is a variant spelling of the name "Britney," which originated as a modern English feminine name derived from the name of the island of Great Britain.

BRITISH The first name British does not have a widely recognized meaning or origin as it is not a conventional or traditional name.

BRIZA Spanish origin and means "breeze" or "gentle wind."

BRONWYN Means "white breast" in Welsh and it originates from the Welsh language.

BROOKLEY The first name "Brookley" is of English origin and means "a clearing near a brook or stream".

BROOKYLN   The name Brooklyn means "brook or stream" and originated as a place name for the borough in New York City.

BRUCHY   Yiddish origin, is a diminutive form of the Hebrew name Bracha, meaning "blessing."

BRYNDLE   The first name Bryndle is of Welsh origin and means "hill" or "mountain."

BRYNJA   Icelandic origin and means "armor" or "protection."

BUSHRA   Means "good news" or "glad tidings" and originates from the Arabic language.

CAIDENCE   Means "rhythm" or "beat" and it is of American origin.

CALEDONIA   Means "from Scotland" and it originates from the Latin term "Caledonii" used by the Romans to refer to the inhabitants of what is now Scotland.

CALIFORNIA   Means "land of the caliph" and originated from the Spanish explorers who named the state after the fictional "Queen Calafia" depicted in a 16th-century novel.

CALIROSE   The first name Calirose is of unknown origin, but it conveys a delicate and gentle nature.

CALLIANDRA   Means "beautiful flower" and has Greek origins.

CALLIEANN   Combination of the names Callie, a diminutive form of the Greek name Calliope meaning "beautiful voice," and Ann, a Hebrew name meaning "grace" or "favor," resulting in a melodic and graceful name.

CALLIEJO   Feminine given name of American origin, likely derived from combining the names Callie and Jo, representing a combination of beauty (Callie) and strength (Jo).

CALVARY   Means "a place of crucifixion" and originates from Calvary Hill, the holy site in Jerusalem believed to be where Jesus was crucified.

CALYPSO   Greek-originated name that means "she who conceals" or "she who hides."

CAMBER   Means "bent, winding river" and has English origins.

CAMBREIGH   Modern American name of uncertain origin, often used as a variant spelling of the name Camberley or as a creatively unique variation of the name Cambria.

CAMBRIELLE   Modern feminine name likely created by combining elements from Cameron and Gabrielle.

CAMBRYN   The meaning and origin of the first name Cambryn is a unique combination of Welsh and English origins, and it is derived from Cambria, which is an ancient name for Wales.

CAMREIGH   American origin and means "bent nose".

CANDELARIA   Means "candlemas" and has Spanish origins.

CAOIMHE   Means "gentle, beautiful" and originates from Irish Gaelic.

CAPRICE   Means "sudden change of mood or behavior" and it originates from the Italian word "capriccio" meaning whim or fancy.

CARALYN   Variant of Carolyn, which is derived from the English name Caroline meaning "free man" and is of Old German origin.

CARAMIA   Means "my dear" in Italian and it is a combination of the words "cara" (dear) and "mia" (my).

CARLEI   English origin and means "strong-willed" or "free person".

CARLYNN   Feminine given name that is a variant of Caroline, derived from the masculine name Carl meaning "man" and Lynn meaning "lake" or "waterfall" ultimately translating to "strong woman of the lake".

CARMELINA   Means "garden of God" and has Latin and Hebrew origins.

CARMILLA   Means "garden, orchard" and originates from the Latin term "carminis."

CAROLE   Means "free man" and has a French origin.

CAROLENA   Variation of the name Caroline, derived from the masculine name Charles, meaning "free man" and of Germanic origin.

CARRIGAN   The first name Carrigan originated as an anglicized form of the Irish surname Ó Corragáin, meaning "descendant of Corragán," which is derived from the old Irish personal name "Corrógán" meaning "spear."

CASILDA   Means "commands in battle" and it originated from Spanish and Basque cultures.

CASSIOPEIA   Means "she who shines upon mankind" and it originates from Greek mythology.

CATALEAH   The meaning and origin of the first name CATALEAH is unknown as it does not have a widely recognized meaning or origin.

CATALEIYA	The first name CATALEIYA originated from the combination of the names Cataleya and Leah, and its meaning is "pure beauty" or "blossom of the night."
CATHARINA	Means "pure" and it originates from the Latin name Katharina, derived from the Greek name Aikaterine.
CATORI	Means "spirit" or "one who sings" and originates from the Native American Hopi tribe.
CAYETANA	Means "pure" and it originated from Spain.
CECEILIA	Means "blind" and has Latin origins.
CEDELLA	African origin and means "gift of God" or "beloved."
CELES	Means "heavenly" and is of Latin origin.
CELESTIAL	Means "heavenly" and has Latin origins.
CELESTINE	Means "heavenly" and originates from the Latin name "Caelestis," derived from "caelum" which means "heaven."
CERENITI	The name Cereniti does not have a widely recognized meaning or origin as it appears to be a unique and uncommon name.
CEREZA	Means "cherry" in Spanish and has its origin in the Latin word "cerasus."
CERSEI	Means "flame" and is of Greek origin.
CHAITHRA	Indian origin and means "born in the month of Chaitra, the first month of the Hindu lunar calendar."
CHAITRA	The first name Chaitra is of Indian origin and it means "month of spring" in Sanskrit.
CHANDRA	Means "moon" in Sanskrit and it originates from Hindu culture.
CHANIYAH	Means "gracious" or "merciful" and is of Hebrew origin.
CHANTAL	Means "song" or "stony place" and originated from Old Provençal.
CHANTZY	Modern Yiddish variant of the name Chana, meaning "grace" or "favor" in Hebrew.
CHARLIEANN	Feminine given name of English origin, combining the names Charlie, a diminutive of Charles meaning "free man," and Ann, meaning "grace" or "favor."
CHARLIEGH	The name "Charliegh" is a modern, creative variation of the name "Charlie," primarily used in English-speaking countries, and derived from the name "Charles" of Germanic origin meaning "free man."
CHARLIEJO	The name CHARLIEJO has no established meaning or origin, as it appears to be a unique or uncommon name.
CHARLIERAE	Modern and unique given name, possibly derived or influenced by combining elements from the names Charlie and Rae.
CHARLIEROSE	Combination of the names Charles and Rose, and its origin is a blending of English and French names.
CHARLOT TEROSE	Means "free woman" and has English and French origins.
CHARMAINE	Means "song" or "charm" and originates from the English language.
CHARNY	The first name Charny is of Hebrew origin and means "determined" or "fierce."
CHAROLETTE	Means "free man" and is of French and English origin.
CHASLYN	Modern, feminine name of American origin, possibly derived from combining the names Charles and Lynn.
CHASSIDY	American origin, means "kindness" or "devotion" and is derived from the word "Chassid" meaning a pious or devout person in Judaism.
CHASTITY	Means purity or virtue, and it originated from the English vocabulary word "chastity" which is derived from the Old French term "chasteté" meaning moral purity or modesty.
CHELSIE	Variant spelling of the name Chelsea, of English origin, meaning "seaport" or "landing place for chalk or limestone."
CHENOA	Means "white dove" and has Native American origins.
CHEROKEE	The name Cherokee is derived from the Cherokee Native American tribe and means "people of a different speech" or "those who live in the mountains."
CHEZNI	The first name "Chezni" is a modern variation of the Irish name "Chesney," meaning "descendant of Seanachaidh" or "storyteller," and it has gained popularity in recent years.
CHIAMAKA	Nigerian Igbo name meaning "God is great" or "God is beautiful" and it is predominantly used by the Igbo people from southeastern Nigeria.

CHIDERA	Means "God is real" and it originated from the Igbo language in Nigeria.
CHIDINMA	Means "God is good" and it originates from the Igbo language in Nigeria.
CHIMAMA NDA	The meaning of the first name Chimamanda is "my God won't fail me" and it is of Igbo origin in Nigeria.
CHIMNORA	Rare Igbo (Nigerian) name meaning "God is gracious."
CHINMAYI	Feminine Indian name of Sanskrit origin meaning "full of knowledge or consciousness".
CHIOMA	Means "good God" or "God is good" in Igbo, and it originates from Nigeria.
CHISOM	Nigerian origin and means "God is with me" or "God follows me."
CHIZARAM	Means "God answers" and has its origin in the Igbo language of Nigeria.
CHIZITEREM	The first name Chiziterem has a Nigerian origin and it means "God sent me."
CHOSYN	The first name "CHOSYN" does not have a widely recognized meaning or origin.
CHOYCE	Means "choice" or "chosen one" and originates from the Old French word "choisir" meaning "to choose."
CHRISETTE	The first name "Chrisette" is derived from the name "Christian" and it means "follower of Christ," with its origin being a combination of the names Chris and Antoinette.
CHRISLEY	The first name Chrisley is of uncertain origin, but it is a modern English variation of the traditional name Chris.
CHRISTABEL	Greek origin and means "beautiful Christian"; it gained popularity due to its use in Samuel Taylor Coleridge's poem "Christabel" published in 1816.
CHRISTELLE	Means "follower of Christ" and originates from France.
CHRYSAN THEMUM	Means "golden flower" and originates from the Greek language.
CHRYSTAL	Variant of the name Crystal, meaning "clear, brilliant" and originated from the English vocabulary word referring to a transparent quartz used as a gemstone.
CHUMY	Given name of Hebrew origin, often used as a nickname for Chaim which means "life" or "living."
CHYENNE	Means "people of a different language" and originates from the Native American Cheyenne tribe.
CHYLOH	Modern American name of uncertain origin and meaning.
CICELY	Means "blind" and has English origins.
CIEYANA	Modern American name of uncertain origin, possibly a variant of the name Cianna or a combination of names like Diana and Ciara.
CILICIA	The name Cilicia originates from ancient Anatolia and it refers to an ancient region situated in modern-day southeastern Turkey.
CINDERELLA	Means "little ashes" and is of French origin.
CINTHYA	Greek origin meaning "from Mount Kynthos" and is derived from the epithet of the Greek goddess Artemis.
CINTIA	The first name Cintia is of Latin origin and means "moon goddess" or "light of the moon."
CIRCE	Means "bird" or "falcon" and originates from Greek mythology, as a powerful enchantress known for her ability to transform her enemies into animals.
CIRILLA	The meaning and origin of the first name Cirilla is "lordly" and it is of Latin origin.
CISNE	Means "swan" in Spanish, and it originates from Spain and other Spanish-speaking countries.
CITLALY	Means "star" in Nahuatl and it originates from Mexico.
CITRINE	Means "a yellow gemstone" and originates from the English word citrine, which refers to a variety of quartz.
CLARABELLE	Means "bright and beautiful" and has English and Latin origins.
CLARICE	Means "bright, clear" and originated from the Latin name Clarus.
CLAUDETTE	Means "little lame one" and originated from the French name Claude, derived from Latin Claudus meaning "lame, crippled."
CLELIA	Means "renowned" and originates from ancient Rome.
CLEOPATRA	Means "glory of her father" and it originates from Ancient Greek.
CLODAGH	Means "river of stones" and is of Irish origin.
CONCEPCION	Means "conception" or "the act of becoming pregnant" in Spanish, and it originates from the Latin word "conceptio" meaning the same.

CONCETTA Means "conception" or "immaculate conception" and has Italian origins.

CONSTANZA Latin origin and it means "steadfast" or "constant."

CONSUELO Means "consolation" in Spanish and it originates from Latin.

CONTESSA The first name Contessa originated from Italian and means "countess," a noble title for the wife or widow of a count or earl.

CORABELLE The meaning of the first name Corabelle is "beautiful heart" and its origin is a combination of the names Coralie and Belle.

CORAIMA Means "beautiful" and it originates from the Guajiro indigenous people in Venezuela.

CORALAI The meaning of the first name Coralai is "coral-like" and it has a Latin origin.

CORALEIGH Modern English name of compound origin, combining the names "Cora" meaning maiden or heart in Greek, and "Leigh" meaning meadow or field in Old English, implying a person with a pure and natural nature.

CORAZON Means "heart" in Spanish and Latin, and it originates from Spanish and Filipino cultures.

CORTANA Means "shortened form of quarter, derived from the English word meaning 'a fourth part'." Its origin is English.

COUMBA The first name Coumba is of African origin and it means "lioness."

COVINGTON Covington is an English surname that originated as a habitational name for someone from a place named Covington, which means "the settlement of Cofa's people."

CRISTEL Variant of the name Christelle or Cristelle, which originated from the French language and is derived from the name Christopher, meaning "bearer of Christ."

CROSLEY Means "cross meadow" and has English origins.

CYBELE Means "mother goddess" and originates from ancient Phrygian mythology.

CYMONE The first name Cymone is of Greek origin and means "one who is like a wave."

CYNIAH The name CYNIAH has no widely recognized meaning or origin as it appears to be a unique name with no historical or cultural significance.

DAGNY Means "new day" in Old Norse and is of Scandinavian origin.

DAHNA Persian origin and means "knowledgeable" or "witty."

DAILANY The first name DAILANY is of uncertain origin and it does not have a widely accepted meaning.

DAISYMAE The name DaisyMae originated from the combination of the name "Daisy," a flower name of English origin, and "Mae," a variation of the name Mary, meaning "pearl" in Hebrew.

DALANIE Modern American origin and its meaning is uncertain as it is a rare name.

DALAYLA Arabic origin and means "captivating" or "alluring."

DALIYA The first name Daliya is of Arabic origin and means "Gentle like the moon."

DALYAH Means "branch" or "tree" and it has Hebrew origins.

DALYLAH Arabic origin and it means "captivating" or "beautiful maiden."

DAMARYS Female given name of uncertain origin, possibly derived from the Greek name Damalis meaning "young cow."

DAMILOLA Means "wealth has built me" and it originates from the Yoruba language in Nigeria.

DANAI The name Danai originates from Greek mythology and means "gift of God."

DANAICA Rare feminine name of uncertain origin, possibly a variation of the name Danae or a modern creation.

DANASIA Means "God is my judge" and is of American origin.

DANDELION English origin and refers to a bright yellow wildflower known for its medicinal properties and vibrant appearance.

DANEIRIS The first name Daneiris is of unknown origin and meaning.

DANELI Hebrew origin and it means "God is my judge."

DANILEIGH Means "God is my judge" and its origin can be traced back to the Hebrew language.

DANITZA Feminine given name of Slavic origin meaning "morning star" or "God is my judge."

DARASIMI Means "God hears me" and it has Yoruba origins in Nigeria.

DARELY The first name Darely is of uncertain origin and meaning.

DARIELYS Modern feminine name of uncertain origin, possibly a creative variation of Daria or a combination of Dariel and Alys.

DARLAH Means "lovely" or "darling" and it possibly originates from the English or American names derived from the word "darling."

DAYAMI	Feminine name of Cuban origin that means "beautiful gift from God."
DAYSI	The name "Daisy" means "day's eye" and originated from the English language.
DEAJAH	Modern American name of uncertain origin, potentially a variant of the name Dajah or a combination of letters from other names.
DEAURI	Rare feminine name of unknown origin, hence its meaning is unclear.
DEBANHI	Modern and unique variation of the name Deborah, likely coined in the United States.
DEBBIE	Diminutive form of Deborah, meaning "bee" in Hebrew, and it originated from the biblical name of a prophetess and judge in the Old Testament.
DEBHANI	Indian origin and it means "divinely beautiful."
DEBRA	Means "bee" and originates from Hebrew.
DECEMBER	Means "tenth month" and originates from the Latin word "decem" meaning "ten."
DEETHYA	The name DEETHYA has a Sanskrit origin and it means "divine light" or "radiance of the gods".
DEIDRE	Means "sorrowful" or "bewailed" and originates from Irish and Gaelic mythology.
DEIRDRE	Means "sorrowful" or "broken-hearted" and originates from Irish Gaelic mythology, particularly from the ancient epic tale "Deirdre of the Sorrows."
DEJANAE	Modern American name of uncertain origin, likely created as a variant of the name Deja with the addition of the suffix -nae for uniqueness or personalization.
DELAILA	Means "born at night" and has Hebrew origin.
DELANEIGH	Modern, unique name of American origin, possibly a combination of the names Delaney and Leigh.
DELARA	Means "adorner" or "beautifier" and has Persian origins.
DELASIA	Modern creation, likely derived from combining the names De-Andre and Asia; it has no widely known meaning or origin.
DELAYNIE	The first name Delaynie is of uncertain origin and meaning, likely a modern variation or unique spelling of the name Delaney.
DELAYZA	Means "noble and kind" and its origin is a combination of the names Delayne and Aza.
DELEIZA	Name of Basque origin meaning "happiness" or "joyful".
DELFINA	Means "dolphin" and it originated from the Latin word "delphinus."
DELILIAH	Means "delicate" or "delicate woman" and originates from the Hebrew name Delilah, which is derived from the word "delil" meaning "weak" or "delicate."
DELMY	Female given name of unknown origin, likely derived from the combination of syllables or letters from other names.
DELPHI	Means "from Delphi," and it originates from Greek mythology and the ancient city of Delphi, which was renowned for its oracle.
DELPHINE	Means "dolphin" and has origins in Greek mythology.
DEMRI	The first name Demri is of uncertain origin and meaning.
DEMYA	The first name Demya has no clear origin or meaning as it is a rare and unique name with no widely recognized etymology.
DENYLA	The first name Denyla is of unknown origin and meaning as it does not have a widely recognized etymology.
DESPINA	Means "Lady" or "Mistress" and has its origin in Greece.
DEVAHNI	Means "divine" and is of Indian origin.
DEVIKA	Feminine Indian name of Sanskrit origin, meaning "little goddess" or "divine."
DEVOIRY	Hebrew origin and it means "a vow or duty" in English.
DEYANI	Feminine given name of uncertain origin, potentially originating from various cultures and languages.
DEYANIRA	Feminine name of Greek origin meaning "devastating, destroyer", derived from the Greek words "dei" meaning "to destroy" and "aniro" meaning "to ravage".
DEZARIAH	Modern and creative variation of the biblical name Zechariah, meaning "God remembers" in Hebrew.
DEZIRAE	The first name Dezirae is of American origin and means "longed-for, desired."
DEZYRE	Means "desire" and has a modern and creative origin.
DHANVI	Indian origin and means "possessing wealth or riches."
DHANYA	Means "fortunate" or "blessed" in Sanskrit and originates from India.

DHATRI	Sanskrit name meaning "goddess of wealth and prosperity," originating from Hindu mythology.
DHEMILLY	Rare Portuguese feminine name of unknown origin.
DHRITI	Means "determination" or "perseverance" and has its origin in Sanskrit, an ancient language of India.
DHRUTHI	Means "steadfastness" or "resoluteness" and is of Indian (Sanskrit) origin.
DHRUVIKA	Feminine Sanskrit name derived from the word "Dhruva," meaning "steady" or "immovable," symbolizing someone who is firm and unwavering.
DHWANI	The first name Dhawani means "sound" or "melody" and has its origin in the Sanskrit language.
DIANELY	The meaning and origin of the first name Dianely is unknown.
DIGIANNIA	The meaning and origin of the first name Digiannia are both unknown.
DILCIA	The first name DILCIA is of uncertain origin and meaning.
DIVIJA	Feminine Indian name meaning "divine" or "celestial" originating from Sanskrit.
DIVINITY	Means "the state or quality of being divine or godlike" and it has English origins.
DIVISHA	Means "divine" and its origin is Sanskrit.
DIVYA	Means "divine" or "divine brilliance" and originates from Sanskrit.
DJAMILA	Means "beautiful" in Arabic and it originated in the Middle East and North Africa.
DJENEBA	Means "daughter of the water" and it originates from the Bambara language spoken in Mali, West Africa.
DJUNA	Means "spiritual, divine" and its origin is uncertain, but it is thought to have African or Native American roots.
DLYLAH	Means "night" and is of Hebrew origin.
DOLLIE	English origin and means "small doll" or "gift of God."
DORCAS	Means "gazelle" and originates from the biblical story of a woman named Dorcas who was known for her acts of kindness and charity.
DOREEN	Means "gift" or "bountiful" and it is of Greek origin.
DOTTY	Means "gift of God" and is of English origin.
DRISHYA	The first name Drishya originates from India and means "vision" or "sight" in Sanskrit.
DRUSILLA	Means "fruitful" or "strong" and has Latin origins.
DRUVIKA	Modern Indian name that means "divine princess" or "Goddess of the forest."
DUCHESS	Means "a noblewoman of high rank" and originated from the English language.
DUHA	Means "midmorning" and originates from Arabic.
DULCEMARIA	Means "sweet Mary" in Spanish and originates from Latin.
DUTCHESS	The first name "Duchess" means a noblewoman or the wife of a duke, and it originated from the English language.
DWIJA	The name Dwiija means "born twice" or "twice-born" and originates from Hindu mythology in India, often associated with the initiation ceremony of Brahmins.
DYNASTY	Means a succession of rulers from the same family or a powerful and influential family group, originating from the Greek word "dynastia."
DYUTHI	Indian origin, means "radiant" or "luminous."
DZEJLA	Means "attractive, gracious" and it originates from the Bosnian-Herzegovinian region of Southeast Europe.
DZIYAH	The first name DZIYAH does not have a widely known meaning or origin as it appears to be rare or uncommon.
EABHA	Means "life" in Irish Gaelic and it is the Irish form of the name Eva.
EASTLYN	Modern, invented name likely derived from the combination of the word "east" and the popular suffix "-lyn," and its meaning is unclear.
ECLIPSE	The first name Eclipse originated from Greek mythology, symbolizing the blocking of light, and is associated with mystery and hidden power.
EDELWEISS	Means "noble white." It originated from German, derived from the words "edel" meaning noble and "weiß" meaning white.
EFRATA	Means "fruitful" and it originates from Hebrew.
EILEITHYIA	The first name Eileithyia comes from Greek mythology and it means "goddess of childbirth."

EILIDH The first name Eilidh is of Scottish origin and it means "radiant."

EIRINI Means "peace" and it originates from Greek.

ELAYAH Unique variant of the biblical name Eliyah, which means "my God is Yahweh" in Hebrew.

ELAYNE Hebrew origin and means "God is my light."

ELAYSIA Uncertain origin and meaning, potentially derived from a combination of elements or created as a modern variation of the name Alyssa.

ELEANORAH Variant of the name Eleanor, originating from the Old French name Alienor, meaning "foreign," "strange," or "the other."

ELEKTRA Means "shining" or "radiant" and originates from Greek mythology.

ELENAROSE Combination of the names Elena and Rose, creating a unique and modern feminine name.

ELEVEN The name Eleven, commonly associated with the character from the TV show Stranger Things, has no widely known origin or meaning in the context of personal names prior to the show's debut in 2016.

ELEXIA Greek origin and it means "defender of mankind."

ELEYNA Variant spelling of the name Elena, which means "bright, shining light" and has Greek origins.

ELHAM Means "inspiration" or "divine communication" and has Persian origins.

ELIANET Means "God has answered" and is of Cuban origin.

ELIANYS Modern American name of uncertain origin, possibly a variant of "Eliana" or a combination of "Eli" and "Anys."

ELIBETH Means "God is abundance" and it is a variant of the name Elizabeth, which has Hebrew origins.

ELICIA Variant of the name Alicia, which means "noble" or "of noble origin," and it originates from the Latin word "alicia."

ELIENAI Means "my eyes have seen God" and originates from biblical Hebrew.

ELISABETTA The name Elisabetta is an Italian variation of the name Elizabeth, derived from the Hebrew name Elisheva, meaning "my God is an oath."

ELIYAHNA Means "my God has answered" and has Hebrew origins.

ELIZABELLA Modern feminine name derived from combining elements of the names Elizabeth and Isabella, and it conveys the meaning of "God is my oath" from Elizabeth and "devoted to God" from Isabella.

ELIZAJANE Combination of the names Eliza and Jane, often used as a given name in English-speaking countries, with Eliza meaning "pledged to God" and Jane meaning "God

ELIZAVETA Female given name derived from the Hebrew name Elizabeth, meaning "God is my oath" and has Slavic origins.

ELLAJO Modern, uncommon feminine name that is likely a combination of the names Ella and Jo.

ELLAMARIE English origin, means "beautiful star of the sea."

ELLARY Modern, unisex name of American origin, possibly derived from the surname Ellery or Eleanor, meaning "resolute" or "shining".

ELLASANDRA Means "a creative combination of the names Ella and Sandra" and is of American origin.

ELLERIE Modern English name of uncertain origin, likely derived from either the Old English words "ellern" meaning "elder tree" or "elloran" meaning "noble one."

ELLIAUNA The meaning and origin of the first name Elliauna is unclear as it is a relatively rare name with limited documented information.

ELLIEANNE Combination of the names Ellie, a diminutive of Eleanor which means "light" or "bright," and Anne, which means "grace," and has English origins.

ELLIEMAE Means "shining light" and it is of English origin.

ELLIEMARIE The first name Elliemarie derives from the combination of the names Ellie and Marie, and it implies a feminine and charming individual.

ELLIEROSE Combination of the names Ellie, derived from the Hebrew name Eli, meaning "my God" and Rose, originating from the Latin word Rosa, meaning "rose flower".

ELLISTON Means "Elias' town" and originates from the Old English name Ælfgar.

ELLOREE Uncertain origin and its meaning is also unknown, but it was first used as a given name in the United States in the early 20th century.

ELLYSON	Elllyson is a modern English name of American origin, derived from the combination of the names Ellie and Mason.
ELNAZ	Means "beloved" and originates from Persian/Iranian culture.
ELNORA	The name Elnora originates from English and is derived from the combination of elements "El," referring to God, and "Nora," meaning "honor" or "light."
ELOAH	Means "God" or "deity" in Hebrew, and it is derived from the Hebrew word "El" meaning "God."
ELSPETH	Means "pledged to God" and it is of Scottish origin.
ELSWYTH	Elswyth is an Old English name meaning "elf strength" or "battle of elves."
ELUNEY	Mapuche name of Native American origin meaning "spiritual light."
ELYCE	Variant spelling of the name Elise, derived from the Hebrew name Elizabeth, meaning "God is my oath."
EMBERLYNNE	Modern American feminine name derived from the word "ember" meaning glowing coals, symbolizing warmth and light.
EMBERROSE	Means "a combination of fiery energy and delicate beauty" and its origin is uncertain, potentially a modern creation or a blend of the English word "ember" and the flower name "Rose."
EMBRACE	"Embrace" means to hold and show affection towards someone or something, and it originated as a virtue name in the English language.
EMERYROSE	The name Emeryrose originated as a combination of the names Emery, meaning "brave" or "powerful," and Rose, a flower associated with love and beauty.
EMIKO	Means "beautiful blessing" and it is of Japanese origin.
EMILENE	Feminine given name of French origin, derived from the name Emile meaning "to strive" or "to excel."
EMILIAROSE	Combination of the names Emilia, derived from the Latin word "aemulus" meaning "rival," and Rose, which comes from the Latin word "rosa" meaning "rose flower."
EMILIJA	Lithuanian origin, means "rival" or "eager" in English.
EMILYROSE	Means "beloved rose" and originates from the combination of the names Emily and Rose.
EMIRETH	Modern invention and its meaning is uncertain.
EMIYAH	The name Emiyah has uncertain origins and a variety of meanings, possibly derived from the Hebrew name Emiyah meaning "nurse" or the Arabic name Amaya meaning "night rain."
EMMAGRACE	Combination of the names Emma and Grace, with Emma meaning "whole" or "universal" and Grace meaning "charm" or "beauty," suggesting someone who embodies both qualities, and it is of English origin.
EMMAJANE	Feminine given name of English origin, combining the names Emma and Jane, usually signifying a combination of elegance and simplicity.
EMMAJEAN	Feminine given name of English origin, derived from combining the names Emma and Jean, which conveys a sense of femininity and strength.
EMMAKATE	The name Emmakate originated as a combination of the names Emma and Kate, and it typically connotes a feminine and strong individual.
EMMALINA	Means "universal; whole" and has Germanic and Latin origins.
EMMALISE	The first name Emmalise originated in the United States and is a variant of the names Emma and Elise, combining their qualities and meanings.
EMMALYNNE	The first name Emmalynne is of American origin and signifies a combination of the names Emma and Lynne, often associated with grace and strength.
EMMASOPHIA	The first name Emmasophia originated from combining the names Emma, meaning "universal" or "whole," and Sophia, meaning "wisdom" or "knowledge," to represent a person who embodies both universal wisdom and wholeness.
EMNET	Ethiopian origin, and it means "honesty" or "trustworthiness".
EMRAKEL	The name Emrakel does not have a specific meaning and origin as it is not commonly found or well-documented.
EMREY	Turkish origin and it means "one who is powerful and respected."
EMUNAH	Means "faith" or "belief" and originates from Hebrew.

EMYLIA Means "rival" or "emulating" and it is a variant of the name Amelia, which has Latin and Germanic origins.

EMYRA The meaning and origin of the first name Emyra is uncertain, as it does not have a widely accepted origin or meaning within a specific language or culture.

EMYRSON Modern variant of the English surname Emerson, which originated from the Old English name Emery, meaning "brave" or "powerful."

ENARA Basque female name meaning "swallow" or "bird," derived from the Basque word "enara" which refers to this migratory bird.

ENDIA The meaning and origin of the first name Endia is uncertain.

ENEDINA Spanish origin and means "ardent and passionate."

ENERGY Unique and dynamic word-derived name that symbolizes vitality and enthusiasm.

ENGLAND Means "from the land of the Angles" and is of English origin.

ENIOLA Yoruba name of Nigerian origin, meaning "a person of wealth."

ENISA Means "friendship" and it originates from Turkish language.

ENMA Japanese origin and it means "the god of the underworld" or "judge of hell" in Japanese mythology.

ENOLA Means "alone" or "solitary" and it is of Native American origin.

ENSLIE Modern variant of the name Leslie, which originated from a Scottish surname meaning "garden of holly."

ENVY Means a feeling of desire or longing for someone else's qualities, possessions, or success, and it originated from the English vocabulary word "envy."

EPHRATA Hebrew origin and means "fruitful" or "abundance," traditionally associated with the biblical city in the Old Testament.

EPIPHANY Means a sudden realization or revelation, and it has its origin in the Greek word "epiphaneia" which translates to "manifestation" or "appearance."

ERANDI Means "mythical flower" and has origins in Nahuatl, an indigenous Mesoamerican language.

ERENDIRA Means "lovely princess" and it originates from the indigenous Huichol language in Mexico.

ERETRIA Means "from the city of Eretria" and originates from Ancient Greek.

ERNESTINA Means "serious" or "honest" and it is of German origin.

ESBEIDY Feminine given name of uncertain origin, possibly a variant of the name Esbeydi or influenced by Spanish and Indigenous American cultures.

ESCARLETH Spanish origin and means "scarlet," a bright red color, symbolizing passion and strength.

ESEOSA Means "God's gift" and originates from the Edo people of Nigeria.

ESMARIE Combination of the names "Esme" and "Marie," and it originated from French and German origins, meaning "esteemed" and "wished for" respectively.

ESMERAY Turkish name, meaning "dark moon."

ESPN Unique acronym originally standing for Entertainment and Sports Programming Network, now a major sports media company.

ESTEPHANY Means "crowned" and has Spanish origins.

ESTHERLINE Feminine name of French origin meaning "star" or "bright, shining light."

ESTRELLITA Estrellita means "little star" and has Spanish origins.

ETHEREAL Means delicate, heavenly, or spiritual, and it originated from the English language.

EUDORA Means "well-gifted" and has Greek origins.

EULA Feminine name of Greek origin, meaning "well-spoken" or "melodious."

EULALIA Means "well-spoken" and originates from ancient Greece.

EUPHEMIA Means "well-spoken" or "eloquent" and originates from ancient Greek.

EUPHORIA Greek origin, signifies a state of extreme happiness and joy.

EURYDICE Means "wide justice" or "wide ruling" and originates from Greek mythology.

EVALINE Means "desired" or "wished for" and is of Latin origin.

EVAMARIA Means "beloved grace" and it is of Hebrew and Latin origins.

EVANI Modern feminine name of Sanskrit origin, meaning "gracious gift of God."

EVANORA Welsh origin and means "white wave."

EVANTHIA Means "flower of bloom" and originates from Greek.

EVELEIGH Modern English name of uncertain origin, possibly derived from a combination of the names Eve and Leigh.

EVELIA Feminine given name of Spanish origin that means "life-giving" or "living one."

EVELYNMAE Modern compound name combining the traditional names Evelyn and Mae, possibly suggesting a combination of timeless elegance and simplicity.

EVELYNROSE Means "beautiful, delicate rose" and likely originated as a combination of the names Evelyn and Rose.

EVEMARIE Compound name of Hebrew origin meaning "life of the sea."

EVENING Means 'the period of time between afternoon and nightfall' and derives from the Old English word 'æfen,' ultimately derived from Proto-Germanic 'abandiz.'

EVERGREEN Means "perennial and vibrant" and originated as a nature-inspired English name.

EVERLIEGH The name Everliegh originated from the combination of the names "Ever" and "Leigh" and means "eternally beautiful meadow."

EVERLYNNE Modern variation of the name Evelyn, derived from the Norman French name Aveline, meaning "desired" or "wished for."

EVERMORE Means "eternally" or "forever" and is of English origin.

EVINA The name Evina has a Slavic origin and it means "life" or "living one."

EVNIKA Russian feminine name meaning "peaceful ruler" and is derived from the word "evnik," which means "victorious" or "winner" in Russian.

EVORA Feminine Portuguese name meaning "olive tree", derived from the city of Évora in Portugal.

EXCELLENCE Virtue name that originated in English-speaking countries, referring to the quality of being outstanding or superior in a particular field or endeavor.

EYLUL The first name Eylül means "September" in Turkish, and it originates from the Turkish language.

EZGI The first name Ezgi originated in Turkey and means "melody" or "song" in Turkish.

EZINNE Means "good mother" or "good woman" in Igbo language of Nigeria, and it originated from the Igbo cultural heritage.

EZLYN Modern origin and its meaning is not widely known.

EZMERELDA Means "emerald" and has Latin origins.

EZRIAH Modern variation of the Hebrew name Ezra meaning "help" or "salvation."

EZTLI The first name Eztlí means "blood" or "redness" and originates from Nahuatl, the language of the Aztecs in ancient Mesoamerica.

FABIHA Means "exceptional" or "extraordinary," and it originates from Arabic.

FABLE The meaning of the first name Fable is "a short literary tale" and its origin is English.

FAITHLYNN Means "faithful lake" and likely originated as a combination of the names Faith and Lynn.

FALAK Means "sky" or "heaven" and has Arabic and Persian origins.

FANTA Means "beautiful" and has its origins in West Africa, specifically in the Manding languages.

FARHIA Somali origin and means "joy" or "happiness."

FARISHTA Means "angel" or "heavenly being" and originates from Persian and Arabic.

FARYAL Persian origin and means "beautiful, enchanting, or splendid."

FATHIMA Feminine name of Arabic origin meaning "one who is cherished and esteemed."

FATIMATA Means "one who weans" and originates from Arabic and West African cultures.

FATIMAZ AHRA Means "the shining one" or "the luminous one" and its origin is Arabic.

FATMA Means "one who abstains" or "one who weans" and originates from Arabic culture.

FATMATA Means "one who abstains from evil" and it originates from the Arabic language.

FATOU Means "a woman born on a Monday" and originates from West Africa, specifically the Wolof language.

FAUSTINA Female given name of Latin origin meaning "fortunate" or "lucky," derived from the Latin word "faustus."

FAVOR Means "act of kindness or preference" and originates from English and Latin roots.

FAWN Means "young deer" and originated as an English word name in the 19th century.

FAYELYNN The first name Fayelynn has a meaning of "fairy" or "fairy-like" and its origin is a combination of the English name Faye and the Welsh name Lynn.

FAYROUZ Means "turquoise" or "precious gem" in Arabic, and it is derived from the Arabic word "fayruz."

FERIHA	Turkish name derived from the Persian word "ferah" meaning joy or happiness.
FEYRE	English origin and its meaning is "magical" or "enchanting."
FEZA	Swahili name meaning "Born at night" and is of African origin.
FIADH	Irish origin and means "wild, untamed spirit."
FILOMENA	Means "loves strength" and has a Greek origin.
FIONNUALA	Means "white shoulder" in Irish Gaelic and originates from Celtic mythology, referring to a legendary swan maiden.
FIRDAUS	Means "paradise" in Arabic, and it is of Persian origin.
FLANNERY	Means "ruler's red eyebrows" and originates from Irish Gaelic.
FLORIDALMA	Combination of the names "Florida" meaning "full of flowers" and "Alma" meaning "soul" in Spanish, and it likely originated in Latin America.
FLOSSIE	Flossie is an English name of Greek origin, meaning "flourishing" or "flower-like."
FLOWER	Means a beautiful and delicate bloom of nature, typically originating from English word use as a literal descriptor for a plant's reproductive structure.
FOLASADE	Means "honor confers a crown" and originates from Yoruba, a language and ethnic group in Nigeria.
FOREVER	Means eternal or everlasting, and it is a modern, creative name often given as a symbolic representation of infinite love or dedication.
FOTINI	Means "light" or "enlightened" in Greek and it is derived from the Greek word "φως" (phos) meaning "light".
FRADEL	The first name Fradel originated from the Yiddish language and means "joyful" or "happiness."
FRAIDY	Yiddish name meaning "joy" or "happiness" and it originates from Jewish culture.
FRANCHESCA	Feminine given name that originated from Italy and is derived from the Italian form of the Germanic name "Francis," meaning "free one" or "from France."
FRANYELI	The first name Franyeli is of Spanish origin and has no specific meaning.
FREIDA	Means "peaceful ruler" and has Germanic origins.
FREYDIS	Means "noble woman" and is of Old Norse origin.
FRIEDA	Means "peaceful ruler" and it originates from Germanic languages.
FRIMET	Means "devoted" and has Yiddish origin.
FURAHA	Means "joy" in Swahili and is of East African origin.
GALADRIEL	Means "maiden crowned with a radiant garland" and has originated from J.R.R. Tolkien's fantasy novel "The Lord of the Rings."
GALAXY	Means "a large system of stars and other celestial objects" and is of English origin.
GARDENIA	Means "a type of fragrant flower" and it originated from the botanical name of a flowering plant native to tropical regions.
GARNET	Means "dark red gemstone" and is of English origin.
GAYATRI	The first name Gayatri is of Sanskrit origin and means "song, hymn or prayer."
GEFFEN	Means "vineyard" in Hebrew and is of Jewish origin.
GEMINI	Means "twins" and originates from the Latin word "gemini," referring to the astrological sign of the zodiac represented by the twins Castor and Pollux in Greek mythology.
GENELLE	Feminine given name of American origin, meaning "genuine" or "courageous spirit".
GENENDY	The first name Genendy has an uncertain meaning and origin as it is very rare and does not have significant historical or cultural documentation.
GENEVIVE	Means "white wave" and its origin is from the Latin name Genoveva.
GENOVEVA	Means "white wave" and has origin in Old German and Spanish.
GEORGETTE	Means "farmer" or "tiller of the earth" and originated from the feminine form of the French name Georges, which is derived from the Greek name Georgios.
GERTRUDE	German origin, means "spear strength" or "strong spear."
GETHSEMANE	Hebrew origin, means "oil press" and is associated with the Garden of Gethsemane mentioned in the Bible.
GETSEMANI	Means "olive garden" and has its origin in Hebrew, specifically from the place named Gethsemane mentioned in the New Testament.
GHALA	Arabic origin and means "precious" or "valuable".
GHINA	Means "melody" or "beautiful song" and originates from Arabic.

GIANNAMARIE Combination of the Italian names Gianna and Marie, meaning "God is gracious" and "bitter" respectively, and it originated as a modern blend name.

GIANNAROSE Means "God is gracious" and originates from the combination of the Italian name Gianna, meaning "God is gracious," and the English name Rose, representing the flower.

GIANNINA Feminine Italian given name derived from the masculine name Giovanni, meaning "God is gracious".

GIAVONNI Variant of Giovanni, an Italian form of John, meaning "God is gracious" and originated from the Hebrew name Yochanan.

GIFT Means a present or a blessing and originated from the African continent.

GINEVRA Means "juniper tree" and it originates from Italy.

GIRASOL Means "sunflower" in Spanish, derived from the words "gira" (turn) and "sol" (sun).

GIRL The first name "Girl" does not have a specific origin or meaning as it is not commonly used as a traditional given name.

GIUSEPPINA Means "God will increase" and it is of Italian origin.

GLADIS Means "swordsman" and has origins in the Old English language.

GLENDA Means "pure and holy" and has origins in both Welsh and Celtic languages.

GLIKA Greek feminine name meaning "sweet" or "charming".

GLORIANA Means "glory of God" and it originated as a poetic name for Queen Elizabeth I of England.

GLORIOUS Means "having great fame, honor, or beauty" and has Latin origins.

GODDESS Means a female deity or supreme being, and it originated from various ancient mythologies and religious traditions.

GOLDYN English origin and means "golden" or "made of gold."

GORGEOUS The first name "Gorgeous" conveys beauty or attractiveness, and it is typically used as a descriptive term rather than a given name; it does not have a specific origin as a first

GOWRI Sanskrit origin and means "yellow or fair complexioned; a Hindu goddess symbolizing purity and radiance."

GRACELEIGH Means "graceful meadow" and has origins in combining the names Grace and Leigh.

GRACEMARIE Means "graceful" and "bitter" and has an English and French origin.

GRACEYN Modern variation of the name Grace, derived from the Latin word "gratia" meaning "grace, favor, kindness."

GRACIANNA The first name Gracianna originated from the combination of the names Grace, meaning "elegance" or "divine favor," and Anna, meaning "gracious" or "merciful," conveying the notion of a graceful and merciful individual.

GRACIOUS Means "kind, forgiving" and it originates from the English language.

GRAYCELYN Modern variation of the name Gracelyn, meaning "graceful" or "lovely" and originated in the United States.

GRAYCIE Means "graceful" and originates from the English language.

GREEICY The first name Greeicy originates from South America and means "graceful and powerful."

GREELEY Means "from the meadow by the grove" and originates from Old English.

GRETHEL Variant spelling of Gretel, originating from the German diminutive of Grete, derived from Margaret, meaning "pearl."

GREYLEIGH The meaning and origin of the first name Greyleigh are not well-defined as it appears to be a modern, invented name combining elements of the color gray and the popular name suffix "-leigh."

GREYS The first name Greys is derived from the English surname Grey, meaning "gray-haired" or "gray-inspired," and it has origins in Old English and Norman French.

GREYSHELL The first name Greysell means "gray shell" or "gray warrior," and its origin is English.

GRIER The first name Grier is of Scottish origin and it means "alert, vigilant."

GRISEL Means "gray warrior" and has Spanish and Scottish origins.

GRISELDA Means "dark battle" and has Germanic origins.

GUILIANA Italian origin and it means "youthful" or "youthful downy one."

GURASEES The first name Gurasees has an origin from the Punjabi language and it possibly means "servant of the guru" or "devotee of the guru."

GURLEEN Means "one absorbed in the Guru's divine light" and it originates from the Sikh religion.

GURMEHAR Punjabi name which means "one who is compassionate and kind-hearted" and originates from Sikh and Indian cultures.

GURNOOR Punjabi origin and means "god's light" or "guru's light."

GURSANJH The meaning and origin of the first name GURSANJH is not available.

GWENEVIERE Means "white phantom" and has Welsh origins.

GWENIVERE Means "white phantom" or "white wave" and it originates from Welsh mythology and Arthurian legends.

GWYNDOLIN Means "shining moon" and has Welsh origins.

GWYNEVERE Means "white phantom" and originates from the Welsh language.

GYPSY Means a free-spirited, wandering individual and has its origin in the English language.

HABIBA Feminine Arabic given name meaning "beloved" or "loved one," and it originates from the Arabic language and Islamic culture.

HADASHA Means "new" or "renewal" and has Hebrew origins.

HADICHA The first name Hadicha is of Arabic origin and means "one who guides and counsels."

HADILYNN Modern American name with no specific origin, likely derived from combining "Hadley" and "Lynn."

HADIYA Feminine given name of Arabic origin meaning "guide to righteousness or gift from God"

HADJA Means "pilgrim" and has Arabic origins.

HADLYN The first name Hadlyn could potentially be of English origin with a meaning, "dweller at the heathery dell."

HAEVYN Means "moonlight" or "radiance" and has no clear origin or etymology.

HAIFA Means "slender, slender-waisted" and originates from Arabic.

HAIZLEIGH American origin and means "dweller by the hedged meadow," combining elements from nature with a modern twist.

HAJAR Feminine Arabic name meaning "emigrant" or "one who leaves her homeland" and is derived from the biblical figure Hagar.

HAJRA The name HAJRA has Arabic origins and means "one who emigrates or migrates to a new place."

HALLELUJAH Means "praise the Lord" in Hebrew and is derived from the Hebrew phrase "Haleluyah," which is composed of "hallelu" meaning "praise" and "yah" meaning "God."

HALONA Feminine Native American name of Lakota origin meaning "fortunate, happy."

HALSEY Means "hall's island" and is of English origin.

HALSTON Unisex name of English origin, meaning "from the halls town" or "hallowed stone."

HANALEI Means "crescent bay" and originates from Hawaiian language and culture.

HANANIAH Hebrew name meaning "God is gracious" and is of biblical origin.

HANIFA Means "true believer" or "one who has true faith" and originates from Arabic.

HANNELORE Means "God's gracious gift" and originates from Germany.

HANVIKA Means "lovely like a swan" and it has Sanskrit origins.

HAPPINESS The meaning of the first name Happiness is a feeling of joy and contentment, and its origin is derived from the English language.

HAPPY Means joyful or content and is of English origin.

HARIR Arabic origin and it means "silk" in reference to its smooth and luxurious nature.

HARLEAUX The first name Harleaux likely originates from French and means "army ruler" or "leader of warriors."

HARLEYANN Combination of the names Harley and Ann, meaning "meadow of the hares" and "grace" respectively, with an American origin.

HARNAAZ Means "God's treasure" and has origins in Punjabi language.

HARPERROSE Modern compound name combining the names Harper, meaning "harp player" or "minstrel," and Rose, a flower symbolizing love and beauty.

HARRIETTE Means "ruler of the home" and is a feminine variant of the name Harriet, which originated from the English language.

HARSHITHA Means "one who brings joy" and it originates from the Sanskrit language.

HARSIRAT Means "one who meditates on the Lord's name" and originates from Punjabi/Sikh cultures.

HARTFORD	Unisex name of English origin meaning "deer crossing the ford."
HARTLEIGH	The first name Hartleigh originates from English and it means "from the deer meadow."
HARTLYN	English origin and means "strong and brave deer".
HARVIE	Means "battle worthy" and it is of Old English origin.
HASANAT	Means "good deeds" and it has Arabic origin.
HASET	The meaning and origin of the first name HASET are currently unknown.
HATHAWAY	Means "dweller near the path" and originates from the Old English words "hæð" (heath) and "weg" (way).
HAUMEA	"Haumea is a Hawaiian goddess of fertility and childbirth, as well as the name of a dwarf planet in our solar system."
HAVILAH	Biblical origin and means "stretch of sand" or "land of gold."
HAVISHA	Means "like Lord Shiva" and it originates from Hinduism.
HAYZEL	Means "a variant spelling of Hazel" and has an uncertain origin, possibly derived from the Old English word "hæsel" meaning "hazel tree."
HAZELEIGH	Modern and unique variation of the name Hazel, derived from the English word for the hazelnut tree.
HAZELEY	The first name Hazeley originated from Old English and it means "meadow of hazel trees" or "a person with hazel-colored eyes."
HAZELGRACE	Means "graceful and wise" and has an English origin.
HAZELMAE	The name Hazelmae likely originated as a combining of the names Hazel and Mae, and it means "hazel tree" or "hazel + pearl."
HAZELYNN	American origin and is a modern combination of the names Hazel and Lynn, meaning "graceful meadow".
HEALANI	Means "haze from heaven" and originates from the Hawaiian language.
HEART	The first name "Heart" signifies love, compassion, and affection, and its origin lies in the English language, derived from the word for the central organ that pumps blood.
HEARTLEY	The first name "Heartley" is of English origin and means "from the meadow of the strong-hearted."
HEARTLYNN	The first name Heartlynn, of unknown origin, likely embodies a heartfelt and loving nature.
HEAVENL EIGH	The meaning of the first name Heavenleigh is "heavenly meadow" and its origin is a modern combination of the words "heaven" and "leigh."
HEILYN	The first name Heilyn has a Welsh origin and it means "bright and radiant."
HEIZEL	German origin and it means "ruler of the house."
HELAENA	Means "sunshine" and has origins in the Greek language.
HELOISA	Means "famous warrior" or "renowned in battle" and originates from Germanic and Portuguese origins.
HENCHY	Irish origin and means "descendant of Cionaodh," derived from the Irish Gaelic name Cionaodh meaning "born of fire."
HENLIE	Means "home ruler" and has English origins.
HENSLEIGH	Name of English origin meaning "meadow of the wild birds."
HENZA	Modern Scandinavian variant of the name Henning, which means "ruler of the home" in Old Norse.
HENZLEY	Means "from the high meadow" and is of English origin.
HEPHZIBAH	Means "my delight is in her" and has Biblical origins, originating from Hebrew.
HERLINDA	Means "beloved warrior" and it has Germanic origins.
HESTIA	Means "hearth" or "fireside" and originates from Greek mythology where Hestia was the goddess of the hearth, home, and family.
HETVI	The first name HETVI is of Indian origin and it means "intelligent" or "sharp-witted".
HEWAN	Amharic origin and it means "God's gift" or "grace" in English.
HEYDI	The name Heydi, a variant of Heidi, is of German origin and it means "noble and kind."
HEYLEN	The first name Heylen is of Dutch origin and means "from Hailin's town" or "descendant of Hailin."
HEYSEL	The name Heyzel is of Hebrew origin and it means "God is my refuge or God has saved."
HIALEAH	Means "pretty prairie" and originates from the Seminole language.

HIKARI	Means "light" in Japanese and it is derived from the Japanese language.
HIKMA	Means "wisdom" and originates from Arabic.
HILDA	Means "battle woman" and originated from Old Norse.
HILDEGARD	Means "battle protection," and it has Germanic origins.
HILINAI	Hawaiian name meaning "seeker of knowledge" or "to search and inquire," derived from the Hawaiian words "hili" (to search) and "nai'a" (to inquire).
HIMAWARI	Means "sunflower" in Japanese and is commonly given to girls, inspired by the bright and radiant nature of the flower.
HINAMI	Japanese name meaning "sunflower" and is derived from the combination of the words "hi" (sun) and "nami" (wave).
HINATA	Means "sunny place" or "towards the sun" and has Japanese origin.
HIRAETH	Means a nostalgic longing for a place that doesn't exist or can't be returned to, and it originates from the Welsh language.
HIRAYA	Means "dream" or "desire" in Filipino and it is of Filipino origin.
HIROMI	Japanese name that means "abundant beauty" or "generous beauty" and can be given to both boys and girls.
HISTORIA	The name "Historia" has its origin in Greek mythology, meaning "history" or "story," reflecting an individual with a strong connection to knowledge and storytelling.
HODAYA	Hebrew name meaning "thanksgiving" or "praise" and it originates from biblical references.
HOKULANI	Means "heavenly star" in Hawaiian and originates from the Hawaiian language and culture.
HOLIDAY	Means "a day of celebration" and it originated as a surname derived from the Middle English word "holi dai," referring to a day of religious observance or festivities.
HONOUR	Means "high respect, esteem, or integrity" and has Latin origins.
HORIZON	Means "the line where the earth seems to meet the sky" and it originates from the English language.
HORTENCIA	Means "garden" or "orchard" and originates from Latin.
HUMAIRA	Means "reddish complexion" and originates from Arabic.
HURAIN	Muslim baby name of Arabic origin, meaning "beautiful-eyed."
HUSNA	Means "beauty" in Arabic and has Islamic origins.
HUXLEIGH	English origin and means "meadow of Hugh's people."
HYACINTH	Means "blue larkspur flower" and originates from the Greek word "hyakinthos."
HYPATIA	Means "highest" or "supreme" and it originates from Ancient Greek.
IBADAT	Means "worship" and originates from the Arabic language.
IBBIE	Diminutive of the English name Isabella, derived from the Hebrew name Elisheba, meaning "God is my oath."
IBTISAM	Ibtisam is an Arabic name that means "smile" or "laughter," originating from the Islamic culture and often given to girls.
IBUKUNO LUWA	Means "blessing of God" in Yoruba language and is of Nigerian origin.
ICELYNN	Modern invented name derived from combining the words "ice" and "lynn," possibly chosen for its unique and icy connotations.
IDALIA	Means "behold the sun" and it has Greek origins.
IDAMAE	Feminine given name of uncertain origin, possibly a variant of the names Idabelle or Ida May.
IDIATOU	Nigerian Yoruba name meaning "chosen one" or "unique" and it is commonly given to girls in the Yoruba tribe.
IFEOMA	Means "good thing" or "beautiful thing" in Igbo language, and it originates from Nigeria.
IFORA	Feminine given name of African origin meaning "wild olive."
IFRAH	Somali origin and means "joy" or "happiness".
IFUNANYA	The Nigerian name Ifunanya means "love inspires" and derives from the Igbo language.
IKHLAS	Means "sincerity" and it comes from Arabic origin.
IKNOOR	The meaning of the name Iknoor is "one who knows the divine light" and it originates from Punjabi.

ILAH	Arabic origin and means "goddess" or "divine" in reference to a female deity.
ILAISAANE	The name Ilaisaane is derived from the Tongan language, meaning "praised or valued one," and it originates from the Polynesian culture.
ILARIA	Ilaria is an Italian feminine name, derived from the Latin word "Hilaris," meaning "cheerful" or "joyful."
ILAYDA	Means "moonlight" and has Turkish origins.
ILENE	Means "light" and is of Hebrew origin.
ILERIOLUWA	Yoruba name meaning "the promise of God" and is of Nigerian origin.
ILINA	Means "light" or "sunshine" and originates from Slavic languages.
ILSE	Means "pledged to God" and originates from the German and Dutch name Elisabeth.
ILUMINADA	Iluminada means "illuminated" in Spanish and is of Latin origin.
ILWAAD	Means "pearl" and its origin is Somali.
IMAGINE	Means to conceive or envision something in one's mind and it originated from the English word "imagine."
IMARA	Means "strong" or "firm" in Swahili, and it originates from the East African region.
IMELDA	Means "universal battle" and originates from Germanic and Old German languages.
IMMACULATA	Means "immaculate" or "pure" and has Latin origin associated with the Virgin Mary.
IMONA	African origin and it means "to be sure" or "reliable".
IMUNIQUE	Modern invented name with no established meaning or origin.
INAYRA	Means "radiant" in Arabic and has roots in various Middle Eastern cultures.
INDIYAH	The first name "Indiyah" is of Arabic origin and means "delicate, affectionate, or full of grace."
INDYA	Means "land of the Indus River" and has Sanskrit origins.
INEISHA	Means "pure, unique" and its origin is from American English.
INFANTGIRL	Infantgirl is not a traditional first name and does not have a specific meaning or origin.
INFINITY	Means limitless or boundless, and it originated from the English language.
INGA	Means "protected by Ing" and it is of Scandinavian and German origin.
INSHA	Means "to create" and has Arabic origins.
INSHIRAH	Arabic origin and means "relief" or "comfort."
INTISAR	Female Arabic name meaning "triumph" or "victory", originating from Arabic and Islamic cultures.
IRELIA	Means "golden princess" and it is of Greek origin.
IRIDESSA	Greek origin, means "rainbow" or "goddess of the rainbow".
ISABEAU	Means "God is my oath" and it originated from the French form of Elizabeth.
ISAMAR	The first name Isamar is of uncertain origin but is likely a combination of the names Isa and Amar, and it is frequently used as a female name in Spanish-speaking countries.
ISAURA	Means "beloved" and it originates from the Ancient Greek name Isaura, derived from the Greek word "Isauros" meaning "from Isauria," a region in ancient Asia Minor.
ISBELLA	Means "devoted to God" and it is a variant of the name Isabella, which originated from Hebrew and Latin.
ISHANVI	Indian origin and means "goddess of knowledge or wisdom."
ISHARA	The name Ishara has Hindi and Sanskrit origins and means "sign" or "symbol."
ISHAREDDY	South Indian name meaning "the warrior who is destined for greatness".
ISHIKA	Feminine name of Indian origin meaning "sacred" or "ray of light".
ISHIMWE	Means "praise" or "joy" in the Kinyarwanda language and originates from Rwanda.
ISHITHA	Indian origin and it means "superior" or "goddess."
ISIOMA	Means "good luck" and it originates from the Igbo language of Nigeria.
ISKRA	Means "spark" or "sparkle" and originates from Slavic languages.
ISLAMAE	The first name Islamae has a Muslim origin and it means "submission to God" or "surrender to God" in Arabic.
ISLAND	The first name Island originates from the English vocabulary word meaning a piece of land surrounded by water.
ISLAROSE	Means "island rose" and it has a modern, coined origin.
ISOLDE	Means "ice battle" and originates from Germanic mythology and literature, particularly the tragic tale of Tristan and Isolde.

ITATI   The first name Itati is of Guarani origin and it means "stone place" or "rocky place."

ITAYETZI   Feminine name of Nahuatl origin meaning "precious and beloved one."

ITOTIANI   Means "sharp rock" in Nahuatl and is of Aztec origin.

ITZABELLA   The first name Itzabella is of Spanish origin and means "devoted to God."

ITZAMARA   Means "bright light" and has its origin in the Maya culture.

IVALEE   The first name IVALEE is of English origin and means "from the yew tree valley."

IVEIGH   The first name Iveigh is of American origin and has no specific meaning as it is a modern invented name.

IVELISSE   The first name "Ivelisse" is of Spanish origin and it means "life".

IVETH   Uncertain origin and meaning, but it is believed to have Spanish or Hebrew roots.

IVYLYNN   Combination of the names Ivy and Lynn, and it likely originated as a modernized form of the name Lynn, meaning "lake" or "waterfall" in Old English, often associated with tranquility and serenity.

IVYMAE   Combination of the name Ivy, derived from the Old English word "ifig" meaning "ivy plant," and the name Mae, a variant of May, derived from the name of the fifth month in the Julian and Gregorian calendars, both of which are of English origin.

IVYMARIE   The meaning of the first name Ivymarie is "a combination of the plant ivy, symbolizing perseverance, and the name Marie, which is of Hebrew origin meaning 'bitterness'.

IVYONNA   Modern and feminine name of unknown origin, possibly a variant of the name Ivy or a combination of Ivy and Yvonne.

IVYROSE   Means "a combination of the nature-derived Ivy and Rose," and its origin is a modern English composite name.

IXCHEL   Means "moon goddess" in Mayan mythology, originating from the indigenous culture of Mexico and Central America.

IYANUOL
UWA   Means "miracle of God" and it originates from the Yoruba language in Nigeria.

IYMONA   Feminine name of unknown origin, meaning "blessed" or "fortunate."

IYONI   The name IYONI has no determined meaning or origin as it does not appear to have a widely recognized or documented background.

IYSIS   The name Iysis has no widely known meaning or origin as it appears to be a relatively rare and unique name.

IZARAYLA   Unique and modern feminine name of uncertain origin, possibly a blend of various influences.

IZUMI   Means "fountain" or "spring" in Japanese and has its origins in the Japanese language and culture.

JACINDA   Means "hyacinth flower" and originates from the Greek language.

JADESOLA   Means "crowned with wealth" in Yoruba and is of Nigerian origin.

JADZIA   The first name Jadzia has a Slavic origin and it means "warrior" or "battle maiden."

JAELIE   Means "heavenly" and it does not have a specific origin or meaning.

JAHLIYAH   The name "Jahliyah" has Arabic origins and means "ignorance" or "foolishness."

JAHNAVI   Means "daughter of the river Ganges" and originates from Sanskrit.

JAHNOVA   Modern, unique name of uncertain origin and meaning.

JAHNVI   The first name Jahnvi is of Sanskrit origin and it means "river Ganga."

JAIANA   Feminine name of American origin, derived from the combination of the names Jaya and Ana, meaning "victorious grace."

JAILAHNI   American origin and its meaning is currently unknown.

JAIYANA   Modern and unique feminine name of uncertain origin, potentially a variation of the name Jana or a combination of other names.

JAKENZIE   The first name "Jakenzie" does not have a widely recognized meaning or origin as it is a rare and unique name.

JAKYRA   The first name JAKYRA is of American origin and its meaning is uncertain.

JALAIAH   American origin and it means "combination of the names Jala and Aiah".

JALILAH   Means "honorable" or "glorious" and it originates from Arabic.

JALYRIC   The name Jalyric has no widely recognized meaning or origin as it is a modern, invented name.

JAMAICA	The first name Jamaica originates from the Caribbean island of the same name and means "land of wood and water".
JAMERIA	Modern American name of uncertain origin, often used as a feminine given name.
JAMILIA	Means "beautiful" or "elegant" and it originates from Arabic.
JAMIRA	Means "beautiful" and is of Arabic origin.
JAMIRACLE	Means "a miraculous outcome" and has an origin derived from combining the names Jamila (Arabic for "beautiful") and Miracle (English for "extraordinary event").
JAMYAH	The name Jamyah likely originated from the African American community and means "beautiful one" or "beloved."
JANAYAH	The first name Janayah, of uncertain origin, means "God is gracious" or "God has answered" and is often used for girls.
JANEAH	Modern origin and is likely a variant of the name Janae, meaning "God has answered" or "God is gracious".
JANEVA	Means "God is gracious" and it is of Hebrew origin.
JANHVI	Means "daughter of Janu" and has origins in Sanskrit.
JANIECE	Modern feminine variant of the name Janice, of Scottish origin, meaning "God is gracious."
JANIELYS	Feminine name of uncertain origin and meaning, possibly created by combining elements from various sources.
JANINA	Feminine given name of Polish origin, derived from the name Jan, which means "God is gracious."
JANIQUE	Means "God is gracious" and has a French origin.
JANIYLA	American origin and holds the meaning "God is gracious."
JANNATUL	Means "paradise" or "garden" and has origins in Islamic and Arabic cultures.
JANUARY	Unisex first name derived from the name of the first month of the year in the Julian and Gregorian calendars, symbolizing new beginnings and fresh starts.
JAONI	Gender-neutral name of Ethiopian origin meaning "gift of God."
JAPJI	The first name Japji is of Indian origin and means "meditation of the soul."
JARETSSI	The first name Jaretssi is of unknown origin and has no widely accepted meaning.
JARETZY	Form of the name Jaritza, of unknown origin, and carries no specific meaning.
JASELYN	The meaning of the first name Jaselyn is "modern invention" and its origin is a combination of the names Jason and Lyn.
JASIBE	Hebrew origin and it means "God is my oath".
JASNOOR	Means "divine light" and originates from Punjabi, a language spoken in the Punjab region of India and Pakistan.
JASREET	The first name Jasreet is of Punjabi origin and means "victorious, brave warrior".
JATAVIA	Modern American female name of uncertain origin, with no widely known or definitive meaning.
JATZIRY	Feminine name of Mexican origin, meaning "beautiful flower" or "precious stone."
JAYLIANIS	The name Jayliani is of American origin and has no specific meaning, as it is a unique and uncommon name.
JAYLINE	American origin and means "beautiful blue jay" or "graceful bird."
JAZAIYAH	Means "God's reward" and has origins in Hebrew and Arabic.
JAZALYN	Modern English feminine given name, likely derived from the combination of the names Jasmine and Lynn.
JAZARA	Feminine name of Arabic origin, meaning "fragrant flower" or "blossom."
JAZHARA	Modern and unique name of uncertain origin, possibly a combination of "Jazz" and "Sahara."
JAZMARIE	Modern invented name combining the elements "Jaz" and "Marie" to create a unique and contemporary feminine given name.
JAZYIAH	The first name Jazyiah is of uncertain origin and meaning, as it does not have a well-established etymology or background.
JEANNIE	Means "God is gracious" and originates from the Hebrew name Jeanne or Jane.
JEDIDAH	Means "beloved of the Lord" and has Hebrew origins.
JEHILYN	The name Jehilyn has no widely recognized meaning or origin.

JEIZY	The first name Jeizy is of uncertain origin and meaning, as it is not a widely recognized or documented name.
JELANY	The first name Jelany is of Arabic origin and means "majestic" or "glorious."
JEMIMA	Hebrew origin, means "dove" and is mentioned in the Bible.
JENAIYA	African origin and means "gift from God" or "God has answered."
JENASIS	Modern invented name of uncertain origin, possibly derived from the word "genesis" meaning "beginning" or "birth."
JENAVIE	Variant of the name Genevieve, of Germanic origin, meaning "woman of the race".
JENAVIEVE	The first name JENAVIEVE is of American origin and means "white wave" or "fair phantom".
JENESSA	Means "God is gracious" and it is derived from the combination of the names Jennifer and Vanessa.
JENIKA	Modern and invented first name of uncertain origin and meaning.
JENOVA	The first name Jenova is of uncertain origin and meaning, but it gained popularity as a fictional character in the video game Final Fantasy VII.
JENTRI	Means "one who is a newcomer" and originated as a modern variation of the English word "gentry."
JERUSALEM	Means "city of peace" in Hebrew and is the capital of Israel.
JERUSHA	Means "possession" or "inheritance" and it originated from Hebrew.
JERZI	The first name Jerzi is of Polish origin and means "farmer" or "tiller of the soil."
JESAAELYS	The meaning and origin of the first name JESAAELYS is unknown as it does not appear to have a widely recognized meaning or traditional origin.
JESSABELLE	Modern and variant form of the name Isabella, derived from the Hebrew name Elizabeth, meaning "God's promise."
JESSAMINE	Persian origin, means "jasmine flower" and is derived from the Persian word "yasamin" or "yasaminah."
JEWELIA	Modern feminine given name of uncertain origin and meaning, possibly derived from the word "jewel" reflecting a precious and unique quality.
JEYMI	American origin and means "beloved" or "precious".
JEZEBEL	Means "impure" or "unexalted" and originated from ancient Hebrew literature, particularly the Bible, where Jezebel was a queen known for her wickedness and idolatry.
JHADE	American origin and has no specific meaning as it is a unique and uncommon name.
JHELANI	Means "mighty" or "great" and originates from Swahili.
JHENESIS	The first name Jhenesis, derived from the name Genesis, conveys the meaning of "beginning" or "origin" and originates from the Hebrew language.
JHERSI	The first name JHERSI is of modern origin and has no clear meaning as it is most likely a variant spelling of the name Jersey or a creative invention.
JHERZEE	Modern American variation of the name Jersey.
JHOSELYN	Feminine given name likely originated from the combination of the names "Jose" and "Lyn," and it generally means "God will increase" or "God will add."
JHOURNI	The meaning of the first name Jhourni is "a journey" and its origin is uncertain.
JHREAM	The meaning and origin of the first name Jhream are unknown as it is a unique and rare name.
JINORA	Means "careful, beautiful light" and originates from a fictional character in the animated TV series "The Legend of Korra."
JOCABED	Means "the glory of the Lord" and it originates from Hebrew.
JOCHEBED	Means "God is glory" and has Hebrew origin.
JOELENE	The name Jolene means "God will increase" and has Hebrew origins.
JOLEIGH	Modern variant of the name Jolie, meaning "pretty" or "beautiful" in French, and it is of French origin.
JOLYNE	Means "cheerful" or "joyful" and it originated from the English language.
JONASIA	Means "God is gracious" and it is of Polish origin.
JOPLIN	Means "a person from Joplin's son" and is of English origin.
JORDIE	Unisex name of English origin, often used as a diminutive form of Jordan, meaning "to flow down" or "descend" in Hebrew.

JOSABETH	Combination of the names Josephine and Elizabeth, and it originated as a creative variation of these traditional names.
JOSHLYNN	Modern, feminine variation of the name Joshua, originating from the Hebrew name Yehoshua meaning "God is salvation."
JOSIEMAE	English origin and is a combination of the names Josie and Mae, meaning "God will increase" and "bitterness" respectively.
JOUDIA	Feminine given name of Arabic origin, meaning "generosity" or "magnanimity."
JOURDYN	Means "modern variant of the name Jordan", originating from England.
JOURNEIGH	Unique modern variation of the word "journey" and likely originated as a contemporary English name.
JOYCELYN	The first name Jocelyn means "Joyful" and has English origins.
JOYLYNN	The first name Joylynn originated from English and conveys the meaning of "one who experiences happiness and joy."
JOZELLE	Means "God will add" and it originates from Hebrew.
JUDAEA	Means "Jewish homeland" and it has Hebrew origins.
JULEAH	The first name Juleah is of Hebrew origin and means "youthful; full of energy and vitality."
JULIANYS	Means "youthful" and has unknown origin.
JULICIA	The first name Julicia is of American origin and means "youthful or energetic."
JULIEANNA	Means "youthful, downy" and is a combination of the names Julie and Anna, derived from Latin and Hebrew origins.
JULY	Means "youthful" or "downy-bearded" and is of Latin origin.
JUMANA	Feminine Arabic name meaning "silver pearl" and it originates from Arabic culture.
JUNEAU	Means "youthful" and originates from the French surname "Junot."
JUNIYAH	Arabic origin and means "young."
JURNEY	The first name Jurney originated in the United States and it means "a unique and unpredictable journey in life".
JURNIE	The name Jurnie originates from the English language and it means "a journey or a trip."
JUWAYRIYA	The first name Juwayriya originates from Arabic and means "little girl with big beautiful eyes."
JYNESIS	Modern and unique variation of the word "genesis," meaning "beginning" or "origin," likely originated in the United States.
KADIATOU	The first name Kadiatou originated from the Fulani language in West Africa and means "pure" or "honest."
KADIJAH	Means "preeminent" or "greatly respected" and originates from Arabic.
KADYNCE	Modern invented name, possibly a variant of Cadence, and it conveys a sense of rhythmic harmony or musicality.
KAELIN	Means "slender" or "mighty warrior" and has Irish origins.
KAHEALANI	Means "the mist from the heavens" and originates from the Hawaiian language.
KAHLEESI	The first name Kahleesi originated from the television series "Game of Thrones" and means "queen" in the fictional Dothraki language.
KAHMYLA	Modern Americanized name with no known origin or specific meaning.
KAIAH	Hebrew origin and carries the meaning "godly, pure, and exalted."
KAIDYNCE	The first name Kaidynce, of uncertain origin, is a modern variation of the name Cadence, possibly derived from the Latin term "cadentia" meaning "to fall" or "rhythm".
KAIHLANY	American origin and means "unique" or "special."
KAILAYA	Indian origin and it means "place of Kailash or abode of Lord Shiva" in Hindu mythology.
KAILEIA	Modern variation of the name Kaila, of Hebrew origin, meaning "crown" or "laurel wreath."
KAILIA	The name Kailia has a Hawaiian origin and means "beautiful and unique."
KAILIANI	Hawaiian name meaning "sea and sky" or "heavenly sea", originating from the Hawaiian language.
KAIOR	The name Kaior has no widely recognized meaning or origin as it appears to be a rare or unique name with limited information available.
KAIULANI	Means "heavenly sea" in Hawaiian and it is of Polynesian origin.
KAIYOMI	Japanese name meaning "beautiful ocean" or "ocean child," combining the elements kai, meaning "ocean," and yomi, meaning "beautiful" or "child."

KALEYAH	Modern invention, combining elements of various names to create a unique and uncommon choice for a baby girl.
KALICIA	The first name Kalicia, of uncertain origin, likely originated as a modern variation or combination of existing names, and its meaning is not widely documented.
KALIESE	American origin and it means "a modern variant of the name Kali, which is derived from the Hindu goddess of destruction and transformation."
KALIONNA	The first name KALIONNA, of unknown origin, does not have a widely accepted meaning.
KALISE	Uncertain origin and meaning.
KALKI	The first name Kalki, of Sanskrit origin, means "destroyer of filth" and is associated with the final incarnation of Lord Vishnu in Hindu mythology.
KALLIOPI	The first name Kalliopi is of Greek origin and means "beautiful voice" or "beautifully voiced."
KALONI	Hawaiian origin and it means "heavenly beauty."
KALYANI	Means "auspicious, beautiful" and originates from Sanskrit.
KALYCE	The name Kalyce has a modern invented origin and does not have an established meaning.
KALYSTA	Means "most beautiful" and it is of Greek origin.
KAMAIYAH	The first name Kamaiyah has no clearly defined meaning or origin as it is a modern invented name.
KAMALANI	Hawaiian origin and means "heavenly child" or "divine child."
KAMARIAH	The name Kamariah likely originated from Arabic or Swahili, and it means "moonlight" or "moon-kissed."
KAMERYN	Originating from the Scottish surname Cameron, the first name Kameryn means "crooked nose" or "bent nose."
KAMIYLAH	Arabic origin and means "perfect" or "complete."
KAMSIYONNA	Means "who is like God" and has an African origin.
KAMYLA	Modern feminine name of uncertain origin and meaning, potentially influenced by names like Kamila or Camila.
KANDICE	Means "glowing white" and it originates from the English language.
KARALEE	Variation of the name Karla, combining the names Kara and Lee, and has American origins.
KARALINE	Modern variation of the name Caroline, derived from the Germanic name Karl meaning "man" or "free man."
KARINE	Means "pure" and it is of Armenian origin.
KARISHMA	Means "miracle" or "gift" and is of Indian origin.
KARISMA	The name Karisma (also spelled Charisma) means "compelling attractiveness or charm" and originates from the Greek word "charis," which represents grace or favor in the original language.
KARLITA	Feminine given name of Spanish origin, often considered a diminutive form of the name Carlos or Carlota.
KARMINA	Means "song" or "poem" and has Latin origins.
KASLYN	Modern variation of the name Kassie, ultimately derived from the Greek name Kassandra, meaning "she who entangles men".
KASSIDI	Means "clever" or "resourceful" and originates from the English language.
KATALAYA	The name Katalaya originated as a modern variant of the name Catalaya, with no specific meaning associated with it.
KATALEIA	Means "beautiful girl" and originates from the Greek language.
KATALIA	Variation of the name Natalia, which is of Latin origin and means "born on Christmas day."
KATARA	Means "clear, pure" and has its origin in Sanskrit.
KATARZYNA	Means "pure" and it originates from the Greek name Aikaterine.
KATELEYA	The first name Kateleya is of unknown origin and meaning.
KATERI	Means "pure" or "clear" and is of Native American Mohawk origin.
KATHALEYA	The first name KATHALEYA is of uncertain origin, but could potentially be a variant of the name Katherine, meaning "pure" or "clean."

KATHALINA	Means "pure" or "innocent" and is of Greek origin.
KATJA	Means "pure" or "chaste" and it is of Slavic origin.
KATNISS	Means "arrowhead" and originates from the fictional character Katniss Everdeen in the Hunger Games trilogy by Suzanne Collins.
KATRIEL	Means "God's angel" and has Hebrew origins.
KATYAYANI	Means "daughter of sage Katyayana" and originates from Hindu mythology and the Hindu goddess Durga.
KAWAILANI	Hawaiian origin and means "heavenly water."
KAWSAR	Means "abundance" or "river in paradise" and originates from Arabic literature and Islamic tradition, specifically referring to a heavenly fountain mentioned in the Quran.
KAWTHAR	Means "abundance" or "goodness" in Arabic, and it originates from Islamic tradition.
KAYHLANI	Means "heavenly sea" and is derived from the combination of the names Kay and Lani.
KAYLAHNI	Means "a combination of the names Kayla and Ahnii" and has no specific origin as it is a contemporary, invented name.
KAYLANA	Means "pure" and has American origins.
KAYLEAH	Irish origin, means "beloved" or "slim and fair."
KAYLIYAH	Uncertain origin and meaning, but it is commonly used as a modern variation of the names Kayla or Kyla.
KAYLONIE	The first name Kaylonie is of American origin and has no specific meaning.
KAYMARIE	Modern, feminine combination of the names Kay and Marie, potentially created in recent years and rooted in English and French origins.
KAYOIR	The first name "Kayoir" does not have a widely recognized meaning or origin as it appears to be a unique or rare name.
KAYRA	Means "precious" and its origin is Turkish.
KAYSLEE	Means "a combination of the names Kay and Lee" and its origin is likely a modern American creation.
KAYSLEIGH	Modern American origin and its meaning is a combination of the names Kay and Leigh, often associated with traits such as independence, strength, and grace.
KAYTLIN	Means "pure" or "clear" and originates from the Irish and Greek names Caitlin and Katherine.
KAYZLIE	The first name Kayzlie likely originated from combining the names Kay and Kylie, and it carries a meaning similar to "pure" or "beautiful."
KAYZLYNN	Modern invented name that does not have a specific meaning or origin.
KEALOHILANI	Means "the heavenly love" and originates from Hawaiian language.
KEARI	Modern variation of the name Kerry, derived from an Irish surname meaning "dark-haired" or "descendant of Ciardha."
KEEVAH	Variant of the Irish name Caoimhe, meaning "gentle, beautiful" and originates from Ireland.
KEHAULANI	The Hawaiian name Kehaulani means "heavenly dewdrop" and originates from the combination of Ke meaning "the" and haulani meaning "dew of heaven."
KEHILANY	Hawaiian name meaning "beautiful ocean" and is of Hawaiian origin.
KEIARA	Unknown origin and meaning, but it is believed to be a feminine variant of the Irish name Ciarán.
KEIGHLEY	The first name Keighley is of English origin and means "from the meadow of the calf."
KEIHLANI	The first name Keihlani is of Hawaiian origin and means "clear sky" or "rising sun.".
KEIKO	Means "blessed child" in Japanese and has its origin in Japan.
KEILEY	Variant spelling of the Irish surname Keely, originating from the Irish Gaelic name Ó Cadhla, meaning "descendant of Cadhla" or "lovely, graceful."
KEILIANY	Hawaiian origin and means "heavenly beautiful."
KEISHLA	The meaning and origin of the first name Keishla is a variant of the name Kayla, of Hebrew origin, meaning "crown of laurels" or "pure."
KEISY	Unknown origin and meaning.
KEKELI	Means "light" or "brightness" and is of Ewe origin, commonly used in Togo and Ghana.
KELAHNI	The first name Kelahni is of American origin and it means "clear water".
KELAYA	Unknown origin and meaning.

KELCIE Means "victorious ship" and it is of Scottish origin.

KELHANI Hawaiian origin and is believed to mean "heavenly warrior" or "heavenly strength."

KELLYANNE Compound name combining the Irish surname Kelly, meaning "warrior" or "bright-headed," with the English name Anne, meaning "grace" or "favor," typically used as a given name for girls.

KENDALYN The meaning of the first name Kendalyn is "valley of the River Kent," and it is a modern combination of the names Kendra and Lynn.

KENISHA Means "beautiful one" and originates from the African-American community.

KENNIDEE The first name Kennidee likely originated as a variant spelling of the name Kennedy and carries the meaning "helmeted chief" or "misshapen head".

KENSLEI The meaning and origin of the first name KENSLEI is a combination of the English name Ken and the Japanese name Sora, reflecting a blend of different cultures.

KENZLIE The meaning and origin of the first name Kenzlie is uncertain, potentially derived from a combination of various names or invented on its own.

KERRINGTON Means "settlement of the royal man" and is of English origin.

KESHVI Indian origin and means "one with beautiful hair".

KETURAH Means "incense" or "fragrance," and it has Hebrew origins.

KETZALY Means "precious jewel" and originates from the Nahuatl language spoken by the indigenous people of Mexico.

KETZIA The name Ketzia has Hebrew origins and means "cassia tree" or "cinnamon."

KEYARI Modern name of uncertain origin and meaning.

KEYIOR Uncertain origin and meaning.

KEYLIANIS Means "beautiful island" and has a Hispanic or Latin origin.

KEYSHA Variant of Keisha and it is of African-American origin, meaning "favorite" or "cassia tree".

KEZIYAH The first name Keziyah originated from Hebrew, meaning "God strengthens" or "God increases."

KHADIDJA The first name Khadidja is of Arabic origin and it means "premature baby" or "early born."

KHAILANI Hawaiian origin and means "royal sea."

KHALEAH Means "beautiful, open-minded" and it has an uncertain origin, possibly a modern variation of the Arabic name Khalilah or an elaboration of the name Leah.

KHAMAYA The first name KHAMAYA is of Indian origin and means "illusion" or "magic."

KHAMORA The name Khamora has an unknown origin and meaning as it does not have a widely recognized or established origin or meaning..

KHAMYA African origin and means "beautiful princess."

KHARIZMA The name Kharizma has a modern origin and its meaning is derived from the word "charisma," symbolizing a captivating and magnetic personality.

KHARMA Means "destiny" or "fate" and it originates from the Sanskrit word "karma," which refers to the consequences of one's actions in Hindu and Buddhist philosophies.

KHAWLAH Khawlah is an Arabic feminine name meaning "gazelle" or "elegant and graceful," derived from the Arabic word "khaul," denoting a type of antelope.

KHEIRA Means "charitable" or "generous" and it has Arabic origins.

KHEMANI African origin and means "strong, mighty."

KHEMISTRY The meaning of the first name KHEMISTRY is unclear, but it is a unique and modern name derived from the word "chemistry."

KHEPRI Egyptian origin, means "he who has come into being" and is associated with the ancient Egyptian god of creation and rebirth.

KHEUMANI The first name Kheumani likely originates from Persian/Iranian origins and means "one who follows the teachings of the supreme leader Ayatollah Khomeini."

KHILYNN The first name Khilynn, of uncertain origin, does not have a widely-known meaning.

KHIONE Means "snow" and is of Greek origin.

KHLANI The name Khelani means "clear water" and is of Hawaiian origin.

KHLEO Means "crown" or "victorious" and it originates from the Greek word "kleos."

KHLOIE Modern variation of the name Chloe, of Greek origin, meaning "blooming" or "green shoot."

KHUSHI	Means "happiness" in Hindi and it is of Indian origin.
KIANI	The first name Kiani has Persian origins and means "kingly" or "royal."
KILLARI	The first name "Killari" does not have a widely recognized meaning or origin.
KIMAYA	Indian origin and means "divine" or "supreme energy".
KIMBERLEIGH	Means "from the meadow of the royal fortress" and it is a modern variation of the name Kimberly.
KIMBRIA	Modern, feminine name of uncertain origin and meaning.
KIMIKO	Means "noble, beautiful child" and has Japanese origin.
KIMIMILA	Means "butterfly" and originates from the Lakota Sioux Native American tribe.
KINDNESS	Virtue that involves being considerate, compassionate, and understanding towards others, with the origin coming from Old English.
KINGSLEIGH	Means "meadow of the king" and has English origins.
KINZA	Arabic origin and means "hidden treasure" or "hidden pearl".
KISWA	Means "covering" or "veil" in Swahili and its origin is from the Swahili language, commonly spoken in East Africa.
KIYARA	Means "beautiful, pure" and has origins in various languages including Hindi and African.
KIYOKO	Means "pure child" and has Japanese origins.
KLAIRA	The first name "Klaira" is of Greek origin and means "bright, clear."
KLARITY	The meaning of the first name Klarity is "clearness, brightness" and its origin is a modern variant of the word "clarity."
KLHOE	Means "blooming" and originates from the Greek name Khloe, derived from the word "khloros" meaning "green" or "blooming".
KLONI	The meaning of the first name Kloni is unknown as it does not have a widely recognized origin or meaning.
KMORA	The name KMORA has no widely recognized meaning or origin, as it appears to be a unique or uncommon name.
KNAVI	Means "angel" and has Hebrew origins.
KNIGHTLEY	Means "from the knight's meadow" and originates from the Old English word "cniht" meaning "servant" or "boy" and "leah" meaning "meadow" or "clearing."
KNOXLEE	Modern surname-derived given name, likely created by combining the surname Knox and the suffix -lee, possibly of English origin.
KNOXLEIGH	Modern English name that has no defined meaning or origin.
KOPELYNN	The meaning and origin of the first name Kopelynn are unknown as it is a rare and unique name.
KORALYNN	Modern name of American origin, combining the elements "kor-" from Corey and "-lynn" from Lynn, with a unique spelling.
KORAYMA	Feminine given name of unknown origin and meaning.
KORINA	Modern variation of the name Corinna, derived from the Greek word "korē" meaning "maiden" or "young girl".
KORTNEY	Unisex name of English origin meaning "courteous" or "knowledgeable."
KOSISOC HUKWU	Igbo origin and it means "As it pleases God" or "God's will is supreme."
KOURTLYN	The meaning of the first name Kourtlyn is "a modern American variant of Courtney, possibly derived from the French and English surname Courtenay."
KOURTNI	Variant spelling of the name Courtney, which originated as a surname and evolved from a locational name referring to individuals who lived near a court, a short form of the Old French "cour(t)."
KOUTURE	The first name KOUTURE originated as a modern feminine variation of the word "couture," referring to high-end, custom-made clothing and fashion design.
KOUVR	Modern, invented name with no known meaning or origin.
KREATION	Modern, creative spelling variant of the word "creation," signifying the act of bringing something into existence.
KRIDHA	The first name Kridha has a Sanskrit origin and means "one who plays or enjoys."
KRISHVI	Indian origin, means "divine" or "able to see the truth."
KRISLEY	American origin and it means "a combination of the names Kris and Ashley."

KRISLYN Modern invented name, likely derived from the names Kristy and Lynn, and its meaning is a combination of their respective meanings.

KRISTAL Means "crystal" and is of Greek origin.

KRISTHEL The first name Kristhel is of Danish origin and it means "follower of Christ".

KRITI Indian origin, means "creation" or "work of art."

KRITIKA Means "a star" and originates from Sanskrit.

KRIVA Feminine given name of Slavic origin meaning "crooked" or "bent."

KRYSTEL Means "crystal" and originates from the Greek word "krustallos."

KRYSTINA Variant of Christina, derived from the Greek name "Christos," meaning "anointed" or "follower of Christ."

KSENIA Feminine given name of Greek origin meaning "hospitable" or "guest" and is derived from the Greek name Xenia.

KULSOOM The first name Kulsoom, of Arabic origin, means "beautiful flower" or "blossom."

KULTURE Means a unique and refined cultural environment, and its origin can be traced back to English and American roots, possibly inspired by the word "culture."

KUMBA Name of African origin, meaning "born on a Tuesday" and is often given to individuals born on that day of the week.

KUROMI Means "black beauty" and has Japanese origins.

KUVIRA The name Kuvira is derived from Sanskrit origin, meaning "brave" or "courageous."

KWYNN The first name Kwynn, of Welsh origin, means "blessed" or "fair."

KYALYNN Modern invented name likely derived from the combination of the names Kylie and Lynn.

KYLEAH Modern feminine variant of the name Kyle, of Scottish origin, meaning "narrow strait" or "channel."

KYLIEANN Feminine given name that is a combination of the names Kylie (an Australian Aboriginal name meaning boomerang) and Ann (a Hebrew name meaning gracious).

KYLIYAH American origin and means "a unique and modern variation of the name Kyla."

KYMBERLEE Modern variant of Kimberly, of English origin, meaning "from the royal fortress meadow".

KYNADEE American origin, means "born of fire" or "fiery one."

KYNSLIE Modern and creative variation of the name Kinsley, likely originated from English and means "king's meadow."

KYOMI Japanese female name, meaning "pure beauty" or "pure love."

KYRIAKI Female given name of Greek origin meaning "belonging to the Lord."

KYRIELLE Means "lordly" or "related to the Lord" and originates from the French language.

LAELIA Means "beautiful" and originates from Latin.

LAENA Means "spear" or "warrior" and has Latin origins.

LAGERTHA The first name Lagerta originates from Old Norse and means "warrior woman."

LAIBA Means "intelligent" or "beautiful" and has Arabic origins.

LAIKLYN American origin and it is a modern invented name, which does not have a widely recognized meaning.

LAILONI Uncertain origin, is a modern and unique variant of the name Laila.

LAINEYJO Means "from the path by the lake" and is a combination of the names Lainey and Jo.

LAIYANI Arabic origin and means "intelligent" or "wise."

LAKEISHA Means "favorite" or "joyful" and has American origin.

LAKEYAH Modern American name likely derived from the combination of "lake" and the suffix "-yah," which has Hebrew roots, meaning "God."

LAKSHMI Means "goddess of wealth and prosperity" and originates from Hindu mythology.

LALISA Means "adorned with grace" and originated from Sanskrit.

LAMYIA The first name Lamyia is of Arabic origin and it means "dark-lipped" or "full-lipped".

LANAIYA The first name Lanaiya likely originated from an American or modern invention, and its meaning is unclear.

LANEIGH Modern variant of the name Lainey, which originated as a diminutive form of the Scottish name Elaine, meaning "bright, shining light".

LANGLEY Means "long meadow" and has English origins.

LANIAKEA Means "immeasurable heaven" and originates from the Hawaiian language.

LANITA Spanish origin and it means "graceful" or "little rock."

LANORA American origin and means "honor" or "light."

LANYAH	Relatively modern and unique name of American origin, its meaning is unknown.
LARAYAH	The name Larayah has a modern American origin, and its meaning is not widely known.
LAREYNA	Feminine given name of uncertain origin, possibly derived from the Irish term "laoire" meaning "calf of the leg".
LARIMAR	Means "sea and sky" and is of Spanish origin.
LAROSE	Means "the rose" and has French origins.
LARYSSA	Means "cheerful" or "from ancient Greece" and originates from the Greek name Larissa.
LASHAY	American origin and it means "promises from God."
LATIFA	Feminine Arabic name meaning "gentle, kind" and it originated from Arabic origins.
LATISHA	Means "joyful" or "happy," and it originates from the feminine form of the male name Latif, which means "kind" or "gentle" in Arabic.
LATOYA	Means "victorious one" and originated from the combination of the popular American names La and Toya.
LATRICE	Means "noble" or "patrician" and has American origin, derived from the combination of the prefix "La-" and the name "Trice."
LAURALEI	German origin and means "crowned with laurel," representing honor and victory.
LAURALYE	Means "laurel wreath" and is a modern variation of the name "Laura" with added creative spelling.
LAURELAI	The name Laurelai originates from the English language and means "crowned with laurels."
LAURELIN	Means "crowned with laurel" and is of English origin.
LAVAEH	The first name Lavayeh is of Persian origin and its meaning is unknown.
LAVANYA	Feminine given name of Indian origin, meaning "beauty" or "grace."
LAWSYN	Modern, creative variation of the name Lawson, which is of English origin and means "son of Lawrence."
LAYANI	The first name LAYANI is of Hebrew origin and means "to answer" or "to respond."
LAYKLEN	American origin and is a modern, creative twist on the name Lachlan, meaning "from the fjord-land" in Scottish Gaelic.
LAYLANY	Means "night beauty" and its origin is uncertain.
LAYLARAE	The meaning and origin of the first name Laylarae are uncertain as it appears to be a unique and uncommon name.
LAYLAROSE	The first name "LaylaRose" is likely a modern combination of the names "Layla," which means "night" in Arabic, and "Rose," a popular English flower name, creating a unique and feminine name.
LAZULI	Means "a gemstone of vivid blue color" and originates from the Persian word "lājward", referring to the gem Lapis Lazuli.
LEAHNA	The first name Leahna is of Hebrew origin and means "weary" or "delicate."
LEANNAH	The first name Leannah, of English origin, means "graceful" or "delicate like a flower."
LEIALOHA	Means "beloved child" in Hawaiian and has its origin in the Hawaiian language.
LEIGHANNA	Variant of the name Liana/Leeanna, of English origin, meaning "graciousness" or "light".
LEIGHLA	English origin and means "meadow or field of Leigh."
LEIGHLANI	Modern fusion of the names Leigh and Lani, potentially of Hawaiian origin, combining the meanings of "meadow" and "heavenly" respectively.
LEIHANA	Hawaiian origin and means "garland of flowers".
LEILAHNI	Means "heavenly child" and originated from the combination of the Hawaiian name "Leilani" meaning "heavenly flower" and the name "Leilah" derived from the Arabic word for "night."
LEILIANA	Feminine name of Arabic origin, meaning "beautiful night."
LEISEL	Means "God is my oath" and originated from the German name Elisabeth.
LEISHA	Modern variant of the name Alicia, derived from the Old German name Adalheidis, ultimately meaning "noble kind" or "noble sort."
LEIYAH	Modern variant of the name Leah, of Hebrew origin meaning "weary" or "delicate."
LEMON	The first name "Lemon" is of Chinese origin and it means "fortunate" or "powerful."
LENKA	Diminutive of Helena, derived from the Greek name Helenē, meaning "torch" or "light," and it originated in Slavic languages.

LEVIAH Means "lion of God" and is of Hebrew origin.

LEWHAT Modern invented name with no known meaning or origin.

LEXANI The meaning and origin of the first name Lexani is uncertain, as it does not have a widely recognized origin or meaning.

LEXUS The meaning of the first name Lexus is "defender of men" and its origin is American.

LEYSI The meaning and origin of the first name Leysi is unclear.

LIAMANI Hawaiian and Swahili origin and means "precious" or "cherished one."

LIELLE Variant of the Hebrew name Liel, which means "mine is God" or "God is mine" and has no specific origin or meaning.

LIESL Means "God's oath" or "pledged to God" and is of German origin.

LIGHT Means illumination or brightness and has origin in English.

LILIBETH Means "a combination of Lily and Elizabeth" and has English origin.

LILIETH Jamaican origin and means "pure one" or "gift of God".

LILINOE Means "fine misty rain" in Hawaiian and it is of Hawaiian origin.

LILIYA Means "lily flower" or "pure" and it originates from Eastern European countries, particularly Ukraine and Russia.

LILIYANA Means "lily" and it is of Bulgarian origin.

LILYANAH Means "pure and graceful" and has various origins, including Hebrew and Arabic.

LILYBELLE American origin, is derived from the combination of the names Lily and Belle and conveys a sense of beauty and feminine charm.

LILYGRACE Means "pure and graceful" and is a combination of the flower name Lily with the virtue name Grace.

LILYJANE Combination of the names Lily and Jane, meaning "pure" and "God is gracious," respectively, and originates from English and Hebrew cultures.

LILYJO Compound name of English origin, combining the names Lily, derived from the flower, and Jo, a diminutive form of the name Joanna or Josephine, meaning "God is gracious."

LILYMAE English origin and means "pure beauty."

LILYMARIE Means "pure beauty" and is a combination of the names Lily and Marie.

LILYROSE Means "a combination of the flower lily, symbolizing purity, and the flower rose, symbolizing love," and is of English origin.

LINEN Means "flax fabric" and has an unclear origin, possibly derived from the Irish surname Linane or a variation of the name Linus.

LINNAEA Means "twinflower" and it has Scandinavian origins.

LINSY American origin and means "from the linden tree island" or "island of linden trees."

LINZIE Variant of Lindsay, originating from Scotland, and it means "from the island of the lime trees."

LIORAH Hebrew feminine name meaning "my light," derived from the Hebrew word "lior" meaning "light."

LIRAEL Means "daughter of the sound of golden bells" and originates from the fantasy novel "Lirael" by Garth Nix.

LISAMARIE Combination of the names Lisa and Marie, and it likely originated as a modern American given name.

LISELI The name Liseli originated in Tanzania and its meaning is "woman of many talents."

LISETTE Means "pledged to God" and originates from the French name Elisabeth.

LIVIENNE The name Liviene, of uncertain origin, means "strong, resilient" and is likely a modern feminization of the name Lévi, derived from the Hebrew name Levi meaning "joined, attached."

LIVINGSTON Means "one who comes from Leving's town" and has Scottish origins.

LIZMARIE Combination of the names Liz and Marie, and it originated as a modern and creative variation of the name Elizabeth.

LOANY The first name Loany originated from the Hebrew name "Leah" and means "weary or tired."

LOCKLYN English origin and means "lake land."

LOKELANI Means "heavenly rose" in Hawaiian and originates from the Hawaiian language.

LOLITA Spanish origin and means "sorrowful" or "grieving."

LORALIE	The name Loralie has German origins and means "alluring enchantress" or "siren of the river."
LORINDA	Means "laurel tree" and has Latin origins.
LORNA	Means "crowned with laurels" and originated from the Scottish and English surnames.
LOUCILLE	French origin and it means "renowned warrior" or "famous fighter".
LOUELLE	Means "renowned warrior" and is of French origin.
LOUETTA	Feminine given name of English origin, meaning "renowned warrior."
LOUJAIN	The first name "Loujain" is of Arabic origin and means "silver" or "shining" in reference to the brightness and beauty associated with the metal.
LOVEAH	The first name Loveah does not have a specific meaning or origin as it seems to be a unique variation or combination of the name "Love" and possibly another name or word.
LOVELEIGH	Modern English name meaning "lovely" or "beautiful" in combination with "love," likely created as a unique variation of more traditional names like "Lovelyn" or "Lovelynn."
LOVETTE	Feminine given name of English origin, meaning "beloved" or "darling."
LOVEYA	Means "beloved" or "loved one" and has a modern, creative origin.
LOVINA	Means "beloved" and has origins in Latin and English.
LOWRY	Meaning "fierce warrior," the first name Lowry is of Irish origin.
LOXLEY	Means "meadow of the wolves" and has English origins.
LOYALTI	Means "faithful and dedicated" and has no specific origin as it is a modern invented name.
LUCETTE	The feminine given name Lucette means "light" or "illumination" and originates from French.
LUCIENNE	Means "light" or "illumination" and has French origins.
LUCILIA	Latin origin, means "light" or "illumination" and is derived from the male name Lucilius, meaning "man of light."
LUCRECIA	Means "profit" or "gain" and it has a Latin origin.
LUCYMAE	Combination of the given name Lucy, deriving from the Latin name Lucia meaning "light," and the English name Mae, a diminutive of Mary, meaning "bitter" or "beloved."
LUDMILA	The first name Ludmila is of Slavic origin and means "favored by the people" or "beloved by the people."
LUDOVICA	Feminine variant of the name Ludovic, derived from the Germanic elements "hlud" meaning "famous" and "wig" meaning "war."
LUISANA	The first name Luisana is derived from the Spanish name Luis and carries the meaning of "renowned warrior" or "famed warrior."
LUJAIN	Arabic origin and it means "silver."
LULAMAE	Means "combination of Lula and Mae" and likely originated as a unique American given name.
LUMINA	Means "light" or "brilliance" and is of Latin origin.
LUNABELLE	Means "beautiful moon" and has its origin in English.
LUNAFREYA	Means "moon princess" and originates from the video game Final Fantasy XV.
LUNAMARIE	Latin origin and implies a combination of the words "luna," meaning moon, and "marie," meaning sea, resulting in a name that evokes the beauty and serenity of the moonlit ocean.
LUNARAE	Modern, feminine name of American origin derived from the celestial term "lunar" symbolizing the moon and "rae" meaning "queen" or "graceful."
LUNARIA	Means "moon-like" and has Latin origins.
LUNAROSE	English origin, signifies a combination of the celestial term "lunar" and the delicate elegance of a "rose."
LUSINE	Means "moon" and originates from Armenian culture.
LUXURY	The first name "Luxury" is a modern English name derived from the word luxury, meaning opulence or extravagance.
LUZELENA	Luzelena, a feminine given name, has an uncertain origin and meaning.
LUZMARIA	Means "bright sea" and originates from the combination of the Spanish words "luz" meaning "light" and "maría" referring to the name "Maria."

LYDIANNA   Means "woman from Lydia" and has its origin in Greek mythology and history.
LYLAROSE   Modern and artistic combination of the names Lyla and Rose, likely created for its aesthetic and unique sound.
LYNDEN   Means "from the linden tree hill" and originates from Old English.
LYNDIE   Variant of the name Linda, derived from the Spanish word "linda" meaning "beautiful" or "pretty."
LYNLEIGH   The first name Lynleigh is of English origin and means "meadow by the lake."
MACARENA   The first name Macarena originated from the Spanish language and refers to a popular Spanish dance and a place name in Seville.
MACKINLEY   Means "son of the learned ruler" and has Irish origins.
MACLAINE   Means "son of Leander" and is of Scottish origin.
MADALINE   English origin and means "tower" or "high, exalted."
MADDALENA   Means "from Magdala" and has biblical origins, referring to Mary Magdalene, a follower of Jesus in the New Testament.
MADDIELYNN   Modern American name, likely created by combining the names Madison and Lynn, and it does not have a specific meaning.
MADELEY   The name Madeley originated from Old English and means "a meadow near a river."
MADIANA   Means "from Hadrian's villa" and has Latin origins.
MADIHA   Means "praiseworthy" or "commendable" and has Arabic origins.
MADYSIN   The first name Madysin originated as a variation of the name Madison and means "son of Matthew."
MAEBELLE   Means "beautiful may" and has a combined origin of English and French.
MAEBRY   Means "compelling happiness" and is of English origin.
MAEDOT   Female given name of Ethiopian origin, meaning "blossom" or "flower".
MAELANI   Means "heavenly flower" and is of Hawaiian origin.
MAELYS   Means "chief, prince" and it originates from Breton, a Celtic language spoken in Brittany, France.
MAESYN   Modern American origin and is a variant spelling of the name Mason, meaning "stoneworker" or "one who works with stone."
MAEVERY   Modern, invented name with no widely known meaning or origin.
MAEVLYN   Modern variation of the name "Maeve," meaning "intoxicating" or "she who intoxicates," of Irish origin.
MAGDA   Means "pearl" and originated as a short form of the given name Magdalena.
MAGDALINE   Means "from Magdala" and is of Hebrew origin.
MAGENTA   Means "vibrant red-purple" and has its origin in the color name, which was named after the Battle of Magenta in 1859 during the Second Italian War of Independence.
MAGGIEMAE   Combination of the names Maggie and Mae, both of which are diminutive forms of Margaret, meaning "pearl" or "child of light," and originate from Greek and Hebrew.
MAGUIRE   The first name Maguire is an Irish surname-turned-given-name, meaning "son of the follower of St. Fiacre."
MAHAILA   Means "God-like" and it is of Hebrew origin.
MAHALIA   Means "tenderness" or "gentleness" and is of Hebrew origin.
MAHATHI   The meaning of the first name Mahathi is "great sound" and its origin is Indian (Telugu).
MAHDIYA   Arabic origin and it means "guided one" or "divine leader."
MAHELET   Hebrew origin and it means "who is like God".
MAHIDEVRAN   Turkish name meaning "moon of the Sultan" and is commonly used in Turkey.
MAHIMA   Means "greatness" or "glory" and has origins in Sanskrit.
MAHLAYA   The name Mahlaya originates from the Arabic language and it means "graceful" or "beautiful one."
MAHLET   Amharic origin and means "special" or "unique."
MAHNOOR   Means "moonlight" and originates from Arabic and Persian languages.
MAHSA   Means "like the moon" and has Persian origin.
MAIJA   Means "beloved" and it originates from Finnish and Latvian cultures.
MAILYN   Uncertain origin and meaning, but it is commonly believed to be a combination of the names Mae and Lynn or a variation of the name Marilyn.

MAIMOUNA	Means "blessed" or "fortunate" and has Arabic and Muslim origins.
MAIREAD	The first name "Mairead" is of Gaelic origin and typically means "pearl," symbolizing purity and uniqueness.
MAIRIN	Gaelic name meaning "bitter" or "sea white", originating from Ireland.
MAITREYI	Means "compassionate" or "loving kindness" and originates from Sanskrit, an ancient language of India.
MAKAELYN	Modern invented name without a specific origin and meaning.
MAKAIAH	The name Makaih means "gift of God" and is of Hebrew origin.
MAKAIYA	Modern American name likely derived as a variant spelling of the traditional Hawaiian name Makai, meaning "toward the sea" or "from the sea."
MAKEDA	Means "greatness" or "queen" and originates from the Ethiopian/Hebrew culture.
MAKENIZE	Modern American name of uncertain origin that possibly originated as a variant of the name McKenzie.
MAKENLEIGH	American origin and it means "son of the beautiful one."
MAKENZY	Scottish origin, means "child of the wise leader" or "comely."
MAKINZIE	Means "child of the wise leader" and originated from the Scottish surname Mackenzie.
MAKYLA	Modern American variation of the name Michaela, meaning "who is like God" and originated from the Hebrew name Michael.
MAKYNLEE	Modern, Americanized spelling of the typically masculine Irish name McCauley, meaning "son of Colla" or "descendant of Colla."
MALAUNI	African origin and it means "strong warrior" or "strength of the army".
MALAYIAH	The first name Malayiah is of uncertain origin and typically used for a girl, with no specific meaning associated with it.
MALAYSHIA	The name Malayshia has no specific meaning or origin as it appears to be a modern and unique creation.
MALEIA	The first name Maleia originated from Hawaiian and it means "calm or serene sea."
MALEIYAH	American origin and means "a unique and beautiful girl."
MALENIA	Greek origin, means "soft, tender" and is a variant of the name Melania.
MALIKAH	Means "queen" in Arabic and it has its origin in the Arabic language.
MALUHIA	Hawaiian name meaning "peace" or "serenity" and is derived from the Hawaiian word "malu" meaning "calm".
MANASVI	Means "intelligent" or "wise" in Sanskrit and has Indian origins.
MANEH	The name "Maneh" has an Armenian origin and means "girl."
MANREET	Means "the enlightened soul" and originates from the Punjabi language.
MARAJADE	Means "beautiful gemstone" and originated from blending the names Mara, meaning "bitter" or "sea" in Hebrew, and the French name Jade, referring to the precious green
MARAKI	Means "bitterness" and it originates from the Amharic language in Ethiopia.
MARANATHA	Means "our Lord has come" and originates from ancient Aramaic, used in early Christian liturgy.
MARCIA	Means "dedicated to Mars" and originates from the Roman name Martius.
MARCIELLA	The name Marciealla means "warlike" and its origin is derived from the Latin masculine name Marcianus.
MARGAERY	Means "pearl" and is of English origin.
MARGEAUX	French origin and it means "pearl."
MARGRET	The first name Margret is of Greek origin and it means "pearl."
MARIAALICE	The first name MariaAlice is of Portuguese and English origin, and it is a combination of the names Maria and Alice, which both have religious and noble connotations.
MARIAAN TONIA	The first name MariaAntonia originates from Spanish and Portuguese languages, and it is a combination of two names: Maria meaning "beloved" and Antonia meaning "priceless" or "invaluable."
MARIACE CILIA	Means "bitter sea" and likely originates from Latin or Spanish roots.
MARIACLARA	The first name Mariaclara originates from the combination of the names Maria and Clara, and it signifies a blend of graceful beauty and clarity.

MARIAEDUARDA	The name Maria Eduarda is of Portuguese origin and combines the classic name Maria with Eduarda, meaning "strong and wealthy."
MARIAELENA	Combination of the names Maria, meaning "bitter" or "beloved" in Hebrew, and Elena, meaning "bright" or "shining" in Greek, resulting in a name that embodies both strength and beauty.
MARIAEMILIA	The name Maria Emilia is a composite name, combining the Latin name Maria meaning "bitter" or "beloved" and the Latin name Emilia derived from the Roman clan name Aemilius meaning "rival" or "equal."
MARIAFERNANDA	Means "bitter grace" and has its origins in Spanish and Portuguese.
MARIAHELENA	Compound name of Spanish and Portuguese origin, meaning "beloved and gracious woman" or "bitter and kind woman".
MARIAINES	The name Mariaines does not have a clear meaning or origin, as it appears to be a unique or rare name without established roots or widely-known background information.
MARIAISABEL	The name Mariaisabel combines the names Maria and Isabel, meaning "bitterness" (Maria) and "God is my oath" (Isabel) respectively, with origins in various cultures including Spanish, Portuguese, and Italian.
MARIAJULIA	The first name Mariajulia originated from the combination of two names, Maria and Julia, and signifies a person who is a combination of strength and grace.
MARIALUISA	Feminine given name of Italian origin, combining the names Maria and Luisa, meaning "bitter" and "renowned warrior" respectively.
MARIAMAWIT	Ethiopian origin and means "gift of Mariam" (referring to the Virgin Mary in Christianity).
MARIANELA	"Marianela" is a Spanish feminine given name meaning "graceful sea" or "beautiful sea," derived from the combination of "María" and "Manuela."
MARIANGEL	The first name Mariangel is of Spanish origin and means "Mary's angel."
MARIAPAULA	Combination of the names Maria and Paula, and it is of Spanish or Portuguese origin.
MARIAPAZ	Means "Mary's peace" and originates from Spanish.
MARIAVICTORIA	Means "Mary of victory" and has Spanish and Latin origins.
MARIAVITORIA	Portuguese name meaning "Mary, the victorious one" and is a combination of the names Maria and Vitoria.
MARICARMEN	Spanish feminine name meaning "beloved Mary" and it is a combination of María (Mary) and Carmen (a reference to the Virgin Mary).
MARICRUZ	Means "Mary of the Cross" and it has Spanish origins.
MARIELENA	Means "bitter sea" and is of Greek origin.
MARIETTA	Means "little rebel" and has Latin origins.
MARIFER	Modern and unique name derived from the combination of two Spanish names, María and Fernanda, representing a person who is a blend of grace and boldness.
MARIGNY	Means "from the sea" and originates from French.
MARILUZ	The meaning of the first name Mariluz is "sea of light" and it has Spanish origins.
MARINETTE	The first name "Marinette" is of French origin, meaning "little sailor" or "from the sea," often used as a nickname for "Marine."
MARIPOSA	Means "butterfly" and has Spanish origin.
MARISABEL	Feminine given name of Spanish origin, created by combining the names María and Isabel, meaning "Mary" and "God is my oath" respectively.
MARISKA	The name "Mariska" is a Hebrew name meaning "star of the sea" or "beloved" and is derived from the name "Maria."
MARISTELLA	Means "star of the sea" and it originates from Italian.
MARIUM	Arabic origin and it means "elevated" or "exalted."
MARKAYLA	Modern American name derived from combining the names Mark, meaning "warrior" or "dedicated to Mars," and Kayla, meaning "beloved" or "pure."
MARLAINA	The first name Marlaina is of Greek origin and means "from the sea," being a variation of the name Marina.

MARLAYSIA	The name "Marlaysia" is likely a modern invention, possibly combining elements of different names or meant to be a unique variation of "Malaysia."
MARLIYAH	Arabic origin and means "bitter" or "sorrowful."
MARSALI	Means "pearl" and has Scottish Gaelic origins.
MARSEILLE	The first name Marseille is of French origin and it is derived from the name of a city in France's southern region, known for its vibrant culture and maritime history.
MARTHINA	Variant of the name Martha, which is of Aramaic origin meaning "lady" or "mistress."
MARYBETH	The first name Marybeth combines the names Mary and Beth, and it originated as a combination of traditional biblical names used together.
MARYCLAIRE	Means "clear and shining of the sea" and has Latin and French origins.
MARYCLARE	The first name Maryclare is of American origin and means "a combination of the names Mary and Clare."
MARYCOL LINS	The name Marycollins is likely a combination of the names Mary and Collins, possibly created by blending two family names together.
MARYELI ZABETH	Means "beloved woman consecrated to God" and is a combination of the names Mary and Elizabeth, both of which have biblical origins.
MARYELLIS	Combination of the names Mary and Ellis, and its origin is a blend of English and Welsh languages.
MARYFRA NCES	Compound name of English origin that combines the names Mary and Frances, typically used as a double-barrelled given name for girls.
MARYGRACE	Compound name combining the traditional name Mary, meaning "bitter" or "beloved' in Hebrew, and Grace, meaning "favor" or "blessing" in Latin, resulting in a name symbolizing a combination of grace and devotion.
MARYJAYNE	The name "Maryjayne" is a compound name of "Mary" which means "beloved" in Hebrew, and "Jayne" which is a variant spelling of "Jane," meaning "God is gracious" in Hebrew, and it originated in English-speaking countries as a combination of these two names.
MARYJEAN	Combination of two names, Mary and Jean, and it originates from English and French origins.
MARYJOY	Means "rejoice, joyful" and originates from combining the names Mary and Joy.
MARYKATE	Combination of the names Mary and Kate, typically given to girls, with Mary being of Hebrew origin meaning "bitter" and Kate being a shortened form of Katherine meaning
MARYKAT HERINE	Compound name of English origin that combines the names Mary and Katherine, typically used to honor both individuals.
MARYKAT HRYN	Combination of the names Mary and Kathryn, likely created as a variant or fusion name in modern times.
MARYLIN	The name Marilyn means "beautiful sea" and it is a combination of the names Mary and Lynn.
MARYLOU	Combination of the names Mary and Lou, it is of English origin and means "bitter drop" or "renowned warrior".
MARYLOUISE	Combination of the names Mary and Louise, and its meaning is "wished-for warrior" or "renowned warrior," originating from the Hebrew name Miriam and the Old German name Ludwig.
MARYMAR GARET	Compound name of two traditional names, "Mary" meaning "bitter" in Hebrew and "Margaret" meaning "pearl" in Greek, and it originates from multiple cultures including Hebrew and Greek.
MARYROSE	Means "a combination of the names Mary and Rose" and has English origins.
MARYRUTH	Combination of the names Mary and Ruth, derived from biblical origins, representing the qualities of devotion and loyalty.
MARYSOL	Means "sea of bitterness and sunlight" and has Spanish and Latin roots.
MARYURI	Spanish origin and it is a combination of the names Mary and Yuri, representing a fusion of cultures, while its meaning is not widely known.
MATHILDE	Means "mighty in battle" and has Germanic origins.
MATTINGLY	Means "strong warrior" and has an English origin.
MAUDE	Means "powerful battler" and its origin can be traced back to Old Germanic and Old English.

MAURIANA	Modern American feminine name with the origin uncertain.
MAWADDAH	Mawaddah is an Arabic name meaning "affection" or "love" and is commonly used in Islamic cultures.
MAYAHUEL	Feminine given name of Nahuatl origin, meaning "agave plant" or "maguey goddess," associated with fertility and sustenance.
MAYARI	Filipino given name derived from the Tagalog goddess of the moon and fertility.
MAYBELLINE	Variant of Mabel, meaning "lovable" or "dear" and originated as a combination of the names May and Belle.
MAYBREE	Relatively new and uncommon name of American origin, combining elements of the names May and Bree to create a distinctive and feminine moniker.
MAYERLY	The first name Mayerly likely originated in the United States and its meaning is unclear.
MAYMUNAH	Means "fortunate" or "blessed" in Arabic, and it has its origins in Islamic tradition.
MAYRANI	Feminine name of uncertain origin, meaning "unique" or "extraordinary."
MAYTAL	Hebrew name meaning "dew drop" or "precious dew," derived from the Hebrew word "tal" meaning "dew."
MAYUKHA	Means "a cluster of rays" and originates from Sanskrit.
MAYUMI	Japanese feminine given name meaning "true beautiful" and originates from the Japanese language.
MAYVIS	The first name Mayvis likely originated as a combination of the names May and Vis, and refers to someone with qualities of grace and vision.
MAZARINE	Means "of the deep blue sea" and has origins in the French language.
MAZURI	Means "excellent" or "beautiful" in Swahili, and it originates from East Africa.
MCCALL	Means "son of gallant warrior" and originates from Scotland and Ireland.
MCKAYLEE	The first name McKaylee originated in the United States and is a variant of the names McKay and Kaylee, meaning "fire" or "slender."
MCKINLEIGH	Modern English name that originated as a combination of the surnames McKinley and Leigh.
MCKINNON	Means "son of the fair one" and originates from Scottish and Irish Gaelic languages.
MCKINSLEY	Means "son of the king's meadow" and it originated from Scottish and English surnames.
MEDINA	Means "city" and originates from Arabic.
MEDLEY	English origin and it means "a mixture or combination of various things or elements".
MEENAKSHI	Means "she with fish-like eyes" and it originates from Sanskrit, an ancient Indian language.
MEGHNA	Means "river" or "cloud" and has origins in Hindu mythology and Sanskrit language.
MEGUMI	Means "blessing" or "grace" in Japanese and is of Japanese origin.
MEHAR	The meaning of the first name Mehar is "blessing" and it originates from Punjabi and Sikh languages.
MEHNAZ	Persian origin and means "like the moon" or "coquettish".
MEHREEN	Means "lively, flourishing" and has Arabic origins.
MEHWISH	Persian origin and it means "moonlight" or "beautiful face".
MEILAH	The first name Meilah is of Hebrew origin and it means "beautiful and graceful."
MEIOMI	Modern name of uncertain origin, possibly derived from a blend of different cultural influences or created for unique appeal.
MEITAL	Means "dewdrop" and has Hebrew origins.
MEIYANI	Javanese name meaning "beautiful and graceful" that is commonly used in Indonesia.
MELEANA	Hawaiian name of Polynesian origin, meaning "heavenly beauty."
MELEK	Turkish origin and means "angel" or "messenger of God."
MELIANI	The first name Meliani is of Indonesian and Malay origin, meaning "gentle and sweet."
MELONA	The first name Melona is of uncertain origin and meaning.
MELROSE	Means "bare promontory" and originates from Old English.
MEMORY	The name "Memory" originated from the English vocabulary word, symbolizing the act or process of remembering or preserving something in one's mind.
MENORAH	Means "lamp" or "candelabrum" and originated from Hebrew.
MENUCHA	Means "tranquility" or "rest" and it has Hebrew origins.
MERELYN	Variant spelling of the name Marilyn, which is of English and Welsh origin and means "beloved lake" or "rebellious woman."

MERIDETH	Welsh origin and means "great ruler" or "protector of the sea."
MERIDIAN	Means "midday" or "highest point" and is of Latin origin.
MERYEM	Arabic origin and it means "beloved" or "loved one."
METZLI	Means "moon" in Nahuatl, the language of the Aztecs.
METZTLI	Means "moon" and originates from the Nahuatl language spoken by the Aztecs in ancient Mexico.
MIAISABELLA	The name Mia Isabella is a combination of two popular names, Mia and Isabella, with Mia meaning "mine" or "beloved" in Italian and Isabella meaning "devoted to God" in Hebrew.
MIAKODA	Means "power of the moon" and has Lakota Sioux origins.
MIALANI	Hawaiian origin and means "heavenly fragrance."
MIANGEL	Modern American name that is a combination of the prefix "mi-" meaning "my" and the name "Angel," which originates from the Latin word "angelus" meaning "messenger" or "angel."
MIAROSE	Modern and creative blend of the names Mia, meaning "mine" or "wished-for child," and Rose, a flower symbolizing love and beauty.
MIASIA	The first name "Miasia" does not have a specific meaning or origin as it is a modern and unique name with no established historical or cultural background.
MIAVICTORIA	Means "mine, victory" and originates from a combination of the names Mia and Victoria.
MICAYLA	Means "who is like God" and it is of Hebrew origin.
MICHAELYN	Contemporary feminine name that is likely a combination of the name Michael and the suffix "-lyn," originating in modern American usage.
MICHELINA	Means "who is like God" and has Italian origins.
MICKAYLA	Variation of the name Michaela and has Hebrew origins, meaning "who is like God?"
MICKIE	Diminutive form of the name Michael, meaning "Who is like God?" and originating from Hebrew.
MIDNA	Fictional character from the video game "The Legend of Zelda: Twilight Princess," with no known origin outside of the game.
MIELA	Means "gracious" or "honey-like" and has origins in both Slavic and Spanish languages.
MIESHA	Means "beloved" and originated from the Russian and Slavic languages.
MIHIKA	The name Miheka means "cloud" and has Indian origins.
MIHRIMAH	Means "sun moon" in Turkish, and it originated from Persia.
MIKEYLA	Modern and feminine variant of the name Michaela, derived from the Hebrew name Michael meaning "Who is like God?"
MIKIAH	Hebrew origin and means "who is like God?"
MILAHNI	Hawaiian origin and means "heavenly caress."
MILAROSE	The first name "Milarose" does not have a widely recognized meaning or origin as it is likely a unique combination or creative invention.
MILAYNA	The first name Milayna is of uncertain origin and meaning.
MILCAH	Means "queen" or "counsel" and originates from Hebrew.
MILEIGH	Modern variation of the name Miley, derived from the Irish surname O'Maolmhuaidh, meaning "servant of Saint Maolmhuire."
MILEYDI	Means "gracious" or "merciful" and it is of Hispanic origin.
MILILANI	Means "heavenly caress" or "cherished one" in Hawaiian, and it is derived from the combination of the words "mili" (to caress, to embrace) and "lani" (heaven, sky).
MILLARAY	Mapuche name meaning "golden flower" and is of indigenous South American origin.
MILLIEMAE	Milliema is an English name meaning "industrious and beloved", being a combination of the names Millie and Mae.
MILUV	The first name Miluv does not have a recognized meaning or origin as it is not a commonly used or documented name.
MINAHIL	Means "spring of clear water" and it originates from Arabic culture.
MINAL	The name "Minal" originated from Sanskrit and means "precious gem."

Note: This answer is based on the most commonly known interpretation of the name and

MINNOW	The first name Minnow is of English origin and it signifies a small freshwater fish, often used symbolically to represent modesty and vulnerability.
MINSA	The name Minsa has no widely recognized meaning or origin.
MIRAJANE	Means "admirable" or "wonderful" and it originates from the combination of the Arabic name "Mira" meaning "princess" and the Hebrew name "Jana" meaning "grace" or "gift from God."
MIREILLE	Means "to admire" and originates from the Provençal region in southern France.
MIROSLAVA	Feminine Slavic name meaning "glorious peace" and its origin can be traced back to Old Slavic roots.
MISAKI	Means "beautiful blossom" in Japanese and it is of Japanese origin.
MISCHA	Unisex name of Russian origin, meaning "who is like God?"
MISGANA	Female given name of Ethiopian origin, meaning "praise" or "thanksgiving" in the Amharic language.
MISK	Arabic origin and it means "fragrance" or "perfume."
MITSUKI	The meaning of the first name Mitsuki is "beautiful moon" and it originates from Japan.
MITZI	Diminutive form of the German name Maria, meaning "bitter," and its origin can be traced back to Latin.
MIYAKO	Means "beautiful night child" and has Japanese origin.
MIYORI	The first name Miyori is of Japanese origin and means "beautiful truth."
MIYOURI	Japanese name meaning "beautiful evening."
MIZUKI	Means "beautiful moon" and is of Japanese origin.
MOHINI	Hindu feminine given name meaning "enchantress" or "delusion" in Sanskrit, originating from Indian mythology.
MOMINA	Feminine Arabic name meaning "believer" or "pious" and has Islamic origins.
MONET	Means "adviser" and has French origins.
MORAYO	Nigerian name meaning "I see joy" or "I have found joy" in Yoruba language.
MORIREO LUWA	Means "I have found grace of God" and originates from the Yoruba language in Nigeria.
MORIYAH	Means "chosen by God" and it originates from Hebrew.
MORRIGAN	Means "great queen" or "phantom queen" and originates from Irish mythology, specifically the goddess associated with battle, sovereignty, and fate.
MORTICIA	Means "deathlike" and originated as a fictional character in the TV show "The Addams Family."
MOTLEY	Meaning "diverse" or "variegated," Motley is of Old English origin and is derived from the Middle English word "motley," which originally referred to a type of multi-colored fabric.
MOXIE	Means "courage, determination, and assertiveness" and it originated from the American English term "moxie," which means to have a strong and positive attitude.
MUBINA	Means "clear, manifest" and it has origins in Arabic and Persian languages.
MUKTA	Means "liberated" or "free" and it originates from Sanskrit, an ancient Indic language.
MUNACHI	Means "God is with us" and is of Igbo origin in Nigeria.
MUNACHI MSO	Means "I am walking/working with God" and originates from the Igbo language in Nigeria.
MUNACHISO	Means "God is with me" and originates from the Igbo language in Nigeria.
MUNIRA	Means "enlightened" or "illuminating" and originates from Arabic.
MUNTAHA	Means "the ultimate goal" and it originates from Arabic.
MUSFIRAH	Means "one who shines or illuminates" and has Arabic origins.
MUSHTAQ	Means "longing, desire" and has Arabic origins.
MUSKAN	Means "smile" in Hindi and it is of Indian origin.
MUSLIMA	Means "one who submits to Islam" and is of Arabic origin.
MWAJUMA	Means "born on Friday" and it originates from Swahili, a Bantu language spoken in East Africa.
MWANGAZA	Mwangaza means "light" in Swahili and is of African origin.
MYAYLA	Native American origin and is believed to mean "beautiful melody" or "sings with grace."
MYKAELA	Feminine given name of Hebrew origin meaning "who is like God".
MYLARAE	The name Mylaray means "my love" and has no origin information available.
MYLIAH	Modern variant of the name "Malia," derived from Hawaiian and Polynesian roots, meaning "calm and serene."

MYLOVE	The name Mylove likely originates from English-speaking countries and conveys a deep affection and devotion towards someone or something.
MYORI	The name Myori has no known meaning or origin as it appears to be a unique or rare name.
MYRAKLE	Means "miracle" or "wonderful" and has a modern origin.
MYRCELLA	The first name Myrcella is of unknown origin and meaning.
MYRIKAL	The name Myrikal has no specific meaning or origin as it is a unique and creative spelling variation of the name Miracle.
MYRNA	Means "beloved" and it has Irish and Scottish origins.
MYRTLE	Means "evergreen shrub" and has its origin in Greek mythology, associated with the symbol of love and immortality.
MYSHA	Arabic origin and it means "life" or "alive."
MYSTIC	Means "of mysterious or spiritual nature" and its origin is English.
MYTHILI	Means "princess of Mithila" and originates from Sanskrit.
NAAMAH	Means "pleasant" in Hebrew and originates from the Old Testament.
NADEZHDA	Means "hope" in Russian and it originates from Slavic languages.
NADIRAH	Means "rare" or "precious" and it has Arabic origins.
NAEVIA	Means "spotless" and has its origin in ancient Rome.
NAFISA	Arabic origin, means "precious gem" or "valuable" and is commonly given to girls.
NAHIARA	Feminine name of Basque origin meaning "one who watches over the valley."
NAHIDA	Arabic origin meaning "brave, courageous."
NAHLANI	Means "strong and powerful" and has origins in the Hawaiian language.
NAIARI	Means "lovely" and is of Basque origin.
NAIAYLA	Modern, unique name of uncertain origin and meaning.
NAIDELYN	Modern feminine given name of uncertain origin, likely created by combining various name elements.
NAIELLE	Hebrew origin and means "God has answered."
NAIEMA	The first name Naiema originated from Arabic and means "gentle" or "kind-hearted."
NAILEA	Means "feminine beauty" and originates from the Hawaiian language.
NAINIKA	Indian origin, means "beautiful-eyed" or "one with beautiful eyes."
NAIYELI	Means "I love you" in Zapotec language and has indigenous Mexican origin.
NAKSHATRA	Means "star" in Sanskrit and originates from Hindu mythology, referring to the 27 lunar mansions or constellations.
NALEAH	The first name Naleah is of Hebrew origin and means "belonging to God" or "God has answered."
NALEDI	Means "star" in the Sotho language, and it originates from the Southern African region.
NALINI	Means "lotus" or "beautiful" and it originates from Sanskrit, an ancient language of India.
NAMIKO	Means "child of the wave" and has Japanese origins.
NANAMI	Means "seven seas" in Japanese and has its origin in Japanese culture.
NANDINI	Means "daughter" or "delightful" and has origins in Sanskrit.
NAOMIKA	The name Naomika likely means "beautiful, pleasant" and originates from Japanese.
NAOMIROSE	The meaning and origin of the first name Naomirose are unknown as it seems to be a combination of the names Naomi and Rose.
NARDOS	Means "fragrant flowers" and originates from Eritrea and Ethiopia.
NARJIS	Means "jewel" or "flower" and has Arabic origins.
NASHALY	Means "graceful" and it is of uncertain origin, potentially a modern creation.
NASHLY	The first name Nashly is of American origin and means "from the ash tree meadow".
NASHRAH	Means "relief" or "joy" and has Arabic origins.
NASIYAH	The name Nasiyah is an Arabic name meaning "onward or advancing" that is typically given to girls.
NASREEN	Means "wild rose" or "gentle breeze" and originates from the Persian language.
NATANIA	Hebrew origin, means "gift of God" or "God has given."
NATIVE	Means "belonging to a particular place or region; indigenous" and originates from the English language.
NATSUMI	Means "beautiful summer" in Japanese and is of Japanese origin.
NATURE	The name "Nature" has an uncommon origin and signifies a deep connection with the natural world.

NAUTICA   Means "related to the sea" and has Latin origins.

NAVAYAH   Modern, creative variation of the traditional name Nava, with Hebrew and Sanskrit origins, symbolizing "beautiful" or "new beginning."

NAVEIGH   Means "new beginning" and has an uncertain origin.

NAVIKA   Means "a new beginning" and originates from the Sanskrit language.

NAWAL   Means "gift" or "blessing" and originates from Arabic culture.

NAXHIELI   The first name Naxhieli is of unknown origin and meaning.

NAYARA   The name NAYARA originates from the Quechua language of South America and means "shining star".

NAYDELIN   The first name Naydelin has an unknown meaning and origin.

NAYONI   Korean name meaning "beautify the world" and is often given to girls.

NAYSA   Means "miracle" or "sign" and has Spanish and Hebrew origins.

NAZANIN   Means "charming, graceful" and originated from the Persian language.

NAZARENE   The name "Nazarene" is derived from the town of Nazareth and typically refers to Jesus Christ as a follower of Christianity.

NAZLI   Means "delicate" or "graceful" and originates from Turkish and Persian cultures.

NDEYE   African origin and means "born on Sunday" or "Sunday's child".

NEAVEH   Modern invented name derived from the word "heaven" spelled backward, gaining popularity in the United States in the late 20th century.

NEBRASKA   Unique and uncommon name of Native American origin, derived from the Otoe Indian word "Nébrathka" meaning "flat water" or "broad river".

NEBULA   Means "cloud" or "mist" and has Latin origins.

NECHY   The meaning and origin of the first name "Nechy" is uncertain as it does not have a widely recognized origin or meaning.

NEFELI   Greek origin and means "cloud" or "bride."

NEFERTARI   Means "beautiful companion" in the ancient Egyptian language and it originates from the royal families of ancient Egypt.

NEFERTITI   Means "the beautiful one has come" and originates from ancient Egypt.

NEHMAT   Nehmat is an Arabic name meaning "blessing" or "gift from God."

NEMESIS   Means "goddess of vengeance" and originates from Greek mythology.

NEREIDA   Means "sea nymph" or "mermaid" and originates from Greek mythology as one of the Nereids, the fifty daughters of Nereus, the god of the sea.

NERIYAH   Means "God is my lamp" and has Hebrew origins.

NESLIHAN   Turkish name meaning "descendant of noble lineage" and originated from the combination of the Turkish words "nesil" (lineage) and "han" (descendant).

NETANYA   Hebrew name meaning "gift of God" or "God's gift," commonly used in Israel.

NETHRA   Feminine given name of Indian origin meaning "eye" or "sight."

NEVADA   The first name Nevada, of Spanish origin, refers to "snow-capped" or "snow-covered," and it is also the name of a U.S. state known for its diverse landscape.

NEVEYAH   Modern American variant of the biblical name Nevaeh, derived from the word "heaven" spelled backwards.

NEYLANI   Hawaiian origin and means "a heavenly beauty."

NEYTIRI   The first name Neytiri originated from the fictional Na'vi language created for the movie Avatar, meaning "warrior" or "hunter."

NEZUKO   Japanese feminine given name, meaning "closed bamboo stalk" and its origin comes from the popular manga and anime series "Demon Slayer: Kimetsu no Yaiba."

NGONE   West African (specifically Wolof) female name meaning "gift" or "present."

NGOZI   Means "blessing" in Igbo language, originating from Nigeria.

NHYIRA   Means "blessing" and it originates from Akan, a language spoken in Ghana and Ivory Coast.

NIAOMI   Variation of the name Naomi, which originated from Hebrew and means "pleasantness" or "delight."

NIAYLA   The first name Niayla is of uncertain origin and meaning, potentially a modern variation or an original creation.

NICHOLETTE   Means "victorious people" and originates from the Greek name Nicholas combined with the feminine suffix "-ette."

NICOLINA   Feminine given name of Italian origin, derived from the masculine name Nicola, meaning "victory of the people".

NIEVE   Means "snow" and it originates from the Spanish language.

NIHARIKA   Means "dew drop" or "someone who is always charming" in Sanskrit and has Indian origin.

NIHIRAREDDY   Sanskrit name meaning "one who is like a diamond;" it is of Indian origin.

NIJAH   Means "success" or "achiever" and has African origins.

NIKAYLA   Means "victorious people" and is a modern feminization of the name Nicholas, originating from Greek and Slavic roots.

NIKOLETTA   Greek feminine form of the name Nicholas, meaning "victory of the people."

NILAYA   Hindi name meaning "abode" or "dwelling," originating from Indian Sanskrit.

NILOUFAR   The first name Niloofar means "Water Lily" in Persian and is of Persian origin.

NIMERAH   Unique and modern name of Arabic origin meaning "soft and gentle breeze".

NIMRAT   The first name Nimrat originated from Punjabi and means "humble and down-to-earth."

NIMUE   Means "lady of the lake" and has Arthurian legend origins.

NINFA   Means "nymph" in Italian and Spanish, originating from Greek mythology.

NIOBE   Means "young woman" in Greek and originates from Greek mythology, as she was a queen who faced tragic loss and was transformed into stone.

NIRALYA   The first name Niralya is derived from Sanskrit origin, meaning "unique" or "unparalleled."

NIRVI   Indian origin and means "blissful, peaceful" in Sanskrit.

NIRVIKA   Means "conqueror of worldly attachments" and originates from Sanskrit.

NISHTHA   Means "dedication" or "loyalty" and it originates from Sanskrit, an ancient Indo-Aryan language of India.

NISSY   Variant of the Hebrew name Nissa and means "miracle" or "God's grace," deriving its origin from the Hebrew language.

NITHYA   Indian origin and means "eternal" or "permanent."

NITZA   Means "flower bud" in Hebrew and it is of Israeli origin.

NIVRITHI   The first name Nivrithi is of Indian origin and means "to walk with knowledge and confidence."

NIYARI   The name Niyari has no specific meaning or origin as it does not appear to be a widely recognized or documented name.

NIZARALY   Means "radiance of God" and is of Arabic origin.

NIZHONI   Means "beautiful" or "she is beautiful" in the Navajo language, and it originates from the Navajo culture.

NOGAYE   Means "courageous" and is of African origin.

NOHEALANI   The Hawaiian name Nohealani means "beautiful mist" and originates from the Hawaiian language.

NOHELY   Native American origin and means "beautiful; light; sun."

NOHEMI   The first name Noemi means "pleasantness" in Hebrew and is of biblical origin, derived from the name Naomi.

NOMI   Means "pleasantness" and has Hebrew origins.

NORAMAE   Unique feminine name of American origin, meaning "modern" or "unique woman".

NORELLE   Variant of the English name Noreen, derived from the Irish name Nóirín, meaning "little honor" or "little noble one".

NOURAH   Means "light" or "brightness" and originates from Arabic.

NOVAHLEE   Modern American name of uncertain origin, possibly a combination of the name Nova and the suffix -lee.

NOVAHLEIGH   "NOVAHLEIGH" is a modern American name created by combining the words "nova" meaning new or star, and "leigh" meaning meadow, resulting in a unique and contemporary name.

NOVALINA   Means "new moon" and has Latin origins.

NOVALISE   The name Novalise has no established meaning or origin as it appears to be a unique and modern name.

NOVARAE	The first name Novarae is of American origin and does not have a specific meaning.
NOVAREIGN	Modern invented name with no widely recognized meaning or origin as it doesn't have a historical usage or background.
NOVAROSE	Modern, feminine given name likely derived from the combination of "Nova," meaning "new" in Latin, and "Rose," a flower symbolizing love and beauty.
NOVEMBER	Means "ninth month" and originates from the Latin word "novem," which means "nine."
NOZOMI	Means "hope" in Japanese and it originates from the Japanese language.
NUBIA	Means "gold," and it originated from the ancient African kingdom of Nubia, located along the banks of the Nile River in present-day Sudan.
NUHAMIN	The first name Nuhamin is of Ethiopian and Amharic origin, meaning "a gift" or "a blessing."
NUSAYBAH	Means "one who has a strong personality" and originates from Arabic.
NYAELA	Swahili origin and means "purposeful" or "intentional".
NYAIRAH	Female name of Arabic origin, meaning "one who shines with brightness and radiance."
NYAMEYE	Means "God has given" in Akan language and originates from Ghana, West Africa.
NYARI	Means "moon" or "moonlight" and originates from the Shona language spoken in Zimbabwe.
NYELI	African origin and its meaning is "gift from God".
NYEMA	Means "grace" or "blessing" and originates from the Shona language spoken in Zimbabwe.
NYMERIA	Means "warrior" or "forging ahead" and originates from the character Nymeria in George R.R. Martin's book series "A Song of Ice and Fire" (popularized by the TV show "Game of Thrones").
NYOTA	Means "star" in Swahili and has African origin.
NYRAREDDY	The meaning and origin of the first name NyraReddy are unknown.
NYROBI	Means "born in Nairobi" and has African origins.
OAKLEYMAE	Modern invented name that likely combines elements of "oak" and "mae," possibly inspired by nature or family names.
OAKLIE	Modern English name of American origin meaning "from the oak tree meadow."
OASIS	Means a fertile or peaceful place, and it originates from the Arabic word "wa□ ah" referring to an isolated spot in the desert with water and vegetation.
OCEANIA	Means "oceanic" and is derived from the Latin word "oceanus," referring to the vast expanse of water on Earth.
OCTAYVIA	Variant of the name Octavia, which is derived from the Latin word "octavus" meaning "eighth," representing the eighth child or the eighth-born.
ODALYS	Means "wealthy and prosperous" and originates from Cuba.
ODILIA	Means "wealthy" or "prosperous" and originates from Old High German.
ODYSSEY	Means a long and eventful journey and originates from Greek mythology.
OHEMAA	Means "queen" and has its origin in Ghana.
OJASVI	Means "radiant" or "full of inner light" and it originates from Sanskrit.
OKALANI	The first name Okalani is of Hawaiian origin and means "heavenly."
OKSANA	Means "praised" or "graceful" and has origins in Slavic languages, particularly Ukrainian and Russian.
OLIVIAGRACE	Means "olive tree" and "God's favor" combined, originating from Latin and English languages.
OLIVIANA	Variant of the name Olivia and originated from Latin.
OLIVIAROSE	Feminine compound name that combines the names Olivia, derived from Latin meaning "olive tree," and Rose, derived from Latin meaning "flower," which symbolizes beauty and grace.
OLOLADE	Yoruba origin and means "wealth has come".
OLUCHI	Means "God's work" and originates from the Igbo language in Nigeria.
OLUWADA RASIMI	Means "God has been good to me" and it originates from the Yoruba language of Nigeria.
OLUWAFU NMILAYO	Means "God has given me joy" and originates from the Yoruba language in Nigeria.

OLUWANI FEMI	Means "God has made me happy" and originates from the Yoruba language in Nigeria.
OLUWATA MILORE	Means "God is enough for me" and is of Yoruba origin in Nigeria.
OLUWATE NIOLA	Means "God remembers one who is worth cherishing" and it has its origin in Yoruba, a language spoken in Nigeria and other parts of West Africa.
OMAIMA	Omaima is an Arabic name meaning "respected, beloved" and is commonly used in Middle Eastern countries.
ONDINE	Means "little wave" and it originates from the Latin word "undina," referring to water nymphs or female spirits associated with bodies of water in folklore and mythology.
ONEIDA	Means "people of the standing stone" and it originates from the indigenous people of the Iroquois Confederacy in North America.
ONESTI	Romanian name meaning "honest" or "sincere," derived from the Latin word "honestus."
ONYINYECHI	Female Igbo name meaning "God's gift" or "God's blessing," originating from Nigeria.
OPALINE	Feminine name of English origin meaning "gemstone" or "opal-like."
ORAH	Hebrew origin and means "light" or "illumination."
ORALIA	Means "golden" or "golden queen" and has Latin origins.
ORCHID	Means a delicate flower and has roots in Greek mythology.
ORLAITH	Means "golden princess" and has Irish origins.
ORLI	Means "my light" in Hebrew and it is a variant of the name Ora, derived from the Hebrew word "or" meaning "light."
ORNELLA	Means "flowering ash tree" and originates from the Italian language.
OSHIAN	Means "ocean" and is a modern variation of the traditional Scottish name Ossian.
OSHUN	Means "goddess of love, beauty, and fertility" and originates from the Yoruba people of Nigeria and Benin.
OSIYO	Means "hello" or "greetings" in the Cherokee language, originating from Native American culture.
OTTILIE	The name Ottillie means "prosperity in battle" and originates from Germanic languages.
OUMOU	Means "gift" or "blessing" and originates from West Africa, specifically in the Malinke ethnic group.
OYINKAN SOLA	Means "honorable wealth has increased" and has Yoruba origins.
OZARA	Female name of Hebrew origin, meaning "help, assistance" or "bound by oath".
OZLEM	The name Özlem means "longing" or "desire" in Turkish and it originates from the Turkish language.
PAISLIE	Modern American variant of the Scottish place name Paisley, derived from the Gaelic word for "church" or "pasture."
PAISLYNN	The meaning and origin of the first name Paislynn is a combination of the names Paisley (Scottish origin) and Lynn (English origin), creating a unique and modern name.
PANDORA	The name Pandora comes from Greek mythology and means "all-gifted" or "all-endowed," referring to the mythological figure who released various blessings and evils into the world.
PARADISE	Means "a place of perfect happiness or bliss," and it originated from the English language as a unique and unconventional name choice.
PARASKEVI	Means "preparation" and originates from Greek.
PARISHA	Indian origin and means "like a fairy, beautiful, charming, or angelic."
PARKLYNN	The first name Parklynn originates from American English and means "a combination of the name Park and the suffix -lynn, indicating a connection to the park or a park-themed name."
PARTHENIA	Feminine given name meaning "virgin" or "chaste" in Greek, and it has origins in ancient Greece.
PASSION	Feminine English name meaning "intense love or strong desire" and is derived from the English word for passionate feelings or enthusiasm.

PATSY   Diminutive form of the name Patrick, originating from Ireland, and means "noble" or "patrician."

PAXLEY   The first name Paxley has a modern origin and is derived from the word "peace" (Pax) combined with the suffix "-ley," meaning "field" or "meadow."

PAYTIENCE The first name "Paytience" is a modern variation of the English word "patience," derived from the Middle English "pacience" and ultimately from the Latin "patientia," meaning endurance or forbearance.

PAYZLEE   The first name Payzlee is of American origin and it means "peaceful meadow."

PEACE   Means tranquility, harmony, and the absence of conflict, and it is derived from the English vocabulary word.

PEACHES   The first name "Peaches" signifies a sweet and fruity nickname that likely originated as a term of endearment.

PEARLIE   Means "precious, small pearl" and is of English origin.

PEREL   The meaning of the first name Perel is "pearl" and it has Hebrew origins.

PERFECT   Means flawless or without fault, and its origin is Latin.

PERIDOT   Green gemstone name of French origin that signifies strength, protection, and balance.

PERPETUA   Means "eternal" or "everlasting" and has Latin origins.

PERSEPHANIE Variant spelling of the name Persephone, which originates from Greek mythology and signifies "bringer of destruction" or "bringer of death."

PERSIA   Latin origin, refers to the historic region in southwestern Asia and means "land of the Persians."

PETRONA   The name "Petrona" is a feminine given name of Italian and Spanish origin, derived from the Latin name "Petronius," meaning "rock" or "stone."

PETUNIA   Means "flower" and originates from the Latin word "petunius," which refers to a type of flowering plant.

PFEIFFER   Means "pipe player" and originates from the German language.

PHAEDRA   Means "bright" or "radiant" and originates from Greek mythology, specifically from the tragic story of Phaedra, the wife of Theseus.

PHEBE   Means "bright, pure" and it has origins in Greek mythology as a variant of the name Phoebe.

PHENIX   Unique and modern English name derived from the mythological creature phoenix symbolizing rebirth and strength.

PHEOBE   Means "bright and shining" and originates from Greek mythology, associated with the goddess Phoebe who represents the moon.

PHOREVER   Playful and unique variation of the word "forever," symbolizing eternal love and commitment.

PHYLLIS   Means "green branches" and has Greek origins.

PIHU   The meaning of the name Pihu is "chirping of a bird" and it originates from the Hindi language.

PIPPIN   Means "youthful" and it originates from the Old English language.

PNINA   Hebrew name meaning "pearl" and it is of Biblical origin.

POETIC   Means having a creative or artistic nature, and it originates from the English language.

POETRY   The name Poetry originated as a creative and poetic term used to describe the art form of expressing emotions and experiences through rhythm and language.

POLETH   The name "Poleth" has no confirmed meaning or origin as it does not appear to have significant cultural or historical roots.

POLLYANNA Feminine given name derived from the character Pollyanna Whittier in the book "Pollyanna" by Eleanor H. Porter, symbolizing an excessively optimistic and cheerful

PORSCHE   Means "offering" and originates from the French surname "Portier."

PORSHA   Feminine given name of unknown origin, possibly derived from the Latin name Portia meaning "pig" or "offering".

PORTIA   Feminine given name of Latin origin, meaning "pig" or "hog" in Latin, which was derived from the Roman family name Porcius.

PORTLYN Uncertain origin, likely originated recently and has no widely recognized meaning.

PRABHNOOR Means "divine light" and is of Punjabi origin.

PRAGYA Sanskrit origin and means "wisdom" or "knowledge."

PRAIRIE The first name Prairie, of English origin, means "a vast, flat grassland" and is derived from the French word "prairie."

PRAISE Means "expression of approval or admiration" and it has an English origin.

PRAJNA Sanskrit origin and means "wisdom" or "insight."

PRANIKA Means "lively" or "energetic" and it originated from the Sanskrit language in India.

PRANSHI The first name Pranshi, of Indian origin, means "supreme" or "the highest."

PRANVI Indian origin and means "sacred life force" or "divine energy."

PRAPTI Feminine Hindu name of Sanskrit origin meaning "attainment" or "achievement."

PRAYER The meaning of the first name "Prayer" is a request or expression of worship towards a higher power, and it does not have a specific origin as it is a unique and uncommon given name.

PREKSHA Feminine given name of Indian origin, meaning "seeing, observing, or insight" in Sanskrit.

PREMA Indian origin and means "love" or "affection" in Sanskrit.

PRESLYNN Modern American feminine name, likely derived as a combination of the names Presley and Lynn.

PRETTY The first name "Pretty" is an English name originated from the Middle English word "praty" meaning cunning, clever, or attractive.

PRICILLA The name Priscilla means "ancient" or "venerable" and it originates from the Latin language.

PRINCESA Means "princess" in Spanish and is of Latin origin.

PRIYANKA Feminine Indian name meaning "beloved" or "beautiful," derived from Sanskrit origins.

PROMYCE The meaning and origin of the first name Promyce are currently unknown as it does not appear to have a recognized meaning or cultural origin.

PROSPERITY Means "great success, wealth, and well-being" and its origin can be traced back to English vocabulary.

PROVIDENCE Means "divine guidance or foresight" and has origins derived from Old French and Latin.

PUALANI Means "heavenly flower" and originates from Hawaiian language.

PUALENA The first name Pu'alena means "soft or delicate blossom" in Hawaiian and it originates from the Hawaiian language and culture.

PURITY Means "innocence" or "cleanliness" and originates from the English vocabulary word.

PURPOSE The name "Purpose" originates from the English language and conveys the meaning of having a clear intention, goal, or reason for one's existence.

PYRRHA Means "red-haired" or "flame-colored" and originates from Greek mythology, particularly from the story of Pyrrha, the wife of Deucalion who survived the Great Flood.

QUEENIE Feminine given name meaning "little queen" and it originated as a nickname derived from the word "queen."

QUETZALY Means "precious quetzal" and originates from Nahuatl, an indigenous Mesoamerican language.

QUINNLEIGH The meaning and origin of the first name Quinnleigh is uncertain as it appears to be a unique or variant name without a widely recognized origin or meaning.

QUINZEL The first name Quinzel is of American origin and its meaning is unknown.

QUORRA The first name "Quorra" is of fictional origin and originated from the 2010 film "Tron: Legacy."

RABAB Means "musical instrument" and has origins in Arabic and Persian cultures.

RABIYA Means "springtime" and is of Arabic origin.

RACQUEL Means "lamb" and is of American origin.

RADHIKA Means "successful" or "prosperous" and originated from Sanskrit, commonly associated with Hindu mythology.

RADIANCE Means a brilliant or glowing quality and originates from the English language.

RAEGHAN Means "queen" and originates from the Irish and Scottish Gaelic name Raighne.

RAELEA Modern, feminine given name of American origin, possibly derived from combining the names Rae and Lea.

RAEMARIE Modern, compound name that combines Rae, derived from the Hebrew tradition meaning "ewe," with Marie, which is a variant of Mary originating from the Hebrew name Miriam, meaning "bitter" or "rebellious."

RAEYAH Arabic origin, meaning "vivid" or "lively."

RAFEEF The name Raf eef is of Arabic origin and means "elevated" or "high-ranking."

RAINAH Means "song or queen" and has origins in Hebrew.

RAINBOW Means a colorful arc in the sky after rain and originates from the English language.

RAIVEN The meaning of the first name Raiven is "mischievous" and its origin is a modern American creation.

RAIYNE Means "queen" or "heavenly" and has an English origin.

RAMATOU LAYE The first name RAMATOULAYE originated from West Africa and it means "the one who thanks God" in the Fulani language.

RAMSIE Means "son of Ram," and it originates from the Old English word "ram" meaning "ram," or "male sheep."

RARITY Means "uniqueness" or "rareness" and originates from English as a vocabulary word name.

RAUNAK Unisex name of Indian origin, meaning "brightness" or "radiance".

RAWLINGS Means "son of Rawlin" and is of English origin.

RAYCHEL Modern variant of the name Rachel, derived from the Hebrew name Rahel meaning "ewe" or "innocent lamb."

RAYELLE Means "counsel of God" and it originates from the combination of the names Ray and Elle.

RAYONNA Means "queenly" or "beautiful song" and has American origins.

REALITY Means the state of being real or truthful, and it is a modern English word name.

REBELLE Means "rebellious" and it originates from the French language.

REGAL Means "royal" and has origins in Latin.

REHAM The first name REHAM is of Arabic origin and it means "compassion" or "mercy".

REIGHLYNN Modern, feminine name of American origin, likely a combination of the names "Reign" and "Lynn," symbolizing power/dominance and a peaceful lake, respectively.

REIGHN The first name Reighn likely originated as a modern spelling variation of the word "reign," meaning to rule or have dominion, and is used as a unique and creative name choice.

REIGNA Means "queen" or "ruler" and is of English origin.

REIGNBOW Modern version of the name Rainbow, inspired by the colorful natural phenomenon, symbolizing beauty and diversity.

REJOICE Means to experience great joy or happiness, and it originates from the English language.

REMEDIOS The first name Remedios derives from Spanish origin meaning "remedies" or "cures."

REMIAH Means "God has lifted up" and has Hebrew origins.

REMINISCE Means to recall or remember past events and experiences, and it originated from the English language.

REMIROSE Feminine given name of English origin, meaning "beloved like a rose."

RENEZMAE The first name RENEZMAE is of American origin and likely does not have a widely recognized meaning as it appears to be a unique or rare name creation.

RENFRI Means "ruler's peace" and originates from the Germanic and Celtic elements "regn" meaning "ruler" or "king" and "frithu" meaning "peace."

RENIYAH The first name Reniyah, of uncertain origin, is mainly used in the African American community and its meaning is currently unknown.

REUT Means "companion" in Hebrew and has biblical origins.

REVEKKA Means "to bind tightly" and has Greek origins.

REVERIE Means "daydream" and originated from the French word for "dream."

RHAENA Feminine name of Welsh origin meaning "queen" or "goddess."

RHAENYRA Means "queen who is born under a blood moon" and it originates from the fictional world of George R.R. Martin's A Song of Ice and Fire series.

RHAPSODY The name Rhapsody originated from Greek mythology and means a work of epic or poetic composition, symbolizing passion and inspiration.

RHEAGAN	The first name RHEAGAN has a meaning of "impulsive ruler" and is of Irish origin.
RHEALYNN	American origin and it means "queenly counselor."
RHIAN	Means "maiden" or "nymph" and has Welsh origins.
RHILEY	Means "courageous and valiant" and has uncertain origins.
RHONDA	Means "noisy" or "rough" in Welsh, and it is of Welsh origin.
RHYLEI	Modern, feminine name of unclear origin, likely created as a variation of Riley or Rylee with an alternate spelling.
RHYLEIGH	Modern feminine name of American origin, possibly derived from the names Riley and Leigh.
RHYLIE	Modern variant of the name Riley, which originated from an Irish surname meaning "courageous" or "valiant."
RHYTHM	Means a strong, regular, repeated pattern of movement or sound, and it originated in English.
RIAS	German origin and it is a short form of the name Elias, meaning "Yahweh is God."
RICHLYNN	Means "powerful ruler" and originates from combining the names Richard and Lynn.
RIDHIMA	Means "full of prosperity and abundance" and has Indian roots.
RILEYANN	The name Rileyann has no specific meaning or origin as it is a combination of the names Riley and Ann.
RINOA	Means "peaceful one" and has no clear origin, but gained popularity due to the character Rinoa Heartilly from the video game Final Fantasy VIII.
RIPLEIGH	The meaning and origin of the first name RIPLEIGH is uncertain, possibly derived from a surname or a variant of the name "Ripley."
RITANYA	Unknown origin and meaning as it does not have a widely recognized etymology.
RITHANYA	The first name Rithanya is of Indian origin and its meaning is "divine, celestial."
RIVERLEIGH	Means "dweller by the river meadow" and has an English origin.
RIVERROSE	Means "a beautiful and flowing flower that blossoms near a river" and has no specific origin as it is a combination of two nature-inspired words.
RIVIERA	Means "coastline" and originates from the Italian word "riviera" which refers to a coastal area.
RIVYN	Welsh origin and means "rebirth" or "to be born again."
RIYASHA	Indian origin and means "the one who shines brightly."
RIZIKI	Means "sustenance" or "provision" in Swahili and has African origins.
ROGUE	Means a deceitful or mischievous person and has its origin in the English language.
ROISIN	Means "little rose" and originates from Ireland.
ROIZA	The first name Roiza is of Hebrew origin, meaning "rose" or "beautiful flower."
ROKHAYA	Means "respected" or "honored" and it originates from West Africa, particularly Senegal.
ROKIA	Means "sunrise" and it originated from West Africa.
ROMELIA	Means "from Rome" and has Latin origins.
ROMILLY	The name Romilly originated from the Old Norse word "rumr" meaning "wide" and "Holme" referring to an island, and it signifies someone who comes from the wide island.
ROMIYAH	Means "from Rome" and has Latin origins.
RONJA	Means "she who brings joy" and is of Swedish origin.
ROSALBA	Female given name of Italian origin, meaning "white rose" or "white color."
ROSALEEN	Means "beautiful rose" and it has Irish origins.
ROSALIYAH	Means "rose" or "graceful" and has uncertain origins, possibly derived from the combination of the names Rosa and Aliyah.
ROSAMARIA	Latin origin and means "rose of Mary."
ROSAMUND	Means "pure rose" and it originates from Old German and Old English.
ROSAURA	Means "golden rose" and has Spanish and Portuguese origins.
ROSEALIE	Variant spelling of the name Rosalie, which is derived from the Latin name Rosalia, meaning "rose" or "rose garden."
ROSEALYNN	Combination of the names Rose and Lynn, and it likely originated as a modern variation or combination of these two names.
ROSEANNA	Means "graceful rose" and has English and Latin origins.
ROSEMINA	Variant of the name Rosamund, which means "horse protector" and originates from Old Germanic.

ROSETTA   Means "little rose" and has Italian origins.
ROSHNI   Means "light" and originates from Hindi and Urdu languages.
ROSMERY   Means "dew of the sea" and has English and Latin origins.
ROSYLN   The name Roslyn means "little rose" and has English and Hebrew origins.
ROULETTE   Means "small wheel" in French and is traditionally associated with the gambling game of the same name.
ROUX   Means "reddish-brown" and originates from French.
ROWENA   Means "famous joy" and it originated from medieval literature and Celtic mythology.
ROZALIA   Means "rose" and it originated from the Latin name Rosa, which comes from the flower of the same name.
ROZALYN   Variant of Rosalind, and it originated from Old German and Latin roots, meaning "gentle horse" or "beautiful rose."
ROZELLA   The first name Rozella likely means "rose" and has Latin origins.
RUANSHI   The meaning and origin of the name RUANSHI are currently unknown.
RUBANI   The first name Rubani is of unknown origin and meaning.
RUBYANN   Combination of the names Ruby and Ann, and it originated as a modern variant of the given name Ruby.
RUBYJEAN   Combination of the names Ruby and Jean and it originates from English and French origins.
RUBYMAE   The name Rubymae originated as a combination of the names Ruby, meaning "deep red precious stone," and Mae, a variant of the name May, meaning "pearl," resulting in a unique and vibrant name.
RUBYROSE   Means "precious flower" and originated as a combination of the names Ruby and Rose.
RUCHAMA   Means "compassionate" or "merciful" and has Hebrew origins.
RUEMANI   Modern invented name with no widely known meaning or origin.
RUFTA   The first name "Rufta" is of Ethiopian origin and means "good path" or "righteousness."
RUHIKA   Means "soulful" or "spiritual" and it originates from the Sanskrit language in India.
RUMAISA   Arabic origin and means "elegant, beautiful, or charming."
RUMOR   Means "a piece of unverified information or gossip" and originates from the English word "rumor."
RUQAIYA   Feminine Muslim name of Arabic origin meaning "elevated, exalted" or "worthy of respect."
RUQAYYAH   Means "gentleness" or "elegant" in Arabic, and it originated from Islamic culture.
RUSHDA   Means "guidance" or "righteousness" and has Arabic origins.
RUSHIKA   Means "ray of light" and originates from Sanskrit.
RUTHANN   Means "graceful" or "compassionate" and is of American origin combining the names Ruth and Ann.
RUTILA   Feminine given name of Latin origin, meaning "reddish" or "little red one."
RUWAIDA   Means "gentle," and it has Arabic origins.
RUWEYDA   Ruweyda is an Arabic name meaning "soft, gentle," typically given to girls, and it originates from Arabic/Islamic culture.
RYELLA   The first name Ryella is of unknown origin and does not have a specific meaning.
RYKLYNN   Modern American name created by combining elements of Ryan and Lynn.
RYLIEGH   English origin and means "a clearing with rye".
RYSA   Feminine given name of Greek origin meaning "rose" or "flower".
SAANVIR   The first name Saanvireddy has no specific meaning or origin as it appears to be a rare
EDDY   and unique name.
SADHANA   The first name Sadhana has origins in Sanskrit and means "spiritual practice" or "devotion."
SADIEJO   Unique and creative combination of the names Sadie and Jo, likely originating as a modern and playful variation.
SADIEMAE   The first name Sadiemae is of English origin and typically refers to a combination of the names Sadie and Mae.
SAESHA   Indian origin and means "girl with a beautiful life".
SAFFRON   Means "a reddish-brown spice" and originates from the Old French word "safran" derived from Arabic "za'faran."

SAFIATOU	Feminine West African name meaning "pure" or "holy" that is commonly used in countries like Mali, Guinea, and Senegal, with Arabic and African origins.
SAFIRA	Means "precious gem" and has origins in both Hebrew and Arabic.
SAGELYNN	Means "wise one" and has a modern origin.
SAHARI	The first name Sahari is of Arabic origin and means "from the desert."
SAHIBA	Means "lady" or "mistress" and it originates from the Indian subcontinent.
SAHILY	Spanish origin and means "the one who walks by the seashore."
SAHMARA	Modern name of unknown origin, often used as a variant of the name Samara, meaning "protected by God" in Hebrew.
SAHORY	The name Sahory does not have a recognized meaning or origin as it is a relatively uncommon name.
SAIDEY	Variant spelling of the name Sadie and is of Hebrew origin, meaning "princess" or "mercy".
SAIESHA	Indian origin and means "one who is full of life and energy."
SAIGELYNN	Modern American name created by combining elements of the names Sage and Lynn.
SAILER	The first name SAILER is of German origin and means "sailor" or "seaman."
SAINABOU	Gambian origin and means "princess" or "queen."
SAIYORI	Japanese name meaning "colorful village" or "small village by the sea."
SAKEENA	Means "calm" or "tranquil" and has Arabic origins.
SALEHA	Means "virtuous" or "pious" and originates from Arabic.
SAMADHI	Sanskrit origin and means "a state of deep meditation or profound contemplation."
SAMANI	The first name Samani is of Arabic origin and it means "one who hears or is attentive".
SAMANVITHA	Means "one who is knowledgeable, righteous, and understanding" and it has origins in the Sanskrit language.
SAMARIYA	Variant of the name Samaria, which originated from the ancient biblical region of Samaria in present-day Israel, and it means "watch mountain" or "guardian."
SAMAYRA	Arabic origin and means "enchanting" or "delightful."
SAMHITA	Means "a collection" or "a compilation" in Sanskrit, and it originates from Hindu mythology and ancient Indian scriptures known as the Vedas.
SAMIHA	Feminine Arabic name meaning "forgiving, generous" with Islamic origins.
SAMIKSHA	Means "to examine" or "to evaluate" and has origins in the Sanskrit language of Hindu origin.
SAMRIDDHI	Means "prosperity" or "wealth" and it originates from Sanskrit, an ancient language of India.
SAMYUKTHA	Means "united" or "joined together" in Sanskrit and has its origins in India.
SANDRINE	Means "defender of mankind" and originates from the French name Alexandrine.
SANSKRITI	Indian origin, means "culture" or "tradition" in Sanskrit.
SAORY	Japanese origin and means "colorful, vibrant."
SAPNA	Indian origin and means "dream" or "vision" in Hindi.
SARABETH	Combination of the names Sara and Elizabeth, and it originated as a modern English given name.
SARAHANN	Combination of the names Sarah and Ann, typically used as a given name for girls; it has a Hebrew and English origin.
SARAHJANE	Combination of the names Sarah and Jane, meaning "princess" and "God is gracious" respectively, and has an English origin.
SARAIYAH	Hebrew origin and means "princess of God."
SARGUN	Punjabi origin and means "one who possesses qualities or virtues."
SARVANI	The first name Sarvani originates from Sanskrit and means "universal" or "complete."
SARYIA	Modern invented name with no specific meaning or origin.
SASKIA	Means "from Saxon origin" and it originated from the Dutch and German cultures.
SATIVA	Latin origin and means "cultivated."
SATURN	Means "god of agriculture and time" and originates from Roman mythology, derived from the Latin word "Saturnus."
SAVREEN	Indian origin and means "encouragement" or "one who motivates others."
SAWDAH	Means "blackness" or "dark complexion" and originates from Arabic.
SAYDIE	Variant of the name Sadie, which is of Hebrew origin and means "princess" or "merciful."

SAYGE Means "wise and knowing" and it is of English origin.

SAYORI Means "small village" in Japanese and is of Japanese origin.

SAYOURI Japanese name meaning "small lily".

SCARLET Combination of the names Scarlett and Rose, and it likely originated as a modern and
TROSE creative name choice.

SEARCY Means "from the ash tree enclosure" and is of English origin.

SECRET The name "Secret" is a modern English word name chosen for its association with
confidentiality and mystery.

SEDNA Means "goddess of the sea" and originates from Inuit mythology.

SEETHA Hindu name meaning "furrow" or "week of Friday" and originates from Sanskrit.

SEFORA Means "beautiful" and it originates from the Hebrew language.

SEHER Turkish origin and means "dawn" or "early morning."

SEHRISH Means "dew on the grass" and has Arabic and Persian origins.

SELAHGRACE Means "pause for divine favor" and it is a combination of the Hebrew word "Selah"
meaning pause or reflection, and the English word "Grace" meaning divine favor or

SELENIA Means "moon goddess" and it has Latin origins.

SELIHOM The first name "Selihom" does not have a widely recognized meaning or origin.

SENECA Means "old" or "aged" and it originated from the Latin language.

SENUA The first name Senua is of African origin and it means "gift from God."

SEOUL Name of Korean origin meaning "capital city," referring to the capital and largest
metropolis of South Korea.

SEPHORA Means "beautiful" and originates from Hebrew.

SEPTEMBER Means "seventh month" and originates from the Latin word "septem" meaning "seven."

SERAIAH Means "Yahweh is ruler" and originates from Hebrew.

SEREIN Means "calmness; serenity" and is of French origin.

SERENDIPITY Means a fortunate and unexpected discovery or occurrence, originating from the Persian
fairy tale "The Three Princes of Serendip."

SERINITI Modern, invented name with no specific meaning or origin.

SETAYESH Means "praise" or "praising" and originates from Persian/Iranian culture.

SEVDA Means "love, affection" and originates from Turkish.

SEYNABOU Feminine given name of African origin, meaning "honored and respected" or "blessed."

SHABNAM Persian origin, means "dew on grass" or "morning dew" symbolizing freshness and purity.

SHADDAI Hebrew name meaning "almighty" or "God" and is often used as a name for the Christian
God.

SHAELYNN Means "gracious" and is of American origin.

SHAHANA Means "royal, majestic" and it is of Persian origin.

SHAHD The name Shahd is an Arabic name that means "honey" and is commonly given to girls.

SHAILI Means "style" or "manner" and has Indian origins.

SHAIRA Means "poetic" or "singer" and has Arabic roots.

SHAKTI Means power or energy, and it originates from Sanskrit, an ancient Indo-Aryan language
in India.

SHALVA Means "tranquility" or "serenity" and has Hebrew origins.

SHAMARA Uncertain origin, but it likely has Arabic or Hebrew roots and means "protected" or "one
who is guarded."

SHAMBHAVI Means "related to Shambhu" and originates from Sanskrit.

SHAMS Means "sun" in Arabic and it has Middle Eastern origins.

SHANAIKA Rare and unique name of uncertain origin, possibly derived from a combination of other
names such as Shanice and Laika.

SHANELLE Feminine name of American origin, meaning "beautiful and admirable" or "gift from God."

SHANIAH Modern and feminine given name of uncertain origin, possibly derived from a blend of
the names Shania and Mariah.

SHANICE Means "God is gracious" and it originated from the United States.

SHANTEL American and French origin and means "stone" or "rocky slope."

SHANYLA The first name "Shanyla" does not have a widely documented origin or specific meaning,
potentially indicating that it is a unique or uncommon name.

SHANZAY   Means "a beautiful princess" and has origins in the Arabic language.
SHARANYA   Means "one who provides shelter" and has origins in the Indian Sanskrit language.
SHARIYAH   Arabic origin and means "divine guidance" or "the path to righteousness."
SHARLENE   Means "free man" and it is derived from the combination of the names Sharon and Charlene.
SHASTA   The first name Shasta is of Native American origin and it means "white mountain" or "singing bird".
SHAYLEIGH   Means "fairy princess" and it has Irish origins.
SHEALEE   American origin and means "meadow, clearing by a small wood."
SHECCID   The name Sheccid is derived from the novel "Sheccid" by Carlos Cuauhtémoc Sánchez and holds no known meaning beyond its use in the book.
SHEKINAH   Means "the dwelling or presence of God" and originates from Hebrew.
SHELIA   The first name "Shelia" is a variant of "Sheila" and has Irish origins, meaning "blind" or "heavenly."
SHEMAIAH   Means "heard by God" and originates from Hebrew biblical sources.
SHERIDAN   Means "wild man" or "seeker" and has an Irish origin.
SHERILYN   Means "beloved" and it is of American origin.
SHERYL   Variant of the name Cheryl, derived from the French name Chérie meaning "darling" or "beloved."
SHEYLI   Feminine given name of uncertain origin and meaning.
SHIFRA   Means "beautiful" or "improvement" in Hebrew and its origin can be traced back to the biblical figure, Shifra, a midwife in ancient Egypt.
SHIORI   Means "bookmark" in Japanese and it originates from Japan.
SHIPHRAH   The name Shiphrah originates from Hebrew and means "beautiful" or "fair."
SHIRIN   Means "sweet" or "sweetheart" and has Persian origins.
SHIVANYA   Indian origin and it means "beloved of Lord Shiva".
SHIVYA   The first name Shivya is of Indian origin and means "divine essence" or "belonging to Lord Shiva."
SHRADDHA   The name Shraddha originated from Sanskrit and means "faith, belief, or trust."
SHRAVYA   Means "famous or celebrated" and originates from Sanskrit.
SHREE   The first name "Shree" is of Sanskrit origin and it means "goddess; glory; radiance; auspicious."
SHRESHTA   Means "the best, superior" and it originates from Sanskrit, an ancient Indo-Aryan language.
SHRESTA   Means "excellent" or "superior" and it originates from Sanskrit, an ancient Indo-Aryan language.
SHREYANVI   Means "auspicious and fortunate" and originates from the Hindu culture.
SHRINIKA   Hindu origin and means "goddess of wealth and prosperity" in Sanskrit.
SHRISHA   Means "lord of prosperity" and originates from Hindu mythology.
SHRIVI   Unique Indian name which means "sacred river" in Sanskrit.
SHTERNA   Means "star" in Yiddish and it is of Hebrew origin.
SHUKRI   Means "thankful" and originates from Arabic.
SHUKRONA   Means gratitude in Pashto language and is of Afghan origin.
SHULAMIS   Hebrew name meaning "peaceful" or "peace." The name originates from the Hebrew word "shalom," signifying peace or wholeness.
SHYLAH   Hebrew origin meaning "daughter of the oath," and it is commonly used as a variant of the name Shiloh.
SIANNY   Modern feminine name of uncertain origin, possibly derived from a variation of the name Sienna.
SIBYL   Means "prophetess" and it comes from the ancient Greek name "Sibylla."
SICILY   Means "from Sicily" and it is an English variant of the Italian place name Sicilia.
SIDDALEE   American origin, derived from combining the name Sidney with the suffix "-lee," and it means "wide island."
SIDDHI   Means "attainment" or "achievement" in Sanskrit and is of Indian origin.
SIDRATUL   The first name Sidratul is of Arabic origin and means "lovely tree."
SIEANNA   Means "God is gracious" and it is of American origin. ·

SIFAT Unisex name of Arabic origin meaning "quality" or "attribute."

SIGNE Scandinavian feminine given name meaning "new victory" or "new sign," derived from Old Norse and Old Swedish.

SIGOURNEY French name meaning "daring victor" and it originated from the surname of Eliza Sigourney, an American poet and essayist.

SIGRID Means "victorious beauty" and it originates from Old Norse.

SILVER Means "the precious white metal" and it derives from the English word for the metal itself.

SIMISOLA Means "rest in wealth" and originates from the Yoruba people of Nigeria.

SINCERITY Means "honesty, truthfulness" and it originated from the English vocabulary word sincerity.

SINCLAIR Unisex name of Scottish origin meaning "clear river."

SINEAD Means "God's gracious gift" and it originates from the Irish Gaelic language.

SINIT The first name SINIT is of Ethiopian origin and means "light" or "illumination".

SINTHIA Variant spelling of the name Cynthia, which is of Greek origin and means "moon goddess" or "from Mount Cynthus."

SISILIA Feminine given name of Latin origin, derived from the name Cecilia, meaning "blind" or "blindness," and often associated with the patron saint of musicians.

SISIRA Means "winter" in Sanskrit, and originates from Indian and Hindu traditions.

SISTINE Means "pertaining to the Sistine Chapel" and originates from the Italian word "Sistina" which is derived from the Latin word "Sistinus."

SITARA Means "star" and originates from various cultures, including Persian, Urdu, and Hindi.

SITHARA Indian origin and means "star; similar to star."

SIYANI Means "knowledgeable" and originates from the Setswana language spoken in Botswana and South Africa.

SKADI Means "goddess of winter, mountains, and hunting" and originates from Norse mythology.

SKAILYNN Modern and creative name, likely a combination of the names Skylar and Lynn, with no specific origins.

SKYELAR The meaning of the first name SkyeLar is "adventurous, sky seeker," and its origin is a modern, Americanized variation of the names Skye and Skylar.

SKYELYNN American origin, combines the elements "sky" and "lynn" to convey the idea of a person with a connection to nature and serenity.

SKYLARROSE Modern American name that combines the names Skylar and Rose, often symbolizing femininity and beauty when merged together.

SKYLEI Modern variation of the name Skylar, likely derived from the English word "sky" which refers to the celestial dome or the heavens above.

SKYLEIGH Means "adventurous and free-spirited" and is of modern English origin.

SKYLIE The first name Skylie originated as a variation of the name Kylie and means "a narrow channel" or "boomerang" in Australian Aboriginal language.

SLOKA The name Sloka originates from Sanskrit and means "verse" or "hymn."

SOCORRO Means "help" or "relief" in Spanish and it has a religious origin, referring to the Virgin Mary as Our Lady of Perpetual Help, who is venerated in Catholicism.

SOFIAROSE The meaning of the first name Sofiarose is a combination of Sofia, meaning wisdom, and Rose, symbolizing beauty and love, and it likely originated as a modern feminine name blending elements of different cultures.

SOKHNA Means "noblewoman" in Wolof language and has its origin in West Africa, specifically Senegal.

SOLARIS Means "of the sun" and derives from the Latin word "solaris" which means pertaining to the sun.

SOLEDAD Means "solitude" in Spanish and it originated from the title of the Virgin Mary, Nuestra Señora de la Soledad, meaning "Our Lady of Solitude."

SOLIANA Feminine given name of Ethiopian origin, meaning "sunshine" or "ray of light."

SOLIELLE Feminine name of French origin which means "sun" or "sunshine".

SOLIHA Arabic origin and means "pious woman."

SOLINE Means "sun" and originates from the Latin name "Sol" which means "sun".

SOLIYANA Means "peaceful" and it originates from the Amharic language spoken in Ethiopia.

SOLOMIA Means "peaceful" and it is of Hebrew origin.

SOLSTICE Means "sun standing still" or "sun stoppage" and it originated from the Latin word "solstitium."

SOLVEIG Means "sun strength" or "house of power" and originates from Old Norse in Scandinavia.

SOLYMAR Means "sun and sea" and has Spanish and Latin origins.

SONALI The female given name Sonali means "golden" or "beautiful" in Bengali and originates from the Sanskrit language.

SONDOS Arabic origin and means "silk brocade" or "fine silk fabric."

SONIYA Means "golden" and is of Indian origin.

SONOMA Native American origin and it means "valley of the moon."

SOPHIAMARIE Meaning: Sophiamarie is a compound name combining the elements of Sophia, meaning "wisdom" in Greek, and Marie, derived from the Hebrew name Miriam, meaning "bitterness" or "beloved."
Origin: It is likely a modern English or American coinage and may have been created by

SOPHIANA Feminine name of Greek origin meaning "wisdom" or "wise."

SOPHIAROSE Modern compound name combining Sophia, derived from the Greek word for wisdom, and Rose, a flower symbolizing love and elegance.

SOPHRONIA The name Sophronia originated from Greek and means "wise" or "sensible."

SORCHA Means "bright" or "radiant" and originates from Irish and Scottish Gaelic.

SOTERIA Female given name of Greek origin meaning "salvation" or "deliverance."

SOUL Means the spiritual or immaterial part of a human being, and it is of English origin.

SOULINE The first name Souline likely originated from the combination of the words "soul" and "line," conveying a deep connection to spirituality or the soul's path.

SOVEREIGN "Sovereign" means a supreme ruler or leader, and it originates from the Latin word "superanus" meaning superior.

SPARKLE Means "to shine brightly or glitter" and has English origins.

SPIRIT The first name "Spirit" is derived from English and has a meaning associated with a person's essence, vital force, or character.

SPRING The name Spring refers to the season and is of English origin.

SPRUHA The name Spruha has Indian origin, meaning "to blossom" or "to grow" in Sanskrit.

SRAVYA Means "fame" or "reputation" and has its origin in the Sanskrit language.

SRESHTA Means "excellent" or "best" in Sanskrit and originates from India.

SRIHITHA Hindu origin and means "one who is loved and favored by the goddess Sri or Lakshmi."

SRINIDHI Means "treasure of God" and has origins in the Sanskrit language.

SRINIKA The first name Srinika has a Sanskrit origin and means "goddess Lakshmi, the beautiful one."

SRISHTI Means "creation" or "existence" in Sanskrit and originates from Indian Hindu culture.

STALEY The first name "Staley" is of English origin and means "from the clearing with the stumps."

STASSI Feminine name of Greek origin, meaning "resurrection" or "rising."

STAVROULA Means "little cross" and has Greek origins.

STEISY The first name "Steisy" is of uncertain origin and meaning.

STELLALUNA The first name Stellaluna is of Italian origin and means "star and moon."

STELLAMAE Means "star of the sea" and it is of American origin.

STELLAMARIE Means "star of the sea" and has Latin and French origins.

STELLAROSE Modern feminine name combining the words "stellar" meaning outstanding or excellent and "rose" symbolizing beauty and love, likely derived from English origin.

STEVIELYNN Modern American name, likely a combination of the names Steve and Lynn or a variant of the name Stephanie-Lynn.

STHEFANY The name Sthefany originated as a variant of the name Stephanie and means "crowned" or "victorious."

STIORRA Variant of the Old English name, "Styra," meaning "guide" or "steer."

STORIE Means "narrative" or "story" and has English origins.

STUTI Means "praise" or "acclamation" and originates from Sanskrit.

SUCCESS Means achieving favorable outcomes or prosperity, and it is derived from the English word for accomplishment or triumph.

SUDIKSHA	Means "good intention" or "pure hope" and originates from the Sanskrit language.
SUHAILA	Means "moonlike" or "beautiful" and originates from Arabic.
SUHANI	Indian origin, means "pleasant" or "beautiful."
SUHEYLA	Turkish name meaning "beautiful halo" or "beautiful crown" and is of Arabic origin.
SUJEY	The name Sujei means "pleasant, beloved" and has Spanish and Hebrew origins.
SUJOOD	The name Sujooh is of Arabic origin and it means "prostration in prayer" or "act of worship".
SUKAINA	Means "tranquility" or "serenity" and is of Arabic origin.
SUKHMANI	Means "peaceful mind" and originates from Punjabi, India.
SULAMITA	Hebrew origin, means "peaceful" or "beloved" and is derived from the Hebrew word "shulamit" which is based on the root word "shalom" meaning peace.
SULEIDY	The first name Suleidy is of Spanish origin and its meaning is not widely documented.
SUMAIYA	Means "high, lofty" and it originates from Arabic.
SUMMERL YNN	Means "a combination of the seasons Summer and Lynn" and its origin is a modern American invention.
SUMMERR OSE	Means "a combination of the warm season and a blooming flower" and its origin is a modern English combination of the words 'summer' and 'rose'.
SUNDUS	Means "silk" in Arabic and is of Arabic origin.
SUNFLOWER	The name Sunflower originated from the English language and represents the vibrant and radiant flower symbolizing positivity, happiness, and adoration.
SUNJAI	Means "sunshine" and has an Indian origin.
SUSEJ	Modern, unusual name of unknown origin and meaning.
SUZETTE	Means "lily" or "little lily" and is of French origin.
SVETLANA	Means "light" or "bright" and it originates from Slavic languages.
SWASTI	The first name "Swasti" derives from Sanskrit origin and means "auspicious" or "blessed."
SYDELLE	Means "princess, noblewoman" and has Hebrew origins.
SYDNIE	Means "from Saint-Denis" and originated from the French surname derived from the Latin name Dionysius, meaning "follower of Dionysus."
SYLPHRENA	The meaning and origin of the first name Sylphrena is unclear as it is a rare name lacking substantial historical information.
SYLVANAS	Means "forest lady" and originates from Latin.
SYLVIANA	Feminine given name of Latin origin meaning "from the forest" or "of the woods."
SYMPHANI	American origin and means "harmony" or "unity."
SYNOVA	The meaning of the first name Synova is "wise and clear thinker," and the origin is uncertain.
SYRIAH	Modern American name of uncertain origin, possibly influenced by the name Syria, with no well-defined meaning.
SYVEN	Means "calm and serene; peaceful" and has an unknown origin.
TABASSUM	Unisex name of Arabic origin, meaning "smile" or "laughter".
TAELOR	Means "tailor" and has English origins.
TAHANI	The first name Tahani is of Arabic origin and means "congratulations" or "best wishes."
TAHIYA	Arabic origin and means "greeting" or "salutation."
TAIMANE	Hawaiian and Polynesian name meaning "diamond" or "precious one" and originated from the Hawaiian language.
TAIYARI	The meaning and origin of the first name Taiyari is "preparation" and it is of Swahili origin.
TAJAE	Means "crown" or "jewel" and it originates from African-American culture.
TAKSHVI	Means "honorable" or "distinguished" and it has its origin in Sanskrit, an ancient language of India.
TAMANA	Means "desire" and has origins in Persian and Pashto languages.
TAMSIN	Means "double or twin" and originates from Cornwall, England.
TAMYRA	The first name Tamyra is of American origin and it means "palm tree" or "date palm".
TANISHA	Means "ambition" and originates from the Sanskrit language.
TANITOLUWA	Means "we are appreciative of God" and it originates from the Yoruba culture in Nigeria.
TAQDEER	Means "destiny" or "fate" and it has its origin in Arabic.
TAQWA	Taqwa is an Arabic name meaning "God consciousness" or "piety" and is commonly used in Islamic cultures.

TARINI	Means "she who is swift" and originates from Sanskrit.
TARTEEL	Means "recitation" and has origins in Arabic/Islamic culture as it is derived from the Quranic term for reciting the verses of the Quran.
TASHYA	Modern variant of the Russian name Tasha, derived from Natasha, which itself is a diminutive form of Natalia, meaning "born on Christmas Day" in Latin.
TASNIA	Feminine name of Bengali origin, meaning "a reminder or a token."
TAYLOUR	Variant spelling of the name Taylor, derived from the Old French occupational name "tailleur" meaning "cutter of cloth" or "tailor".
TAYSHA	Means "a lively woman" and has Native American origins.
TEAGEN	The first name Teagan means "attractive" or "beautiful" and has Welsh and Irish origins.
TEAGHAN	Means "attractive" or "beautiful" and has Irish origins.
TEHILA	Means "praise" or "song of praise" in Hebrew and has biblical origins.
TEIGHLOR	The meaning and origin of the first name Teighlor is a modern variation of the name Taylor, derived from an English occupational surname for a tailor.
TELESIA	Samoan origin, means "seer" or "prophetess".
TEMILADE	Nigerian origin and it means "mine is the crown of joy" or "mine is worthy of the crown".
TEMILOLUWA	Means "God is mine to be praised" and originates from the Yoruba language in Nigeria.
TEMPEST	Means "violent storm" and originates from the Latin word "tempestas" meaning "stormy weather."
TENILLE	The name Tenille originated from the combination of the names Ten and Danielle and means "from the estate of the patron" or "God is my judge."
TENNESSEE	Means "land of the big bend" and originates from the Native American word "Tanasqui."
TERESITA	Means "little Theresa" and originates from Spanish.
TEYANA	Means "fairy queen" and it has origins in African and American cultures.
THAIS	Means "beloved" or "one who is loved" and originates from Ancient Greek.
THALEIA	Means "to blossom" or "to bloom" and originates from ancient Greece.
THALIANA	Variation of the Greek name Thalia, meaning "blooming" or "to flourish," and is derived from the Greek word "thallo."
THASWIKA	Modern Indian name of unknown meaning.
THELMA	Means "will, volition" and it originated from a fictional character in Marie Corelli's novel "Thelma" (1887).
THEODOSIA	Greek origin and means "gift of God".
THEORY	The first name "Theory" is derived from the English vocabulary word, referring to a systematic explanation or framework of ideas used to understand a subject or
THISTLE	Means "a prickly plant" and its origin can be traced back to Old English.
THIYA	The name THIYA originated from Tamil Nadu, India and it means "a gifted, talented, or accomplished person."
THOMASIN	Means "twin" and it originated from the medieval masculine name Thomas.
THRISHIKA	Feminine name of Indian origin meaning "goddess."
TIARAOLUWA	Yoruba origin and typically given to a female child, meaning "God's crown of wealth."
TIARI	The name Tiari has no commonly known meaning or origin.
TIEGAN	Modern variant of the Irish name Teagan, meaning "attractive" or "beautiful," and it originated from the Gaelic word "teg" which translates to "poet."
TIEGHAN	The first name Tieghan is of Irish origin and means "attractive, beautiful, and graceful."
TIERNEY	Means "descendant of Tighearnach" and it originates from the Irish surname Ó Tighearnaigh or Mac Tighearnáin.
TIFERET	The Hebrew name Tiferet means "beauty" or "glory" and it has roots in Jewish mysticism and the Kabbalah tradition.
TIGERLILY	Means "a bold and vibrant flower" and is of English origin.
TIMBERLEE	Modern American name, combining the word "timber" which refers to wood, and the suffix "-lee" which means meadow, indicating a peaceful or nature-inspired personality.
TIMIA	Feminine given name of uncertain origin and meaning.
TINZLEY	Modern American name deriving from "Tinsley," meaning "shining meadow," and is typically used for girls.

TISSAIA Uncertain origin and meaning, possibly derived from the ancient city of Tissa in Macedonia or from the Persian word "tisya" meaning "miracle" or "wonderful."

TIWATOPE Means "God is worthy of thanks" and originates from the Yoruba language spoken in Nigeria.

TOMIRIS The first name Tomiris is of Persian origin and it means "iron lady."

TONANTZIN Means "our honored mother" and originates from the Nahuatl language of the Aztecs.

TOPANGA Means "where the mountains meet the sea" and originated from the Native American Chumash tribe in the Topanga Canyon, California.

TRANIYAH The first name Traniyah meaning "a unique and modern name" has an unclear origin but is possibly a variant of the name Tania.

TREZURE Means "a valuable possession" and it has an origin in English.

TRICIA The name Tricia originated as a diminutive form of Patricia and means "noble" or "of noble birth".

TRISHIKA Indian origin and it means "one who is skilled in three arts."

TRIXIE Latin origin and it means "bringer of joy" or "she who makes things enjoyable".

TROIAN Greek origin and it means "from Troy," referencing the ancient city of Troy in Greek mythology and history.

TRULEIGH The meaning and origin of the first name Truleigh is uncertain, as it is a rare name with no commonly known etymology or cultural background.

TRULOVE Means "faithful love" and has English origins.

TRUVEYA Modern and unique baby girl name of uncertain origin, possibly a combination of other names.

TSION The first name Tsion is of Hebrew origin and it means "a sign or token."

TSIREYA Name of Native American origin meaning "winter moon."

TSUMUGI Japanese name meaning "spinning silk" and is often used for girls.

TSUNADE Means "legendary shinobi" and originates from Japanese folklore and mythology.

TUESDAY Means "day of the week" and originated as a modern English name, derived from the Old English word "Tiwsdæg" meaning "Tiw's day," which refers to the Norse god of war, Týr.

TULIP The first name Tulip originated from the English word for a type of flower and symbolizes beauty and love.

TULSA Unisex name of Native American origin meaning "old town" or "town of the old ones".

TVISHA Indian origin and it means "brightness" or "radiance."

TWYLA Means "woman with double strength" and originates from the English language.

TYASIA The first name Tyasia has a modern American origin and its meaning is unclear or unknown.

TYLASIA Modern American name that does not have a widely known meaning or origin.

TYLAYA The first name Tylaya has an uncertain meaning and origin.

TYMBER Modern, unique variation of the name Timber, with no specific meaning or origin.

TYNSLEE Modern American name of unknown origin, possibly created as a variant of existing names.

TYONNA Means "princess" and has an uncertain origin.

TZILA Hebrew name meaning "shade" or "shadow".

TZIPORA Means "bird" in Hebrew and originates from the Old Testament, specifically from the story of Moses and his wife in the Book of Exodus.

TZIREL Means "bird" and it has Hebrew origin.

TZIVIA Hebrew origin, means "deer" or "gazelle" and is often associated with grace and beauty.

TZURTY The first name TZURTY has no widely recognized meaning or origin, as it is a rare or unique name without historical cultural significance or documented etymology.

UJIN Korean name that means "bright and precious" and is typically given to those believed to bring hope and good fortune.

UMAIZA Means "bright and beautiful" and it originates from Arabic.

UMMEHANI The name Umehani means "mother of Hani" and it is of Arabic origin.

UNGWA Means destiny or fate in the Hausa language and is of African origin.

UNITY Means "the state of being united or joined as one" and originates from the English language.

URSA — Feminine given name derived from Latin, meaning "bear" or "little bear," often associated with the constellation Ursa Major or Ursa Minor.

URSULA — Means "little she-bear" and has Latin origins.

URVI — Indian origin and means "earth" or "goddess of the earth" in Sanskrit.

UTA — Means "prosperous" or "wealthy" and has German origins.

UWASE — Female given name of African origin meaning "beautiful one" or "beloved" in the Kinyarwanda language.

VAGMI — Vagmi is an Indian Sanskrit name meaning "eloquent or wise speaker".

VAIDEHI — Feminine Indian name meaning "belonging to Videha," which refers to a kingdom in Hindu mythology, and is commonly used in Hindu culture.

VAISHNAVI — The first name Vaishnavi originates from Hindu mythology and means "devotee of Lord Vishnu" or "goddess Lakshmi."

VALERIANA — Feminine given name of Latin origin, meaning "strong" or "valiant."

VALESKA — The first name Valeska originated from Germany and means "ruler of all."

VALLEY — Means a low area of land between hills or mountains, and its origin lies in the English language.

VALLOLET — The first name Vallolet does not have a widely recognized meaning or origin, as it appears to be a rare or uncommon name.

VALYRIA — Unique and fictional name created by author George R.R. Martin for his fantasy series, "A Song of Ice and Fire," which inspired the television show "Game of Thrones."

VAMIKA — Hindu name of Sanskrit origin, meaning "goddess Durga" or "belonging to Durga."

VANITY — The name Vanity originates from the English vocabulary word, signifying excessive self-admiration and self-centeredness.

VARENYA — Means "deserving of praise" and has its origin in the Sanskrit language.

VARNIKA — Indian origin, means "colored" or "brilliant."

VARSHINI — Feminine Indian name meaning "one who brings rain" or "goddess of rain" in Sanskrit.

VARVARA — Female given name of Greek origin meaning "foreign, stranger, barbarian".

VASHTI — Means "beautiful" or "good" and originates from the Hebrew language.

VASILIKI — Means "royal" or "regal" and it has Greek origins.

VASILISA — Feminine given name of Slavic origin meaning "royal" or "queenly."

VEDANSHI — Means "part of divine knowledge" and originates from Sanskrit, an ancient language of India.

VEDHIKA — The first name Vedhika has its origins in India and it means "knowledge, wisdom" in Sanskrit.

VEDIKA — The name Vedika has Indian origins and it means "knowledge" or "wisdom" in Sanskrit.

VEEKSHA — Unique and modern Indian name derived from Sanskrit, meaning "desire" or "aspiration."

VELMA — Female given name meaning "protected" or "desire for protection" that originated from Greek mythology.

VELVET — The first name Velvet, of English origin, means a luxurious fabric typically associated with softness and elegance.

VELZY — The name Velzy has no specific meaning or origin, as it is not a commonly used or recognized name.

VENBA — The name Venba originated from the Tamil language and it means "poem" or "song."

VENEZIA — Means "Venice" and has Italian origins.

VENICE — Means "from Venice" and is of Italian origin.

VENITA — Means "blessed" or "desired" and has Hindi and Latin origins.

VENNELA — Telugu name meaning "moonlight" that is commonly used in South India.

VERALYNN — Modern American feminine name derived from the combination of the names Vera, meaning "truth" or "faith," and Lynn, derived from the Old English word for "lake" or

VERONA — The first name Verona is of Latin origin and means "from Verona," a city in northern Italy.

VERSAVIA — The meaning and origin of the first name Versavia is currently unknown as it does not appear to have any established historical or cultural references.

VESNA — Means "spring" in Slovene and has Slavic origins.

VIANKA — Feminine given name of Slavic origin, meaning "grace of God."

VIBHA — Means "radiant" or "shining" in Sanskrit and originates from India.

VICTOIRE	Means "victory" in French and has its origin in Latin.
VIDYA	Means "knowledge" or "learning" in Sanskrit and is of Indian origin.
VIELKA	Means "great" and it has Spanish and Latin origins.
VIKTORIYA	Feminine given name of Slavic origin meaning "victory" or "conqueror."
VINAYA	Means "modesty" or "discipline" and has its origin in Sanskrit.
VINTAGE	Means "classic, old-fashioned, or of high quality" and it originated as a word to describe wines of a particular year or era.
VIRADHYA	Means "respected" or "honored" in Sanskrit and is of Indian origin.
VIRIDIANA	Means "green" and originates from the Latin word "viridis" meaning "green."
VIRSAVIYA	Means "strength" and it originated from the Slavic language.
VIRTUE	Means moral excellence or goodness and originates from the English language.
VISENYA	Means "beloved" or "chosen one" and it originates from the fictional world of George R.R. Martin's "A Song of Ice and Fire" series.
VITALIA	Latin origin, means "life-giving" or "vital" and is typically used for girls.
VITTORIA	Means "victory" and it originates from Italian, derived from the Latin word "victoria."
VIVI	Latin origin and means "alive, lively, vibrant."
VIVICA	Means "alive" or "full of life" and it is of Scandinavian origin.
VLADA	Means "ruler" or "prince" and is of Slavic origin.
VRINDA	The name "Vrinda" originates from Hindi and Sanskrit, and it means "tulsi" or "a cluster of flowers."
VUNG	The first name Vung, of Vietnamese origin, means "victory" or "triumph."
VYLETTE	Feminine given name of English origin, derived from the word "violet" which symbolizes beauty and modesty.
WAFA	Means "loyalty" or "faithfulness" and has Arabic origins.
WAJIHA	Means "distinguished" or "illustrious" and originates from Arabic.
WANDA	Means "a Slavic tribal goddess" and has its origin in Slavic mythology.
WAVERLEIGH	The first name Waverleigh, of English origin, means "meadow of waving grass" or "from the quaking or waving meadow.".
WELLESLEY	Means "woodland clearing" or "meadow near a spring" and originates from an Old English surname referring to a location in England.
WESLEIGH	Means "from the western meadow" and it originated as a variant of the name Wesley, which is derived from an English surname.
WESLYNN	Modern variant of the names Wesley and Lynn, combining elements from both names to create a unique and gender-neutral name.
WESTLYNN	Means "from the western waterfall" and has a combination of English and Old English origins.
WHISKEY	Type of alcoholic beverage made from fermented grain mash, and is of English origin.
WHISPER	Means to speak in a soft, hushed voice, and its origin is English.
WHITLEIGH	English origin and means "from the white meadow."
WHYNTER	The first name Whyn-ter is of American origin and means "winter" or "white" referring to the season or color.
WIKTORIA	Means "victory" and originates from the Latin word "victoria."
WILHEMINA	The name Wilhelmina is of German origin, meaning "resolute protector" or "willful helmet," and it is a feminine form of the name Wilhelm.
WILLAMAE	Combination of the names William and Mae, and it originates from English and Germanic origins.
WILLAMINA	Means "resolute protection" and originated as the feminine form of the name William.
WILLOUGHBY	Means "farm near the willows" and originates from Old English.
WILLOWG RACE	English origin, combines the gracefulness of a willow tree with the virtue of grace, representing a strong and elegant presence.
WILLOWMAE	The first name Willowmae is of English origin and it combines the names "Willow" and "Mae," meaning a person with the qualities of both the willow tree and the month of May.
WINDSOR	The first name Windsor originated as an English surname derived from the Old English words "win(n)" meaning "friend" and "s□ t"meaning "seat," and it signifies a person with a friendly nature.

WINSLET Means "from the Wynn's hill" and originated as an English surname before becoming a modern given name.

WINSOME Means "attractive" or "charming" and originated from the Old English word "wynsum."

WINTERROSE Means a combination of the seasonal name "Winter" and the flower name "Rose," likely created as a unique and evocative modern name choice.

WISTERIA Means "climbing plant with purple flowers" and its origin is English.

WRENLIE The first name "WRENLIE" does not have a widely recognized meaning or origin as it appears to be a unique or uncommon name.

WRENLYNN Means "songbird that resides near the lake" and originated as a combination of the names Wren and Lynn.

WYNNE Means "fair" or "blessed" and originates from Welsh and English origins.

WYOMING Means "at the big river" and originated from the Native American term for Dak□ ótaSioux tribe.

XANDRIA Means "defender of mankind" and is a feminine variation of the name Alexander, originating from Greek.

XANTHI Greek name meaning "blonde, yellow" and it comes from the Greek word "xanthos" which means yellow or golden-haired.

XENOVIA Means "foreigner" and has Greek origins.

XIADANI Feminine name of Nahuatl origin meaning "flower that comes from the sand."

XILEI Chinese name meaning "happy and elegant," derived from the Mandarin words xi (happy) and lei (elegant).

XILENIA Modern and unique feminine name of uncertain origin and meaning.

XIOLANI Hawaiian name meaning "heavenly or royal one" and is of Polynesian origin.

XOCHI Means "flower" in Nahuatl, an indigenous language of Mexico.

XOCHILT Means "flower" and it originates from the Nahuatl language of the Aztecs.

XOCHIQU ETZAL Means "flower feather" and originates from the Nahuatl language, spoken by the Aztecs in ancient Mesoamerica.

XOIE Modern and unique female given name of uncertain origin that conveys a sense of elegance and mystery.

XOLA Means "stay in peace" and originates from the Zulu and Xhosa languages of South Africa.

YACHET The meaning and origin of the first name YACHET are currently unknown.

YAELIS Means "God will ascend" and it is of Hebrew origin.

YAHRITZA The first name YAHRITZA likely originated in Puerto Rico and its meaning is unknown or unclear.

YAHVI Means "divine" or "of the Lord" and it has its origin in Sanskrit.

YAILIN The first name Yailin is of uncertain origin and meaning, possibly a variation of the name Yalina or influenced by Gaelic names.

YALDA Persian origin and means "longest night," symbolizing the winter solstice and the celebration of rebirth and light.

YALIT Modern Hebrew name that means "unique" or "special."

YAMINAH Means "right-handed" in Arabic and its origin can be traced back to Arabic and African cultures.

YANAISY Cuban name that likely originates from a combination of Spanish and indigenous Taíno influences, meaning "unique" or "one of a kind."

YANARA Female name of Indigenous American origin meaning "gift from God" or "butterfly".

YANELY The first name "Yanely" is of Hebrew origin and it means "God has answered" or "Yahweh has responded."

YANETH The first name Yaneth, of uncertain origin, is typically considered a variation of Janet or Janeth and may have originated from Hebrew, Scottish, or English names.

YAQEEN YAQEEN is an Arabic name meaning "certainty" or "conviction," derived from the Arabic word for "belief" or "faith."

YARIELIS Modern invented name of uncertain meaning and origin.

YARIZEL Uncertain origins and meaning.

YARYNA Ukrainian name meaning "peaceful" or "calm", originating from the Slavic word "yaru" which translates to peace or tranquility.

YASANIY	The first name Yasaniy has an unknown meaning and origin as it does not appear to have any established etymology or cultural background within readily available sources.
YASEMIN	Turkish name meaning "jasmine flower", derived from the Persian word "yasaman" ultimately of Arabic origin.
YASHIKA	Means "successful" or "one who brings fame," and it originates from the Sanskrit language in India.
YASNA	Means "holy" or "sacred" and it originates from the Persian language.
YATZARY	Hebrew origin and means "God remembers" or "God has answered".
YAZ	Gender-neutral, informal abbreviation for the given name Yasmin or Yazid, possibly of Arabic or Persian origin.
YEIMY	Feminine given name of uncertain origin, with no readily available meaning or established cultural background.
YELIANNY	The first name YELIANNY is of uncertain origin but is commonly used in Latin America, particularly in Venezuela.
YELITZA	Means "beautiful flower" and originates from the indigenous Arawak language of Venezuela.
YEMARIAM	Means "gift of Mary" and originates from Ethiopian culture.
YEMAYA	Female given name of Yoruba origin meaning "mother of the fish" and it is derived from the Yoruba goddess of the sea and motherhood.
YENNEFER	Means "white enchantress" and originates from the fantasy world of Andrzej Sapkowski's Witcher series.
YENTY	Hebrew name meaning "gift of God" and it is of Hebrew origin.
YESBETH	Modern English name derived from merging the names "Yes" meaning affirmation or agreement, and "Beth" a diminutive of Elizabeth meaning "God is my oath."
YESLIN	Modern and unique name of uncertain origin, with no widely accepted meaning or historical background.
YETZALI	Means "warrior" and it originates from the Nahuatl language spoken by the indigenous peoples of Mexico.
YEXALEN	Unique and modern name of unknown origin, likely created in recent times.
YEYETZI	Means "he/she who maintains order" and originates from the Nahuatl language used by the indigenous people of Mexico.
YIDES	The first name Yides is of Yiddish origin and means "a Jewish woman who is deeply religious and righteous."
YILDIZ	The first name Yildiz is of Turkish origin and means "star" or "shining star".
YISETH	Feminine name of unknown origin and meaning.
YIYI	The first name YIYI is of Chinese origin and its meaning is "double happiness" or "joyful and happy."
YLVA	Means "she-wolf" and has Scandinavian origins.
YNEZ	Variant of the name Inez, derived from the Greek name Agnes, meaning "pure" or "chaste."
YOADAN	Means "God's chosen gift" and originates from the Amharic language spoken in Ethiopia.
YOATZI	The baby girl name Yoatzi has an Aztec origin and means "noble one."
YOJANA	Means "plan" or "strategy" and originates from Sanskrit, an ancient Indian language.
YORLENY	The first name YORLENY is of uncertain origin and meaning, but it is believed to have been influenced by Spanish or Latin American naming traditions.
YOSTINA	Feminine given name of Coptic origin meaning "faithful" or "devoted."
YOSUANI	The first name Yosuani is of Cuban origin and means "gift of God."
YOUMNA	Means "blessed" and has Arabic origins.
YOUSRA	Means "ease" or "wealth" and is of Arabic origin.
YOYO	The first name YOYO is of Chinese origin and it is typically derived from a Chinese term "yōuyōu" which means "friendly, pleasant".
YSABELLE	The meaning and origin of the first name Ysabelle is "God's promise" and it is of Hebrew origin.

YUKI	Japanese origin and means "snow" or "happiness."
YUKTHA	Indian origin, means "perfectly composed" or "intelligent" in Sanskrit.
YULANI	Means "heavenly flower" and is of Hawaiian origin.
YULEINI	Feminine name of Russian origin, meaning "born at Christmas."
YULEISY	Cuban origin and means "born on Christmas."
YULEYSI	The first name Yuleysi is of Greek origin and its meaning is "bright, cheerful, and full of life."
YULIETH	Feminine given name of Spanish origin, possibly derived from "Juliet" or "Julia," meaning youthful or full of youth.
YUMIKO	Means "beautiful child" in Japanese and originated in Japan.
YUMNA	Means "blessed" and is of Arabic origin.
YUNALESCA	The first name Yunalesca likely originates from a fictional character in the video game Final Fantasy X, and its meaning is not specified.
YUNIZA	Yuniza is an Indonesian name meaning "unique" or "unmatched" and originates from the Malay culture.
YURIANA	Means "youthful" and it has Russian origins.
YURIDIA	Russian origin and means "peaceful" or "calm."
YURITZI	Feminine name of Aztec origin, meaning "flower of the earth."
YUVIKA	Means "young girl" or "maiden" and originates from Sanskrit in India.
YVAINE	Feminine given name originated from French, meaning "evening star" or "first star of the evening."
YVIE	Variant of the name Yvette and has French origins, meaning "yew wood."
YZABELLA	The meaning and origin of the first name YZABELLA is a variant spelling of Isabella, derived from the Hebrew name Yiscah meaning "God is my oath."
ZABIBU	Swahili name meaning "grape" or "grapevine," typically given to girls born in Tanzania or other Swahili-speaking areas.
ZAEDA	Arabic origin and it means "prosperous" or "successful."
ZAFEERA	Feminine Arabic name meaning "victorious" or "successful."
ZAHAVA	Means "golden" in Hebrew.
ZAHIRAH	Means "radiant" or "bright" and originates from Arabic.
ZAHRIAH	The first name Zahriah is of Arabic origin and means "blossoming, flourishing."
ZAHRIYA	The first name Zahriya is of Arabic origin and means "flower," symbolizing beauty and delicacy.
ZALAIYA	Means "to find peace" and it is of Arabic origin.
ZAMAYA	The name Zamaya has no widely recognized meaning or origin as it is a rare and uncommon name.
ZANOVAH	Modern female name with uncertain origin, possibly a creative variation of existing names.
ZANOVIA	The first name Zanovia is of Greek origin and it means "God's gift of life."
ZANYIAH	Modern American name derived from combining the word "zany" which means eccentric or humorous, with the suffix "-iah" which is often used in names of African or Hebrew origins, creating a unique and playful name.
ZAPHIRA	Hebrew name meaning "beautiful" or "sapphire" and it originates from the Hebrew Bible.
ZARAE	The meaning and origin of the first name Zarae is unknown as it has no well-documented origin or meaning.
ZARAIAH	Hebrew origin meaning "God remembers" or "God has remembered."
ZAREYAH	Means "radiant, shining" and has origins in Arabic.
ZARYAH	Modern invented name with uncertain origins, often seen as a variation of the name Zahara or Zahrah, meaning "flower" or "blooming" in Arabic.
ZAYLIA	Modern and unique name of unknown origin, likely created as a variant of the name Zaylee or a combination of names.
ZAYNAH	Arabic origin and it means "beautiful, graceful."
ZAYNEB	Feminine Arabic name meaning "beauty and grace" originating from Islamic tradition.
ZEINETH	Uncertain origin and meaning.
ZELAIA	Means "from the yellow meadow" and has Basque origin.

ZELYIANA	Modern and unique female name of uncertain origin, possibly derived from a combination of various sounds or elements.
ZENAIDA	Means "of Zeus" in Greek and it originated from the ancient Greek name "Zenaida".
ZENAYA	Means "strong" or "powerful" and it originated from Arabic.
ZENEYDA	Spanish variant of the name Zenaida, meaning "of Zeus" in Greek, and is of Greek origin.
ZENOBIA	Means "life of Zeus" and originates from ancient Greek.
ZENYAH	Rare and modern variation of the name Zenia, meaning "hospitality" or "hospitable" in Greek.
ZERUIAH	Means "my gumdrop" and originates from Hebrew.
ZEYA	Russian origin and means "prominent, radiant, or bright."
ZHAMIRA	Means "princess" and has an Arabic origin.
ZHARA	Means "radiant" or "shining" and has Persian origin.
ZHOE	Variant spelling of the name Zoe, which is of Greek origin and means "life."
ZIRACHI	The name Zirachi has no widely recognized meaning or origin.
ZIRAILI	Rare feminine given name of unclear origin and meaning.
ZIRWA	Female Arabic name meaning "highest point" or "pinnacle" that is of Arabic origin.
ZLATA	Feminine Slavic name meaning "golden" or "golden-haired" that originates from a Slavic language.
ZNIYAH	Unknown origin and meaning as it does not have a specific history or documented etymology.
ZOEJANE	Means "life-giving and gracious" and is of Greek and Hebrew origin.
ZOELI	Modern and unique name of uncertain origin, possibly derived from the Greek name Zoë meaning "life".
ZOEMY	Modern invented name with no specific meaning or origin.
ZOHARA	Means "radiant" or "bright" and originates from Hebrew.
ZOHEMY	Means "blessing" and it has uncertain origins.
ZOILA	Means "life" and it originates from Greek and Spanish.
ZUHRI	Means "bright" or "luminous" and has Arabic origins.
ZULAIKHA	Means "beautiful" or "brilliant" and originates from Arabic and Islamic traditions, primarily associated with the story of Zulaikha and Yusuf (Joseph) in the Quran and other Abrahamic religious texts.
ZULEIMA	Arabic origin and means "peaceful, serene."
ZULEYMI	The first name Zuleymi is of Arabic origin and means "beautiful and radiant."
ZULMA	Means "peaceful" and it originated from Arabic.
ZUNAIRA	Arabic origin and it means "flower found in paradise."
ZUNAISHA	Means "a woman filled with grace and radiance" and has Arabic origins.
ZURIAH	Means "God is my rock" and originates from Hebrew.
ZURISADAI	Means "my rock is the Almighty" and is of Hebrew origin.
ZURIYAH	Means "my rock" or "my strength" and has Hebrew origins.
ZURMANI	Masculine name of Arabic origin meaning "winning, victorious".
ZUZANNA	Feminine given name of Hebrew origin meaning "lily" or "graceful".
ZUZU	The first name Zuzu is of Arabic origin and means "little gem."
ZYANYA	Nahuatl origin, meaning "forever, always" and is primarily used in Mexican culture.
ZYIAH	Uncertain origin and meaning, possibly derived from Hebrew, Arabic, or African origins.
ZYNECIA	Modern and unique name of uncertain origin and meaning.

1,000 most popular names for boys.

AARON   Means "high mountain" and originates from Hebrew.

ABDIEL   Means "servant of God" and has biblical origins.

ABDIRAHMAN   Means "servant of the Most Merciful" and has a Muslim origin.

ABDUL   Means "servant of" or "slave of" in Arabic, and it is commonly used as a prefix in Arabic names to emphasize devotion to Allah.

ABDULAZIZ   Means "servant of the All-Powerful" and originates from Arabic.

ABDULLAH   Means "servant of Allah" and originates from Arabic.

ABDULRAHMAN   Means "servant of the merciful" and has Arabic origin.

ABELARDO   Means "noble and resolute" and originates from the Germanic name Adalhard.

ABHIRAM   Indian origin and means "delightful, charming" in Sanskrit.

ABNER   Means "father's light" and is of Hebrew origin.

ABRAHAM   The meaning of the name Abraham is "father of many" and it is of Hebrew origin.

ABRAM   Means "exalted father" and it has Hebrew origins.

ACHILLES   Means "pain" or "lipless" and originates from Greek mythology.

ADITYA   Means "sun" in Sanskrit and it originates from ancient Indian mythology.

ADNAN   Means "settler" or "one who stays," and it has Arabic origins.

ADOLFO   Means "noble wolf" and originates from the Germanic language.

ADONAI   The first name "Adonai" is of Hebrew origin and means "my Lord" or "my God," often used as a reverential title for God in Jewish tradition.

ADONIS   Means "lord" or "ruler" and it originates from Greek mythology, referring to a handsome youth beloved by the goddess Aphrodite.

ADRIAN   Male name of Latin origin meaning "man of Adria" or "from the Adriatic Sea."

ADRIEL   Hebrew name meaning "my God is my helper" and is of biblical origin.

ADVAITH   Means "unique" or "the one and only" and originates from Sanskrit.

ADVIK   Means "unique" or "one who is unique" and originates from Hindu mythology.

AGASTYA   Means "fast, quick" and it originates from Sanskrit, an ancient Indian language.

AGUSTIN   Means "respected" or "venerable" and originates from the Latin name Augustinus, derived from the Latin word "augustus" meaning "great" or "exalted."

AHMARI   Modern variant of the Arabic name Amir, meaning "prince" or "leader," with Arabic roots.

AHMED   Arabic name meaning "praiseworthy" or "commendable," originating from the Arabic root word "◻ amd"which translates to "praise" or "commendation."

AIDEN   Means "little fire" and is of Irish origin.

AIYDEN   Variant of the name Aidan, of Irish origin, meaning "little fiery one" or "born of fire".

AKIVA   Means "protected" or "guarded" and it has Hebrew origins.

AKSEL   Means "father of peace" and has Scandinavian origins.

ALBERT   Means "noble and bright" and originated from Germanic roots.

ALDO   Means "old, wise" and it originates from Germanic and Italian languages.

ALEJANDRO   Means "defender of mankind" and has its origin in Spanish.

ALEKSANDER   Means "defender of mankind" or "protector of men" and originated from the Greek name Alexandros, which is a combination of the words "alexein" (to defend) and "andros" (man).

ALEX   Unisex name of Greek origin meaning "defender of the people."

ALEXANDER   Alexander means "defender of the people" and originates from the Greek name Alexandros.

ALEXAVIER	Means "defender of mankind" and is a combination of the names Alexander and Xavier.
ALEXZANDER	Means "defender of mankind" and is derived from the Greek name Alexander.
ALFONSO	Means "noble and ready" and originates from the Germanic name Adalfuns, which was derived from the elements adal meaning "noble" and funs meaning "ready".
ALFREDO	Means "elf counselor" and originated from Old English and Germanic roots.
ALISTAIR	Means "defender of mankind" and originated from the Scottish Gaelic name Alasdair.
ALISTER	Means "defender of mankind" and has Scottish and Gaelic origins.
ALONZO	Means "noble and ready" and it originated from a Spanish and Italian variation of the name Alfonso.
ALPHA	Means "first" or "beginning" and it is of Greek origin.
ALVARO	Means "elf warrior" and has Spanish and Portuguese origins.
AMADEUS	Means "lover of God" and originates from Latin.
AMADO	Means "loved" or "beloved" in Spanish, originating from the Latin word "amatus."
AMAURI	Means "strength" and is of French origin.
AMBROSE	Means "immortal" or "divine" and originates from the Ancient Greek name Ambrosios derived from "ambrotos" meaning "immortal" or "not subject to death."
AMEN	Means "so be it" and originates from the Hebrew language.
AMIR	Male name of Arabic origin meaning "prince" or "commander".
AMOS	Means "burden-bearer" and originates from Hebrew.
ANDERS	Means "strong and manly" and originates from Scandinavian countries.
ANDERSON	Meaning "son of Andrew," Anderson is a surname-turned-first name of Scandinavian origin.
ANDREW	Meaning "manly" or "brave," Andrew is of Greek origin and is derived from the name Andreas.
ANGEL	Means "messenger" or "one who is like an angel" and has Latin origins.
ANSON	English origin and means "son of a nobleman" or "son of Agnes."
ANTHONY	Means "priceless" and originates from Latin.
ANTOINE	Means "priceless" or "invaluable" and originates from the Greek name Antonios.
ANTONIO	Spanish and Italian origin, meaning "highly praiseworthy" or "worthy of praise."
ANTWAN	Variant of the name Antoine, derived from the Greek name Antonios, meaning "priceless" or "highly praiseworthy," and it has its origin in France.
APOLLO	Means "destroyer" or "to destroy" and has its origins in Greek mythology, where Apollo was the god of sun, music, healing, and prophecy.
ARCHER	The first name Archer, of English origin, means "one who uses a bow and arrow" or "bowman."
ARCHIBALD	Means "genuine, bold" and originates from Old High German.
ARCHIE	The name Archie originates from Scotland and means "true and bold" or "genuine and courageous."
ARES	"Ares" is a Greek masculine name referring to the Greek god of war in Greek mythology.
ARJUN	Means "bright, shining" and it originates from Indian/Bengali mythology, where Arjuna was a hero and warrior prince in the Hindu epic Mahabharata.
ARLO	Means "army, hill" and has English and Spanish origins.
ARMANI	Unisex name of Italian origin meaning "son of Armand".
ARNOLD	Means "eagle power" and is of Germanic origin.
ARTEM	Greek origin and means "gift of Artemis," referring to the Greek goddess of the hunt and wilderness.
ARTHUR	The name Arthur originates from Celtic and means "bear-like" or "courageous."
ARTURO	Means "noble and courageous" and originates from the Latin name 'Artorius,' possibly derived from the Celtic word 'artos' meaning "bear."
ARYEH	Means "lion" and it originates from Hebrew.
ASHER	Asher means "happy" or "blessed" and is of Hebrew origin.
ASHTON	Unisex name of English origin meaning "ash tree town."
ATHARV	Means "knowledgeable" and it originates from Sanskrit, an ancient language of India.
ATLAS	Means "bearer of the heavens" and its origin can be traced back to Greek mythology, where Atlas was a Titan who was condemned to hold up the celestial spheres on his shoulders.

ATREUS Means "fearless" and originates from Greek mythology, being borne by a tragic and bold character in the Trojan War.

ATREYU The first name Atreyu originates from the popular fantasy novel "The Neverending Story," and it means "son of all" or "warrior."

ATTICUS Means "man of Attica" and it originates from ancient Greece.

AUGUST Means "great" or "venerable" and is of Latin origin.

AUGUSTINE Latin name meaning "great" or "venerable," and it is of Roman origin.

AUGUSTUS Means "great" or "venerable" and it originated from Ancient Rome as a title given to Roman emperors, with the most well-known being Octavian, the first emperor of Rome.

AUSTIN Meaning "great" or "magnificent", Austin is of English origin and derived from the Latin name "Augustine".

AVROHOM Hebrew name meaning "father of many nations", originating from the Old Testament patriarch Abraham.

AXEL Means "father of peace" and originates from Scandinavian and Germanic languages.

AYANSH Means "part of the parents" and has Indian origin.

AYCE The first name "Ayce" is of American origin and means "gift of God."

AYUB Means "patient" or "one who bears trials" in Arabic and is of Hebrew origin, derived from the biblical character Job.

AZAEL The meaning of the first name Azael is "God strengthens" and its origin is Hebrew.

AZIZ Means "powerful" or "beloved" and has its origins in Arabic language and culture.

AZLAN Means "lion" and originates from Arabic and Malay cultures.

AZRAEL Means "helper of God" and originates from Hebrew and Islamic traditions.

BAKER The first name Baker originated as an occupational surname, derived from 'baecestre' in Old English, meaning "baker," indicating someone who bakes bread or other baked goods professionally.

BANKS Means "one who dwells by the riverbank" and has an English origin.

BARRETT Surname-derived given name meaning "bear strength" and is of English origin.

BASIL The name Basil has Greek origins and means "royal" or "kingly."

BASTIAN Means "venerable" or "revered" and is of German origin.

BAXTER Means "baker" and it originated as an occupational surname in medieval England.

BAYRON Spanish origin and means "bearer of victory".

BEAU Means "handsome" or "beautiful" in French, and it originates from the French word "beu" which means "beautiful."

BECK English origin, means "brook" or "stream."

BECKAM Means "stream" or "homestead by the brook" and originated from the English surname Beckham.

BECKETT Means "dweller near the brook" and it originated from the Old English word "bece" meaning "brook" or "stream."

BECKHAM English origin and means "homestead by the stream," derived from the combination of the Old English words "beo" (bee) and "ham" (homestead or village).

BELLAMY Gender-neutral name of French origin meaning "beautiful friend."

BENAIAH Means "God has built" and it originates from Hebrew.

BENEDICT Means "blessed" and has Latin origins.

BENICIO Means "blessed one" and originates from Latin.

BENJAMIN Hebrew name meaning "son of the right hand" and is of biblical origin.

BENJI Diminutive form of Benjamin, meaning "son of the right hand" or "son of the south," and it originated from the Hebrew name Binyamin.

BENNETT Bennett is of English origin and means "blessed".

BENSON English origin and its meaning is "son of Ben," derived from the medieval given name Benjamin.

BENTLEY Means "from the bent-grass meadow" and is of Old English origin.

BERNARDO Means "brave as a bear" and has Germanic origins.

BISHOP Means a high-ranking clergyman or overseer and has English origins.

BJORN Means "bear" and originates from Old Norse.

BLAINE Means "thin" or "slender" and is of Gaelic origin.

BLAKE Meaning "black" or "dark," Blake is a gender-neutral name of Old English origin.

BOAZ   Means "strength" or "swiftness" and originates from Hebrew, often associated with a biblical figure in the Old Testament.

BOBBY   Pet form of the name Robert, meaning "bright fame" and originating from the Germanic elements "hrod" (fame) and "beraht" (bright).

BODEN   Means "shelter" or "dwelling" and is of English origin.

BODHI   Means "enlightenment" in Sanskrit and is of Indian origin.

BODIE   Masculine name of Irish origin, meaning "descendant of Bodhan" or "messenger."

BOSTON   The meaning of the name Boston is "from the town of Boston" and it is of English origin.

BRADEN   The meaning of the name Braden is "from the wide valley" and it is of Irish origin.

BRADFORD   Means "from the broad ford" and has English origins.

BRADLEY   Means "broad clearing" and originates from Old English.

BRAEDYN   Means "from the broad valley" and is of Scottish origin.

BRANCH   The first name "Branch" originates from the Middle English word "braunche," meaning a division or offshoot, and symbolizes strength, growth, and connection to one's family

BRANDON   Means "hill covered with broom" and has English origins.

BRANTLEY   Modern American name derived from an English surname meaning "clearing where burnt brushwood remained."

BRAULIO   Means "shining" or "brilliant" and has Origin in Latin.

BRAXTON   Modern English name that originally came from an English surname meaning "Brock's town."

BRAYAN   The name Brayan originated as a variant of the name Brian and means "strong, virtuous, or noble" in English and Irish.

BRAYDEN   Modern English name of Celtic origin, meaning "broad valley".

BRAYLON   Means "son of the brave one" and is of American origin.

BRECKEN   Scottish origin and means "freckled".

BRENDAN   Means "prince" and is of Irish origin.

BRENNAN   Brennan is an Irish name meaning "descendant of Braonán" or "teardrop" in Gaelic, and it is derived from the old Irish surname Ó Braonáin.

BRENTLY   Means "hilltop meadow" and originates from Old English.

BREWER   Means "one who brews or sells beer" and originates from an English occupational surname.

BRIGGS   The first name Briggs is of Scottish origin and means "son of a bridge builder."

BRIGHAM   Means "dweller by the bridge settlement" and is of Old English origin.

BROCK   Means "badger-like" and originates from Old English.

BRODY   Scottish name meaning "ditch" or "muddy area," ultimately derived from the Gaelic word "bròdhaig."

BROGAN   Means "descendant of the shoe maker" and has Irish origins.

BRONSON   Means "son of the brown one" and it originates from a surname derived from Old English.

BROOKS   Surname turned first name that means "stream" or "small river" and originates from Old English.

BRUNO   Means "brown" in Germanic and Italian, and it originated from the Germanic name "Brun" which referred to someone with dark hair or complexion.

BRYANT   Means "strong" or "high hill" and is of Old English origin.

BRYCE   Means "descendant of Brice" and originates from the Welsh name "Brice."

BRYER   English origin and means "of the briar, a thorny shrub or bush."

BRYSON   BRYSON means "son of Brice" and is of English origin.

BURKE   Means "from the fortress" and originates from the Gaelic surname Ó Broin, derived from the Irish word "brog" meaning "fortress" or "stronghold."

BYRON   Means "from the barns" and originates from the Old English word "byre," meaning barn.

CADEN   Means "spirit of battle" and is of Welsh origin.

CAESAR   Means "to cut, to seize" and originated from the Latin word "caedere" meaning "to cut".

CALEB   Means "faithful" or "devotion to God" and originates from Hebrew biblical traditions.

CALLAHAN   Means "bright-headed" and is of Gaelic origin.

CALLAN   Means "battle" and is of Scottish origin.

CALLUM   Means "dove" or "dovekeeper" and originates from Scotland and Ireland.

CALVIN — Means "bald" and originates from the French surname 'Cauvin' derived from the Latin word "calvus" meaning "hairless."

CAMDEN — Unisex name of Scottish origin meaning "winding valley."

CAMERON — Means "crooked nose" and is of Scottish origin.

CANNON — The name Cannon originates from the English language and its meaning refers to a powerful weapon or artillery used in warfare.

CANYON — Means "deep valley" and has its origin in the English language.

CARL — Means "free man" and originates from various languages, including Old English and Germanic.

CARLOS — Spanish name meaning "free man" and is derived from the Germanic name Karl.

CARLTON — The first name Carlton is of English origin, meaning "from the Carl's town" or "settlement of free peasants."

CARSON — Unisex name of Scottish origin meaning "son of Carr."

CARSTEN — German name of Scandinavian origin, meaning "Christian" or "follower of Christ."

CARTER — Carter means "transporter of goods by cart" and originated as an English occupational surname for someone who drove a cart.

CASEY — Casey is an Irish name meaning "brave in battle" and is derived from the Gaelic surname Ó Cathasaigh.

CASPIAN — Means "from the Caspian Sea" and originated from the name of the large saltwater lake situated between Europe and Asia.

CASSIAN — Means "belonging to the ancient Roman gens Cassia" and originates from Latin.

CASSIUS — Means "hollow" or "empty" and originated from the Roman family name Cassius, which was derived from the Latin word "cassus."

CASTIEL — Name of Hebrew origin meaning "shield of God" or "my cover is God".

CAYSEN — American origin and it means "son of Casey".

CECIL — Means "blind" and has origins in both the English and Welsh languages.

CEDAR — Means "strong and sturdy tree" and it originates from the Hebrew word "kedem" meaning ancient or old.

CEDRIC — Means "ruler" or "chief" and has English and Gaelic origins.

CHAIM — Means "life" in Hebrew and it has its origin in Jewish culture.

CHANCE — Means "luck" or "fortune" and originated from the English language.

CHANCELLOR — Means "chief secretary" or "one who keeps records" and its origin is French.

CHANDLER — Means "candle maker" and originated as an occupational surname in England.

CHANNING — Means "young wolf" and has English origins.

CHARLES — Means "free man" and is of Germanic origin.

CHASE — Means "to hunt or pursue" and is of English origin.

CHESTER — Old English origin, means "fortress" or "walled town."

CHEVY — Means "horseman" and is of American origin.

CHOZEN — Means "chosen" and its origin is uncertain.

CHRIS — Short form of the name Christopher, meaning "bearer of Christ" and originating from Greek.

CHRISTIAN — Means "follower of Christ" and is of Latin origin.

CHRISTO PHER — Means "bearer of Christ" and has Greek origins.

CLARENCE — Means "bright and clear" and it originated from Latin.

CLAYTON — Name of English origin meaning "clay settlement" or "town built on clay."

CLIFFORD — Means "lives near a steep cliff" and is of Old English origin.

CLIFTON — Means "settlement near a cliff" and has English origins.

CLINT — Means "settlement on the hill" and originated from Old English.

CLYDE — Means "from the river Clyde" and originates from the Scottish Gaelic term "Cluaidh", referring to the famous river in Scotland.

CODY — Means "helper" and is of Irish origin.

COHEN — The name Cohen originates from Hebrew and means "priest" or "religious leader."

COLEMAN — Means "young servant" and originates from a combination of Old English and Irish elements.

COLESON Means "son of Cole" and originates from the English surname Cole, derived from the Old English word "col," meaning "coal" or "charcoal."

COLSTON Means "from the coal town" and has English origins.

COLT Means "young horse" and originates from Old English.

COLTER Colter is of English origin and means "swarthy or dark-haired."

COLTON Means "from the coal town" and originated as a surname in Old English.

CONAN Means "little wolf" and originates from Irish and Scottish Gaelic.

CONLEY The name Conley originated as an Irish surname derived from the Gaelic Ó Conghaile, meaning "descendant of Conghal."

CONNOR Means "lover of hounds" and is of Irish origin.

CONRAD Means "brave counselor" and has Germanic origins.

CONSTAN Means "steadfast" or "unwavering" and originates from the Latin name "Constantinus,"
TINE derived from the word "constans" meaning "constant" or "steadfast."

CONWAY Means "holy river" or "holy watercourse" and originates from Irish and Welsh origins.

COOPER Means "barrel maker" and originated as an occupational surname in medieval England.

COPELAND Means "from the land by the hilltop" and originated as a surname derived from Old English.

CORBIN Means "raven" and has English and French origins.

CORDELL Means "rope maker" or "maker of cords" and has English origins.

COREY Meaning "from the hollow," Corey is a unisex name of Irish and Gaelic origin.

CORMAC Means "charioteer" or "son of defilement" in Gaelic and originates from Ireland.

CORNELIUS Means "horn" or "horn-bearer" and originates from the Latin name "Cornelius," derived from "cornu," meaning "horn."

CORTEZ Spanish origin and it means "courteous" or "polite."

CRAIG Means "rocky hill" or "dweller by the crag" and originates from the Scottish Gaelic word "creag."

CRAWFORD The first name Crawford originated from Scotland and means "ford at the crow's ford."

CREW The first name "Crew" is of English origin and means "group of people; team; companion."

CRISTIAN Spanish and Italian form of the name Christian, derived from the Latin word "Christianus" meaning "follower of Christ."

CRISTOBAL Spanish origin and means "bearer of Christ" or "Christ-bearer".

CRISTOFER Greek origin and means "bearer of Christ."

CROIX The first name Croix originates from French and it means "cross."

CROSBY Crosby is an English surname turned first name meaning "by the town crossed by streets" and originating from a place called Crosby in England.

CRUZ Meaning "cross" in Spanish, it is of Latin origin and is often used as a surname denoting someone who lived near a cross.

CULLEN Cullen is an Irish name meaning "holly tree" and was originally a surname derived from the Gaelic O Cuilinn.

CURTIS Means "courteous" and originates from old French.

CYLAS Masculine given name of Greek origin meaning "renowned and noble in battle."

CYPRESS Means "evergreen tree" and is of English origin.

CYRUS Means "Sun" and originates from Persia.

DAEMON Means "divine power or spirit" and has its origin in Greek mythology, derived from the word daimon, referring to a supernatural being or deity.

DALLAS Means "meadow dwelling" and originates from a Scottish surname.

DALTON Means "from the valley town" and has English origins.

DAMIAN Means "to tame or subdue" and has origins in Greek and Latin.

DAMON Means "to tame" or "one who subdues" and originates from Greek mythology, derived from the name of a loyal friend of Pythias in the story of Damon and Pythias.

DANDRE The name Dandre originated from the combination of the names Dan and Andre, and it carries the meaning of "God is my judge" or "manly and courageous".

DANIEL Means "God is my judge" and is of Hebrew origin.

DANILO Means "God is my judge" and has Slavic origins.

DARIO Means "possessor of wealth" and it originated from ancient Persia.

DARWIN	The name Darwin originates from Old English and means "dear friend" or "friend of the deer."
DASHIELL	The name Dashiel is of Irish origin and means "adversary" or "cheerful."
DAVID	Means "beloved" or "uncle" and has Hebrew origins.
DAWSON	Means "son of David" and is of Scottish origin.
DAX	Means "leader" or "guiding light" and is of French origin.
DEACON	The name "Deacon" originates from English and means "a religious official or servant."
DEAN	Means "dweller of a valley" and is of English origin.
DEANDRE	Means "from the family of Andrew" and originates from American culture.
DEANGELO	Italian origin and means "of the angel" or "from the angel."
DECKER	Means "roofer" or "thatcher" and has English origins.
DECLAN	Declan is an Irish name meaning "man of prayer" or "full of goodness," derived from the Gaelic word "Deaglán," which was the name of a fifth-century saint.
DEKLYN	Modern American spelling variant of the traditional Irish name Declan, derived from the Gaelic name "Deaglán" meaning "full of goodness."
DEMARCUS	The first name "Demarcus" is of American origin and refers to an individual who is the son of Marcus or has a similar association with the name Marcus.
DEMARI	Means "son of Mary" and has American origins.
DEMARION	Means "of Mars" and has an uncertain origin, possibly emerging from a combination of the name De- and the name Marion.
DEMETRI	Means "follower of Demeter" and its origin can be traced back to ancient Greek mythology.
DEMETRIUS	Means "devoted to Demeter" and originates from Greek mythology.
DEMPSEY	Means "proud" or "proudly judged" and originates from Ireland.
DENNIS	Means "from Dionysus" and is of Greek origin.
DENVER	Means "green valley" and originates from a surname derived from the Old English words "denu" (valley) and "ofer" (riverbank).
DENZEL	Means "from the high stronghold" and originated from the Cornish surname which derives from the place name "St. Denys" in France.
DEONTE	The name Deonte originated from America and it means "of divine and immortal nature."
DEREK	Means "ruler of the people" and originates from Old Germanic.
DESEAN	Means "God is gracious" and is of American origin.
DESHAWN	DESHAWN is an American name of African-American origin, meaning "God is gracious".
DESMOND	Gaelic name meaning "man from south Munster" and is of Irish origin.
DEVANSH	The Hindu name "Devansh" means "part of god" and has origins in Sanskrit.
DEVON	Unisex name of English origin meaning "from Devonshire," a county in England.
DEVONTE	The name Devonte originated in the United States, and it means "belonging to Devon."
DEWAYNE	The first name DeWayne is of American origin and means "from Wayne's homestead."
DEXTER	Means "skillful" or "right-handed" and originated from a Latin surname meaning "dexterous" or "skillful".
DHRUV	Means "fixed" or "firm" in Sanskrit and has its origin in Hindu mythology, referring to the North Star.
DIEGO	Means "supplanter" and originates from the Hebrew name Ya'aqov (Jacob) through the Spanish language.
DIESEL	The name Diesel originated as a surname derived from the German word "tiesel," meaning "resolute" or "bold."
DILLON	Means "faithful, loyal" and has Irish origins.
DIMITRI	Means "follower of Demeter" and has Greek origins.
DOMINGO	Means "Sunday" in Spanish and originates from the Latin word "dies Dominicus" meaning "Lord's day."
DOMINIC	Means "belonging to the Lord" and is of Latin origin.
DOMINIQUE	Means "belonging to the Lord" and is of French origin.
DONALD	Means "world ruler" or "ruler of the world" and originates from Scottish and Gaelic languages.

DONOVAN	Gaelic name meaning "dark-haired prince" and has Irish origins.
DONTAE	American origin and is derived from the combination of the English name Don and the Italian name Dante, meaning "gifted" or "enduring."
DORIAN	Means "of the sea" and has Greek origins.
DOUGLAS	Means "dark water" and has Scottish origins.
DRAKE	Means "dragon" and its origin is English.
DUNCAN	Means "dark warrior" and originated from Scotland and Ireland.
DWAYNE	Means "dark" or "swarthy" and originated from the Irish surname Ó Duibhín, meaning "descendant of Dubhán."
DWIGHT	Means "white or fair" and has English origins.
DYLAN	Welsh name meaning "son of the sea" and is derived from the Welsh god of the sea, Dylan.
EASTON	Easton is an English surname turned first name meaning "east town" or "east settlement."
EDISON	Means "son of Edward" and has English origins.
EDMUND	Means "wealthy protector" and it originates from Old English.
EDRICK	English origin and it means "wealthy ruler" or "ruler with great riches".
EDSON	Means "son of Edward" and has English and Portuguese origins.
EDWARD	Edward means "wealthy guard" or "guardian of prosperity" and originates from Old English.
EDWIN	Edwin means "friend of wealth" and is of Old English origin.
EFRAIN	Means "fruitful" or "abundant" and has Hebrew origins.
EITHAN	Means "strong" or "enduring" and has Hebrew origins.
ELEAZAR	Means "God has helped" and originates from the Hebrew language.
ELI	"Eli" is a Hebrew name meaning "ascended" or "my God", and is often used as a short form of names such as Elijah.
ELIAS	Greek name meaning "Yahweh is God," derived from the Hebrew name Eliyahu.
ELIEL	Means "my God is God" and it originates from Hebrew.
ELIEZER	Means "my God is help" and is of Hebrew origin.
ELIJAH	Means "my God is Yahweh" and is of Hebrew origin.
ELLIOTT	The first name Elliott is of English origin and means "greatly admired" or "the Lord is my God."
ELTON	Means "from the old town" or "from the village by the river," and it originated from Old English.
EMILIANO	Masculine name of Italian and Spanish origin, meaning "rival" or "eager" in Italian.
EMMANUEL	Emmanuel means "God is with us" in Hebrew and is of Christian origin, taken from the Bible.
ENOCH	Biblical name of Hebrew origin meaning "dedicated" or "initiated."
ENRIQUE	Spanish name meaning "ruler of the home" and originates from the Germanic name Heinrich.
ENZO	Means "ruler of the estate" and originates from Italy.
EPHRAIM	Means "fruitful" and it is of Hebrew origin.
ERICK	Scandinavian origin and means "eternal ruler" or "ever-powerful."
ERMIAS	Means "pillar" or "strength" and originates from the Ethiopian Amharic language.
ERNESTO	Means "serious" or "resolute" and is of Italian and Spanish origin.
ESDRAS	Means "helped by God" and has its origin in Hebrew.
ESTEBAN	Spanish male name meaning "crown" or "crowned" and has origins in the Hebrew name Stephen.
ETHAN	Means "strong, firm" and originates from Hebrew.
EUGENE	Means "noble" and originates from the Greek name Eugenios.
EVANDER	Means "good man" or "good-hearted" and originates from Greek mythology, referring to a legendary hero and founder of the city of Pallantium.
EVERARDO	Means "ever brave" and it originates from Old Germanic languages.
EVERETT	Means "brave as a wild boar" and has English origins.
EVREN	Turkish origin and it means "cosmos" or "universe."
EZEKIEL	Means "God strengthens" and it originates from Hebrew.
EZEQUIEL	Means "God strengthens" and originates from the Hebrew name Yehezqel.

EZRA	Hebrew name meaning "helper" or "helper of God," originating from the Bible.
FABIAN	Means "bean grower" and it originates from the Latin name Fabianus, derived from the Roman family name Fabius.
FAHAD	Means "panther" or "cheetah" and its origin can be traced back to Arabic and Islamic cultures.
FAISAL	Means "decisive" or "resolute" and originates from Arabic.
FARHAN	Means "happy" or "joyful" in Arabic, and it originated from Islamic culture.
FEDERICO	Means "peaceful ruler" and it is of Italian and Spanish origin.
FELIX	Means "fortunate" or "lucky" and has Latin origins.
FERNANDO	Fernando means "brave traveler" and is of Spanish origin.
FIDEL	Means "faithful" and it has Latin origins.
FILIP	Means "lover of horses" and originated from the Latin name "Philippus" which means "lover of horses" in Greek.
FINLEY	Means "fair-haired hero" and originated from Ireland and Scotland.
FINN	Meaning "fair" or "white," Finn is a common name in Ireland and Scandinavia often used as a given name or surname.
FINNEAS	Means "fair-haired warrior" and originates from the Irish and Hebrew languages.
FINNEGAN	Means "fair" or "white", and its origin is Irish.
FINNICK	Means "fair leader" and is of Irish origin.
FISCHER	The first name Fischer is of German origin, meaning "fisherman."
FISHER	Means "one who lives near a fisherman's cottage" and has English origins.
FITZGERALD	Means "son of Gerald" and originates from Ireland.
FLETCHER	Means "arrow-maker" and has originated from the Middle English occupational surname for a person who made and sold arrows.
FLYNN	Gaelic name meaning "son of the red-haired one," originated in Ireland.
FORD	Means "from a ford" and has origins in Old English.
FORREST	Means "dweller near the woods" and originates from an English surname derived from the Old French word "forestier," meaning "forest keeper or guardian."
FOSTER	Means "one who looks after or fosters" and is of Old English origin.
FRANCISCO	Means "free man" and has Spanish and Portuguese origins.
FRANK	Germanic origin and means "free man" or "sincere," often associated with honesty and straightforwardness.
FRANKLIN	Means "free landowner" and it originated from an English surname derived from the Middle English word "franklin," referring to a free man who owned land.
FREDDY	Diminutive form of Frederick, meaning "peaceful ruler," and it originated from Germanic and English languages.
FREDERICK	Means "peaceful ruler" and originates from Germanic and Old English origin.
FREDRICK	The name Frederick means "peaceful ruler" and it originates from the Germanic elements "frid" meaning "peace" and "ric" meaning "ruler".
GABRIEL	Means "God is my strength" and has Hebrew origins.
GAEL	Means "one who is generous" and it originates from Gaelic/Celtic languages.
GATLIN	Means "one who comes from the land of the goats" and has English origins.
GAUGE	Means a measuring instrument, and its origin is derived from the English vocabulary word "gauge" referring to a tool for measuring or estimating dimensions.
GAVIN	Meaning of the first name Gavin: A Welsh name meaning "white hawk" or "little falcon", of Celtic origin.
GENARO	Means "noble warrior" and has Spanish roots.
GENTRY	Means "noble" or "gentleman" and originates from English aristocratic rank and title.
GEOFFREY	Means "peaceful ruler" and originates from Germanic roots.
GEORGE	Means "farmer" and is of Greek origin.
GEOVANNY	Spanish origin and it means "God is gracious."
GERARDO	Spanish name meaning "brave with a spear" and originated from Germanic roots.
GERMAN	The first name "German" originated from the Latin name "Germanus" meaning "brother" and is derived from the Latin word "germen" meaning "sprout" or "bud."
GERSON	The name GERSON originates from Hebrew and means "exile" or "stranger."
GIANCARLO	Means "God's gracious gift" and its origin can be traced back to Italy.

GIANLUCA Means "John the Wolf" and has Italian origins.

GIBSON Means "son of Gilbert" and has an English origin.

GIDEON Means "mighty warrior" or "one who cuts down", and it originates from the Hebrew language.

GILBERT Means "bright pledge" and originates from Germanic and Old English roots.

GIORGIO Means "farmer" and it has Italian and Greek origins.

GIOVANNI Giovanni is an Italian name meaning "God is gracious" and is the Italian form of the name John.

GIUSEPPE Means "God shall add" in Italian and has its origin in Hebrew.

GONZALO Means "battle" or "war" and it originates from Spanish and Portuguese cultures.

GORDON Scottish origin and it means "spacious fortification" or "hill fort".

GRADY Grady means "noble" or "renowned" and has Irish origins.

GRAEME Means "gray home" or "gravelly homestead" and originates from Scotland.

GRAHAM Means "gravelly homestead" in Old English, derived from the words "grāf" (gravel) and "hām" (homestead).

GRANGER Means "farmer" or "someone who lives by a granary" and has English origins.

GRANT The name Grant originated from Scotland and means "tall, large".

GRAYSON Means "son of the bailiff" and originates from Old English.

GREGORY Means "vigilant, watchful" and has Latin origins.

GREYSEN Means "son of the servant of Gregory" and is of American origin.

GRIFFIN Means "strong lord" and has Welsh origins.

GUILLERMO Means "will, desire, protection" and has Spanish origins.

GUNNER Means "warrior" or "soldier" and has Scandinavian origins.

GUSTAVO Spanish and Italian name meaning "staff of the Goths" and is of Germanic origin.

GUY French origin and means "guide" or "leader."

HAKEEM Means "wise" or "judicious" and it has Arabic origins.

HAMILTON Means "beautiful mountain" and is of Scottish origin.

HAMPTON The first name Hampton originates from the Old English language meaning "enclosed settlement."

HAMZA Means "strong" or "steadfast" and it has Arabic origins.

HANSEL German diminutive form of the given name Hans, meaning "God is gracious," and it originated from the Germanic language.

HARLAN Means "from the hare's land" and it originates from Old English and Old Norse.

HARLEM Unisex name of African American origin that refers to a neighborhood in New York City known for its rich cultural history and influence on the arts.

HAROLD Means "ruler of an army" and originates from Old English.

HARRISON Harrison means "son of Harry" and is of English origin.

HARVEY French origin and means "battle-worthy" or "strong and worthy of battle."

HASHIM Means "destroyer of evil" and it has Arabic origins.

HASSAN Means "handsome" or "good" in Arabic, and it is of Arabic origin.

HAWKINS Means "son of hawk," and it originates from the English surname, derived from the medieval given name "Hawkyn."

HAYES Means "hedged area" and originates from Old English.

HEATH Means "heathland dweller" and originates from Old English.

HECTOR Means "holding fast" and originated from Greek mythology as the name of a Trojan hero.

HENDRIX Means "son of Hendrick" and is of Dutch origin.

HENRY Means "ruler of the home" and originated from Germanic roots.

HERBERT Means "bright army" and originates from Germanic roots.

HERIBERTO Means "illustrious warrior" and has Spanish and Germanic origins.

HERNAN Means "ardent" or "passionate" and has its origins in Spanish and Portuguese.

HEZEKIAH The first name Hezekiah originates from the Hebrew language and means "God gives strength" or "Yahweh strengthens".

HIRO Means "generous" or "abundant" in Japanese and has its origin from the Japanese language.

HOLDEN Modern English name of unknown origin, meaning "hollow valley".

HOLLIS HOLLIS means "dweller at the holly trees" in Old English, and is of English origin.

HOUSTON Meaning "hill town," Houston is a name of Scottish origin that is inspired by a town in Renfrewshire, Scotland.

HOWARD Means "brave heart" or "high guardian" and originates from Old English.

HOYT Means "spirit of the woods" and it has American origin.

HUCK Means "lucky, fortunate" and originates from the Germanic name Hug, which means "mind, heart, spirit."

HUDSON Meaning "son of Hudde," Hudson is of English origin and can also refer to "son of Hugh."

HUGO The name Hugo originates from Germanic and means "bright in mind and spirit."

HUMBERTO Spanish name meaning "bright warrior" and it originated from Germanic roots.

HUNTER Means someone who hunts and it originated as an English occupational surname for those who hunted wild animals for a living.

HUNTLEY Huntley is of Old English origin, meaning "meadow of the hunter."

HUSSEIN Means "handsome" or "good" and has Arabic origins.

HUXLEY Unisex name of English origin meaning "from Hucca's wood or meadow."

HUXTON English origin and means "from the enclosed settlement."

HYRUM Hebrew origin and it means "my brother is exalted."

IAN "Ian is a Scottish name meaning 'gift from God'."

IBRAHIM Means "father of many nations" and originates from the Arabic language.

IDRIS Gender-neutral name of Arabic origin that means "interpreter" or "one who interprets dreams," and is also associated with the prophet Idris in Islamic tradition.

IGNACIO Spanish male name derived from the Latin name Ignatius, meaning "fiery" or "ardent".

IGNATIUS Means "fiery" and is of Latin origin.

IKER Means "visitation" or "caregiver" and it has Basque origins.

ILYAS Means "god is my god" and originates from Arabic and Hebrew roots.

IMRAN Means "prosperity" or "prosperous" and it originates from Arabic and Islamic cultures.

IRVING Means "green river" or "friend of the sea" and originated from a Scottish and English surname.

ISAAC Means "he will laugh" and originates from Hebrew.

ISAIAH Means "Yahweh is salvation" and is of Hebrew origin.

ISHMAEL Means "God will hear" and it originates from Hebrew.

ISIDRO Means "gift of Isis" and has Spanish and Portuguese origins.

ISMAIL Means "God will hear" and it has Arabic and Hebrew origins.

ISRAEL Means "God contends" and is of Hebrew origin.

ISREAL Means "God perseveres" and is of Hebrew origin.

ITZAE Means "water sorcerer" in Mayan culture and originates from the Yucatan Peninsula in Mexico.

IVERSON Means "son of Ivor" and has Scandinavian origins.

IZAAK Means "laughter" or "he will laugh" and originates from the Hebrew name Yitzhak, deriving from the Old Testament figure Isaac.

IZAYAH The name Izayah has a Hebrew origin and means "Yahweh is my salvation."

JACEON Modern American name with uncertain origin, possibly derived from the combination of the names Jason and Jayceon.

JACK Means "God is gracious" and is of English origin.

JACKSON English name meaning "son of Jack", derived from the Middle English personal name Jakke, which is a pet form of John.

JACQUES French origin and it means "supplanter" or "to seize by the heel."

JAHAZIEL Means "God beholds" and originates from Hebrew.

JAHEIM Means "raised up, exalted" and has African-American origins.

JAHMIR Means "a noble and honorable individual" and its origin is uncertain, possibly derived from Arabic or Hebrew origins.

JAHSEH The first name Jahseh is of American origin and means "God raises" or "God exalts."

JAHZIEL Hebrew name meaning "God's sight" or "God shines."

JAIME Spanish name meaning "supplanter" and is the Spanish form of James.

JAIRUS Biblical name of Hebrew origin meaning "he enlightens," referencing a biblical character known for seeking enlightenment and healing.

JAKARI Jakari is an African American name of unknown origin, meaning "young at heart" or "just and true."

JAKHARI	Means "young man" or "youthful" and its origin is African, specifically Swahili.
JAKHI	Means "god is gracious" and has African American origins.
JAKOB	The name Jakob originated from the Hebrew name Yaakov, meaning "supplanter" or "holder of the heel."
JALEN	Means "from the high or lofty" and is of American origin.
JAMAL	Means "beauty" or "handsome" and has Arabic and Islamic origins.
JAMARCUS	The first name Jamarcus is of African American origin and its meaning is derived from combining the name elements "Jamal" and "Marcus," resulting in a combination of their respective meanings and associations.
JAMES	Means "supplanter" and is of Hebrew origin.
JAMESON	"Jameson means 'son of James' and is of English origin."
JAQUAN	Jaquan is of American origin and means "a combination of the names Jason and Quan."
JARED	Hebrew name meaning "descent" or "to descend."
JARVIS	The name Jarvis originated from Old French and means "servant or steward of the spear."
JASAI	Unknown origin, does not have a widely known meaning.
JASPER	Name of Old French origin meaning "treasurer" or "bringer of treasure."
JAVION	Modern American name of uncertain origin, possibly a combination of the names Jason and Avion.
JAWAD	The Arabic name Jawad means "generous" or "noble" and is of Islamic origin.
JAXON	Modern American name derived from the surname Jackson, meaning "son of Jack."
JAXSON	Means "son of Jack" and is a modern variant of the name Jackson, which is of English origin.
JAXSTON	Means "son of Jack" and has American origins.
JAXTYN	The name Jaxtyn originated in modern times and is a variant of the name Jaxon/Jackson, meaning "son of Jack" or "God has been gracious."
JAYCEON	Modern American name derived from the combination of "Jay" and "ceon," possibly inspired by the name "Jason" or "Jayden."
JAYCOB	Variant spelling of Jacob, derived from the Hebrew name Ya'aqov, meaning "supplanter" or "heel grabber".
JAYDEN	Modern name of American origin that is a combination of the names Jay and Aiden, signifying an interpretation of "thankful" or "God has heard".
JAYVIAN	American origin and it means "God is gracious".
JAYVON	The first name Jayvon is of American origin and its meaning is derived from combining the names Jay and Devon, possibly symbolizing a variation or blend of the two names.
JAZIAH	Means "God has apportioned" and it has Hebrew origins.
JAZIEL	Means "God divides" and it is of Hebrew origin.
JEDIDIAH	Means "beloved of the Lord" and has Hebrew origins.
JEFFERSON	The name Jefferson originated as a surname meaning "son of Jeffrey" and now commonly refers to someone named after Thomas Jefferson, the third President of the United States.
JEFFERY	Means "peaceful ruler" and is of Germanic origin.
JEFFREY	Means "peaceful ruler" and originated from the Old German name Geffrey, which was derived from the Old French name Geoffrey.
JENNINGS	Jennings is an English surname-derived first name, meaning "son of John" and dating back to medieval times.
JENSEN	Meaning "son of Jens," Jensen is a Danish and Norwegian surname turned first name.
JEREMIAH	Means "God will exalt" and has Hebrew origins.
JEREMY	Means "appointed by god" and is of biblical origin.
JERICHO	Means "city of palm trees" and is of Hebrew origin.
JERMAINE	Jermaine means "brother" and has English and French origins.
JEROME	Means "sacred name" and originated from the Greek name Hieronymos.
JERONIMO	The first name Jeronimo is of Spanish origin and it means "sacred name," often associated with Saint Jerome.
JESUS	Means "God is salvation" and originates from the Greek name Iesous, which was derived from the Hebrew name Yeshua.

JETHRO	The first name Jethro originally derives from Hebrew and means "excellence" or "abundance."
JETT	Meaning "jet black" or "black gemstone," the name Jett is of English origin and is inspired by the dark, sleek mineral.
JETTSON	Means "son of Jett" and it has no specific origin as it is likely a modern creation or variant of the surname Jett.
JIMMY	Diminutive form of the name James and originated in medieval England.
JIRAIYA	Means "young thunder" and has its origin in Japanese folklore and mythology.
JIREH	Means "God will provide" and is of Hebrew origin.
JOAO	Means "God is gracious" and it originates from the Hebrew name Yochanan.
JOAQUIN	Means "God will establish" and it comes from the Hebrew name Yochanan, which later evolved into the Spanish name Joaquín.
JOHN	Means "God is gracious" and originates from the Hebrew name Yochanan.
JOHNATHAN	Means "gift of God" and originates from the Hebrew name Yehohanan (Yahweh has been gracious).
JOHNNIE	Unisex name meaning "God is gracious," and is a variation of the name John, which originates from Hebrew.
JOHNPAUL	Compound name combining the names John and Paul, with the origin being derived from Hebrew (John) and Latin (Paul) origins.
JOHNSON	The first name Johnson, of English origin, means "son of John" or "God is gracious".
JONAH	Means "dove" in Hebrew and originates from the biblical story of the prophet who was swallowed by a whale and later saved.
JONATHAN	Means "gift of God" and is of Hebrew origin.
JORDAN	Means "to descend" and has biblical origins, referring to a river in Israel where Jesus was baptized.
JORGE	Spanish name meaning "farmer" or "husbandman," originating from the Greek name Georgios.
JOSE	Means "God will increase" and originates from the Hebrew name Yosef.
JOSELUIS	Means "God will increase" and it is a combination of the names Jose and Luis.
JOSEPH	Means "God will increase" and originates from Hebrew.
JOSHUA	Means "God is salvation" and originates from the Hebrew name Yehoshu'a.
JOSIAH	Meaning "Yahweh supports," Josiah is a Hebrew name originating from the Bible, where it was the name of a king of Judah known for his religious reforms.
JOVANNI	Means "God is gracious" and it is of Italian origin.
JUAN	Spanish name meaning "God is gracious" and is of Hebrew origin.
JUANCARLOS	Spanish origin and is a combination of the names Juan and Carlos, meaning "gracious gift of God who is strong and noble."
JUANPABLO	Spanish masculine given name that originated in Latin America, combining the names "Juan" and "Pablo" to create a compound name.
JUDE	Means "praised" or "from Judaea" and has Hebrew and Greek origins.
JUELZ	Modern American name of uncertain origin meaning "strong" or "brave."
JULIAN	Name of Latin origin meaning "youthful" or "downy-bearded."
JULIUS	Means "youthful" in Latin and is of Roman origin.
JUNIOR	Latin origin and means "younger" or "son" denoting a child with the same name as their father, usually used as a suffix to the given name.
JUSTICE	Means "righteousness" and comes from the Latin word "justitia."
JUSTUS	Latin name meaning "fair" or "just," and is derived from the Roman family name Iustus.
KABIR	Means "great, powerful" and originates from Arabic and Persia.
KACEY	English origin and means "vigilant" or "alert."
KADYN	Modern Americanized spelling variant of the traditional Irish name Caden, meaning "battle" or "companion."
KAEDEN	The meaning of the name Kaeden is "fighter" and it originates from American English.
KAHLIL	Means "friend" or "companion" and has Arabic origins.
KAI	Unisex name of Hawaiian origin meaning "ocean" or "sea".
KAIRO	Means "victorious" or "triumphant" and originated from the Maori language.

KAISER   Means "emperor" or "ruler" and originates from the German language.

KAIUS   Means "rejoice" and originates from the Latin language.

KAIZEN   Means "continuous improvement" in Japanese and is often associated with the business philosophy focused on constant and incremental progress.

KALEL   Means "voice of God" or "strong voice" and has Hebrew origins.

KAMARI   Swahili name meaning "like the moon" and is often given to boys or girls.

KAMARION   Uncertain origin, is a modern American name likely created by combining elements from different cultural sources.

KAMDYN   Modern variation of the name Camden, derived from a place name in England meaning "winding valley."

KAMREN   Variation of the name Cameron and originates from Scotland, meaning "crooked nose."

KANAN   Sanskrit origin, means "forest" or "dweller of the forest."

KAREEM   Kareem is an Arabic name meaning "generous" or "noble", and it is of Islamic origin.

KARMELO   Basque origin and it means "orchard" or "garden of fruit."

KARTIER   Modern, creative spelling variation of the name Cartier, which is of French origin and means "cart driver" or "carrier of a cart".

KASEN   Modern American name of uncertain origin, possibly derived from the Japanese word for "spring."

KASHMIR   Unisex name of Arabic origin meaning "from the beautiful land".

KAYSON   Means "rejoice" or "son of Kay" and has American origin.

KEATON   Surname turned first name of English origin meaning "place of hawks".

KEEGAN   Means "small fire" and is of Irish origin.

KEITH   Means "wooded area" or "forest" and originated from Scotland.

KEKOA   Hawaiian name meaning "brave" or "courageous" and is of Hawaiian origin.

KENDRICK   Means "royal ruler" and is of Old English origin.

KENTRELL   Means "slender, small village" and has American origins.

KENYON   The first name Kenyon originated from the Gaelic language and means "blond-haired or fair one."

KEYON   Means "God is gracious" and it has African American and Irish origins.

KHALIL   Meaning "friend" or "companion" in Arabic, Khalil is a popular name in the Muslim world, especially among Arabic-speaking populations.

KHAMARI   Modern American name of uncertain origin, likely derived from a combination of other popular names such as Kamari and Khaleem.

KHAZA   The name KHAZA meaning "leader" originates from Arabic/Islamic culture.

KHYREE   African origin and it means "honorable ruler."

KINGSLEY   Means "from the King's meadow" and originates from Old English.

KINGSTON   Means "king's town" and originates from Old English and Old Norse.

KIPTON   The first name Kipton is an American name of uncertain origin, most likely a modern variant of the name Kip.

KLAY   Modern variant of the name Clay, derived from the English word for "earthen clay" and has an English origin.

KNIGHT   Means "warrior" or "servant of the king" and originates from the English language.

KNOWLEDGE   Means having an understanding or awareness about various subjects, and it is a modern English word name derived from the Middle English term "knawliche," meaning "cognition" or "knowledge."

KNOX   Means "round hill" and it originates from a Scottish surname derived from the Gaelic word "cnoc" meaning hill or hillock.

KOBE   Means "tortoise" or "door" in Japanese, and is also associated with the NBA basketball star Kobe Bryant.

KODA   Means "friend" or "companion" and originates from Native American cultures, particularly the Sioux tribe.

KOLBY   Old Norse origin and means "dark haired".

KOLSON   The name KOLSON originated from the Scandinavian language and it means "son of Cole" or "victorious people."

KOLTEN The first name KOLTEN is of German origin and means "coal town" or "coal settlement."

KORBEN The first name "Korben" is a modern variation of the name Corbin, derived from the Latin word "corvus" meaning "raven," and it has English and French origins.

KRISHIV The first name Krishiv is of Indian origin and means "someone who is lord Krishna's blessing and manifestation."

KRISHNA Sanskrit name meaning "black" or "dark" and is a popular name in Hinduism, given to the eighth avatar of the god Vishnu.

KRISTOPHER Variation of the name Christopher, which means "bearer of Christ" and derives from the Greek name Christophoros.

KROSS The first name Kross, of American origin, means "cross" or "crossing" and is often associated with religious or symbolic significance.

KURT Means "bold counselor" and it has Germanic origins.

KYLIAN Means "warrior" or "little church" and it has Irish and Dutch origins.

KYLO Means "sky" and is of American origin.

KYMANI Name of Jamaican origin meaning "adventurous" or "adventurer."

KYREN American origin and means "little dark one."

KYRIE Means "lord" or "lord have mercy" in Greek and is of Christian origin.

KYZER The name "Kyzer" originated from the German word "Kaiser" meaning emperor or ruler, symbolizing power and authority.

LACHLAN Means "land of lochs" and is of Scottish origin.

LANCE Means "a warrior or knight with a lance" and it originates from the Old French word "lance" meaning "a spear or lance."

LANDON Meaning "from the long hill," Landon is of English origin.

LANGSTON Means "long stone" and originates from English and Old Norse.

LARS The first name Lars has Danish and Norwegian origins and it means "crowned with laurel" or "from Laurentum."

LAVON Means "white" in Hebrew and is of Hebrew origin.

LAWRENCE Means "from Laurentum" and originated from the ancient Roman city Laurentum.

LAZARUS Means "God is my helper" and originates from the Greek name Lazaros, derived from Hebrew Eleazar.

LEANDER Means "lion man" or "lion of a man" and has Greek origins.

LEANDRO Spanish and Portuguese masculine given name meaning "lion-like" and originating from the Greek name Leandros.

LEDGER Means "bookkeeper" or "scribe" and originated from Old English, ultimately derived from the Middle English word "leger" or "ligger," which referred to a person who kept records or accounts.

LEGEND Means a traditional story sometimes popularly regarded as historical but unauthenticated, originating from the English word for a story handed down from earlier times.

LELAND Meaning: From a surname which was derived from a place name meaning "fallow land" in Old English. Origin: English.

LEMUEL The name Lemuel has Hebrew origins and means "devoted to God" or "belonging to God".

LENNOX The meaning of the first name Lennox is "place with elm trees" and it has Scottish origins.

LEON Means "lion" and has origins in Greek and Germanic languages.

LEONARDO Means "brave lion" and originates from Italy.

LEONEL Means "lion" or "lion-like" and has Spanish and Portuguese origins.

LEONIDAS Means "lion's son" and has Greek origins.

LEOPOLD Means "bold people" and originates from the Germanic language.

LEROY Means "the king" and originates from French.

LESTER Means "from the fort by the river," and it originated as a surname in England.

LEVI Means "attached" in Hebrew and has biblical origins.

LEVIATHAN Means "great sea monster" and derives from the Hebrew word "livyathan," mentioned in the Bible as a powerful creature symbolizing chaos and untamed forces of nature.

LEVITICUS Means "belonging to or pertaining to Levites" and has its origin in the Hebrew Bible, specifically the book of Leviticus.

LEXINGTON Unisex name of English origin referring to a town in Massachusetts, USA.

LIAM Means "resolute protector" and originates from Irish and Gaelic languages.

LINCOLN Means "town by the pool" and originates from Old English.

LINKIN English origin and means "lives near a bank or slope."

LINUS Greek origin and means "flaxen" or "fair-haired," referring to a person with light-colored hair.

LISANDRO Means "liberator" and is of Greek origin.

LLOYD Means "grey-haired" or "grey-haired warrior" and originates from the Welsh language.

LOCKE Old English origin and it means "from the fortified place; a lock or fastening."

LOGAN Means "dweller at a little hollow" and has Gaelic origins.

LORENZO Italian origin and means "renowned warrior."

LOUIS Means "renowned warrior" and originates from the Germanic name Hludowig, composed of the elements "hlud" meaning "fame" and "wig" meaning "warrior".

LUCAS Means "light" and is of Greek origin.

LUIS Means "renowned warrior" and originates from the Germanic name Hludowig, which was brought to Spain by the Visigoths.

LUKE Means "light-giving" and originates from the Latin name "Lucas" which means "from Lucania."

LUTHER Means "famous warrior" or "army of the people" and originated from Germany.

MACKLIN Means "son of the bare one" and originates from the Scottish and Irish surnames MacGilleFhinnein or MacGilfinnan.

MADDOX Means "fortunate" or "blessed" and it originated from Welsh and Cornish languages.

MAGNUS Means "great" or "mighty" and originates from Latin.

MAHDI Means "guided one" and originates from Arabic Islamic traditions.

MAHMOUD The first name Mahmoud has Arabic origins and means "praiseworthy" or "commendable."

MAISON French name meaning "house" or "home", originating from the French word for "house".

MAKOA Means "brave" or "fearless" and has Hawaiian origins.

MAKSIM Masculine name that is of Slavic origin and means "the greatest" or "the greatest one."

MALACHI Hebrew name meaning "my messenger" or "my angel," and it is of biblical origin, originating from the Book of Malachi in the Old Testament.

MALAKAI Means "my messenger" or "messenger of God" and has Hebrew origins.

MALCOLM Means "follower of Saint Columba" and originated from Scotland.

MALIK Arabic name meaning "king" or "master", and it is of Islamic origin.

MAMADOU The first name Mamadou is of West African origin meaning "given by God" or "praised by God".

MANOLO Spanish diminutive of Manuel, originating from the Hebrew name Immanuel meaning "God is with us."

MARCELO Means "young warrior" and it originates from Latin.

MARCUS Means "battle" or "warlike" and is of Latin origin.

MARLON Name of English origin meaning "little hawk" or "falcon."

MARQUEZ The first name Marquez, of Spanish origin, means "nobleman" or "lord."

MARQUIS Means "nobleman" and originates from the Latin word "marcus" meaning "hammer" or "warrior".

MARSHALL Means "caretaker of horses" and originated from Old French and Old English.

MARTIN Means "warrior" and originates from the Latin name Martinus, derived from Mars, the Roman god of war.

MASON Means "worker in stone" and is of English origin.

MASSIMO The Italian name Massimo means "greatest" and originates from Latin.

MATEO Means "gift of God" and has Spanish and Portuguese origins.

MATHIAS Means "gift of Yahweh" and has origins in Hebrew and Greek.

MATIAS Hebrew origin, means "gift of God" or "God's gift."

MATTHEW Means "gift of God" and originates from the Hebrew name Matityahu.

MAURICIO Means "dark-skinned" and originates from Latin.

MAURO Means "dark-skinned" or "Moorish" and it has Latin origins.

MAVERICK Means "an independent, non-conformist person" and originates from the surname Maverick, derived from the term "maverick" referring to an unbranded stray calf in the language of southwest United States cattle ranchers.

MAVRICK	Means "a free-spirited and independent individual" and has its origin in American English.
MAXIMIL IANO	Means "greatness" or "greatest" and has Latin origins.
MAXIMUS	Means "greatest" and it originates from Latin.
MAXWELL	Scottish surname turned first name meaning "Mack's stream" and originates from the Old English words "mæcg" (Mack) and "well" (stream).
MAZEN	Means "rain clouds" in Arabic and it is of Arabic origin.
MCCOY	The first name McCoy, of Irish origin, means "son of Aodh" or "fire."
MEKHI	Masculine given name of Swahili origin, meaning "who is like God."
MELVIN	The first name Melvin, of English origin, means "council protector" or "friend of the council."
MEMPHIS	Masculine given name of Greek origin, meaning "established and beautiful".
MENACHEM	Means "comforter" or "consoler" and originates from Hebrew.
MENDEL	Means "comfort" or "comforter" and originated from the Hebrew language.
MESSIAH	Means "anointed one" and has Hebrew origins.
MEYER	Means "bringer of light" and it has German and Jewish origins.
MICAH	Hebrew name meaning "who is like God" and is of biblical origin.
MICAIAH	Means "Who is like the Lord?" and originates from Hebrew.
MICHAEL	Means "who is like God" and originates from the Hebrew name Mikha'el.
MICHEAL	Means "who is like God" and has origins in Hebrew.
MICHELA NGELO	Means "angelic messenger" and it originated from Italian.
MICKEY	Diminutive form of the name Michael, meaning "who is like God," and has American origins.
MIGUEL	Means "Who is like God?" in Spanish and Portuguese and is of Hebrew origin.
MIGUELA NGEL	Means "who is like God" and has Spanish origins.
MIKEL	Basque variant of the name Michael, meaning "Who is like God?" in Hebrew.
MIKHAIL	Means "who is like God" and originates from Hebrew.
MILAN	Means "gracious" and originates from the Slavic word for "beloved".
MILES	Means "soldier" and is of Latin origin.
MILTON	Means "settlement with a mill" and is of Old English origin.
MISAEL	Means "who is like God" and is of Hebrew origin.
MITCHELL	Masculine given name of English origin meaning "who is like God".
MOHAMED	Arabic origin and means "praised" or "worthy of praise", commonly used in Islamic culture.
MOISES	Means "drawn out of the water" in Hebrew and is of biblical origin, referring to the prophet Moses who was saved from the Nile River as a baby.
MONTE	Means "mountain" and it has Italian and Spanish origins.
MONTGOM ERY	Montgomery means "mountain belonging to the ruler" and has English origins.
MORDECAI	Means "warrior" or "devotion to God" and originates from the Hebrew Bible, particularly the book of Esther.
MORDECHAI	Means "warrior" or "given by God" and has biblical origins.
MORRISON	Means "son of Morris" and originates from the Scottish and Irish surnames Mac Murchadhain or O Muireadhaigh.
MOSHE	Means "drawn out of the water" and has Hebrew origins.
MUHAMMAD	Means "praiseworthy" and it originates from Arabic.
MUSA	Means "to draw out" or "to save" and originates from the Arabic language, derived from the Hebrew name Moses.
MUSTAFA	Means "chosen one" or "the chosen" in Arabic, and it is of Arabic origin.
NAFTALI	Means "my struggle" or "my wrestling" and originates from Hebrew.
NASH	Means "by the ash tree" and is of English origin.
NATAN	Means "gift of God" in Hebrew and is of biblical origin.
NATANAEL	Means "gift of God" or "God has given" and originates from Hebrew.
NATHAN	Means "gift of God" and comes from the Hebrew name נָתָן (Natan).

NATHANIEL Means "gift of God" and is of Hebrew origin.

NAZIR Means "observer" or "supervisor" and originates from Arabic.

NEHEMIAH Means "Yahweh comforts" in Hebrew and is of biblical origin, stemming from the Old Testament figure who rebuilt the walls of Jerusalem.

NEIL Means "champion" and has origins in both Irish and Scottish cultures.

NELSON Means "son of Neil" and originates from the Old English language.

NESTOR Means "wisdom" and originates from Greek mythology, specifically from Nestor, the wise king of Pylos in Homer's Iliad and Odyssey.

NEYMAR Means "sea boy" and has Brazilian Portuguese origins.

NIALL Means "champion" or "cloud" and has Irish and Scottish origins.

NICHOLAS Male given name of Greek origin meaning "victory of the people."

NICO Greek origin and typically means "victory" or "people of victory."

NICOLAS Means "victory of the people" and is of Greek origin.

NIGEL The name Nigel, which originated from the Latin name Nigellus, means "champion" or "black-haired" and is of English origin.

NIKHIL Means "whole, complete" and originates from the Sanskrit language.

NIKITA Means "unconquered" or "victorious" and has Russian origin.

NIKLAUS Means "victorious people" and originates from the Germanic name Nikolaus.

NIKOLAI Means "victorious" and originated from the Russian and Slavic languages.

NOAH Means "rest" or "comfort" in Hebrew and is of biblical origin, being the name of a character in the Old Testament who built an ark to survive a great flood.

NOLEN The name Nolen originated from Irish and it means "champion" or "descendant of Nuallán."

NORMAN Means "northern man" and originates from Old Germanic and Old Norse languages.

OBADIAH Means "servant of Yahweh" and originates from Hebrew.

OBED Means "worshipper" in Hebrew, and it originates from the Old Testament of the Bible, as it is the name of a character mentioned in the Book of Ruth who was the son of Boaz and Ruth.

OCEAN Means "large body of salt water" and originates from the Latin word "Oceanus," which was the name of a titan in Greek mythology who was believed to be the divine personification of the World Ocean.

ODIN Norse origin, means "fury" or "inspiration" and is derived from the Old Norse word "óðr."

OLIVER Means "olive tree" and originates from the Latin name "Oliverus" derived from the word "oliva" meaning "olive".

OMARI Swahili name that means "God is high" or "populous nation."

OMARION Arabic origin and it means "eloquent or flourishing."

ONYX Means "precious gemstone" and has Greek origins.

ORION Greek name meaning "son of fire" or "hunter," originating from Greek mythology as a legendary hunter renowned for his strength and beauty.

ORLANDO Means "famous land" and has Latin origins.

OSCAR Oscar means "divine strength" and originates from Old English and Old Norse.

OSIEL Means "divine strength" and has its origins in Hebrew.

OSIRIS Greek name meaning "powerful" or "strong", derived from the Egyptian god of the afterlife and the underworld.

OSMAN Means "protection" or "one who is protected," and it originates from Arabic.

OSVALDO The first name Osvaldo originated from the Germanic name "Ansaldo" meaning "divine ruler" and it is commonly used in Spanish and Italian-speaking countries.

OTTO Means "wealthy" or "prosperous" and has Germanic origins.

OWEN Welsh name meaning "young warrior" and comes from the Gaelic name Eoghan.

OZIAS Means "strength of God" and originates from Hebrew.

PARKER Meaning: Occupational surname meaning "keeper of the park" or "park keeper."

PATRICK Means "nobleman" and originated from the Latin name Patricius, which means "noble" or "inheritance."

PATTON	Means "from the warrior's town" and has an English origin.
PAUL	Means "small" or "humble" and comes from the Latin name Paulus.
PAXTON	"Paxton" is an English name meaning "peace town" and is of Old English origin.
PEDRO	Meaning "rock" or "stone" in Spanish, Pedro is a popular name of Spanish and Portuguese origin.
PERSEUS	Means "destroyer" or "hero" and it originates from Greek mythology, as Perseus was a legendary hero who slew the Gorgon Medusa.
PETER	Means "rock" or "stone" and is of Greek origin.
PHARAOH	Means "great house" or "palace" in Egyptian, and it originated from the ancient Egyptian title given to the ruler of Egypt.
PHILIP	Means "lover of horses" and it originated from the Greek name Philippos, derived from the elements "philein" meaning "to love" and "hippos" meaning "horse".
PHINEAS	Means "oracle" or "the Nubian" and originates from Hebrew biblical times.
PHOENIX	Gender-neutral name meaning "a mythical bird that rises from its own ashes" and is of Greek origin.
PIERCE	"Pierce" is an English surname turned first name meaning "son of Piers" or "rock" and originates from medieval England.
PIERSON	Surname-derived first name of English origin, meaning "son of Peter."
PORTER	Porter means "gatekeeper" or "doorkeeper" and is of English origin.
PRANAV	Means "sacred syllable OM" and has its origin in the Sanskrit language.
PRESTON	Means "from the priest's town" and is of Old English origin.
PRINCE	The name "Prince" originates from the English language and signifies a royal or noble title given to a son of a monarch or a ruling family.
PRINCETON	Means "the prince's town" and originates from the English language.
QUADIR	Means "capable, powerful" and it originates from Arabic.
QUENTIN	Means "fifth" and originated from the Latin name Quintinus.
QUEST	Means a search or a journey for knowledge or truth, and its origin is English.
QUINCY	Means "estate of the fifth son" and originates from an English surname.
QUINTON	Means "the fifth" and has Latin origins.
RAFAEL	The first name Rafael is of Hebrew origin and means "God has healed" or "God has cured."
RAGNAR	Means "warrior" and originates from Old Norse.
RAHEEM	Arabic origin, means "merciful" or "compassionate."
RALPH	Means "wolf counsel" and originates from Old Norse and Old English.
RAMIRO	Means "supreme judge" or "wise ruler" and it has Spanish and Portuguese origins.
RAMSES	Means "son of Ra" and has its origins in ancient Egyptian culture.
RANDY	Means "shield of wolves" and is of English origin.
RANSOM	Means "redemption" or "rescue," and it has its origins in Old English.
RAPHAEL	Means "God has healed" and it originates from Hebrew.
RASHAD	Means "rightly guided" in Arabic and it has an Islamic origin.
RAYMOND	"Raymond" is a masculine given name of Germanic origin that means "advice" or "protector."
REGINALD	Means "ruler's advisor" and it originates from Old English and Germanic languages.
REID	Scottish surname that means "red-haired" or "ruddy complexion," and is often used as a first name in modern English-speaking countries.
REMINGTON	Name of English origin meaning "from the raven farm," derived from the Old English words "hraefn" (raven) and "tun" (farm).
REUBEN	Means "behold, a son" and has Hebrew origins.
REVAN	Means "one who is blessed with divine grace" and its origin is uncertain, but it gained popularity through the Star Wars Expanded Universe character named Revan.
REYANSH	The name Reayansh means "part of Lord Vishnu" and originates from the Sanskrit language.
REYNALDO	Means "ruler's advisor" and has Spanish and Portuguese origins.
RHETT	Means "enthusiasm" or "counsel" and it originates from the Welsh language.
RHODES	Surname-turned-first name meaning "from the island of roses" and derived from the Greek island of the same name.

RHYDER	The meaning of the first name Rhyder is "horseman" and it is of Old English origin.
RHYS	Welsh name meaning "enthusiastic" or "ardor," derived from the Old Welsh word "Rhys" meaning "ardor" or "passion."
RICARDO	Means "powerful ruler" and originates from the Spanish and Portuguese languages.
RICHARD	Means "strong ruler" and originated from Germanic languages.
RICKY	Ricky means "dominant ruler" and is a diminutive form of the name Richard, of Old German origin.
RIDGE	Means "a long, narrow elevated land formation" and originates from Old English.
RIGGINS	Means "son of Rigan" and has English origins.
RIGOBERTO	Means "bright fame" and originates from Germanic origins.
RIOT	Means a state of disorder, chaos, or violence, and originated from the Old Irish word "riod" meaning wild or vehement.
RISHI	Means "sage" or "seer" and originates from Sanskrit, an ancient Indo-Aryan language from India.
RIVER	Means "a natural flowing watercourse" and originates from the English word for a body of water.
ROBERT	Means "bright fame" and originates from Germanic roots.
ROCCO	The first name Rocco originated from Italy and means "rock" or "rest."
ROCKWELL	Means "rocky well" and has English origins.
RODERICK	Means "renowned ruler" in Old German, and it has Gaelic and Old Germanic origins.
RODNEY	Means "island clearing" and is of Old English origin.
RODOLFO	Means "famous wolf" and originates from Germanic roots.
RODRIGO	Means "renowned ruler" and originated from the Germanic elements "hrod" (fame) and "ric" (ruler).
ROGELIO	Means "famous spear" and originates from the Spanish and Portuguese languages.
ROMAN	Means "from Rome" and originates from the Latin name "Romanus."
ROMEO	Means "pilgrim to Rome" and originates from Italian and Latin.
RONIN	Means "a samurai without a master" and is of Japanese origin.
RORY	Means "red king" and is of Irish origin.
ROSCOE	The first name Roscoe is of English origin and means "deer forest" or "wood of the roe deer."
ROWDY	Means "noisy, disorderly" and originated as a descriptive word used to refer to a boisterous or mischievous person.
ROYAL	Means "belonging to a king or queen" and originated as a medieval English surname referring to someone of royal descent or bearing regal qualities.
ROYCE	Means "son of the king" and originated from Old French.
RUDRA	Means "the howler" or "the roaring one" and originates from Hindu mythology.
RUGER	The first name Ruger is of American origin and means "famous warrior" or "shooter."
RYAN	Means "little king" and originates from Irish Gaelic.
RYDER	English origin and means "horseman" or "messenger".
SAINT	Means "holy" or "sanctified" and has Christian origins.
SALMAN	Means "safe" or "peaceful" and it originated from Arabic and Persian languages.
SALVADOR	Salvador means "savior" in Spanish and is of Latin origin.
SAMSON	Means "sun" or "bright sun" and its origin can be traced back to Hebrew biblical times.
SAMUEL	Means "God has heard" and is of Hebrew origin.
SANTANA	Spanish name meaning "holy" or "saint," often used as a surname indicating ancestry from the Spanish word for "saint."
SANTIAGO	Spanish name meaning "Saint James," originating from the name of the apostle James the Greater in the Christian religion.
SANTINO	Means "little saint" and originated from Italian.
SANTOS	Spanish and Portuguese name meaning "saints" or "holy" acquired from the Latin word "sanctus."
SAWYER	Meaning "woodcutter", Sawyer is an English occupational surname turned given name.
SCOTT	The name Scott originated from Scotland and means "from Scotland" or "one who comes from a Scottish province."

SEAMUS	Means "supplanter" and originates from Ireland.
SEBASTIAN	Means "venerable" or "revered" and originates from the Latin name Sebastianus, derived from the Greek name Σεβαστος (Sebastos) meaning "from Sebastia."
SEKANI	Means "laughing" or "joyful" and originates from the Shona language spoken in Zimbabwe.
SEMAJ	American origin and is a modern variation of the name James spelled backwards.
SERGIO	Spanish and Italian name meaning "servant" or "attendant," derived from the Latin name Sergius.
SHALOM	Hebrew name meaning "peace" or "harmony" and is often used as a traditional Jewish greeting.
SHANE	Irish origin and means "God is gracious" or "gift from God".
SHAURYA	Means "bravery" or "courage" and originates from the Sanskrit language of India.
SHAWN	Irish origin and means "God is gracious."
SHELDON	Means "steep valley" and originates from Old English.
SHEPARD	Means "sheep herder" and originates from the Old English word "sceapweard."
SHEPHERD	Means "a person who tends to and cares for sheep" and has English and German origins.
SHIMON	Means "hearkening, listening" and it originates from Hebrew.
SHIV	The first name "Shiv" is of Indian origin and means "auspicious; sacred" in Sanskrit.
SHIVANSH	The name Shivaansh means "an incarnation or reflection of Lord Shiva" and has Indian origins.
SHLOK	Indian origin and means "a verse or hymn in Sanskrit literature."
SHULEM	Hebrew origin and means "peaceful" or "complete."
SIDDHARTH	Means "one who has attained enlightenment" and it originates from Sanskrit, an ancient Indo-Aryan language.
SILAS	Means "man of the forest" and has Hebrew origins.
SIMCHA	Hebrew name meaning "joy" and is often given to children born during celebrations or happy occasions.
SIMEON	Means "hearkening" or "hearing" in Hebrew and is of biblical origin.
SIMON	Means "he who hears" and originates from the Hebrew name "Shimon" meaning "heard" or "listening."
SINCERE	Means "genuine" or "honest" and it originated from the English language.
SLADE	Means "valley" or "dweller in the valley" and originates from Old English.
SMITH	The first name Smith is of English origin and it refers to a person who works with metal, specifically a skilled metalworker or blacksmith.
SOLOMON	Means "peaceful" and originates from the Hebrew language.
SONNY	"Sonny" is an English name meaning "son" and is often used as a nickname for boys named after their fathers.
SPENCER	Means "steward" or "dispenser of provisions" and originates from the English occupational surname for someone in charge of a household's provisions.
STANLEY	Means "stone clearing" and originates from Old English.
STEFANO	The first name Stefano is of Italian origin and means "crowned" or "crowned with laurels."
STEPHEN	Means "crown" or "crowned" and comes from the Greek name Στέφανος (Stephanos), meaning "crown" or "wreath."
STERLING	Means "genuine, high quality" and originated from the Old English word "stēorling" meaning "little star."
STETSON	Means "son of Stephen" and originates from Old English.
STEVEN	Means "crown" or "crowned one" and originates from the Greek name Stephanos.
STONE	Means "strong, unyielding" and has English origins derived from the Old English word "stan."
STRATTON	The first name Stratton originated as a surname of English origin, meaning "town by the Roman road".
STRYKER	Means "one who strikes" and originates from the Old English word "strica" meaning "to strike" or "to smite."
STUART	Means "stewart" or "keeper of the estate," and it is of Scottish origin.
SULAIMAN	Means "man of peace" or "one who is peaceful" and has Arabic origins.

SULLIVAN	Sullivan means "black-eyed one" in Irish Gaelic and originated from the Irish surname Ó Súilleabháin, meaning "descendant of Súilleabhán."
SULTAN	Means "ruler" or "king" and originates from Arabic and Turkish.
SUMMIT	Contemporary English name derived from the word summit, representing the peak or highest point.
SYED	The first name Syed commonly used in Islamic cultures means "leader" or "noble" and is of Arabic origin.
SYLUS	The first name SYLUS is of Greek origin and means "forest" or "woodland."
SYLVESTER	Means "from the forest" and has Latin origins.
TADEO	Means "gift of God" and originates from the Hebrew name Thaddeus.
TAHJ	Means "crown" and is of Arabic origin.
TANNER	Means "a person who works with leather" and originates from the Old English word "tannere."
TATUM	Unisex name of English origin meaning "cheerful or full of spirit; brings joy."
TAYSOM	Modern masculine name of uncertain origin, possibly a variation of the surname Taysum or derived from the Cornish word "taisum" meaning "peace" or "quiet."
TEDDY	Diminutive form of Theodore, meaning "gift of God," and originated from the United States as a nickname for President Theodore Roosevelt.
TERRANCE	Means "smooth" or "soft," and it originated from the Latin name Terentius.
THADDEUS	Means "courageous heart" and it has biblical origins, derived from the Aramaic name "Thaddai."
THATCHER	Means "one who repairs thatched roofs" and has English origins.
THEO	Means "God's gift" and it is derived from the Greek name Theodoros.
THEODORE	Means "gift of God" and it originates from the Greek name "Theodoros" composed of the elements "theos" meaning "god" and "doron" meaning "gift."
THERON	Means "hunter" or "hunting ruler" and has its origins in Ancient Greek.
THIAGO	Portuguese and Spanish origin, means "may God protect and guard."
THOMAS	Means "twin" and originates from the Aramaic word "t'om'a," meaning "twin."
THOR	Means "thunder" and originates from Norse mythology, where Thor is the god of thunder and strength.
THORIN	Means "thunder" or "thunder god" and has Scandinavian origins, derived from the Old Norse name Þórir.
TIAGO	Portuguese variant of the name James, derived from the Latin name Iacomus, meaning "supplanter".
TIBERIUS	Roman name of Latin origin meaning "from the Tiber River."
TIMOTHY	Means "honoring God" and originates from the Greek name Timotheos, derived from timao meaning "to honor" and theos meaning "God."
TITUS	Means "honorable" and derives from the Latin word "titulus" which means "title" or "inscription."
TOBIAS	Hebrew origin, means "God is good" and is derived from the biblical figure in the Old Testament.
TOMMY	Diminutive of the name Thomas, meaning "twin," and has English origins.
TOWNES	Means "from the town" or "from the settlement" and it is of English origin.
TRAVIS	Name of Old French origin meaning "crossing" or "crossroads."
TRAVON	Modern American origin and means "fair town" or "from the fair town."
TRAYVON	Means "from a combination of the names Tray and Von" and has African-American origins.
TREMAINE	Means "from the town of Tremayne" and originated as an English surname.
TRENTON	Modern English name derived from the city of Trenton in New Jersey, meaning "town by the Trent River."
TREVOR	Means "steadfast and true" and has English origins.
TREYSON	Means "son of three," and it is of English origin.
TRIPP	Means "traveler" or "one who goes on a journey" and originated as a surname derived from the Old French word "trippes," meaning "tripe" or "intestines."

TRISTAN	Means "sorrowful" in Old French and is of Celtic origin.
TRITON	The first name Triton, of Greek origin, means "son of Poseidon" and refers to a mythical god associated with the sea and marine life.
TROY	Means "from the ancient city of Troy" and originated from Greek mythology.
TRUETT	Means "loyal, true" and has English origins.
TRUMAN	Means "loyal man" and it originates from Old English, derived from the words "tru" meaning "true" and "mann" meaning "man."
TUCKER	Tucker is an English name that means "fabric pleater" or "cloth-drawer" and is derived from the Old English word "tucian."
TURNER	Means "one who works with a lathe or turner of wood" and originated from the occupational surname derived from Middle English.
TYLER	Means "tile maker" and originated as an English occupational surname.
TYRELL	Means "stubborn or willful" and is of English origin.
TYSHAWN	Means "peaceful one" and it originated in America.
TYSON	Meaning "son of Ty" or "firebrand," Tyson is an English surname turned first name originating from Old French, derived from a Norman French nickname.
TZVI	Means "gazelle" in Hebrew and has biblical origins.
ULYSSES	Means "wrathful" or "one who is full of anger" and originates from the Latin form of the Greek name Odysseus, the legendary hero from Homer's epic poem, the Odyssey.
UNKNOWN	The meaning of the first name UNKNOWN is that it is of English origin and refers to something that is not known or recognized.
URIJAH	Means "God is my light" and originates from the Hebrew language.
UZIEL	Means "God is my strength" and has Hebrew origins.
UZZIAH	Means "strength of God" and it has origins in Hebrew.
VAUGHN	Welsh name meaning "small" or "junior" and is of Welsh origin.
VEDANT	Means "knowledge of the Vedas" and originates from Sanskrit.
VERNON	Means "alder tree" in French and originated from a Gaulish word, ultimately derived from Latin.
VICENTE	Means "conquering" or "victorious" and has Spanish and Portuguese origins.
VICTOR	Means "conqueror" and originates from Latin.
VIHAAN	Means "dawn" or "morning" and originates from Sanskrit.
VINCE	Shortened form of the name Vincent, which is derived from the Latin name "Vincentius" meaning "conquering" or "prevailing," and originated from the Roman name "Vincens."
VINCENT	Male name of Latin origin meaning "conquering" or "victorious."
VIRGIL	Means "flourishing" or "staff bearer" and it originates from the Roman name Vergilius.
VITO	Means "life" and originates from Italian.
VLADIMIR	Means "ruling with peace" and originates from the Slavic languages.
WALKER	Means "cloth washer" and has English origins.
WALLACE	Means "foreigner" or "stranger" and originates from Old French.
WARNER	Means "defender" or "protector" and originated from Germany.
WARREN	The name "Warren" originated from Old English and means "enclosed or protected place," often referring to a game park or a rabbit warren.
WATSON	Means "son of Watt," and it has Scottish and English origins.
WAYLON	Means "land by the road" and has English origins.
WELLS	Means "from the well" and has English origins.
WESLEY	Means "western meadow" and originates from Old English.
WESSON	Means "son of Wess" and has English origins.
WESTLEY	Means "from the western meadow" and it originates from Old English.
WESTON	Means "from the western town" and has Old English roots.
WILDER	Means "wild animal, untamed" and originates from the Old English word "wieldra," meaning "untamed" or "in the wild."
WILLEM	Means "will, desire" and it originates from the Dutch and Germanic languages.
WILLIAM	Means "resolute protector" and has origins in Germanic and English languages.
WILSON	Wilson is an English surname-derived name meaning "son of Will" or "son of William," originating from the Middle Ages in England.

WINSTON Means "joyful stone" and is of English origin.

WITTEN Means "from the white one's farm" and has English origins.

WOLF German origin, signifies strength, courage, and loyalty.

WOLFGANG Means "wolf path" and originates from Germanic languages.

WOODROW Means "lives near a row of trees" and originates from the Old English words "wudu" (wood) and "raw" (row).

WYATT Meaning "brave in battle," Wyatt is an English name derived from the Old English words "wīg" (war) and "heard" (brave or hardy).

XANDER Shortened form of the name Alexander and it originates from Greek language meaning "defender of mankind."

XAVIER Means "bright" or "new house" and originates from the Basque region in Spain.

XZAVIER Means "bright, new house" and originates from the Basque language.

YAAKOV Means "supplanter" and is of Hebrew origin.

YAHYA Means "God is gracious" and its origin is Hebrew.

YANDEL The first name Yandel is of American origin and means "one who is creative and innovative."

YASIR Arabic origin and means "rich" or "prosperous."

YAZAN Means "to deem worthy" or "sharp intellect" and originates from Arabic origin.

YECHIEL Means "God lives" and has Hebrew origins.

YEHOSHUA Means "God is salvation" and it originates from Hebrew.

YEHUDA Means "praised" and it originates from the Hebrew language.

YERIK The name Yerik originates from Kazakhstan and means "ever ruler" or "eternal ruler".

YESHUA Hebrew origin, means "salvation" and is an alternate form of the name Jesus.

YISROEL Means "he who struggles with God" and it originates from Hebrew.

YITZCHOK Means "laughter; he will laugh" and originates from Hebrew.

YONATAN Hebrew name meaning "God has given" and it originates from biblical times.

YOUSEF Means "God will add" and it has Arabic origins.

YUSUF Arabic origin and it means "God increases" or "God will add."

ZACH Shortened form of the Hebrew name Zachariah, meaning "God has remembered" and it originates from biblical times.

ZACHARIAH Means "Yahweh has remembered" and is of Hebrew origin.

ZACHARY Means "God has remembered" and is of Hebrew origin.

ZACKERY Means "God has remembered" and originates from the Hebrew name Zechariah.

ZAHIR Means "evident" or "manifest" and originates from Arabic language.

ZAIDYN Arabic origin and means "increasing" or "abundance."

ZAIRE Name of African origin meaning "river that swallows all rivers".

ZAKAI Hebrew name meaning "pure" or "innocent" and originating from the Bible.

ZAKARIYA Arabic name meaning "God remembers" and is derived from the Hebrew name Zechariah.

ZAVIAN Means "gift of God" and has origins in both Hebrew and Latin.

ZAYN "Zayn" is a modern Arabic word name meaning "beauty" or "grace" and it originated from the Arabic language and Islamic culture.

ZAYVION American origin and it means "blessed" or "gift from God."

ZEALAND Means "from the sea land" and has Dutch origins.

ZEKE Nickname derived from the biblical name Ezekiel, meaning "God strengthens," and it has Hebrew origins.

ZEPHANIAH Zephaniah means "Yahweh has hidden" in Hebrew and is of biblical origin.

ZEPHYR Means "west wind" and has its origin in Greek mythology.

ZEPPELIN Means "a large German airship" and is of German origin.

ZEUS Means "god" and originates from Greek mythology, where Zeus was the king of the gods and the god of sky and thunder.

ZIGGY Means "victorious protector" and its origin is a diminutive form of the German name Siegfried or Sigmund.

ZION Means "a place of peace and harmony" and is of Hebrew origin.

ZURIEL Hebrew origin and means "God is my rock" or "rock of God."

ZYAIRE Modern American name of uncertain origin, possibly a variant of the name Zyair.

ZYION Uncertain origin and does not have a widely recognized meaning.

4,000 more names for boys.

ABANOUB Means "ancient and honorable" and originates from Egypt.

ABBOTT The first name Abbott, of English origin, means "father" or "leader."

ABDIAS Means "servant of God" and has Hebrew origins.

ABDIFATAH Means "servant of the conqueror" and it has Somali origins.

ABDIMALIK Means "servant of the King" and originates from Arabic and Somali cultural backgrounds.

ABDINASIR Somali masculine name, meaning "servant of the victorious" or "servant of the one who gives success."

ABDIRIZAK Somali origin and it means "servant of the generous one."

ABDOUL Arabic origin and means "servant of Allah."

ABDOULAYE Male given name of Arabic origin meaning "servant of God."

ABDOULIE Means "servant of God" and originates from the Muslim tradition.

ABDOURA HMANE Male given name of Arabic origin meaning "servant of the merciful," often used in Islamic cultures.

ABDULAHAD Means "servant of the one who is praised" and it originates from Arabic.

ABDULHADI Arabic origin and it means "servant of the guide" or "servant of the leader".

ABDULHA KEEM Means "servant of the wise" and it originates from Islamic tradition, specifically from Arabic language.

ABDULKARIM Arabic origin and means "servant of the generous" or "servant of the noble."

ABDULLATEEF Arabic origin and means "servant of the kind and gentle."

ABDULMALIK Means "servant of the King" and it originates from Arabic.

ABDULRAHIM Means "servant of the Most Compassionate" and has Arabic origins.

ABDULSALAM Means "servant of peace" and is of Arabic origin.

ABDULSA MAD The first name Abdulsamad has Arabic origins and means "servant of the All-Praiseworthy."

ABDULWA HAB Means "servant of the Giving" and originates from Arabic.

ABDURAH MON Arabic origin and it means "servant of the Most Gracious."

ABEDNEGO The first name Abednego, of Hebrew origin, means "servant of God" and is derived from the Biblical figure mentioned in the Book of Daniel.

ABELINO Means "breath" or "vanity" and has Spanish and Portuguese origins.

ABHAY Means "fearless" or "brave" and originates from Sanskrit.

ABHAYRAM The first name Abhayram originates from Sanskrit and means "fearless and compassionate."

ABHIMANYU Sanskrit name meaning "fearless warrior," derived from Hindu mythology and the Mahabharata epic.

ABHINAV Means "new and innovative" and originates from Sanskrit, an ancient Indian language.

ABHIR The first name Abhir is derived from Sanskrit origins and means "brave" or "fearless."

ABHYANT Means "confident" or "fearless" and originated from Sanskrit, an ancient Indo-Aryan language spoken in the Indian subcontinent.

ABID Arabic origin and it means "worshiper" or "one who is devoted to God."

ABIMAEL Means "my father is God" and has Hebrew origins.

ABOUBACAR Means "father of Bakr" and originates from Arabic and African cultures.

ABSALOM Means "father of peace" and originates from Hebrew biblical sources.

ABSHIR Means "messenger of good news" and originates from Arabic.

ABUBAKR Means "noble and esteemed" in Arabic, and it originates from Islamic tradition as the name of the first caliph after the Prophet Muhammad.

ABUZAR Means "greatly renowned" and is of Arabic origin.

ACESON The first name Aceson is of American origin and it means "one who excels, achieves greatness, or is a leader in their field."

ACESTON The name Aceston has no widely recognized meaning or origin as it is a very rare and uncommon name.

ACETYN The first name Acetyn has no commonly known meaning or origin, as it is not a widely recognized or documented name.

ACEYN Uncertain meaning and origin, possibly derived from the combination of "ace" meaning "exceptionally skilled" and "yn" as a suffix; it does not have a widely recognized cultural or historical background.

ACHIM The first name Achim is of Hebrew origin and means "he will establish" or "God will establish".

ACRE The first name Acre comes from the English word which refers to a unit of land measurement, and is derived from the Latin word "ager" meaning "field."

ACYN The first name ACYN is of uncertain origin and meaning, as it does not have clear established origins or widely known meanings.

ADALBERTO The first name Adalberto, meaning "noble and bright ruler," originated from the Old High German elements "adal" (noble) and "beraht" (bright).

ADEDAMOLA Means "crown settles joyfully" and originates from the Yoruba culture in Nigeria.

ADEDAYO Means "crown of joy" in Yoruba language and originates from Nigeria.

ADEJARE "Adejare means "crown has overcome" in Yoruba and is of African origin."

ADELSO Means "noble" or "noble wolf" and has Spanish origins.

ADEM Means "man" or "earth" and it is of Turkish and Arabic origin.

ADEMIDE Means "the crown has come" and is of Yoruba origin.

ADENIYI Means "crown has value" or "royalty has worth" and has Yoruba origins in Nigeria.

ADEWALE Means "crown has come home" and originates from the Yoruba language in Nigeria.

ADEYEMI The first name Adeyemi has a Yoruba origin and it means "royalty befits me" or "the crown suits me".

ADHRIT Sanskrit-origin name meaning "one who is supported or protected by a higher power."

ADHVAITH Means "unique" or "one and only" and has origins in the Sanskrit language.

ADHYANSH Hindi name that means "part of God" and is of Indian origin.

ADHYUTH Adhyuth is an Indian name meaning "incomparable" and derived from Sanskrit origin.

ADIEN Modern variation of the name Aidan, derived from the Irish name Aodhán meaning "little fire" or "fiery one."

ADITHYA Means "sun god" and has its origin in Hindu mythology.

ADLAI Means "my ornament" or "God is just" and originates from Hebrew.

ADOLPH Means "noble wolf" and originates from Germanic languages.

ADONIJAH Hebrew name meaning "my lord is Yahweh," and is derived from the Bible.

ADONIRAM Means "my Lord is exalted" and has Hebrew origins.

ADRIUS Means "man of Adria" and has origins in Latin.

ADRYEN The first name Adryen has no widely accepted meaning or origin as it is a relatively rare and uncommon name.

ADVAITH REDDY The first name "Advaitreddy" is of Indian origin and it means "unique king" or "one who is incomparable in his rule or leadership".

ADVAY Means "unique" or "non-dual" and it originates from Sanskrit, an ancient Indian language.

AEGON Means "ruler" or "lord" and it is of Greek origin.

AELIUS Roman origin and means "sunlight" or "sun".

AENEAS Means "praiseworthy" and originates from Greek mythology, specifically from the epic poem "The Aeneid" by Virgil, where Aeneas is a Trojan hero and the legendary ancestor of the Romans.

AENGUS Means "one strength" or "true vigor" and originates from Irish mythology.

AETHER Greek origin, means "the heavenly substance or the personification of the upper air regarded as a light or invisible substance, encompassing the universe".

AFRAZ Means "noble" or "honorable" and is of Persian origin.

AGAMJOT Means "inner divine light" and originated from Punjabi, a language spoken in the Punjab region of India and Pakistan.

AGAMVEER	Means "brave and fearless" and it originates from the Punjabi language in India.
AGASTHYA	Means "one who is fast" and it originates from Sanskrit.
AHIJAH	The Hebrew name AHIJAH means "Yahweh is my brother" or "my brother is Yahweh," originating from the Hebrew Bible.
AHKEEM	Means "wise, intelligent" and has Arabic origins.
AHLEGEND	The name "Ahlegend" does not have a recognized meaning or origin as it appears to be a rare or unique name.
AHLIAS	The name Ahlias has no specific meaning and is not of known origin.
AHLIJAH	Means "Yahweh is my God" and it is a variant of the biblical name Elijah.
AHMADOU	West African name of Arabic origin meaning "most commendable" or "praiseworthy".
AHMADUL LAH	Muslim name of Arabic origin, meaning "the praised one of Allah" or "one who is highly praised by God".
AHMAUD	Arabic origin and means "praiseworthy" or "one who is highly esteemed."
AHMIER	The name Ahmier has an uncertain meaning and origin, potentially having a combination of Arabic and English influences.
AHNAF	Arabic origin and it means "one who stays on the right path."
AHRON	Means "enlightened" or "exalted" and has Hebrew origins.
AHSAIAS	Hebrew origin and means "God has made."
AHSAN	Means "excellence" or "the best" and has Arabic origins.
AHZAI	Modern and unique name of uncertain origin and meaning.
AHZIRE	Modern invented name with no specific meaning or origin.
AIDONEUS	Means "ruler of the underworld" and originates from Greek mythology, referring to Hades, the god of the underworld.
AIMILIOS	Means "rival" or "emulating" in Greek and it is derived from the Latin name Aemilius.
AIRION	The first name Airion is of uncertain origin and meaning.
AIRMIESS	The first name AIRMIESS does not have a commonly known meaning or origin as it appears to be a unique and uncommon name.
AJIT	Means "invincible" and originates from Sanskrit.
AKASH	Unisex name of Sanskrit origin meaning "sky" or "space."
AKHIL	Means "whole" or "complete" and has its origin in the Sanskrit language.
AKING	Yoruba origin and means "warrior" or "chief."
AKOREDE	Means "one who brings happiness" and it originates from the Yoruba culture in Nigeria.
ALASDAIR	Means "defender of the people" and it originated from Gaelic language.
ALASSANE	Means "defender of mankind" and originates from Arabic and African cultures.
ALASTOR	Means "avenger" and originates from Greek mythology, specifically as a name for the spirit of blood feuds and justice.
ALBEIRO	Spanish origin and means "noble and bright," often associated with someone who exhibits these qualities.
ALBION	Means "white" or "high hills" and it originates from the ancient Greek word "albus."
ALBORZ	The first name Alborz originates from Persian/Iranian mythology and refers to a mythical mountain range believed to be the home of the gods.
ALBY	Variant of the name Albert, which originates from Old German and means "noble and bright."
ALCIDES	Means "strength" or "power" and has its origin in Greek mythology, referring to the son of Zeus and Alcmene, who was known for his exceptional bravery and courage.
ALDAHIR	The name Aldahir likely originates from the Arabic language and means "noble and honorable."
ALDAIR	Means "old ruler" and it has Germanic origins.
ALDOUS	Means "old and wise" and it has English origins.
ALDRIC	Means "ruler of all" and has Germanic origins.
ALEISTER	Means "defender of the people" and is of Scottish origin.
ALEKAI	The meaning and origin of the first name Alekai is Hawaiian in origin and it means "defender of the people".
ALEKSEY	Masculine given name of Russian origin, meaning "defender of mankind" or "protector of the people."

ALEXEI	Means "defender of the people" and originated from Greek and Russian roots.
ALFIE	The first name "Alfie" is a diminutive of the name Alfred, of English origin, and it means "wise counselor".
ALHAJI	Means "pilgrim" in Arabic and it is commonly used as a title for those who have completed the Hajj pilgrimage to Mecca.
ALHASSAN	Means "the handsome" or "the beautiful" and has Arabic origins.
ALIEU	Means "exalted" or "noble" and originates from Africa, particularly in the Mandinka language.
ALIOUNE	The first name Alioune is of West African origin and typically means "noble," "lofty," or "exalted."
ALMIGHTY	Means having infinite power and authority, and it likely originated from English vocabulary, symbolizing strength and dominance.
ALONTE	Modern Americanized variant of the Spanish name Alonzo, derived from the Germanic name Alfonso meaning "noble and ready."
ALOYSIUS	Means "famous warrior" or "renowned warrior" and has Latin origins.
ALPARSLAN	The first name Alparslan, of Turkish origin, means "heroic lion" or "valiant lion."
ALPHEUS	Means "white, pure" and is of Greek origin.
ALPHONSE	Germanic origin and it means "noble and ready for battle."
ALUCARD	Play on the name Dracula spelled backwards, commonly used in popular culture to indicate a vampire or a character inspired by Bram Stoker's novel.
ALVEY	The first name Alvey is of English origin, derived from the Old English elements "ælf" meaning "elf" and "wīg" meaning "war," suggesting a meaning of "elf-warrior."
ALWALEED	Means "the one who finds and directs towards God" and it has Arabic origins.
ALYUS	The name Alyus does not have a widely known meaning or origin, as it appears to be a rare or unique name without established linguistic roots or cultural associations.
AMARJAE	Modern invented name that may be a combination of the names Amar and Jae.
AMAZI	Means "surprised" in Zulu and Xhosa languages and is of South African origin.
AMAZIAH	The meaning of the name Amaziah is "the strength of God" and it is of Hebrew origin.
AMEDEO	Means "lover of God" and has Italian origins.
AMENADIEL	Means "faithful to God" and it originates from Hebrew.
AMILCAR	Means "one who seeks protection" and it originates from the Phoenician and Carthaginian cultures.
AMILLEON	Unique name of unknown origin and meaning.
AMILLIEON	Means "desire for a million" and is of American origin.
AMIRION	The first name Amirion is of uncertain origin, but it may be a modern variation of the name Amari combined with the suffix -ion.
AMIRIYON	The first name "Amiriyon" is of American origin and its meaning is currently unknown as it is a rare name.
AMIRKHAN	Means "noble leader" and originates from the Arabic and Persian languages.
AMIRUS	Unique name of Arabic origin, meaning "prince" or "commander" in Islamic tradition.
AMITAI	Hebrew origin, means "my truth" or "my honesty."
AMJAD	Means "excellence" or "glory" and is of Arabic origin.
AMNEN	Arabic origin and means "peaceful, trustworthy."
AMONTAE	Unknown origin and does not have a commonly attributed meaning.
AMROM	The first name Amrom is of Hebrew origin and means "exalted nation."
AMUNRA	Means "hidden sun god" and originates from Ancient Egyptian mythology.
ANAKYN	Modern variant of the name Anakin, derived from the fictional character Anakin Skywalker in the Star Wars franchise created by George Lucas.
ANANTH	Masculine Indian name meaning "eternal" or "infinite," derived from the Sanskrit word "ananta."
ANASTACIO	Means "resurrection" and originates from Greek.
ANCHOR	The first name Anchor originated from Old English, and it symbolizes stability, strength, and steadfastness.
ANDRANIK	The first name Andranik has Armenian origins and means "righteous and brave man".
ANDROS	Means "man" or "warrior" and has Greek origins.

ANDUIN Means "swift-flowing river" and has its origin in Tolkien's fictional Middle-earth in "The Lord of the Rings" series.

ANFERNEE Means "man who overcomes" and it is of American origin.

ANGELGA BRIEL Hebrew origin, means "messenger of God" or "angel Gabriel."

ANGELITO Means "little angel" in Spanish, and it is a diminutive form of the name Ángel.

ANIKETH Sanskrit name meaning "undefeatable" or "unconquerable" and its origin can be traced back to ancient Indian culture and mythology.

ANIRUDH Means "unstoppable" or "one who cannot be restricted" and originates from Hindu mythology.

ANIRVED Modern Indian name that means "unstoppable" or "invincible," derived from Sanskrit origins.

ANMOL Anmol means "priceless" or "invaluable" in Hindi and is of Indian origin.

ANSELMO Masculine given name of Germanic origin meaning "divine helmet."

ANTARES Means "rival of Mars" and derives from the Greek words "anti" (opposite) and "Ares" (the Greek god of war).

ANTAVIOUS Modern American name with an uncertain origin, often used in African-American communities.

ANTHEM Means "a rousing or uplifting song" and has its origin in the English language.

ANTHONY JAMES Combination of the names Anthony and James, and it likely originated as a unique given name or as a combination of two family names.

ANTHUAN Modern variation of the name Anthony, of Latin origin, meaning "priceless" or "highly praiseworthy."

ANTIONE Means "invaluable" or "priceless" and has its origin in France.

ANUBIS Male given name of ancient Egyptian origin, derived from the Egyptian god of mummification and the afterlife.

ANVITH Means "one who is unique" and it originates from the Indian subcontinent.

AODHAN Means "little fire" and originates from Ireland.

APOLINAR Means "devoted to Apollo" and originates from the Latin name Apollinaris.

AQUILES Means "he who has strong potential" and has origins in Greek mythology, as it was the name of the hero in the Trojan War, Achilles.

ARAFAT Means "a person who has excellent knowledge" and has Arabic origin.

ARAGORN Means "noble ruler" and originates from J.R.R. Tolkien's fictional Middle-earth in his epic fantasy series, "The Lord of the Rings."

ARAMIS The first name Aramis is of French origin and means "from Aramithea" or "follower of Saint Thomas".

ARCANGEL Means "archangel" and has its origin in the Spanish and Italian languages.

ARCH Greek origin, means "ruler" or "leader" and is often used as a short form of the name Archibald or Archer.

ARCHANGEL Means "chief angel" and derives from Greek and Christian origins as the highest-ranking angel in heaven.

ARCHIMEDES Means "master planner" and originates from ancient Greek.

ARCTURUS Means "guardian of the bears" and has its origin in Greek mythology.

ARDIAN Male name of Albanian origin, meaning "gold" or "golden".

ARELIO Spanish name meaning "golden eagle" and is derived from the Latin name Aurelius.

ARGENIS The name Argenis originated from Greek mythology and means "silvery," "white," or "shining."

ARHUM The meaning and origin of the first name Arhum is unknown.

ARINJAY Male name of Indian origin, meaning "victorious in acquiring knowledge and wisdom."

ARINZE The first name Arinze originated from the Igbo language in Nigeria and means "dear to the king" or "the king is respected".

ARISTEO Means "bestowed with excellence" and has Greek origins.

ARISTIDES Means "the best and noblest," originating from Ancient Greek.

ARISTOS Means "the best" or "excellent" in Greek, and it is derived from the Greek word "aristos" meaning "best" or "most excellent."

ARISTOTLE The first name Aristotle, of Greek origin, means "the best purpose" or "the best goal."

ARJUNKR Hindu name meaning "victorious, black-complexioned Lord Krishna," combining the
ISHNA names of the warrior Arjuna and the deity Krishna.

ARJUNREDDY Means "bright, shining warrior" and originated from India.

ARKHAM Means "from the town of Arkham" and its origin can be traced back to H.P. Lovecraft's
fictional works.

ARKYN The first name Arkyn originated from a combination of the words "ark" and "kin" and it
means "someone who is connected to or part of a sacred vessel or protector."

ARLINGTON Means "town of eagles" and has English origins.

ARMOND Means "noble protector" and has origins in both Germanic and French languages.

ARNEZ Masculine given name of uncertain origin, potentially derived from various sources
including Spanish, English, or African-American cultural influences.

ARNULFO Means "eagle-wolf" and has Germanic origins.

AROLDO Germanic origin and means "ruler and power of the eagle."

ARSALAN Means "lion" and has Persian and Arabic origins.

ARSENIO Means "strong" or "virile" and has origins in Spanish and Portuguese.

ARSHIV The first name Arshiv has an uncertain origin and meaning.

ARSLAN Masculine given name of Turkic origin, meaning "lion" or "brave warrior."

ARTHAS Means "noble guardian" and it originates from Old High German.

ARTIMUS Means "gift of Artemis" and is of Greek origin.

ARTIST Means a person who creates and produces art, and its origin is derived from the English
language, primarily used as a unique or creative name choice.

ARTORIUS Means "bear king" and has origins in ancient Roman and Celtic cultures.

ARTREUS Means "noble and courageous" and originates from Greek mythology.

ARTYOM Means "great strength" or "brave" and originated from Greek mythology, being
associated with the god Apollo.

ARVAND Persian name meaning "swift river" and is derived from the ancient Persian word "Arvand
Rud."

ARYAMAN Means "noble" or "the best" in Sanskrit and originates from ancient Indian mythology,
where Aryaman was one of the Adityas or solar deities.

ARYANSH Means "part of the noble or superior race" and it originated from Sanskrit.

ARYASH Modern Indian name, derived from Sanskrit, meaning "noble and respected."

ARYAVEER Means "noble hero" and originates from Sanskrit in India.

ASAHD Means "lion" or "powerful" and originates from Arabic and Hebrew.

ASANTE Ghanaian name meaning "thank you" or "gratitude", typically given to children born on a
Friday in the Akan culture.

ASAPH Means "gatherer" or "collector" and has Hebrew origins.

ASAUN American origin and it means "healer" or "physician."

ASHFORD Means "ford by the ash trees" and originates from Old English.

ASHISH Male given name of Sanskrit origin meaning "blessings" or "benedictions".

ASHKAN Means "a prince" and it originates from ancient Persian/Iranian culture.

ASHOT Means "undefeated" or "victorious" in Armenian, and it has ancient origins in Armenian
history and culture.

ASHRAF The name Ashraf originates from Arabic and means "noble" or "honorable".

ASHRIEL Hebrew origin and it means "God is my happiness" or "fortunate."

ASIM Means "guardian" or "protector" and has Arabic origins.

ASKARI Means "soldier" in Swahili and has origins in Eastern Africa.

ASMODEUS Means "wrath of God" or "one who judges" and is of Hebrew origin.

ASRITH Means "dependent" or "protected" and is of Indian origin.

ASTA Scandinavian name meaning "divine beauty" or "love" and is of Old Norse origin.

ASUKULU Name of African origin meaning "warrior" or "fighter."

ATEF The given name Atef is of Arabic origin, meaning "noble" or "kind".

ATHANASIUS Means "immortal" and it originates from the Greek language.

ATHARVR The first name Atharvreddy is of Indian origin and typically means "descendant of
EDDY Atharva" or "one who follows the path of Atharva."

ATHIRAN	Means "one who reflects intelligence and knowledge" and originates from the Sanskrit language.
ATHOS	Means "immortal" or "from Mount Athos" and is of Greek origin.
ATIGUN	Means "mountain" and is of Inuit origin.
ATTILIO	Means "father" or "paternal" and originates from the Latin name Atilius, derived from the word "aetus" meaning "ancestral."
ATWOOD	Means "dweller near the wood" and originates from Old English.
AUDEMAR	Masculine French given name, derived from the Old Germanic elements "auda" meaning "wealth" and "mar" meaning "fame," implying a person of prosperous fame or renowned wealth.
AUDI	Means "noble strength" and originates from Germany.
AUKAI	The Hawaiian name Aukai means "sailor" and originates from the Hawaiian language.
AULDEN	Means "old friend" and has English origins.
AUNDRE	Means "strong, courageous" and originates from the French form of the name Andrew or Andre.
AURELIANO	Means "golden" or "gilded" and it is of Latin origin.
AUZEIR	Modern French name of unknown origin, with no specific meaning.
AVANEESH	Means "lord of the earth" and originates from the Sanskrit language.
AVENIR	Means "future" in French and has origins in the Latin word "advenire," meaning "to come" or "to arrive."
AVETIS	The first name Avetis, of Armenian origin, means "good news" or "gospel".
AVIGDOR	Means "father of the fence" in Hebrew and originated from Jewish biblical traditions.
AVINASH	Masculine Indian name that means "indestructible" or "unconquerable" in Sanskrit.
AVIYON	Modern American name of uncertain origin, possibly a variation of the Hebrew name Aviya meaning "my father is Yahweh."
AVONDRE	Modern American name of uncertain origin, potentially created as a unique variation or combination of other names.
AVRUM	Hebrew name meaning "exalted father," and it is a variant of the name Abraham.
AVYAANR EDDY	The meaning and origin of the first name Avyaanreddy are not available as it does not appear to have a widely recognized meaning or origin.
AVYION	The name Avyion likely originated in the United States and its meaning is not readily available.
AVYUKTH	Means "clear, insightful" and originates from Sanskrit.
AVYUKTH RAM	Male Indian name that means "clear, distinct" in Sanskrit.
AVYUKTH REDDY	Traditional Indian name meaning "intelligent and fearless king".
AWS	The first name AWS does not have a recognized meaning or origin as it is commonly known as an abbreviation for the Amazon Web Services.
AXETON	Modern name with an unclear origin, likely created as a unique and distinctive name.
AYAANREDDY	Indian origin and likely means "eternal, superior, or without limits" combined with the surname Reddy, which is a prominent caste in southern India.
AYANSHR EDDY	Sanskrit name meaning "gift of God" with roots in Indian culture.
AYDRIEN	Modern variant of the name Adrian, derived from the Latin name Adrianus meaning "from Adria" or "dark one," which may refer to the dark or black sea.
AYDYN	Modern variation of the name Aidan, derived from a combination of Irish and Gaelic origins meaning "little fire" or "fiery one."
AYHAM	Means "generous" or "blessed" and originates from Arabic.
AYINDE	Means "one who is praised" and it originates from the Yoruba culture in Nigeria.
AYOMIDE	Unisex Yoruba name meaning "my joy has arrived" and is of Nigerian origin.
AYOMIKUN	Yoruba origin and means "joy becomes sufficient" or "joy is filled up."
AYOUB	Means "God restores" and originates from Arabic and Hebrew.
AYRTON	English origin and means "from the town near the river Ayr."
AYSUN	Means "beautiful as the moon" and is of Turkish origin.

AZAIUS	The meaning and origin of the first name Azaius is uncertain and possibly of Hebrew origin.
AZARIEL	Hebrew name meaning "God is my help" or "helped by God."
AZARION	Means "fire" or "flame" and originates from the Persian language.
AZARIUS	Modern, invented name with no widely recognized meaning or origin.
AZAZEL	Means "God strengthens" in Hebrew and has biblical origins.
AZEKIAL	Means "God strengthens" and it has Hebrew origins.
AZREAL	The first name "Azrael" means "helper of God" and is of Hebrew origin.
AZTLAN	The first name "Aztlan" derives from Aztec mythology and represents the legendary ancestral homeland of the Aztecs.
BABACAR	Means "father of all" or "father of people" and is of African origin.
BABYBOY	The first name "Babyboy" is a modern, non-traditional name of English origin typically used as a term of endearment or nickname for a young boy or child.
BAELFIRE	The name Baelfire has a mythical origin and refers to a powerful or magical fire associated with demonology and witchcraft.
BAER	Means "bear" in German and has origins in Germanic and Old Norse languages.
BALDEMAR	The name Baldermar means "famous ruler" and its origin can be traced back to Old High German and Old Norse languages.
BALDOMERO	The first name Baldomero has a Spanish origin and means "brave and renowned".
BALDWIN	Means "brave friend" and originates from Old Germanic.
BALTAZAR	The first name Balbazar means "Baal will protect the king" and it is of Hebrew origin.
BALTHAZAR	Means "God protects the king" and has its origins in the Hebrew language.
BANGALY	Means "one who is born on Tuesday" and has origins in the Mandinka language of West Africa.
BANKSTON	The first name Bankston is of English origin and means "from the bank settlement" or "town by the river bank."
BARACK	Means "blessed" or "blessing" in Arabic and Swahili, and it is of African origin.
BARAKA	Swahili name that means "blessing" or "good fortune" and originates from the East African region.
BARKON	The meaning and origin of the first name "BARKON" are not readily available, as it does not have a well-established origin or widely recognized meaning.
BARNABAS	Means "son of encouragement" and originates from the Greek name "Barnabas" (Βαρνάβας) found in the New Testament of the Bible.
BARTHOLOMEW	Means "son of Tolmai" and has its origins in Aramaic and Hebrew.
BARTOLO	Means "bright ruler" and is of Spanish and Italian origin.
BARUCH	Means "blessed" and has Hebrew origins.
BASHIR	Means "bringer of good news" and originates from Arabic.
BASSAM	Means "one who smiles" and it is of Arabic origin.
BAUDELIO	Means "brave ruler" and has Germanic origins.
BAVLY	The first name BAVLY has an uncertain meaning and origin as it is a rare name without a commonly known etymology.
BAYOU	Unique and exotic name of French origin, deriving from the Choctaw word "bayuk," which means "small stream" or "river."
BEARETT	Modern English name of uncertain origin, possibly derived from the surname Barrett meaning "brave as a bear."
BEAUDEN	Means "beautiful valley" and it originates from the French language.
BEAUMONT	Means "beautiful mountain" and has French and Latin origins.
BEAUREGARD	Means "beautiful gaze" or "beautiful look" and has French origins.
BEHR	Modern variation of the German surname "Bär," which means "bear" in English and derived from a byname given to someone who exhibited bear-like qualities or
BENEDETTO	Means "blessed" or "the blessed one" and originates from Italian.
BENIGNO	Means "kind" or "benevolent" and has origins from Latin and Italian.
BENJIMAN	The first name Benjamin means "son of the right hand" and originates from Hebrew.
BENNIE	The first name "Bennie" is a diminutive form of the name "Benjamin," meaning "son of the right hand" and originating from the Hebrew name "□ □ □ □ □ □ □ □ □ □ ".

BENNINGTON	Means "town associated with Benno" and originates from Old English.
BENTZION	Means "son of Zion" and has Hebrew origins.
BENTZY	Yiddish name of German origin, derived from the name Bentsion meaning "blessed" or "fortunate."
BENZION	Means "son of Zion" and originates from Hebrew.
BEOWULF	Means "bee wolf" and it originates from Old English.
BEREKET	Means "abundance" or "blessing" and has origins in several cultures, including Turkish, Amharic (Ethiopian), and Eritrean.
BERENGER	Means "brave as a bear" and has French and Germanic origins.
BERIC	Slavic origin and means "brilliant ruler or ruler of the people."
BERNABE	Means "son of consolation" and it originates from the Greek name Barnabas.
BERNARDINO	Means "bold as a bear" and has Italian and Spanish origins.
BETZALEL	Means "in the shadow of God" and it originates from Hebrew biblical tradition.
BEXTYN	Modern, unique and uncommon first name of unknown origin and meaning.
BEZALEL	Hebrew name meaning "in the shadow of God" and has its origins in the Old Testament.
BHARGAV	Means "descendant of Bhrgu" and originates from Sanskrit, an ancient Indo-Aryan language.
BHODI	Means "enlightenment" and has origins in both Sanskrit and Pali languages.
BILOL	The first name Bilol comes from Uzbek origin and means "loving" or "affectionate".
BINYAMIN	Means "son of the right hand" and originates from Hebrew.
BIRCH	The first name Birch originates from the Old English word "birce," meaning "birch tree," symbolizing resilience, renewal, and growth.
BIRUK	Means "one who is blessed" and originates from the Ethiopian language, Amharic.
BISMARCK	Means "protector in battle" and originates from Germanic elements "bis" meaning "protector" and "marka" meaning "border, borderland."
BISON	Bison means "wild ox" and originates from the Middle English word "bisont" derived from the Latin word "bison."
BLANTON	The first name Blanton is of English origin and means "from the town near the field."
BLESSED	Means to be filled with divine favor or protection and is of Latin origin.
BLEU	French-origin name meaning "blue," often used as an unconventional and artistic choice for a boy.
BLUE	Meaning "the color of the sky or sea", the name Blue is of English origin and has gained popularity as a modern and unique choice for a baby name.
BOCEPHUS	The first name "Bocephus" is a nickname for William Randall Hank Williams Jr., originated from his father's nickname, "Bocephus," and it implies a sense of rebelliousness and uniqueness.
BOGDAN	Means "given by God" and it originates from Slavic origin.
BOHANNON	The first name Bohannon is of Irish origin and means "descendant of Buadhachán," which translates to "victorious" or "triumphant."
BOHDI	Means "enlightenment" and originates from the Sanskrit word "bodhi," which is often associated with the wisdom achieved by Gautama Buddha.
BOLIVAR	Means "warrior" and it originated from Spanish and Latin American history, particularly associated with the Venezuelan military and political leader Simón Bolívar.
BOLUWATIFE	Yoruba name meaning "God's gift" or "to be rich in love", originating from the Yoruba-speaking people in Nigeria.
BONAVEN TURE	Means "good fortune" and originates from the Latin phrase "bona ventura."
BONIFACIO	Means "fortunate, good fate" and originated from Latin.
BORJA	Means "tower" or "fortress" and has Spanish origins.
BOUDREAUX	The first name Boudreaux is of French origin, derived from the surname Baudouin, and it means "bold ruler."
BOWDEN	Means "little cabin" and originates from Old English.
BOWIN	The first name Bowin originated from Scotland and means "small and attractive."
BOWMAN	Means "archer" and is of English origin.
BRADDOCK	The first name Braddock is of English origin and means "broad oak."

BRAELIN American origin and means "proud chief."

BRAESON Means "son of brave heart" and has uncertain origins, possibly a modern variant of the name Brayson.

BRANDER The first name "Brander" is of Scottish origin and means "proud chief" or "fiery sword".

BRANSEN The first name Bransen is of Dutch origin and means "son of Brand" or "descendant of the fiery one."

BRAVERY Means having courage or fearlessness, and it is of English origin.

BRAY Means "hill" or "dweller near a hill" and originates from Old English.

BRAZOS Means "arms" in Spanish and it originated from the Brazos River in Texas, United States.

BREGMAN Surname of Eastern European Jewish origin that was later used as a first name, meaning "farmer" or "ploughman".

BREKKEN The first name Brekken is of Norwegian origin and means "hillside dweller" or "from the slope."

BRENHAM Means "homestead of fire" and has English origins.

BRENTEN Means "hill" or "dweller near the burnt land" and originated from the Gaelic and English language.

BREX The name BREX does not have a widely-known meaning or origin as it does not appear to be a commonly used or recognized name in any specific culture or language.

BREXTYN The name Brextyn is an invented name of American origin, likely derived from the word Brexit with an added suffix for uniqueness.

BREYLEN The first name Breyleen means "Brotherly" or "Like a brother" and its origin is uncertain.

BREYNER Means "brave warrior" and originates from the Germanic language.

BREYON Modern name of uncertain origin, with variations found in both African-American and French cultures.

BRINTON The name "Brinton" originated from the Old English surname meaning "town near the burnt land," referring to a settlement near a burned area.

BRIXON Means "wooden settlement" and has English origins.

BRIXTEN Means "the beloved one" and it has modern origins as a variant of the name Braxton.

BROCKTON The first name Brockton originated from an English surname, meaning "town of badgers" or "settlement by the brook," and it is now used as a masculine given name.

BRONXTON Modern, masculine name of American origin, likely derived from the borough in New York City called The Bronx.

BRONZE The name "Bronze" originates from the English language and conveys the image of a precious alloy, symbolizing strength and durability.

BROOKSTON Means "town near a brook" and has an English origin.

BROWN The first name Brown is of English origin and it derived from the Old English word "brun," meaning "brown-haired" or "brown complexion."

BRUIN Means "bear" and originates from Dutch and Old English.

BRYCESON The first name Bryceson is of English origin and it means "son of Bryce" or "descendant of Bryce".

BRYLAN American origin and it means "from the hills."

BRYSTON English origin and means "bubbling spring," symbolizing someone with a lively and energetic personality.

BUCHANAN Means "victorious" or "from the cannon's seat" and has origins in Scotland.

BUCKLEY Means "clearing of the bucks" and is of English origin.

BUDDY Term of endearment meaning "friend" or "companion," and it originated as a nickname given to close friends or acquaintances.

BUFORD Masculine given name of English origin, meaning "ford near the hills" or "man from the ford by the hill."

BUKHARI The first name Bukhari has Arabic origins and it means "from the city of Bukhara."

BURECH The first name BURECH does not have a widely recognized meaning or origin.

BURHAN Means "proof" or "evidence" and it originates from Arabic.

BURTON Means "fortress settlement" and originated from Old English.

BUSTER The first name "Buster" is a nickname given to someone who breaks things or is a troublemaker, and it originated in English-speaking countries in the late 19th century.

CAEDMON	Means "wise warrior" and originates from Old English.
CAEDON	Means "spirit of battle" and has origins in Celtic and Gaelic languages.
CAELEN	Modern variation of the Irish name Caolán, meaning "slender" or "fair-haired."
CAELUM	Means "heaven" or "sky" and originates from Latin.
CAINAN	Means "possession" or "spear" and is of Hebrew origin, derived from the biblical figure mentioned in the Old Testament.
CALCIFER	The first name Calcifer is of fictional origin and gained popularity through the character of a fire demon in the book "Howl's Moving Castle" by Diana Wynne Jones.
CALDWELL	English origin, means "cold well" referring to someone living near a well with cold water, or a person who is reserved or stoic.
CALEDON	Means "from a rocky and fortified place" and has Scottish origins.
CALHOUN	The first name Calhoun is of Scottish and Irish origin, meaning "warrior" or "fierce spirit."
CALIBER	Means "quality or measurement of excellence" and originates from the English vocabulary term referring to the diameter of a firearm's ammunition.
CALIXTO	Means "most beautiful" and has its origin in Latin.
CALLAGHAN	Means "bright-headed" and has Irish origins.
CALLOWAY	Surname turned first name of English origin, meaning "pebbly place" or "grove with a stony surface".
CALOGERO	Means "beautiful old man" in Italian and originates from Greek.
CALVERT	Means "cowherd" and originates from Old English.
CAMBRIDGE	Unique English place name meaning "bridge over the River Cam" that has been used as a given name since the 19th century.
CAMP	English origin and means "enclosed place" or "camp."
CAMPION	Means "champion" or "winner" and it originated from the English surname Campion derived from the Old French word "champiun" meaning "warrior" or "fighter."
CANDIDO	Means "pure" or "innocent" and it originates from the Latin word "candidus."
CAPTAIN	Title and occupation derived from the Latin word "capitaneus," meaning leader of a military unit.
CARDIER	The first name "Cardier" does not have a widely recognized meaning or origin as it appears to be a rare or uncommon name.
CARLISLE	Carlisle is an English name that means "from the protected tower" and is derived from a place name in Cumbria, England.
CARLITO	Diminutive form of the name Carlos, meaning "man" or "warrior", and originated from Spanish and Portuguese.
CARMICHAEL	The first name Carmichael is of Scottish origin and means "friend of Michael" or "devotee of Saint Michael."
CARNELL	Means "defender of the fortress" and has an English origin.
CASANOVA	The first name Casanova originates from Italian and means "new house" or "new home" in reference to someone associated with luck or good fortune.
CASHEL	Means "castle" and has Irish origins.
CASHMERE	Luxury fiber obtained from the undercoat of certain goats, and the name is derived from the region of Kashmir in India where the fiber is traditionally produced.
CASHTEN	Means "town of warriors" and has English and Celtic origins.
CASIMIR	Means "proclaimer of peace" and originates from Slavic and Polish cultures.
CASMIR	Means "peacemaker" in Polish, and it originates from the Slavic name Kazimierz.
CASTEN	Variant of the name Karsten, which originated from the Old Norse language and means "Christian."
CASTOR	Greek origin and means "beaver."
CASYN	American origin and means "curly-headed one" or "curly-haired one."
CATARINO	Means "pure" or "innocent" and it has Latin origin.
CAYLIX	The name Caylix has no established meaning or origin as it appears to be a rare or unique name with no significant historical or cultural background.
CAYLUS	The first name Caylus is of French origin and means "from a town in France."
CAYMAN	Means "alligator" and is of Spanish origin.
CEASAR	The first name Caesar means "long-haired" and has Latin origin.

CEPHAS Means "rock" and originates from the New Testament, where it was given to Simon Peter by Jesus.

CERULEAN The first name Cerulean is of English origin and means "sky blue."

CESUR Turkish name meaning "brave" or "courageous."

CHADWICK Means "from the warrior's town" and is of Old English origin.

CHALINO Mexican origin and means "little Chalo," derived from the Spanish name "Gonzalo" which means "battle or war."

CHAMBER LAIN Means "chief officer of the household" and originates from the medieval English term for a person in charge of managing the household of a noble or royal family.

CHAMP Means "champion" and originated as a nickname for someone who excels in a particular field or sport.

CHAMPION Means "one who excels or is victorious" and it originates from the Old French word "champion" which referred to a person who fought on behalf of another in combat.

CHANOCH The name Chanoche means "dedicated" or "educated" and originates from Hebrew.

CHAPLIN The name Chaplin originates from English and means "clergyman, chaplain" referring to a member of the clergy.

CHAPMAN Means "merchant" or "trader" and it originates from Old English.

CHARBEL Means "beautiful work of God" and it originates from the Aramaic language.

CHARLEM AGNE Means "Charles the Great" and originated from Old High German, composed of the elements "karal" meaning "free man" and "magan" meaning "mighty, strong."

CHARLTON The first name Charlton is of English origin and means "settlement of free men" or "farm of the churls."

CHARMING Means "pleasant, charismatic, and captivating" and originates from the English language.

CHARVIK Sanskrit origin and means "intelligent" or "knowledgeable."

CHASETON The meaning and origin of the first name Chaseton is uncertain as it is a rare, modern variant of the name Chayse or Chase, which are derived from English vocabulary words referring to a hunt or pursuit.

CHASTEN Means "to discipline or correct" and has English or French origins.

CHAUNCEY Means "chancellor" and has its origins in Old French.

CHAYSON The meaning of the first name Chayson is "son of Chay" and it has origins in English and Gaelic.

CHEICK The first name CHEICK is of African origin and means "noble" or "leader."

CHEIKH Arabic origin and it means "leader" or "ruler".

CHESKEL Means "God will protect" and has Yiddish and Hebrew origins.

CHESTON Means "from the town by the chestnut trees" and it has English origins.

CHETAN Means "consciousness" or "soul" and originates from Sanskrit, an ancient language of India.

CHEZKY Hebrew name meaning "God has remembered" and it is of Jewish origin.

CHICAGO The first name Chicago is of American origin and derived from the name of a city in Illinois, known for its vibrant culture and distinctive architectural landmarks.

CHIDOZIE Nigerian name meaning "God establishes" or "God fixes" in the Igbo language.

CHIDUBEM Means "God is my guide" and it originates from Igbo, a language spoken in Nigeria.

CHIKAMSO Nigerian name meaning "God is with me" in the Igbo language.

CHINEDU Means "God leads" and it originates from the Igbo language of Nigeria.

CHIP Diminutive form of Charles, meaning "free man" and it originated from Old German.

CHIRON The name Chiron originates from Greek mythology and means "skilled" or "handicraftsman," referring to the wise centaur who taught heroes such as Achilles and

CHRISEAN Modern American name that combines the elements "Chris," a diminutive of Christopher, and "Sean," of Irish origin, meaning "bearer of Christ" or "gift from God."

CHRISHAWN Variant of the name Shawn, derived from the Irish name Seán, meaning "God is gracious."

CHRISTAIN The name Christian means "follower of Christ" and originates from the Latin name Christianus, derived from the Greek word Christianos.

CHRISTENSEN Means "son of Christen" or "son of Christian" and is of Danish origin.

CHRISTI ANJAMES Compound name derived from the English name Christian, meaning "follower of Christ," and the name James, originating from the Hebrew name Yaakov meaning "supplanter."

CHRISTOBAL Means "follower of Christ" and it originates from the Spanish language.

CHRISTOFER Means "bearer of Christ" and it is derived from the Greek name Christophoros.

CHRISTOPH Greek origin, means "bearer of Christ."

CHUKWUE BUKA Means "God is mighty" and it originates from the Igbo language of Nigeria.

CHUKWUE MEKA Means "God has done great" in Igbo language and originates from Nigeria.

CHUKWUKA Means "God is supreme" and it originates from the Igbo people of Nigeria.

CHURCH Surname-derived name meaning "belonging to the church," originating from the Old English word "cirice" and the Old Norse word "kirkja."

CICERO The first name Cicero, of Latin origin, means "chickpea" or "pea," and it was derived from the Roman cognomen Cicero, famously associated with the Roman philosopher, orator, and politician, Marcus Tullius Cicero.

CISCO Means "from the Church" and its origin is Spanish.

CLANCY Gaelic name meaning "red-haired warrior" and is of Irish origin.

CLARKSON The first name Clarkson, derived from an English surname, means "son of Clark" or "son of the cleric."

CLEMENT The first name Clement is of Latin origin and means "merciful" or "gentle."

CLEVELAND The meaning of the first name Cleveland is "land of cliffs," and it originates from Old English.

CLOVIS The first name Clovis originated from the Germanic language and it means "renowned warrior."

CLUTCH The first name "Clutch" is a contemporary English name that conveys a sense of being reliable, resourceful, and poised under pressure.

COAST The first name "Coast" has the meaning of "seashore" and is of English origin.

COASTAL Means relating to or located near the coast, and it is likely a modern, creative take on nature-inspired names.

COBAIN Means "ravine dweller" and originates from the Gaelic language.

COBI Short form of the Hebrew name Jacob, meaning "supplanter" or "holder of the heel," and is of Spanish origin.

COBURN The first name Coburn is of Scottish origin and means "lives at the hillside stream."

COLESTON Means "town of charcoal," and its origin can be traced back to Old English.

COLMAN Means "dove" and it originated from an Old English surname derived from the Latin personal name Columba.

COLSEN Means "son of Nicholas" and has English origins.

COLUMBUS Means "dove" and its origin is derived from the Latin language.

CONLAN Means "hero" or "brave" and originates from Irish Gaelic language.

CONNELL Gaelic name that means "strong wolf" and is derived from the Irish name Conall.

CONROY Means "hound of the plain" and it is of Irish origin.

CORBETT The first name "Corbett" is of English origin and it means "raven" or "dark-haired."

CORDAE The first name Cordae originates from Spanish origin and its meaning is "rope maker."

CORINTHIAN Means "from Corinth" and it originates from the Greek region of Corinth.

CORLEONE Means "lion-like" and is of Italian origin.

CORTLAND Means "land of the court" and has English origins.

CORVO The first name Corvo, of Italian origin, means "crow" or "raven" and is associated with intelligence and mystery.

COSIMO Means "order, beauty" in Greek and it is derived from the Italian name Cosmo, which is of Latin origin.

COSMO Means "order, beauty" and comes from the Greek word "kosmos" meaning "world" or "universe."

COSTNER The first name COSTNER is of English origin and means "town of cottages or cottar's settlement".

COTTON The first name Cotton originates from English and it refers to a person with a surname derived from the Old English word "cotun," meaning "cottage" or "enclosure."

COULSON Means "son of Cole" and it originates from English and Scottish surnames.

COULTER Scottish origin, meaning "one who lives near the coal-mining settlement or has black hair."

COURAGE Means bravery or boldness, and it is derived from the English word "courage" which comes from the Old French word "corage," ultimately stemming from the Latin word "cor," meaning heart.

COURTEZ Variant spelling of the Spanish name Cortez, derived from the Spanish word "cortés" meaning "courteous" or "polite," and it originated from the medieval ages as a descriptive surname for individuals exhibiting courteous behavior.

COURTLAND Masculine name of English origin meaning "land of the court" or "courtier's land".

COYOTE The first name Coyote has Native American origins and means "trickster" or "mischievous one."

CRASH The first name "Crash" is of American origin and typically conveys a daring and risk-taking persona, often associated with extreme sports and adrenaline-fueled activities.

CREEDENCE Means "belief, trust, confidence" and originated from the English word "creed."

CREIGHTON Masculine given name of English origin meaning "settlement near a hill."

CRISANTO Means "golden flower" and originated from Greek and Spanish languages.

CRISTHIAN Means "follower of Christ" and has origins in Christian and Spanish cultures.

CRISTHOFER Means "bearer of Christ" and it is a variation of the name Christopher, which originates from Greek and has biblical associations.

CRIXUS Means "one with curly hair" and originates from Ancient Rome.

CROCKETT The first name Crockett derives from an English surname and means "one who dwells near a small river."

CRUISE Means "journey" and it originates from the English vocabulary word related to sailing or flying.

CRUZITO The meaning and origin of the first name Cruzito is a diminutive form of the Spanish name Cruz, derived from the word "cross" and its origin is Latin.

CUAUHTE MOC Means "falling eagle" and originates from the Nahuatl language, spoken by the Aztecs in ancient Mexico.

CUPID Means "desire" or "passion" and originates from Roman mythology, where Cupid was the god of love.

CUTLER Means "one who makes or sells knives or cutlery" and its origin can be traced back to medieval England.

CUTTER Means "one who cuts" or "carves" and derives from the English occupational surname historically given to someone who worked as a cutter of cloth or leather.

CYNCERE The first name Cyncere is of American origin and means "a unique and creative individual."

CYPHER Means "codebreaker" and has a modern origin as a variant of the word "cipher," which refers to a secret or disguised way of writing a message.

CYPRIAN Means "from Cyprus" and has Latin origins.

CYXX Unique and modern name of unknown origin, possibly created for its originality and distinct sound.

DAECARI Unknown origin and meaning.

DAESHAWN The first name Daeshawn is of American origin and its meaning is a combination of elements from the name Dae (meaning "great") and Shawn (a variant of Sean, which means "God is gracious").

DAGIM Means "fish" and originates from Amharic, a language spoken in Ethiopia.

DAGMAWI Means "to build or construct" and originates from Amharic, which is a Semitic language spoken in Ethiopia.

DAGOBERTO Means "shining ruler" and has Germanic origins.

DAIQUAN Means "big influence" and is of American origin.

DAIVIK Means "divine, godly" and originates from Sanskrit, an ancient language of India.

DAIVON Modern variant of the name Devon, derived from an English surname, ultimately originating from the Celtic word "dubno" meaning "deep" or "dark".

DAKARAI Means "happiness" in Shona and originates from Zimbabwe.

DAKAVION American origin and likely a modern creation with unknown meaning.

DAKSH Means "competent" or "able" in Sanskrit and originates from ancient Indian (Hindu) mythology.

DALESSANDRO The first name Dalessandro is of Italian origin and means "son of Alessandro" or "descendant of Alessandro."

DAMACIO Spanish origin and means "tame" or "subdued."

DAMARCO Means "from the market" and has Latin origins.

DAMARIAN Means "from the sea" and originated from the combination of the names "Damaris" and "Marian."

DAMARIUS Means "he who tames" and has origins in Greek and Latin.

DAMASCUS Means "well-watered place" and originates from the ancient city in Syria, known for its fertile land and abundant water sources.

DAMEON The first name Dameon, of Greek origin, means "to tame" or "gentle" and it is a variant of the name Damon.

DAMERE The first name Damere originated from the English language and means "gifted ruler."

DAMIRI The name Damiri has Arabic origins and means "conscientious" or "one who follows a righteous path".

DAMONEY The first name Damoney is of American origin and is derived from combining the word "da" (slang for "the") and the name "Money," creating a distinctive and modern-sounding name.

DAMONIE Means "to tame" and is of Greek origin.

DANGER The first name "Danger" conveys a sense of risk or peril, while its origin can be traced back to the English language and is predominantly used as a unique and non-traditional name choice.

DANSBY The first name Dansby is of American origin and means "from the dance hall settlement."

DANTES The first name Dantes is of Italian and French origin and it means "enduring" or "steadfast."

DANYAL Means "God is my judge" and originates from Hebrew.

DAQUARIUS The first name Daquarius is of American origin and is derived from the combination of the name Da- and -quarius, with "Da" being a prefix often used in African-American naming customs, and "quarius" possibly influenced by the astrological sign Aquarius, symbolizing innovation and individuality.

DARECK Polish origin and it is a variant of the name Derek, meaning "ruler of the people."

DARICKSON Means "son of Derek" and originates from the English language.

DARIKSON The first name Darikson likely originates from combining the names Derek and Jackson, and its meaning may be a blend of their respective meanings.

DARIOUS Means "possessor" or "wealthy" and has Persian origins.

DARIUSH Means "possessor of wealth" and originates from Persian language and culture.

DARKIEL Contemporary, masculine given name of unclear origin that is not widely recognized or documented.

DARRAGH Means "oak tree" and has Irish origins.

DARROW The first name Darrow is of English origin and it means "from the small deer."

DARSHAN Indian origin and means "vision" or "to see with clarity."

DARSHIL Indian origin and means "one who is able to see or perceive clearly."

DARTAGNAN The first name D'Artagnan means "from Artagnan" and originates from the French place name, Artagnan.

DARYAN Modern variation of the Persian name Dariush, meaning "possessing goodness" or "upholder of the good."

DARYEL Means "beloved" and originates from the Hebrew name Dārīyāh.

DASHAUN Means "God is gracious" in American origin, often used as a modern variation of the name Shaun or Deshawn.

DASTAN Means "story" or "legend" in Persian, and it is commonly used in Central Asian countries.

DAUNTE Means "steadfast" or "enduring" and originated from the Latin name Dante, derived from the medieval Italian poet Dante Alighieri.

DAVANTE Means "beloved" or "cherished" and has American origins.

DAVARI The first name Davari is of Persian origin and means "judge" or "someone who gives verdicts."

DAVEION The meaning and origin of the first name Daveion is uncertain, as it is a modern variant of the name David with no specific origin.

DAVEY Diminutive form of the name David, of Hebrew origin meaning "beloved."

DAVIDSON Means "son of David" and has Scottish origins.

DAVILUCCA The first name Davilucca is of uncertain origin and meaning as it does not have a distinct etymology or widely recognized background.

DAVINCI Means "from Vinci" and originated from the Italian surname of the renowned artist and polymath, Leonardo da Vinci.

DAVISON The first name Davison is of English origin and means "son of David."

DAVONTAE Means "beloved gift" and has originated from American English.

DAVYON The first name "Davyon" originated as a modern variation of the name "David," meaning "beloved" in Hebrew.

DAWENS The first name Dawens has no widely recognized meaning or origin.

DAWENSKY The first name Dawensky holds no specific meaning or origin as it is a rare name with no widely-known associations.

DAWENSLEY Unique English first name of unknown origin and meaning.

DAWIT Means "beloved" or "cherished" and originates from the Amharic language in Ethiopia.

DAWOUD Means "beloved" and originates from Arabic.

DAWUD Means "beloved" and originates from Arabic and Hebrew.

DAXTEN The meaning of the first name Daxten is "from the town of Dax" and it has an English origin.

DAXYN The meaning and origin of the first name Daxyn are unknown as it is a modern and invented name with no known origins.

DAYMEIN Variant of the name Damian, which means "to tame" and can be traced back to Greek origins.

DAYMIAN Means "tamer" and its origin can be traced back to Greek mythology.

DAYREN The name Dayren originated from the English language and its meaning is derived from the combination of "day" and "ren," representing a person who brings joy and excitement to others during the day.

DEADRIAN The first name Deadrian originated from combining elements of the English word "dead" and the name "Adrian," and it likely signifies a unique individual with a blend of contrasting qualities.

DEAGLAN Masculine name of Irish origin meaning "full of goodness" or "full of virtue."

DEAKYN The meaning and origin of the first name Deakyn is a modern invented name with no known origin or specific meaning.

DEANTHONY Means "of Anthony" and has an American origin.

DEARIES The first name Dearies likely has a sentimental or affectionate connotation and its origin is unknown.

DEAUNDRE Means "beloved leader" and it is of American origin.

DECARLOS Modern American name that combines the prefix "De-" meaning "of" or "from" with the name Carlos, which is derived from the Old German name Karl meaning "free man."

DECHLAN Irish origin, means "full of goodness" or "loving"

DECKLYN Modern American name likely derived from the Gaelic surname Ó Dubhshláine, meaning "descendant of Dubhshláine."

DECORIAN The first name Decorian is of Latin origin and means "belonging to God" or "devoted to God".

DEIBY Variant of the name David, which originated from the Hebrew name ⬜ ⬜ ⬜ ⬜ (Dawid), meaning "beloved" or "uncle."

DEIMOS Means "terror" or "dread" in Greek, and it originates from Greek mythology as the name of the personification of dread and son of Ares and Aphrodite.

DEIVID   Variation of the name David, originating from Hebrew and meaning "beloved" or "friend."

DEJOUR   Means "from the day" and it is of French origin.

DEJUAN   Means "divine grace" and is of American origin.

DEKHARI   The first name Dekhari has an unknown origin and meaning as it does not have a widely recognized history or etymology.

DELBERT   Means "bright day" or "noble and shining" and has English and Germanic origins.

DELEON   Means "of the lion" and has Spanish origins.

DELOREAN Means "from the meadow of the laurel tree" and is of American origin.

DELUCA   The first name DeLuca originated from Italy and typically means "son of Luke" or "of the Lucanian region."

DELVONTE Means "from the town of Delvin" and has an English origin.

DEMARQUIS Means "of noble descent" and it originates from the combination of the French name prefix "De-" meaning "of" or "from," and the name "Marquis," which refers to a noble title.

DEMARYIUS Uncertain origin, but it is a modern American name likely invented by blending elements from various sources.

DEMAURI   The first name Demauri originated from combining the prefix "De-" meaning "of" or "from" and the name "Mauri," which refers to an ancient North African people.

DEMECO   The first name Demeco is of African origin and means "man of peace" or "peaceful ruler."

DEMETRICE Unisex name of Greek origin meaning "devoted to Demeter," the ancient Greek goddess of agriculture and fertility.

DEMETRIOUS Greek origin, means "devoted to Demeter" or "follower of Demeter."

DEMONTAE Means "mountain or of the mountain" and has American origins.

DENHAM   The name Denham originated from English and means "dweller at the estate in the valley."

DENILSON Means "son of Daniel" and it originates from the combination of the Portuguese element "de" meaning "of/from" and the name Nelson.

DENNISON Means "son of Dennis" and is of English origin.

DENTON   Denton is an English surname turned first name, meaning "town in a valley," derived from Old English elements "denu" (valley) and "tun" (enclosure, settlement).

DEQUINCY Means "from the estate of the nobleman" and originates from Old French.

DERVIN   Irish origin and its meaning is "gifted friend".

DESHUN   Means "male child born on a sunny day" and it originates from the Yoruba language spoken in Nigeria.

DESIDERIO Means "desired" or "longed for" and it originates from Latin.

DESTRY   Means "war horse" and has origins in Old French.

DETRICK   German origin and means "ruler of the people."

DEUCE   Means "second son" and originated from the English word used in card games to represent the number two.

DEVAUGHN Means "from the little dark one" and originates from Irish and Gaelic roots.

DEVEREAUX Male given name that originated from the Old French surname Devreux, referring to a person from Évreux in Normandy.

DEVLIN   The first name Devlin is of Irish origin and means "fierce bravery" or "descendant of Damhlaic, a follower of St. Columba."

DEWEY   Welsh origin and means "beloved" or "sorrow."

DEYVIS   The first name Deyvis originated from Latin America and means "beloved."

DEZMIN   Modern variation of the name Desmond, which originated from the Irish surname ó Deasmhumhnaigh, meaning "man from South Munster."

DHAIRYA   Means "courage" or "patience" and has its origin in Sanskrit.

DHANUSH   Means "bow" or "archery" and has origins in Sanskrit and Hindu mythology.

DHANVITH Dhanvith is an Indian name meaning "wealthy and knowledgeable" in Sanskrit origin.

DHARIUS   Modern variant of the name Darius, derived from the ancient Persian name Dārayavahush, meaning "possessing goodness" or "wealthy ruler."

DHARSHAN Sanskrit name meaning "vision" or "sight," originating from Hinduism and often associated with spiritual enlightenment and insights.

DHEER	Means "patient" and has its origin in Indian culture.
DHEERAN	Indian origin and means "brave" or "courageous".
DHRUVAN	Means "steadfast" and originates from Sanskrit.
DHRUVREDDY	Means "steadfast king" and has Indian origins.
DHYEY	The first name DhYey is of Indian origin and means "one who is focused and determined."
DIAMANTE	Meaning "diamond," Diamante is of Italian origin and signifies a precious and valuable gemstone.
DIANTE	The first name "Diante" is of American origin and it means "ahead" or "in front."
DICE	English origin and means "son of Denis."
DIERKS	Means "brave ruler" or "people's ruler" and originates from the Dutch and German languages.
DIETER	Means "warrior of the people" and it is of German origin.
DIETRICH	Means "ruler of the people" and has German origins.
DIEUDONNE	The first name Dieudonné means "gift from God" and has its origin in French.
DILLINGER	The first name Dillinger derives from the German surname meaning "son of Dill," typically given to someone who originated from a place named Dill or had associations with the herb dill.
DILLION	The meaning of the first name DILLION is "faithful" and it is of Irish and Gaelic origin.
DIMITRIOS	Means "devoted to Demeter" and originates from Greek mythology.
DINERO	Means "money" and has Spanish origins.
DIONDRE	Means "divine man" and it is of American origin.
DIONICIO	Means "follower of Dionysus" and has Greek origins.
DIONTAE	The name DIONTAE originated from the combination of the names Dion and Tae, and it means "God is my judge" or "God has judged."
DIONYSUS	Greek origin, means "Zeus's divine son" and is associated with the Greek god of wine, fertility, and ecstatic revelry.
DIRK	The name Dirk originated as a diminutive of the Germanic name Theodoric, meaning "ruler of the people," and is often associated with Dutch and Flemish cultures.
DIVYANSH	Means "a part of the divine" and is of Hindu origin.
DJANGO	The first name Django, of Romani origin, means "I awake" or "I am awake" and gained popularity due to the influential jazz guitarist Django Reinhardt.
DJAY	Modern variation of the name DJ, and its origin is derived from the term "DJ," which refers to a disc jockey who plays and mixes music at events or on the radio.
DJIBRIL	Means "messenger" or "archangel Gabriel" and originates from the Arabic language.
DKARI	The name DKARI does not have a widely recognized meaning or origin as it appears to be a unique or uncommon name.
DKARTER	The meaning of the first name DKARTER is not known and its origin is also unclear as it does not appear to have any known linguistic or cultural roots.
DKHARI	The first name DKHARI is of Sanskrit origin and means "one who is victorious or successful."
DMARCO	The first name D'Marco is of American origin and means "from the land of Mark."
DMITRI	Means "belonging to Demeter" and originates from Greek mythology.
DMONI	The first name DMONI, of unclear origin, does not have a widely recognized specific meaning.
DMYTRO	Means "warrior" or "of the earth" and originates from the Ukrainian variant of the name Demetrius.
DODGE	The first name Dodge, of American origin, means "skilled or quick in evading or eluding."
DOMINQUE	Means "belonging to the Lord" and is of French origin.
DOMINUS	Means "master" or "lord" and originates from Latin.
DONATELLO	Means "gift of God" and originated from Italian.
DONATI	Donati is of Italian origin and means "given by God."
DONAVON	Means "strong fighter" and has Irish and Gaelic origins.
DONTAVIOUS	Means "enduring, steadfast" and it originated as an American combination of the names Don and Octavius.

DONTAVIUS Means "enduring, steadfast" and has an American origin.

DORUK Means "summit" or "peak" and has Turkish origin.

DOVBER Means "bear-like" and it is of Hebrew origin.

DOYLE Means "dark stranger" and originates from Ireland, derived from the Gaelic surname Ó Dubhghaill.

DRACARYS Means "dragonfire" in High Valyrian and gained popularity through its association with Daenerys Targaryen from George R.R. Martin's "A Song of Ice and Fire" series and the television show "Game of Thrones."

DRAGAN Slavic origin and means "dear" or "beloved."

DRAIDEN Uncertain origin and meaning.

DRAVYN Means "strong one" and has uncertain origins, but it is possibly derived from the Old English word "dragan" meaning "to carry" or from the Old Norse name "Drafn."

DRAYTON Means "settlement of the dragon" and has English origins.

DRAYVEN Modern English name believed to be a variant of the name Draven, which is derived from the Old English word "draefend" meaning "hunter" or "one who hunts".

DREDEN Means "from the valley of turning" and it has uncertain origins.

DREQUAN The name Drequan originated in the United States and it means "a modern and unique name derived from combining 'Dre' and 'Quan'."

DRESDEN Means "people of the riverside forest" and originates from the Old Sorbian language in Germany.

DRESEAN Means "ambitious" and has an American origin.

DREUX French name of uncertain origin, often associated with the Breton region, meaning "oak tree."

DREVON The first name Drevon is of American origin and means "a modern and unique variation of the name Devon."

DREXEL Means "castle stronghold" and it originates from the Old English word "dæxel."

DREXLER The first name Drexler is of German origin and means "flexible or versatile builder."

DREYDAN Modern variant spelling of the name Dryden, which is of English origin and means "dry valley."

DRIN The first name Drin does not have a widely recognized meaning or origin.

DUBLIN Means "black pool" and originates from the Gaelic word "dubh" meaning black and "linn" meaning pool or lake.

DUDLEY Means "meadow of the people" and has English origins.

DUNAMIS Means "power" in Greek and has origins in the Bible, specifically in the New Testament.

DUPREE The first name Dupree has French origins and it means "of a noble lineage."

DURHAM Means "hill island" and originated from Old English.

DUSTY Meaning "covered with dust" or "gritty," Dusty is a nickname-turned-first name derived from the English word dust.

DUTCH Means "from the Netherlands" and originated as a nickname for individuals with Dutch ancestry or by those who come from the Netherlands.

DYAMI Means "eagle" and originates from the Native American Hopi tribe.

EARNEST Means "serious," "sincere," or "determined," and it is of English origin.

EAST The first name East derives from Old English origins and means "the direction of the sunrise."

EBENEZER Means "stone of help" and originates from the Hebrew language.

EBRAHEEM Arabic origin and means "father of nations" or "a prophet's name" in Arabic/Islamic context.

EDAHI The first name Edahi is of Native American origin meaning "one who is blessed."

EDERSON Portuguese origin and it means "son of Eder."

EDINSON Means "son of Eduardo" and has Spanish and English origins.

EDREI Means "mighty, powerful" and has Hebrew origins.

EDSEL Means "noble offspring" and has an English origin.

EDU Diminutive form of the male given name Eduardo, of Spanish and Portuguese origin, meaning "wealthy guardian" or "guardian of riches."

EFRAYIM	The name Efraim means "fruitful" or "very fruitful" in Hebrew and has biblical origins.
EFREM	Means "fruitful" or "productive" and originates from Hebrew.
EHITAN	The name Ehitán is of Edo origin in Nigeria and it means "royalty" or "crowning of a king."
EIDER	The first name "Eider" is of Basque origin and means "beautiful."
EIVOR	The first name Eivor is of Old Norse origin and means "eternal warrior."
EKAMJOT	Means "divine light" and has origins in Punjabi, a language spoken in Punjab region of India and Pakistan.
EKAMVEER	Means "brave and unique" and has a Punjabi origin.
EKANSH	Means "the whole" or "complete" and it originates from Sanskrit.
EKKO	"EKKO is a modern Scandinavian name meaning 'echo'."
EKLAVYA	Sanskrit origin, meaning "solemnized; self-taught hero" and is derived from the Hindu epic, Mahabharata, where Eklavya was a skilled archer who learned his skills on his own.
ELADIO	The first name "Eladio" is of Greek origin and means "man from Greece."
ELCHANAN	Means "God has been gracious" and has Hebrew origins.
ELCHONON	Means "God is gracious" and has Hebrew origin.
ELDAR	Means "ruler of the Elephants" and has Persian and Arabic origins.
ELDEN	The first name Elden, of English origin, means "old and wise protector" or "from the elves' valley."
ELDRIDGE	Means "noble ruler" and has English origins.
ELEFTHERIOS	Means "liberator" or "freedom" in Greek, and it originates from ancient Greek mythology and history.
ELHADJI	Means "the pilgrim" in Arabic and is commonly used in Senegal and other West African countries, often given to boys who have completed the Muslim pilgrimage to Mecca.
ELIAKIM	Means "God will establish" and originates from Hebrew.
ELIANTTE	The meaning and origin of the first name Eliantte is uncertain as it does not have a widely recognized origin or meaning.
ELIASJAMES	Name of English origin that combines the Hebrew name Elias, meaning "Yahweh is God," and the English name James, meaning "supplanter."
ELIGH	Hebrew origin and its meaning is "God is my oath" or "pledged to God".
ELIHU	Means "my God is He" and its origin is Hebrew.
ELIJAHJAMES	Compound name of English origin meaning "Yahweh is my God" combined with "supplanter" or "may God protect."
ELIMELECH	The meaning of the first name Elimelech is "my God is king" and its origin is Hebrew.
ELIOENAI	Means "my God has answered" and it has Hebrew origins.
ELISHAMA	Means "God has heard" and it originates from Hebrew.
ELIUD	Means "God is my praise" and originates from Hebrew.
ELIXANDER	The name Elixander likely has a modern variant of Alexander and originates from the Greek name Alexandros, meaning "defender of men."
ELIYAS	Hebrew origin and means "Jehovah is my God."
ELIYOHU	Hebrew name meaning "My God is Yahweh" and has origins in biblical literature and Jewish tradition.
ELIZANDRO	Modern name of uncertain origin, potentially influenced by the names Elisa and Alejandro.
ELJAY	The first name Eljay is an English-originated name meaning "noble" or "birdlike," often associated with masculine individuals.
ELNATAN	Means "God has given" and originated from Hebrew.
ELNATHAN	Means "God has given" and it originated from Hebrew.
ELOHIM	The first name Elohim has Hebrew origins, meaning "God" or "gods" and is often used as a reference to the divine.
ELROY	Means "the king" or "the ruler" and has English and Old French origins.
ELSHADDAI	The first name ElShaddai is of Hebrew origin and means "God Almighty."
ELUZER	The first name "Eluzer" is of Hebrew origin and it means "God is my help."
ELWOOD	Means "from the old forest" and has Old English origins.
EMEKA	Means "great deeds" or "merciful" and is of Igbo origin in Nigeria.
EMERICK	German origin, derived from the Germanic elements "amal" meaning "work" and "ric" meaning "ruler," with the overall meaning of "ruler of work" or "powerful and industrious ruler."

EMIGDIO Spanish given name meaning "immigrant," derived from the Latin word "emigrantem."

EMILSON Means "son of Emil" and originates from Scandinavia.

EMIRHAN Turkish name meaning "Ruler's Khan" or "Prince" and it is derived from the Turkish words emir (ruler) and han (khan or prince).

EMMAUS The name Emmaus originated from biblical times and it refers to a town mentioned in the New Testament as the place where Jesus appeared after his resurrection.

EMMETTE The first name Emmette originated as a variant spelling of the English name Emmett, meaning "universal" or "whole."

EMPEROR Means "ruler" or "sovereign" and originates from the Latin word "imperator."

ENAEL Hebrew origin and means "God is gracious."

ENDRI Masculine Albanian name, derived from the Greek name Andreas meaning "manly" or "courageous."

ENDYMION Means "to dive into" or "to enter into" and originates from Greek mythology.

ENEKO Means "my little one" in Basque and is of Basque origin.

ENLIL Means "lord" or "ruler" and originates from ancient Mesopotamia, where Enlil was worshipped as a god of air, wind, and storms.

ENMANUEL The first name "Enmanuel" derives from the Hebrew name "Imanu'el" which means "God is with us" and is often associated with the birth of Jesus in the Bible.

ENRICO The first name Enrico is of Italian origin and means "ruler of the home" or "ruler of the household."

EOGHAN Means "born of the yew tree" and has Irish Gaelic origins.

EPHREM Means "fruitful" or "productive" and has origins in biblical and religious traditions, particularly in Christianity and Ethiopian culture.

EPHRIAM Means "fruitful" or "abundant" and has Hebrew origins.

EPIFANIO Means "manifestation" or "appearance" and originates from Greek.

ERAGON Means "dragon" and originates from the fantasy novel series "Inheritance Cycle" written by Christopher Paolini.

ERASMO The first name Erasmo originates from Greek and means "beloved."

ERDEM Means "virtuous" or "honorable" in Turkish, and it is derived from the Turkish word "erdem" which translates to "virtue" or "worthiness."

ERFAN Means "knowledgeable" or "wise" and it originates from Persian/Iranian culture.

ERICKSON The first name Erickson is of Scandinavian origin and it means "son of Erik".

ERIKSON Means "son of Erik" and has Scandinavian and Germanic origins.

ERIOLUWA Yoruba name meaning "God's gift" or "God's promise" and is of Nigerian origin.

ERLING Means "descendant of the nobleman" and originates from Old Norse.

ERNIE Diminutive form of the name Ernest, of Germanic origin, meaning "serious" or "resolute."

ESAIAS Means "God is my salvation" and originates from Hebrew.

ESCANOR The first name Escanor originated from Arthurian legend and means "splendid," referring to his character's exceptional strength and pride.

ESGAR Means "spear of God" and has Germanic origins.

ESKO The Finnish name Esko means "God's helmet" and originates from the Finnish word "eskola," which refers to an annual summer camp for children organized by the Evangelical Lutheran Church of Finland.

ESNEIDER The first name Esneider is of Spanish origin and means "spear of God" or "God's spear."

ESTIVEN Variation of the name Stephen, which is of Greek origin and means "crown" or "crowned."

ESTUARDO Spanish variant of the name Edward, meaning "wealthy guardian" and it originates from Old English.

ESVIN Means "friend of God" and its origin can be traced back to Germanic languages.

ETHANIEL The first name Ethanial means "gift of God" and is derived from the Hebrew name Ethan.

ETHANJAMES Modern English compound name, combining the Hebrew name Ethan meaning "strong" or "enduring" and the given name James, derived from the Hebrew name Ya'aqov meaning "supplanter" or "heel grabber."

ETHANMA ETHANMATEO is likely a combination of the names Ethan and Mateo, possibly created as
TEO a unique or modern variation of traditional names.

ETHIC	Means "moral principles or values" and is of Greek origin.
ETIENNE	The first name Étienne means "crown" or "garland" in French, and it originates from the Latin name "Stephanus" which means "crown" or "crowned one."
EUSEBIO	Means "pious" or "devout" and it originates from the Greek name Eusebios.
EUSTACE	Means "fruitful" or "productive" and originates from the Greek name Eustachius/Eustathios.
EVANGELOS	Means "bringer of good news" or "messenger of good news" in Greek, and it originates from the Greek word "evangelion" meaning "good news" or "gospel."
EVARISTO	The first name Evaristo, of Spanish and Portuguese origin, means "well-pleasing" or "acceptable" in Greek.
EVERHETT	Means "brave boar" and it is of Old English origin.
EVERTON	Means "from the boar enclosure" and it has English origins.
EVRHETT	The first name Evrhett is of uncertain origin and does not have a specific meaning.
EXODUS	Means "a mass departure or journey" and originates from ancient Hebrew, primarily associated with the biblical story of the Israelites' escape from slavery in Egypt.
EYDAN	Hebrew origin and it means "fiery and passionate."
EYOAB	Eyoab is an Ethiopian name meaning "one who shines like a star" and is of Amharic origin.
EYOEL	Means "God will be his salvation" and it is of Ethiopian origin.
EYOSIAS	The first name Eyosias is of Amharic origin and it means "God saves" or "God rescues" in Ethiopia.
EZANA	The first name Ezana has Ethiopian origins and means "he has increased" or "he has become bigger" in the Amharic language.
EZECHIEL	Means "God strengthens" and it originates from the Hebrew language.
EZEKEIL	Means "God strengthens" and it originates from the Hebrew language.
EZEKIAS	Means "God strengthens" and it originates from Hebrew.
EZEKIELJAMES	Means "God strengthens" and is of Hebrew origin.
EZEQUIAS	Means "God strengthens" and it originates from Hebrew.
EZERA	Variant of the biblical Hebrew name Ezra, meaning "help" or "assistance", originating from the Hebrew language.
EZERIAH	The name Ezeriah, derived from Hebrew origin, means "God is my helper" or "God has helped me."
EZRAJAMES	Combination of the Hebrew name Ezra, meaning "helper," and the English name James, meaning "supplanter," originally from the Bible.
EZRIEL	The first name Ezriel is of Hebrew origin and means "God is my help."
FABRIZIO	Means "craftsman" or "blacksmith" and originates from the Latin name Fabricius.
FAIZAN	Means "blessings" or "abundance" and has origins in Arabic and Urdu languages.
FALCON	The first name Falcon is of English origin, meaning "bird of prey" and symbolizing speed, agility, and strength.
FAOLAN	Means "little wolf" and has Irish origins.
FARAZ	Means "elevation, height" and has Persian origins.
FARID	Means "unique" or "peerless" and originates from Arabic and Persian languages.
FAROOQ	Means "one who distinguishes between right and wrong" and has Arabic origins.
FATEH	Means "victorious" and originates from Arabic and Persian languages.
FAUSTO	Means "lucky" or "fortunate" in Italian, and it is of Latin origin.
FAWKES	The first name Fawkes originated from the English surname "Fawkes," meaning "fox," derived from the Middle English word "faux."
FELICIANO	Means "fortunate" or "lucky" and originates from Latin.
FENRIR	The first name "Fenrir" originates from Norse mythology and refers to a monstrous wolf, symbolizing chaos and destruction.
FERDINAND	The name Ferdinand originated from Germanic roots and means "brave traveler" or "bold voyager."
FERGUS	Means "man of force" and originates from Gaelic.
FERGUSON	The first name Ferguson is of Scottish origin and means "son of Fergus."
FERMIN	Means "firm, resolute" and has Spanish origins.

FERRARI FERRARI is an Italian surname turned first name meaning "blacksmith" or "metalworker" and is associated with luxury sports car manufacturer Enzo Ferrari.

FESTUS Means "merry, festive" and originates from the Latin word "festus" meaning "joyous, festive."

FIDENCIO Spanish masculine name meaning "faithful" or "trustworthy," derived from the Latin word "fides" which means "faith."

FIELDING Means "one who lives in or near a field" and originated from an English surname that derived from a place name.

FIELDS Means "open land" and is of English origin.

FILIBERTO Means "bright, illustrious" and is of Italian and Spanish origin.

FINAN Means "fair-haired" and has Irish and Scottish origins.

FINCH English and Scottish name meaning "a person who lived by a finch's habitat" or "a bright or beautiful person" and it originates from the Middle English word "fink" or "finke."

FINDLEY Name of Scottish origin meaning "fair warrior".

FINESSE Means skillful and refined in behavior, originating from the French word meaning delicacy or subtlety.

FINLAN Means "fair-haired hero" and originates from Ireland.

FINNBAR Means "fair-haired warrior" and originates from the Irish language.

FITZPATRICK Means "son of Patrick" and has an Irish origin.

FITZWILLIAM Means "son of William" and has English origin.

FLAVIO Means "blond" or "yellow-haired" and originates from the Latin name Flavius.

FLORENTINO The first name Florentino originated from the Latin name Florentinus and it means "flourishing" or "blooming."

FLORIN Means "flower" and originates from Latin.

FOLARIN The first name Folarin originated from the Yoruba culture in Nigeria and it means "walking with glory."

FORBES The first name Forbes originated from a Scottish surname meaning "field" or "farm" and often symbolizes someone who is proud and successful.

FOREIGN Unique and unconventional name that is likely of English origin, suggesting an individual who is different or stands out from the norm.

FORTUNE Means "luck" or "fate" and is of Latin origin.

FOUAD Means "heart" or "one with an excellent heart" and it originates from Arabic.

FOWLER Means "bird-catcher" and originated from an occupational surname for someone who caught birds for food or sport.

FRABIAN The first name Frabian is of uncertain origin and meaning.

FRANCISZEK Means "free man" and it originates from the Latin name Franciscus.

FRANCOIS The first name François means "free man" in French and originates from the Latin name Franciscus, meaning "Frenchman" or "from France."

FRASER Means "strawberry-bearing" and originates from Scotland.

FRAZIER The first name Frazier, of Scottish origin, means "free man" or "strawberry" and it is derived from the Old French name "Fraser."

FRIEDRICH Means "peaceful ruler" and originates from Germanic and Old High German languages.

FRITZ The first name Fritz is of German origin and it means "peaceful ruler" or "peaceful ruler of the people."

FROYLAN The first name Froylan is of Spanish origin and means "flowered meadow."

FULLER The first name Fuller originated as an occupational surname in medieval England, meaning "one who played the role of a fulling mill worker."

FULTON Means "settlement by a field" and it originates from the Old English surname "Fugol-tun" meaning "bird settlement."

FURQAN Means "criterion" or "the one who distinguishes between right and wrong" in Arabic, and it is of Arabic origin.

FUTURE Means anticipation of what is to come and originated as a modern English word name.

FYODOR Means "gift of God" and originates from the Slavic language.

GABRIAN The first name Gabrian is of uncertain origin, but it is likely a modern invention derived from the name Gabriel, meaning "God is my strength."

GAETANO	Means "from Gaeta" and originates from Italy.
GAHEL	Breton origin, means "generous and kind."
GAINES	English origin and means "from the district of Gainsborough" or "from the town of Gaines."
GALDINO	Portuguese and Spanish name, derived from the Germanic elements "wald" meaning "rule" and "win" meaning "friend", and it means "ruler's friend".
GALLAGHER	The first name Gallagher is of Irish origin and means "brave and spirited; descendant of foreign helper."
GAMALIEL	Means "reward of God" and originates from Hebrew.
GANZA	The first name GANZA originates from the Swahili language, meaning "treasure" or "valuable possession."
GARDNER	Means "one who tends to or works in a garden" and is of English origin.
GARRUS	Means "youthful" and has origins in ancient Rome.
GASPAR	Means "treasurer" or "bearer of treasure" and originates from the Hebrew name "Gizbar."
GATES	Surname-derived first name meaning "someone who lived by the gates" and is of Old English origin.
GATSBY	Means "from the nobleman's stronghold" and is of English origin.
GAURIK	The first name Gaurik is of Sanskrit origin and means "belonging to Lord Ganesha" or "golden-colored".
GAUTAM	Means "enlightened" and its origin can be traced back to Sanskrit.
GAUTHAM	Means "knowledgeable" or "enlightened" and it originates from the Sanskrit language of ancient India.
GAWAIN	Means "white hawk" and derives from the Welsh name "Gwalchgwyn."
GEDALYA	Means "God is great" and has Hebrew origins.
GEORDI	Variant of the name Jordy/Jordan and originated as a diminutive form of the name George.
GEOVONNI	Means "God is gracious" and it is of Italian origin.
GERALT	Means "spear ruler" and has Old High German origins.
GEREMIAS	The first name "Geremias" is a variant of the biblical name "Jeremiah," which is of Hebrew origin and means "exalted by the Lord."
GERSHON	Means "exile" and has Hebrew origins.
GERVONTA	The first name Gervonta is of American origin and is derived from the combination of the names Gerald and Lavonta.
GHAITH	Means "rescuer" or "helper" and it originates from Arabic.
GHAZI	Means "victorious" or "conqueror" and originates from Arabic.
GHOST	English origin and refers to a spirit or apparition, often associated with the supernatural and the deceased.
GIACOMO	Means "supplanter" and is of Italian origin.
GIANFRANCO	The first name Gianfranco originated in Italian and it means "God is gracious."
GIANMARCO	Means "God is gracious" and has an Italian origin.
GIBRAN	Means "strong" or "powerful" and has Arabic origins.
GIDON	Means "feller" or "warrior" in Hebrew and is of biblical origin, referencing the Old Testament figure Gideon who led the Israelites to victory against the Midianites.
GILDARDO	The first name Gildardo has Hispanic origins and means "brave ruler" or "ruler with a golden sword".
GILEAD	Means "hill of testimony" and it originated from Hebrew.
GIORNO	Giorno is an Italian name meaning "day" and is derived from the Latin word "diurnus."
GIVENCHY	French origin and means "place at the edge of a village" or "a settlement near the river."
GLAUK	Greek origin and means "bright blue" or "gleaming."
GODFREY	Means "God's peace" and originated from Old English and Old Germanic languages.
GODWIN	The meaning of the first name Godwin is "friend of God" and it has Old English origins.
GOKU	Means "aware of emptiness" and originates from Japanese anime and manga series, Dragon Ball.
GOTEN	Means "Palace of Enlightenment" in Japanese and it is derived from a character in the Dragon Ball series.

GRACESON	The first name Graceson originates from combining the English word "grace" which means elegance or divine favor, and the suffix "-son" indicating "son of," resulting in a name meaning "son of grace" or "graceful son."
GRAESYN	Means "graceful or graceful son" and it has a modern American origin.
GRAFTON	English origin, means "town of the grove," derived from the Old English words "grafwudu" (grove) and "tun" (town).
GRAINGER	Means "grain farmer" and has English origins.
GRAYLEN	Modern American name of uncertain origin, often believed to be a combination of the names Gray and Lynn.
GRAYSTON	The first name "Grayston" is of English origin and means "gray stone," referring to someone with a strong and dependable nature.
GREATNESS	Greatness means exceptional, superior or truly outstanding, and the name likely originated as a descriptor of someone who embodies these qualities.
GRESHAM	The name Gresham has English origins and means "grazing homestead", derived from the Old English words "gres" (grass) and "ham" (homestead).
GREYDON	Means "son of a grey-haired man" and is of English origin.
GREYLAN	Means "graceful or noble land" and has an American origin.
GRIEZMANN	Means "son of a gray man" and originated from Basque language and culture.
GRIFFEY	Welsh origin, means "descendant of the fierce lord" or "son of the griffin."
GRIZZLY	The first name Grizzly likely originated as a nickname inspired by the powerful and fearsome characteristics of the grizzly bear.
GROVER	Means "great grove" and originates from an English and Scottish surname.
GRYPHON	Means "mythical creature" and it originates from Greek mythology.
GUDIEL	Spanish name meaning "God is majesty" and is of biblical origin.
GUNTHER	Means "warrior" and it originates from Old Norse and Germanic languages.
GURBAAZ	Punjabi name meaning "brave and fearless" that is derived from the words "gur" (meaning guru or wisdom) and "baaz" (meaning falcon or eagle).
GURFATEH	Punjabi origin and means "victorious through spiritual knowledge or grace."
GURJAAP	Means "meditating or remembering the Guru" and it has origin in Punjabi and Sikh communities.
GURKIRAT	Sikh name meaning "one who sings praises of the Guru," originating from Punjabi language.
GURNIWAZ	The name Gurniwaz has a Punjabi origin and its meaning is "one who remains absorbed in the Guru's praises."
GURSAHIB	Means "Master of the Guru" and originates from Punjabi, a language spoken in Punjab, India.
GURSEHAJ	Means "God's lion" and originates from the Punjabi language used in Sikh culture.
GURSHAAN	Means "one who meditates on the Lord" and it has its origin in Punjabi Sikh Indian culture.
GURTAJ	The first name Gurtaaj means "crown of the guru" and has Punjabi and Sikh origins.
GURVEER	Means "brave and wise" and has Sikh origins.
GUTHRIE	The first name Guthrie is of Scottish origin and means "windy place."
GUZMAN	Means "good man" and originates from Spanish.
HAAHEO	Means "pride" in Hawaiian and is of Polynesian origin.
HABAKKUK	Means "embrace" and it originates from the Hebrew language.
HAFEZ	Means "guardian" or "memorizer" and has Arabic origin.
HAGGAI	Means "festive" or "festive pilgrim" and has Hebrew origins.
HAIDER	Means "lion" in Arabic and is of Islamic origin.
HAITHAM	Means "lion" and has Arabic origins.
HAJIN	The first name Hajin is of Korean origin and means "beautiful treasure" or "precious and valuable person."
HALCYON	Halcyon means calm, peaceful, and prosperous, and originates from Greek mythology where Halcyon was a bird believed to calm the sea during its nesting period.
HAMID	Means "praised" or "praiseworthy" and it has Arabic origins.
HAMIDOU	Means "praiseworthy" or "thankful" and originates from Arabic.

HANDSOME	Means physically attractive or good-looking and originated as a descriptive English surname that evolved into a given name.
HANZO	The meaning of the name Hanzo is "leader" or "ruler" and it originated from Japan.
HARDIN	The first name Hardin is of English origin and means "valley of hares."
HAROUN	Means "exalted" or "high" and originates from Arabic.
HARTMAN	Means "strong man" and is of German origin.
HARUN	Means "exalted" or "high mountain" and originates from Arabic.
HASIBULLAH	Male Arabic name meaning "God's reckoning" and is of Islamic origin.
HASKELL	Hebrew origin and means "wise, one who understands."
HASNAIN	Arabic origin and means "two beautiful or full moons," typically used as an honorific title referring to the Prophet Muhammad and his two grandsons, Hasan and Husayn.
HASSIAH	Hebrew name meaning "God has judged" or "God has saved," with its origin being the bible.
HASTINGS	Surname turned first name of Old English origin meaning "son of Hæsta".
HAWK	The name Hawk refers to a bird of prey and has English origin, derived from the Old English word "hafoc."
HAWTHORNE	Means "thorn bush" and originated from the Old English words "haga" (enclosure or fence) and "þorn" (thorn).
HAYATO	Means "falcon person" in Japanese and it has Japanese origins.
HAYDN	Means "heathen" or "pagan" and originates from Welsh and Anglo-Saxon sources.
HAYNES	The first name Haynes is of English origin and means "from the enclosed meadow," referring to someone living near or from a fenced-in field.
HAYSTEN	The first name Haysten is of American origin and means "born of hay fields."
HAYWARD	Means "keeper of the hedge" and has English origins.
HAYWOOD	Means "enclosed wood" and originates from Old English.
HAZAIAH	The meaning of the first name HAZAIAH is "God sees" and its origin is Hebrew.
HAZIQ	Arabic origin, means "intelligent" or "sharp-witted."
HEBER	Means "enclave" or "associate" and originates from Hebrew.
HEINRICH	Means "ruler of the household" and originates from Germanic roots.
HELIOS	Means "sun" in Greek and originated from Greek mythology where Helios was the god of the sun.
HENDERSON	Means "son of Henry" and has Scottish and English origins.
HENDON	The first name Hendon is of Old English origin and means "hill of hinds" or "moor of deer."
HENOK	Hebrew origin, meaning "dedicated" or "initiated," often associated with biblical figures.
HENRICK	German and Old Norse origin, meaning "ruler of the home" or "ruler of the household."
HERCULES	Masculine given name meaning "glory of Hera" in Greek mythology, derived from the name of the mythological hero known for his great strength and adventures.
HERMES	Means "messenger of the gods" and originates from Greek mythology.
HERMINIO	Means "little Hermes" and has Spanish and Portuguese origins.
HERSCHEL	Means "deer" or "stallion" and has Hebrew origins.
HERSHY	Yiddish origin, meaning "deer" or "beloved," and is often used as a nickname for the Hebrew name Hersh or Hershel.
HESHY	Hebrew nickname derived from the name Hershel, meaning "deer" or "stag" in Yiddish and originating from Eastern European Jewish communities.
HETANSH	Means "part of the heart" and originates from the Sanskrit language.
HEWITT	The first name Hewitt is of English origin and means "bright in mind and spirit."
HEZEKAI	Means "God strengthens" and has Hebrew origins.
HEZEKIYAH	Means "God strengthens" and originates from Hebrew biblical literature.
HICKORY	American origin and refers to a type of hardwood tree, symbolizing strength and durability.
HIEU	The first name Hieu has origins in Vietnamese culture and it means "understanding" or "knowledgeable."
HILLEL	Means "praise" or "praised one" and has Hebrew origins.
HIROSHI	Means "generous" or "abundant" in Japanese and its origin is Japanese as well.
HOBART	Means "bright or shining mind" and it originated from an English surname, derived from the village of Hobart in Lincolnshire, England.

HOLSTYN	Rare and modern English-originated name that does not have a widely known meaning or origin.
HOMER	Means "security" or "pledge" and originates from the Greek language.
HORACIO	Means "man of time and hour" and is of Latin origin.
HORUS	Means "the one who is above" and originates from ancient Egyptian mythology, referring to the god of the sky and kingship.
HOVHANNES	The first name Hovhannes is of Armenian origin and means "gift of God."
HOWELL	Means "eminent and noteworthy" and has Welsh origins.
HOWIE	The first name "Howie" is a diminutive form of the male given name "Howard," originating from English and meaning "brave heart" or "noble protector."
HRIDAYA	Means "heart" in Sanskrit and originates from India.
HUCKLEB ERRY	The name Huckleberry, meaning "sweet berry," originates from English literature and gained popularity as the given name of the adventurous character Huckleberry Finn created by Mark Twain.
HUCKSON	Huckson is an uncommon English name derived from the combination of "Huck," a diminutive of Henry or Hugh, and "son," indicating "son of."
HUCKSTON	The first name Huckston originated as an English surname meaning "from Huxstone," referring to someone from Hucks Stone, which may have been a place known for its prominent rock formation or used as a personal name.
HUESTON	Variant of the name Houston, derived from a place name meaning "hill town" in Old English.
HUEY	Means "bright in mind and spirit" and originates from the Germanic name Hugh.
HUGHES	Means "heart, mind, spirit" and it is of French and Old German origin.
HUGHIE	Means "bright in mind and spirit" and is of Scottish and English origin.
HUNT	Means "to pursue, search, or capture" and is of English origin.
HUNTING TON	The first name Huntington, derived from an English surname, suggests a sense of strength and belonging as it means "from the hunter's settlement" or "town near the huntsman's estate".
HUSAYN	Means "handsome" or "good" and it originates from Arabic language and Islamic traditions, notably associated with Imam Husayn ibn Ali, a significant figure in Shiite Islam.
HUTCHINSON	Means "son of Hugh" and has English origins.
HUTCHISON	The first name Hutchison originated as a Scottish patronymic surname, derived from the given name Hugh and the suffix "son" meaning "son of Hugh."
HUXEN	The meaning and origin of the first name HUXEN are uncertain as it does not have a widely recognized or established origin or meaning.
HUZAIFA	Means "intelligent" or "wise" and is of Arabic origin.
ICARUS	Means "to ascend" and it is of Greek origin, derived from the mythological figure who flew too close to the sun.
ICHIRO	Means "first son" in Japanese and its origin is Japanese.
IFEANYI	Means "nothing is impossible with God" and originates from the Igbo language of Nigeria.
IFEANYI CHUKWU	Means "nothing is impossible with God" and originates from the Igbo people of Nigeria.
IFEDAYO	Yoruba name of Nigerian origin meaning "love brings joy."
IGANZE	The first name Iganze is of African origin and means "one who brings joy" or "happiness."
IKAIKA	The first name Ikaiaka means "strong" or "mighty" and it is of Hawaiian origin.
IKECHUKWU	Means "God's strength" and originates from the Igbo tribe in Nigeria.
IKTAN	The meaning and origin of the first name Iktan is unknown, as it does not have a widely recognized origin or meaning in any specific language or culture.
INFANTMALE	The name "Infantmale" does not have a specific meaning or origin as it is an unusual compound word that combines the words "infant" and "male," possibly used as a placeholder or placeholder name.

INIGO Means "fiery" or "ardent" and has Spanish and Basque origins.

INIOLUWA Yoruba name meaning "God's property" or "God's possession".

INMER The first name Inmer originates from Hebrew and its meaning is "spoken of God" or "dedicated to God."

INNOCENT Means "pure" or "innocent" and has Latin origins.

IOANE Means "God is gracious" and originates from Hebrew.

IOSIF Means "God will increase" and its origin is from the Hebrew name Yosef, meaning "may Jehovah add/give increase".

IOSUA The first name "Iosua" is of Hebrew origin, meaning "God is salvation" or "Yahweh is salvation."

IRAM Means "bright city" and it is derived from Arabic origins.

IREMIDE The first name "Iremide" is of Yoruba origin and it means "my goodness has come."

IREOLUWA IREOLUWA means "blessing of God" in Yoruba and is of Nigerian origin.

IRETOMIWA Yoruba name meaning "hope has returned" and is of Nigerian origin.

IROH Means "mystery" or "mystical" and has its origins in Japanese language and culture.

IRTAZA Arabic origin and means "one who seeks or yearns for forgiveness."

ISHAANR Unique Indian name meaning "lord of the north" with Ishaan being a Sanskrit name and
EDDY Reddy denoting a Telugu-speaking community.

ISIDORE Means "gift of Isis" and has Greek origins.

ISKANDER Means "defender of mankind" and has its origin in the ancient Greek name Alexander.

ISOM The name Isom originated from the Hebrew name "Isaiah" and means "God is salvation."

ISRAFIL Means "the angel who blows the trumpet" and originates from Islamic mythology.

ISSACHAR Means "reward" or "there is a reward" and is of Hebrew origin.

ITACHI Means "weasel" or "ferret" and is of Japanese origin.

ITHIEL Means "God is with me" and it originates from Hebrew.

IYAD Arabic origin and it means "support" or "reinforcement."

IZAIAS Hebrew origin and means "God is salvation."

IZAIYAH Modern variant of the biblical name Isaiah, meaning "Yahweh is salvation", and it originated from Hebrew.

IZAYUS The first name Izayus does not have a recognized meaning or origin, as it appears to be a unique and uncommon name.

IZEAH Modern American variation of the Hebrew name Isaiah, meaning "Yahweh is salvation."

IZHAAN Means "young, growing" and is of Arabic origin.

IZIR Arabic origin and means "prosperous" or "successful".

IZMAEL Means "God has heard" and it originates from Hebrew.

IZYAIS Unique and expressive name of unknown origin, possibly created or derived from a combination of various other names or words.

JABARE Means "brave" and it has an African origin.

JABEZ Means "sorrow" or "borne in pain" and has Hebrew origins.

JABRAYLEN African-American origin, has no specific meaning but likely originated as a modern invented name.

JABRIL Means "servant of God" and it is of Arabic origin.

JACAERYS Means "healer" and is of unknown origin.

JACEION The meaning and origin of the first name Jaceion is unknown as it does not have a recognized meaning or origin.

JACERE The first name Jacere has no widely recognized meaning or origin as it is not a commonly used name.

JACHAI Thai origin and means "victory" or "triumph".

JACIEON The name JACIEON has no widely recognized meaning or origin as it is not commonly found in established name databases.

JACINTO Means "hyacinth flower" in Spanish and it originates from the Greek name Hyakinthos.

JACKMAN The first name Jackman likely originated as a patronymic surname meaning "son of Jack."

JACKSTON Means "son of Jack" and is a variant spelling of the surname Jackson, which originates from English and Scottish origins.

JACOLBY Modern variant of the name Jacob, of Hebrew origin, meaning "supplanter" or "holder of the heel."

JACORI Modern American name with uncertain origins, likely a variant of the name Jacory.

JACORIAN Means "a modern American name with unknown origins or meaning."

JADIS Feminine given name of French origin, meaning "a long time ago" or "formerly," popularized by the character of the White Witch in C.S. Lewis's "The Chronicles of

JAEDYN Modern name of American origin that is likely a variant of Jadon, meaning "thankful" in Hebrew.

JAEGER Means "hunter" and originates from the German language.

JAEVION Uncertain origin, conveys an essence of uniqueness and individuality.

JAFET Means "may he enlarge" and it is of Hebrew origin.

JAHCARI Means "one who is strong and brave" and has an African origin.

JAHCERE The first name "Jahcere" is of American origin and does not have a specific meaning.

JAHIEM Means "elevated by God" and it has African and Hebrew origins.

JAHKAI Modern American name likely created by combining elements from various African, Jamaican, or Rastafarian origins, with no specific documented meaning.

JAHKING The first name Jahking is of African origin and it means "God is gracious" or "God's gift."

JAHKOR The name Jahkor has a contemporary origin and meaning, often associated with an African-American cultural context, and it may be a variation of the name Jacob or an invented name combining elements of Jah (meaning God) and Kor (meaning dedicated or committed).

JAHLEEL Means "God waits" and it has biblical origins.

JAHMANI African origin and means "strong and faithful warrior" or "one who has faith in God."

JAHMARION American origin, and it means "combination of Jah and Marion, possibly referring to an appreciative or devoted follower or lover of God."

JAHMARLEY The name "Jahmarley" has a combination of origins, with "Jah" derived from the Hebrew word for God and "Marley" being associated with the iconic Jamaican musician Bob Marley, resulting in a name that signifies a connection to spirituality and reggae music.

JAHMEIR The first name Jahmeir is of Hebrew origin and is believed to mean "God will uplift, exalt."

JAHSIAH The first name Jahsiah is of Hebrew origin and means "God has healed" or "God's gift of healing".

JAHSIER Modern and unique first name of uncertain origin, potentially derived from a combination of various cultural influences.

JAISHAUN The first name Jaishaun is of American origin and its meaning is a combination of "Ja" meaning "supplanter" and "Shaun" meaning "God is gracious", indicating one who is a gracious usurper.

JAISHON The first name Jaishon is of American origin and it means "God is gracious."

JAIVIN The meaning and origin of the first name Jaivin is uncertain, as it is a modern and rare name with no established historical or cultural background.

JAIYCE Means "a variant spelling of Jayce, a modern invented name without a specific origin or meaning."

JAKADEN The meaning and origin of the first name Jakaden are currently unknown as it does not appear to have a widely recognized meaning or origin.

JAKAURI Modern American name of uncertain origin, possibly a variant of the name Ja'Kauri.

JAKAYDEN Modern American name of uncertain origin, possibly derived from combining elements of different names or variations of "Jacob."

JAKOBIE Means "supplanter" and has Hebrew origin.

JAKYLIN Modern name of uncertain origin, likely derived from a combination of various name elements.

JALIL Means "illustrious" or "exalted" and has Arabic origins.

JAMAINE Variant of the name Jamal, which originated from Arabic and means "beautiful" or "handsome".

JAMARIOUS The first name Jamarious is of American origin and its meaning is a combination of the names James and Marious, suggesting a person who is a blend of strength and charm.

JAMERSON The first name Jamerson likely originated as a variant of the surname Jameson and means "son of James" or "son of Jamie."

JAMESLEY	Means "supplanter's meadow" and originates from the combination of the names James and Lee.
JAMICHAEL	The meaning of the first name JAMICHAEL is a modern American name derived from the combination of the names "James" and "Michael."
JAMIER	Means "he who supplants" and originates from the English surname derived from Jacob, meaning "holder of the heel" or "supplanter."
JAMIESON	Meaning: Son of James.
JANGELO	Modern and unique name of Filipino origin, likely derived from combining the prefix "Jan" (meaning "God is gracious") with the popular suffix "-gelo" (derived from the Spanish "Angel").
JAPHETH	Means "enlarged" or "may he extend" and has its origin in Hebrew biblical texts.
JAQUAVION	The first name Jaquavion, of American origin, means "distinguished and unique individual" or "one who stands out".
JAQUEZ	Spanish-originated name, meaning "God has shown favor."
JASEAN	American origin and it means "God is gracious."
JASHAWN	Modern American name that likely originated as a creative variation of the names Jason and Shawn.
JASHON	Hebrew origin and means "God is gracious."
JASIAS	Greek origin and means "healing" or "to heal."
JASRAJ	Masculine Indian name meaning "king of melody" or "lord of fame," derived from the combination of the Sanskrit elements "jasa" (fame, glory) and "raj" (king, ruler).
JASUR	The first name JASUR is of Uzbek origin and it means "brave" or "courageous".
JATAVIOUS	The first name JATAVIOUS has an unclear meaning and origin, as it does not have a widely recognized etymology or historical background.
JATHNIEL	Means "God has given" and it originates from Hebrew.
JATNIEL	The first name Jatniel is of Hebrew origin and means "God has given."
JAVARION	The name Javarian is a modern American invention, likely derived from the combination of the prefix "Ja-" and the name "Davarian."
JAVARIUS	The first name Javarius is of American origin and means "a modern invented name."
JAVAUGHN	The first name Javaughn has a modern origin and means "God is gracious" or "gift from God".
JAVONTE	The first name Javonte is of American origin and is derived from a combination of the names "Ja" and "avonte," with "Ja" being a short form of the name "Jason" and "avonte" having an unknown meaning.
JAXCEN	Modern creation with an American origin.
JAYANTH	The first name Jayanth, of Indian origin, means "victorious" or "one who triumphs."
JAYCEION	Unique and modern American name with no established meaning or origin.
JAYDIS	Unknown origin and meaning.
JAYJAY	The name JayJay originated as a modern, creative variation of the name Jay, and it conveys a playful and energetic personality.
JAYMAR	Modern American name, likely a variant of the combination of the names Jay and Mar, and its meaning is not specifically known.
JAYMESON	Variant of the name Jameson, derived from the Hebrew name Jacob meaning "supplanter."
JAYQUAN	American origin and means "a modern variant of the name Jaquan, derived from combining the names Jay andquan."
JAYSEAN	Means "gift from God" and it is a modern invented name combining the elements "Jay" and "Sean."
JAYSION	Modern invented name derived from the combination of the names Jay and Jason.
JAYTHAN	The meaning of the first name Jaythan is "gift of God," and it originates from the combination of the names Jay and Nathan or as a variation of the name Jonathan.
JAZAIRE	Meaning "great warrior" in French, Jazaire is a unique and modern name with no specific historical origin.

JEANLUC	Means "God is gracious" and originates from the combination of the names Jean and Luc.
JEANPAUL	The first name Jean-Paul means "John-Paul" in French and it originates from combining the names Jean (John) and Paul, frequently used together as a double-barreled first name in France.
JEANPIERRE	The first name Jean-Pierre means "God is gracious" in French, and it has a Latin and Hebrew origin.
JEBEDIAH	The name Jebadiah means "beloved of Yahweh" and it has Hebrew origins.
JEDIAH	Means "beloved by the Lord" and it originates from Hebrew.
JEDREK	The first name Jedrek is of Slavic origin and means "man of strength" or "powerful warrior".
JEHOSHA PHAT	Means "God has judged" and comes from Hebrew origins.
JEINER	The first name Jeiner originates from Spanish and it carries the meaning of "God is gracious."
JEIREN	The meaning and origin of the first name Jeiren are currently unknown.
JEKAI	Means "a noble, victorious person" and has origins in the Shona language of Zimbabwe.
JENCARLOS	Combination of the names Jennifer and Carlos, originating from Spanish and possibly Latin American cultures.
JENDRY	Means "God is gracious" and has Slavic origins.
JENTZEN	The first name Jentzen originates from the combination of the German name "Jens" and the English surname suffix "-tzen," meaning "son of Jens" or "son of John."
JEPTHA	Means "God will open" and it originates from Hebrew.
JERALD	Means "ruler of the spear" and it originates from the English and Old French name "Gerald" derived from Germanic elements.
JEREMIYAH	Means "appointed by God" and derives from the Hebrew name Yirmeyahu.
JERETH	Uncertain origin and meaning, possibly derived from Welsh, Irish, or Hebrew backgrounds.
JERIEL	Means "founded by God" and has Hebrew origins.
JERIMYAH	Variant spelling of Jeremiah, meaning "appointed by God" or "God will uplift," originating from the Hebrew name Yirmeyahu.
JERMARI	The first name JERMARI originated from the combination of the names Jeremy and Mari, and it means "appointed by God" or "gift from God."
JERMIAH	Hebrew origin and means "appointed by God."
JERMICHAEL	American origins and is a combination of the names Jeremy and Michael, meaning "beloved gift from God."
JERMONI	Means "from the sea" and has an unknown origin.
JESAIAH	Hebrew origin, means "God supports" or "Yahweh saves."
JESHURUN	Means "upright one" and originates from Hebrew.
JESSEJAMES	The first name JesseJames has a meaning of "gift of God" and originated from the combination of the biblical name Jesse and the notorious outlaw Jesse James.
JETZIEL	Modern Hebrew name meaning "God will protect" and has no specific origin or cultural significance.
JEVAUN	Means "God is gracious" and it has Jamaican origins.
JEYDER	The name JEYDER is relatively obscure with an unknown origin, making its meaning and etymology difficult to determine.
JEYKO	Uncertain origin and meaning.
JEYVIER	Modern name of uncertain origin, likely a variation or combination of other names.
JEZREEL	Means "God has planted" and originates from Hebrew origins.
JHACARI	Unknown origin but is believed to be a modern invented name with no established meaning.
JHASAI	Unique name of African origin that means "happy" or "joyful".
JHAYCO	Uncertain origin and meaning, as it is a unique and uncommon name.
JHAZIEL	The name Jhaziel originated from Hebrew and it means "God sees" or "God's vision".
JHEREMY	Variant of the name Jeremy and has an unclear origin, but likely derives from the Hebrew name Yirmeyahu meaning "appointed by God" or "God will uplift."

JHETTSON The meaning and origin of the first name JHETTSON is a modern invented name likely derived from the more traditional name "Jackson."

JHEYDEN Modern variation of the name Jayden, which is of American origin and means "thankful" or "God has heard."

JHOAN Variant spelling of the name Johan, which originated from the Hebrew name Yohanan meaning "God is gracious."

JHONATAN Means "God has given" and is a variant of the name Jonathan, which is of Hebrew origin.

JHONATHAN Variant spelling of the name Jonathan, which originates from the Hebrew name Yehonatan meaning "God has given" or "gift of God."

JHONJAIRO Spanish name meaning "God is gracious" and is likely a variation of the name John.

JHONNY Variant spelling of the name Johnny, which is a diminutive form of John and originated from the Middle English personal name Jonny, a nickname for John.

JHORDY Variant spelling of the name Jordy, which is a modern English name of uncertain origin and meaning.

JHOSEP The first name JHOSEP is of Filipino origin and is a variant spelling of Joseph, meaning "God will add" in Hebrew.

JHOSTIN The first name Jhostin likely originated as a variant of the name Justin, meaning "just" or "fair," with an added unique spelling.

JHOSUA Means "God is salvation" and is of Hebrew origin.

JHOVANY Spanish origin and its meaning is "God is gracious".

JIARUI Means "outstanding and sharp" and it has Chinese origins.

JIAYIR Means "excellent and virtuous" and it has Chinese origins.

JIBREEL Means "God is my strength" and has Arabic origins.

JIHAD Means "struggle" or "effort" and originates from Arabic.

JIOVONNI Italian origin and it means "God is gracious."

JOACHIM Means "established by God" and is of Hebrew origin.

JOAKIM The first name Joakim is of Hebrew origin, meaning "raised by Yahweh" or "established by God."

JOAOGABRIEL Portuguese name meaning "God is gracious" and it is typically used in Brazil and other Portuguese-speaking countries.

JOAOLUCAS The first name JoaoLucas is of Portuguese origin and it means "God is gracious, bringing light."

JOAOMIGUEL Means "God is gracious" and it originated from the combination of the Portuguese names Joao and Miguel.

JOAOPEDRO The first name Joaopedro is of Portuguese origin and means "gift of God."

JODECI Means "combination of two names" and is of American origin.

JOESEPH The first name Joeseph, derived from the Hebrew name Yosef, means "God will add" and has biblical origins.

JOESIAH The name Joesiah is an uncommon variation of the Hebrew name Josiah meaning "Yahweh supports" or "God heals."

JOESPH The first name Joseph means "may God add/increase" and it has Hebrew origins.

JOHANDER Modern invented name of uncertain origin, possibly combining elements of "Johan" and "Alexander."

JOHNANT HONY Means "God is gracious" and is a combination of the names John and Anthony, both derived from Hebrew and Latin origins respectively.

JOHNATAN Means "God has given" and it is of Hebrew origin.

JOHNDAVID The first name "JohnDavid" is a combination of the biblical names John and David, often given to honor both figures, with John meaning "God is gracious" and David meaning "beloved," originally derived from Hebrew origins.

JOHNHENRY Means "God's gracious gift" and it originated as a combination of the biblical names John and Henry.

JOHNKERRY The first name Johnkerry originates from the United States and is a combination of the names John and Kerry, potentially a variant of the Irish surname Ó Ciaráin meaning "descendant of Ciarán", or possibly derived from the Gaelic word "ciar" meaning "dark or

JOHNLUCAS	English origin and it combines the masculine names John, meaning "God is gracious," and Lucas, meaning "light-giving."
JOHNLUKE	Combination of the biblical name John and the common name Luke, often used as a compound name.
JOHNMARK	Means "gift of God" and is of biblical origin, derived from the combination of the names John and Mark, often used to refer to John, the apostle, and Mark, the evangelist, in the New Testament.
JOHNMIC HAEL	Combination of two traditional biblical names, "John" meaning "God is gracious" and "Michael" meaning "Who is like God," indicating someone who is grateful and heavenly.
JOHNPATRICK	Combination of the names John and Patrick, of English origin, meaning "God is gracious" and "noble."
JOHNSTON	Means "son of John" and has Scottish origins.
JOHNTHO MAS	Compound name that combines the traditional names John and Thomas, possibly indicating a combination of their respective meanings and origins.
JOHNWESLEY	Compound name of biblical origin, combining the names "John" and "Wesley," typically given as a homage to the co-founder of Methodism, John Wesley.
JOHNWIL LIAM	The name JohnWilliam combines the names John and William, possibly indicating a combination of their meanings and origins from various cultures.
JOMAR	Filipino origin and means "God will lift up" or "God will rise."
JONPAUL	The name Jonpaul typically means "God is gracious" and is a combination of the names John and Paul, originating from Hebrew and Latin respectively.
JONUEL	Modern masculine name of Hebrew origin, meaning "God is gracious."
JORAVAR	The first name JORAVAR likely has an origin in Punjabi Sikh culture and its meaning is not readily available.
JOSAFAT	Means "God has judged" and originates from Hebrew.
JOSAPHAT	The name JOSAPHAT derives from the Hebrew name "Yehoshaphat" meaning "Yahweh has judged," and it is of biblical origin.
JOSEANGEL	Spanish origin and means "God will increase" or "God's messenger."
JOSEANT ONIO	The first name Joseantonio combines the Spanish names Jose and Antonio, carrying the meaning "God will add; highly praised" and originates from Spanish and Portuguese cultures.
JOSEDEJESUS	Means "God will add" and originates from the combination of the Hebrew name "Yosef" (meaning "to add") and the Spanish name "Jesús" (meaning "Jesus").
JOSEGABRIEL	Combination of the Spanish name "Jose," meaning "God will add or multiply," and the name "Gabriel," which originates from Hebrew, meaning "God is my strength."
JOSEJUAN	Combination of the names Jose and Juan, with Jose being of Hebrew origin meaning "God will increase" and Juan being of Spanish origin meaning "God is gracious."
JOSEJULIAN	Combination of the names Jose and Julian, and its origin is derived from Spanish and Latin roots.
JOSEMANUEL	The name Josemanuel originates from Spanish and Portuguese origins and means "God is with us."
JOSEMARIA	The first name "Josemaria" originates from Spain and combines the names "Jose," derived from Joseph meaning "God will add/increase," and "Maria," referring to the Virgin Mary, resulting in a name that signifies devotion to both Joseph and Mary.
JOSEMIGUEL	The first name José Miguel means "God will increase" or "God will add" and has Spanish and Portuguese origins.
JOSEPHUS	Masculine given name of Hebrew origin meaning "he will add" or "God will increase," which gained popularity due to the biblical figure Joseph in the Old Testament.
JOSIYAH	Means "God supports" or "God heals" and its origin can be traced back to Hebrew.
JOSMAR	Means "God will add" and is of Hebrew origin.
JOSPEH	The name Joseph means "God will increase" and originates from Hebrew.
JOTHAM	Means "Yahweh is upright" in Hebrew and has origin in the Bible.
JOUD	Means "generosity" in Arabic and its origin is Islamic.
JOYNER	The first name "Joyner" is of English origin and means "someone who works with or creates joy."

JOYSON Means "son of Joy" and has English origins.

JOZHIEL Unique boys' name of uncertain origin, potentially of Hebrew or Slavic roots, meaning "God is my strength."

JOZSEF Hungarian name meaning "God will add" or "God will enhance" and originates from the Hebrew name Yosef meaning "May he add, God shall add."

JRAE American origin and it is a modern, unique name with no commonly known meaning.

JSHAUN American origin and its meaning is a modern variation of the name Shaun, derived from the Hebrew name John, meaning "God is gracious."

JSIAH Modern variation of the biblical name Isaiah, meaning "salvation of the Lord," and is primarily of Hebrew origin.

JUANANT ONIO The name Juan Antonio is a combination of the Spanish names "Juan" and "Antonio," with Juan meaning "God is gracious" and Antonio meaning "priceless" or "invaluable," originating from the Hebrew and Latin languages.

JUANDAVID The first name Juandavid is of Spanish origin and is a combination of two names, Juan meaning "God is gracious" and David meaning "beloved".

JUANDIEGO The first name Juandiego is of Spanish origin and combines the names Juan and Diego, meaning "God is gracious".

JUANJOSE The first name Juanjose is of Spanish origin and means "God is gracious; may he add."

JUANMANUEL Means "God is gracious" and originates from a combination of the Spanish names Juan and Manuel.

JUBRAN The first name Jubran originates from Arabic and its meaning is "to comfort" or "to console."

JUDSEN Variant spelling of the name Judson, which is of English origin and means "son of Jordan" or "descendant of Judd."

JUJHAR Means "mighty, courageous" and has its origin in Punjabi, a language spoken in the Punjab region of India and Pakistan.

JULIOCESAR The name JULIOCESAR originated from Latin and its meaning is "youthful ruler."

JULIOUS Means "youthful" or "downy-bearded" and its origin is derived from the Latin name Julius, ultimately originating from the Roman family name Julius.

JUNAID Means "warrior" or "soldier" and it has Arabic origins.

JUSTEN Means "just" or "fair" and it is of Latin origin.

JUVENAL Means "youthful" or "young at heart" and originates from ancient Rome.

JUVENTINO Means "youthful" and originates from the Latin word "Juvenis."

JVEON The first name JVEON does not have a commonly recognized meaning or origin as it does not appear to be a traditionally used name.

KACEYON Uncertain origin and does not have a widely recognized meaning.

KADAFI The meaning of the first name KADAFI is "one who is strong, powerful, or able to conquer" and its origin is Arabic.

KADMIEL Means "God is my east" and has Hebrew origins.

KAHIAU Means "selfless generosity" and originates from the Hawaiian language and culture.

KAICYN The meaning and origin of the first name Kaicyn is unclear, as it does not have a widely known or documented derivation.

KAILASH Means "abode of Lord Shiva" and originates from Sanskrit.

KAIMANA Hawaiian name meaning "power of the sea" and it originates from the Hawaiian language.

KAIMIR Means "strong and powerful" and has Russian and Slavic origins.

KAIMONI Hawaiian origin and means "the seeker of knowledge."

KAINALU Means "rippling sea" in Hawaiian and is of Polynesian origin.

KAINOAH The name Kainoah has Hawaiian origins and means "the thoughtful one" or "deep thinker."

KAIQUE Means "sea" or "ocean" and originates from the Tupi-Guarani language spoken by indigenous people in Brazil.

KAISHAWN The first name Kaishawn is of American origin and is derived from a combination of two names, Kai meaning "sea" in Hawaiian and Shawn meaning "God is gracious" in Hebrew, expressing the idea of a person who is divine and graceful like the sea.

KAIVION	The meaning of the first name Kaivion is unknown, as it is a unique name with no widely recognized origin or meaning.
KAIYAIR	The meaning of the first name Kaiyair is uncertain, but it is believed to have originated as a unique modern name with no specific cultural or linguistic origin.
KAIYZEN	The name Kaiyzen originated from the Japanese word "kaizen" meaning continuous improvement or change for the better, and it carries the meaning of constant growth and striving for excellence.
KAIZIER	Modern variation of the name Kaiser, meaning "emperor" in German, and is of German origin.
KAJAI	The name Kajai originated in the African country of Ghana and means "born on a Monday."
KAJUN	Means "spirited" and originated in the United States.
KAKASHI	Means "scarecrow" in Japanese and it originated from Japanese folklore and literature.
KALAB	Variant of the Hebrew name Caleb, meaning "faithful" or "devotion," and it originates from the Bible.
KALADIN	The first name Kaladin is of uncertain origin and meaning, but gained popularity through a fictional character in the Stormlight Archive series by Brandon Sanderson.
KAMSIYO CHUKWU	Nigerian Igbo name meaning "Let me live in God's presence" or "As I have said at my father's place, I say here" in Igbo language.
KANALOA	Means "god of the sea" in Hawaiian and originates from Hawaiian mythology.
KANDHAN	South Indian name meaning "son of Kanda" with origins in Hindu mythology.
KANEKI	The first name Kaneki originated from Japan and its meaning is "golden valley" or "golden tree."
KANISHK	Means "gold" or "wealth" and originates from the Sanskrit language in India.
KANOA	Means "the free one" and it has origins in the Hawaiian language.
KANTON	The first name "Kanton" has no widely accepted meaning or origin as it is a fairly rare name.
KANYE	Means, "let's give" or "to give" and it originated from the Yoruba tribe in Nigeria.
KAPONO	Means "the righteous one" in Hawaiian and originates from the Hawaiian language.
KARDIAIR	Means "heart of the air" and is of Greek origin.
KARSTON	German origin and means "Christian" or "follower of Christ."
KARTHIK	Indian origin and typically means "one who is intelligent and has divine attributes" or "a deity associated with war and victory" in Hindu mythology.
KARTHIKEYA	Means "son of Krittika" or "war god," and it originates from Hindu mythology where Karthikeya is a prominent deity and the son of Lord Shiva and Goddess Parvati.
KARTIKEYA	Means "son of Krittika" and originates from Hindu mythology, where Kartikeya is the god of war and the commander of the celestial armies.
KARVER	The meaning and origin of the first name KARVER is uncertain as it does not appear to have a commonly accepted or documented meaning or origin.
KASHDEN	The meaning and origin of the first name Kashden are uncertain as it does not have a widely recognized etymology or background.
KASHINDI	African origin and means "one who shines brightly."
KASHIUS	The name Kashiuss means "destroyer" and has an uncertain origin, potentially derived from Latin or Greek.
KASHMEIR	Means "from the Kashmir region" and has a Persian/Sanskrit origin.
KASHMIERE	Means "from Kashmir" and is of Persian origin.
KASHSTON	Means "wealthy town" and its origin is a combination of the English word "cash" and the suffix "ton" meaning town or settlement.
KASHTIAN	The first name Kashtian has an uncertain meaning and no specified origin as it is a rare name with limited available information.
KASHTYN	Modern spelling variation of the name Kastyn, inspired by traditional English names with a unique twist.
KASHUS	The first name Kashus is of uncertain origin and meaning.
KASTIN	Variant spelling of the name Caston, derived from a surname of English origin meaning "from the Roman fortification".

KAULDER	The name "Kaulder" is a rare and modern English name with no widely known meaning or origin.
KAVEH	Means "ancient Persian warrior" and its origin is from the ancient Persian language.
KAWHI	The first name Kawhi is of Native American origin and means "one who is strong and powerful."
KAWIKA	Means "David" in Hawaiian and is of Hawaiian origin.
KAWLIGA	The first name "KAWLIGA" is of Native American origin, meaning "wooden effigy or idol."
KAYCION	The meaning and origin of the first name Kaycion is unknown, as it does not appear to have any established meaning or historical origin.
KAYDIN	Modern origin, is a variant of the name Caden and means "fighter" or "friend."
KAYODE	Means "he brings joy" and originates from the Yoruba people of Nigeria.
KAYSAUN	African origin and its meaning is uncertain.
KAYVEON	Means "strong and courageous" and is of unknown origin.
KAZIM	Means "one who restrains or controls" and originates from Arabic.
KAZIMIR	Means "famous destroyer" and is of Slavic origin.
KAZUKI	Means "peaceful tree" and has Japanese origin.
KAZUYA	Means "peaceful valley" and originates from Japanese culture.
KEALOHA	Hawaiian name meaning "the love."
KEANAN	Means "ancient" or "wise" and has Irish origin.
KEAWE	Means "the descending" in Hawaiian and is of Hawaiian origin.
KEIJI	Japanese given name with the meaning "respectful, revered second son" and originates from Japanese culture.
KEILIJAH	Modern invented name with no known origin, likely created by combining elements from various existing names.
KEIMARI	The first name Keimari is of uncertain origin and meaning.
KEISHON	The first name Keishon is of American origin and it means "gift from God."
KEITHEN	Means "descendant of Caoithín" and has Irish origins.
KEIZER	Means "emperor" and is of Dutch origin.
KELECHI	Means "thank God" in Igbo and it is of Nigerian origin.
KEMAL	Means "perfection" or "completeness" and originated from Arabic.
KEMET	Means "black land" or "Egypt" in ancient Egyptian, and it originates from the ancient Egyptian civilization.
KEMONTE	Uncertain origin and meaning, most likely a modern and unique name creation.
KEMPER	Means "warrior" and originates from Germanic and Dutch surnames derived from occupational names for a shield-bearer or shield-maker.
KENDARIOUS	Modern American name, believed to be a variation or combination of the names "Kendall" and "Darius," typically given to baby boys.
KENDARIUS	The first name KENDARIUS is of American origin and means "spear ruler" or "divine ruler."
KENDER	Means "bold and adventurous" and originated from the fantasy book series, Dragonlance, by Margaret Weis and Tracy Hickman.
KENDRIEL	American origin and it means "combination of Kendall and Gabriel, meaning 'valley of the river Kent' and 'God is my strength' respectively."
KENECHU KWU	Means "God's power" or "God's strength" in Igbo language and has its origin in Nigeria.
KENG	The first name Keng originated from Cambodia and it means "strong" or "powerful."
KENJIRO	Means "intelligent second son" and has origins in Japanese culture.
KENLIN	Means "sharp/wise ruler" and its origin can be traced back to the combination of the names Ken and Lin.
KENNARD	Means "brave leader" and has English origins.
KENSHIN	Means "humble truth" and originated in Japan.
KENSTON	The first name Kenston originated in England and means "from the king's town."
KENTAVIOUS	Means "brave leader" and is of American origin.
KENYATTA	Means "musician" in Swahili and is of Kenyan origin.
KEOKI	The name Keoki originated from Hawaiian culture and means "George."
KEONDRE	Modern variant of the name Deandre, derived from the combination of the prefix Ke- meaning "descendant of" and Andre, which is of Greek origin and means "manly" or

KEONTAE   Modern American name likely derived from a combination of Kion (meaning "king") and Tae (a variant of the name Taya, meaning "gift").

KERIM   The first name Kerim carries the meaning of "generous" or "noble" and has Turkish origins.

KERVENS   Means "from the town of Caravan" and has Haitian Creole origins.

KERVENSON   Haitian Creole name meaning "strength and determination" and is derived from the French name Cervantes.

KERWIN   The first name Kerwin derives from an anglicized form of the Irish surname Ó Ciaráin, meaning "descendant of Ciarán," which itself means "dark-haired" or "black" in Irish.

KESHAV   Means "one who has beautiful hair" and it originates from Sanskrit.

KESHON   Modern American name of unknown origin, possibly a variation of the name Keisha.

KESSLER   Means "barrel maker" or "cooper" and is of German origin.

KETCH   The name Ketch originated as a surname derived from the occupation of a "ketchman" or "ketcher," referring to someone who caught kestrels (small falcons) for sport or hunting.

KETCHER   The first name KETCHER does not have a widely known meaning or origin as it is not a commonly recognized name.

KEVEN   The name KEVEN, meaning "handsome" or "gentle," is a variant spelling of the name Kevin derived from the Irish name Caoimhín.

KEVION   The meaning of the first name Kevion is "handsome" and it has an American origin.

KEYANDRE   Modern American origin and does not have a widely recognized meaning.

KEYDEN   Means "son of Aodhán" and is of Irish origin.

KEYMANI   Modern American name of uncertain origin, possibly a variation of the name Kamani.

KEYMARION   Modern American name of uncertain origin and meaning.

KEYNER   Variant of the name Keaner, derived from the Irish surname Keaney, meaning "ancient" or "distant."

KEYONTAE   Modern, invented name with an uncertain origin and meaning.

KEYSHAWN   Means "God is gracious" and has American origins.

KEYVON   The first name Keyvon likely originated from Persian and it means "royal" or "noble."

KHACE   American origin and has no commonly known meaning.

KHAEL   The first name Khael typically has a modern origin and its meaning is not widely known.

KHAIDYN   Modern variant of the traditional Irish name Caden, meaning "spirit of battle," and is of Gaelic origin.

KHAIRO   Arabic origin, meaning "noble" or "excellent."

KHAIZER   Means "emperor" or "ruler" and originates from Arabic and Persian languages.

KHALEIL   Means "friend" or "companion" and originated from Arabic.

KHAMARION   Modern and unique blend of the names Khamari and Marion, with an unclear origin and meaning.

KHAMRYN   Modern American name of uncertain origin, possibly a variant of the name Cameron.

KHAOS   Means "primordial force of chaos" and originates from Greek mythology.

KHARSON   Uncertain origin and meaning as it does not have a well-established etymology or cultural background.

KHARTER   American origin and means "explorer" or "pioneer".

KHAYDEN   Modern origin and its meaning is derived from combining the elements "khay," meaning "crown" or "king," and "den," indicating "a shelter" or "a valley," resulting in a name that can be interpreted as "royal sanctuary" or "king's haven."

KHAYIR   Means "good" or "benevolent" and is of Arabic origin.

KHAYRI   Means "generous" or "charitable" and it originates from Arabic.

KHAZIER   Modern American name of uncertain origin, possibly a creative variation of the name Kazimir.

KHIARI   African name meaning "king" or "royalty", of Swahili origin.

KHING   Means "powerful ruler" and originates from Chinese or Thai cultures.

KHINGSTON   Modern variation of the English name Kingston, meaning "king's town," originating from Old English.

KHOI   Means "dwarf" in Vietnamese and it is of Vietnamese origin.

KHOSEN   Means "faith" or "believe" and originates from the Zulu language of South Africa.

KHROME The first name Khrome has an innovative, modern feel and likely originated as a variant spelling of the word "chrome," which symbolizes strength, beauty, and sophistication.

KHYAIR Arabic origin and it means "excellent" or "generous".

KHYLIN Modern American name of uncertain origin, likely a variation or combination of other names such as Kyler or Dylan.

KHYREIN The meaning and origin of the first name KHYREIN is unknown.

KIDUS Ethiopian origin and means "holy" or "saint" in Amharic.

KIEFER Means "barrel maker" and it originates from Germany.

KIERIAN Means "dark-haired" and is of Irish origin.

KIERYN Modern American name of uncertain origin, often used as a variant of Kieran or Kyler.

KIJANI Means "green" in Swahili and is of African origin.

KILLUA The first name Killua is of Japanese origin and means "to kill gently".

KIMBLE The first name Kimble, of English origin, means "leader of warriors" or "chief of war."

KINCADE Means "battle chief" and originates from the Scottish Gaelic surname "Mac Einneid."

KINCAID The first name Kincaid originated from Scottish Gaelic and means "head of the battle."

KINDRED Means "family or relatives" and has English origins.

KINGDAVID Means "kingly" or "beloved ruler" and originates from the combination of the titles "king" and the biblical figure "King David".

KINGDOM Means a realm or domain ruled by a king, and it originated as a surname used predominantly in English-speaking countries.

KINGJOSIAH Modern, creative combination of the word "king" symbolizing power and leadership, and the biblical name "Josiah" meaning "God supports" or "healed by Yahweh," giving an ambitious and religious connotation to the name.

KINGSON Means "son of a king" and has African origins.

KIPLING Means "from the Kippax meadow" and originated as a surname in the English region of Yorkshire.

KIRKLAND The first name Kirkland derives from Old Norse and means "church land" or "land belonging to the church."

KIROLOS Egyptian origin and means "crowned with laurel" or "victorious."

KIRUBEL Ethiopian origin and means "gift from God."

KIVON The name Kivon originated from African-American roots and means "a noble or princely spirit."

KIYANSH The first name Kiyansh is of Persian origin and it means "god's grace" or "blessing from God".

KIYEN Unknown origin and meaning.

KIYOSHI Means "pure" or "clear" in Japanese and it has its origins in this language as a popular masculine given name.

KLEIN The first name Klein, of German and Jewish origin, means "small" or "little."

KLEVER Means "intelligent" or "wise" and originates from the Dutch and German language.

KLOUD Means "a cloud" and it has modern origins, likely influenced by its association with the word "cloud" in English.

KNOXTON American origin and conveys the meaning of "from the town of hills."

KNOXVILLE The first name Knoxville is of Scottish origin and it means "from the hill."

KODIAK Means "a strong and powerful bear" and originates from the Native American Alutiiq language.

KOEHN The first name Koehn is of German origin and means "bold and courageous."

KOHL Means "coal" in German and it is derived from the Germanic word "kol" which also means "coal".

KOHLER Means "charcoal burner" and originates from the German language.

KOHLSON The first name Kohlson originated from English and has a Germanic origin, meaning "son of Kohl."

KOJI The first name Koji originated from Japan and means "light" or "radiant".

KOLESYN The first name Kolesyn is of Slavic origin and means "a person who loves horses" or "horse enthusiast."

KOLSTEN	The first name Kolsten is of Scandinavian origin and means "coal town or settlement."
KONSTANTINOS	Means "constant" or "steadfast" and it originates from Greek.
KORVIN	The first name Korvin is of Hungarian origin and means "raven" or "crow."
KOSTAS	Means "strong, steadfast" and it is derived from the Greek name Konstantinos.
KOTARO	Means "large or great boy" in Japanese and has origins in the Japanese culture.
KOVU	Means "scar" in Swahili and gained popularity due to its use as a character name in Disney's animated film "The Lion King II: Simba's Pride."
KOZMO	Unknown origin, could refer to someone with a cosmic, otherworldly nature.
KRATOS	Means "strength" or "power" and originates from Greek mythology, where Kratos was the god of strength and power.
KREEK	Variant spelling of the English word "creek" which refers to a small stream or narrow channel of water, and it is an English nature-inspired name.
KRISHIV REDDY	Unique Indian name meaning "redemption by Lord Krishna" and is likely a combination of the names Krish and Reddy.
KRISTOFF	Means "bearer of Christ" and is of Scandinavian origin.
KRITHIK	The first name Krithik has Indian origins and means "supreme ruler" or "one who is victorious."
KRIYANSH	Means "Lord Krishna" and it originates from Hindu mythology and Indian culture.
KRYSTIAN	Means "follower of Christ" and has Polish and Slavic origins.
KUBA	Polish diminutive form of Jakub, meaning "supplanter" and originating from the Hebrew name Yaakov.
KUIPER	The first name Kuiper has Dutch origins and means "cooper" or "barrel maker."
KURRENCY	The name KURRENCY does not have a widely recognized meaning or origin as it is a modern English name influenced by the word "currency" and coined for uniqueness or creative purposes.
KUSH	Sanskrit origin and it means "son of lord Rama" or "happiness."
KUSHAL	Means "skilled" or "competent" in Sanskrit, originating from India.
KUZEY	Means "north" in Turkish and originates from the Turkish language.
KWABENA	Means "born on a Tuesday" and originates from Akan, a language spoken in Ghana and Cote d'Ivoire.
KWADWO	Means "born on a Monday" and originates from the Akan people of Ghana in West Africa.
KWAKU	Means "born on Wednesday" and originates from the Akan people of Ghana.
KWAME	Means "born on a Saturday" and it originates from the Akan language of Ghana.
KWASI	Means "born on Sunday" in Akan and Ewe languages, originating from the Akan people of Ghana and Ivory Coast.
KYCION	Modern and unique variation of the name Kyson, likely originating in the United States.
KYESON	Modern American invention, and its meaning is not readily available.
KYHEEM	Modern, invented name of American origin, without a widely recognized meaning.
KYJUAN	The meaning and origin of the first name Kyjuan is uncertain, as it does not have a widely recognized origin or meaning.
KYMIR	Uncertain origin, likely means "unique" or "one of a kind."
KYNDRIX	The first name Kyndrix has a modern and unique sound, likely derived from the combining of different elements or created for its originality.
KYNGSTEN	Modern variation of the name Kingston, which originated from Old English and means "king's settlement."
KYRILLOS	Means "Lordly" or "masterful" and it originates from Greek.
KYSIN	The name Kysin does not have a widely recognized meaning or origin, as it appears to be a rare or unconventional name with limited historical usage.
KYSTON	The name Kyston originated from English and it means "from the town of the cheese dairy" or "from the cheese farm".
KYZAIR	Uncertain origin and meaning, possibly derived from a combination of different cultures or created as a unique name.

LADARIAN Means "from the valley of the river Darien" and its origin can be traced back to American English.

LADARIUS The first name LADARIUS is of American origin and means "one who is a combination of strength and nobility."

LAFAYETTE Means "faithful and loyal" and has French origins.

LAITHAN Means "lion" and is of English and Arabic origin.

LAJUAN The first name "LaJuan" is of American origin and typically denotes a person who is gracious or of compassionate nature.

LAKENDRICK American origin and its meaning is a combination of the elements "lake" referring to a water body and "Kendrick" meaning "royal ruler" or "champion."

LAMELO The name LaMelo originated from American culture and it means "the loved one" or "loving."

LAMONTE Means "the mountain" and it is of Spanish and Italian origin.

LANCELOT Means "servant of the land" and originates from Old French.

LANDIS Means "from the land" and has German origins.

LANGDON Means "long hill" and originated from Old English.

LARSEN Means "son of Lars" and is of Scandinavian origin.

LASZLO Means "glorious rule" and originates from Hungary.

LATHAM English origin and it means "from the barnyard."

LATHEN English origin and it means "from the barn settlement."

LATRELL Means "from a modern combination of the prefix La- and the name Terrell" and has American origins.

LATROY Modern variation of the name Latre, of unknown origin, likely created from various name elements or as a creative respelling.

LAUTARO Means "swift hawk" and is of Mapuche origin from Chile and Argentina.

LAVELLE Variant of the French name LaVal, meaning "the valley," and it originated from a surname derived from a geographical feature in France.

LAVERNE Means "of alder trees" and it originated from the French word "l'auburne".

LAWAIA Hawaiian origin and meaning "guide or leader."

LAWLER LAWLER is an English surname derived from the Old French "l'avaleur" meaning "swallower" or "devourer," possibly used as a nickname for a voracious eater.

LAWTON The name Lawton typically means "hillside settlement" and has originated from Old English.

LAYTH Means "lion" and it is of Arabic origin.

LAZER The first name "Lazer" is a Hebrew name meaning "God is my help" and it is a variant of the name Eliezer.

LAZLO Means "glorious ruler" and originates from Hungary.

LEAVITT The name Leavitt is an anglicized form of the Hebrew name Levi, meaning "joined" or "attached," often associated with the biblical tribe of Levi.

LEBRON Means "the brown-haired one" and originates from Germanic roots.

LEDUAR Spanish origin and is a variant of Edward, meaning "wealthy guardian" or "rich guard".

LEFTY The first name "Lefty" is derived from the term used to describe a left-handed person and is often used as a nickname or informal name.

LEGENDARY Means "extraordinary or iconic" and does not have a specific origin as it is a word used to describe something of great significance or fame.

LEGION Means a large group or multitude and is of Latin origin.

LEIBISH Means "beloved" or "dear" and it originates from Yiddish.

LENSKY Means "lion" in Russian and is of Russian origin.

LEOMAR Spanish origin and means "lion of the sea."

LEONCIO Means "lion-like" and has Spanish origin.

LEONHART Means "lion-strong" and is of Germanic origin.

LEONZO The first name Leonzo is of Italian origin and means "lion."

LEOVANNI Means "lion of God" and it is of Italian origin.

LESTAT Means "eternal" or "everlasting" and has its origin in French literature, popularized by a character in Anne Rice's "The Vampire Chronicles" series.

LEUL   Means "lion" in Amharic and originates from Ethiopia.

LEVENTE   Means "brave" and it originates from Hungarian.

LEVEON   The name Le'Veon originated in the United States and has an African-American origin, meaning "handsome village."

LEXIEL   The meaning and origin of the first name Lexiel are unknown as it does not have a widely recognized or documented historical background.

LEYLAND   Means "meadow land" and has English origins.

LIAMGAEL   Modern and unique combination name likely derived from Liam (Irish origin meaning "strong-willed warrior") and Gael (Irish origin meaning "stranger" or "foreigner").

LIBRADO   Means "liberated" and originates from Latin.

LINWOOD   Means "near the linden tree" and it originated from Old English.

LISIATE   The name Lisiāte is female in origin and it is of Tongan descent, meaning "beautiful sunshine."

LIZARDO   Means "lizard" and it originates from Spanish and Portuguese languages.

LLEWELYN   Welsh origin and means "leader of the people" or "lion-like."

LLEWYN   Means "leader" or "lion-like" and it has Welsh origins.

LOCHLAINN   Means "land of lakes" and originates from Irish Gaelic.

LOCKSLEY   Means "meadow of locks" in Old English and is of English origin.

LOFTON   Means "enclosed settlement" and has English origins.

LOGIC   Means "reasoning" or "rational thinking" and is derived from the English word "logic."

LOIC   Means "fierce warrior" and has Breton origins.

LONG   The first name "Long" is of Vietnamese origin and means "dragon" or "prosperous."

LOUAY   Means "warrior" or "lion" and is of Arabic origin.

LOUDEN   Means "loud" or "noisy" and it is of English origin.

LOUKAS   Means "man from Lucania" and originates from the Greek language.

LOVENSKY   The first name "Lovensky" is a modern variant of the name "Lovenski," which originated from the Slavic language and means "beloved" or "one who is loved."

LUAR   Means "moonlight" and originates from the Galician language spoken in the northwest region of Spain.

LUCARIO   The name Lucario has Latin origins and means "bright one" or "bringer of light."

LUCIFER   The meaning of the first name Lucifer originates from Latin and means "light bringer" or "morning star," but is commonly associated with Satan in Christian theology.

LUCIOUS   The meaning of the first name Lucious is "light" or "illumination," and it originates from the Latin name Lucius.

LUDWIG   German origin and means "famous warrior" or "famous in battle."

LUISANGEL   Spanish origin and it combines the names Luis and Angel, meaning "warrior angel" or "angelic warrior."

LUISCARLOS   The name Luiscarlos likely originates from Spanish origins and means "renowned warrior" or "famous warrior".

LUKASEY   The meaning and origin of the first name Lukasey are uncertain as it is a rare variant of the name Lucas.

LUKYAN   Means "light" or "shining" and it has Russian origins.

LUMIERE   Meaning "light" in French, Lumiere is a name popularized by the character Lumière in Disney's "Beauty and the Beast."

LUQMAN   Arabic origin and it means "wise" or "intelligent."

LUXON   Means "light" or "enlightened" and it is derived from the Latin word "lux" which also means "light."

LUXTEN   The meaning and origin of the first name LUXTEN is a modern English name with no established meaning or origin.

LYFE   Modern English name that means "life" and is likely a variation of the word itself.

LYNFORD   The first name Lynford has English origins and means "ford by the lime trees."

LYNX   The first name Lynx is derived from the animal of the same name, symbolizing strength and stealth.

LYSANDER   Means "liberator of men" and is of Greek origin.

MACALLAN   The first name Macallan, of Scottish origin, means "son of the love, son of the bald one."

MACALLISTER	The first name Macallister originates from Scotland and means "son of Alasdair."
MACARIUS	The name Macarius originated from Ancient Greek and means "blessed" or "happy".
MACARTHUR	Scottish origin and means "son of Arthur."
MACAULAY	The first name Macaulay, of Scottish origin, means "son of righteousness" or "son of a servant of Saint Columba."
MACKINNON	The first name Mackinnon is of Scottish origin and means "son of the fair born" or "son of the beautiful one."
MACKSEN	Modern variation of the traditional name Maxon, derived from the English and German surnames meaning "son of Mack" or "son of Max."
MACLEAN	Means "son of Leod" and has Scottish Gaelic origins.
MACLIN	Surname derived from the Scottish and Irish Gaelic name Mac Gille Eoin, meaning "son of the servant of John."
MACOY	The first name "Macoy" is of Filipino origin and it means "son of a Terminator."
MACRAY	The first name Macray is of Scottish origin and its meaning is "son of Rath," signifying a connection to a prominent Scottish clan or family.
MADSEN	Danish origin and means "son of Mads."
MAGDIEL	Hebrew name meaning "God is great" and is derived from the Bible.
MAGIZHAN	Means "happiness" or "joy" and has Tamil origin.
MAHAMAD OU	The first name Mahamadou originates from West Africa and means "praised one" or "the one who is praised."
MAHER	Means "skilled" or "talented" and originates from Arabic.
MAHMUD	Means "praiseworthy" or "worthy of praise" and has Arabic origins.
MAIKOL	Variant of the name Michael, with German and Hebrew origins, meaning "who is like God?".
MAJID	Means "glorious" or "noble" and has Arabic origins.
MAJOUR	The first name Majour does not have a commonly known meaning or origin as it does not appear to be a widely recognized name.
MAKARIOS	The first name Makarios is of Greek origin and means "blessed" or "happy."
MAKAVELI	The first name Makaveli is of uncertain meaning and origin, but it gained popularity as the adopted stage name of American rapper Tupac Shakur, who took inspiration from the Italian philosopher Niccolò Machiavelli.
MAKSYMI LIAN	Means "greatest" or "'greatest energy" in Latin, and it has Polish origins.
MALACHITE	Means "royal stone" and is derived from the gemstone of the same name, known for its vibrant green color and believed to have healing and protective properties.
MALAKHAI	Means "messenger of God" and originates from Hebrew.
MALAKYE	The first name Malakye is of uncertain origin, but it is commonly accepted as a modern variant of the biblical name Malachi, meaning "my messenger" or "messenger of God."
MALAQUIAS	Means "messenger of God" and originates from the Hebrew name Malakhi.
MALIKHI	Means "my king" and it is of Hebrew origin.
MALIQUE	Means "kingly" or "royal" and it originated from Arabic.
MALKIEL	Means "God is my king" and it originates from Hebrew.
MALOSI	Means "strong" or "powerful" and it originates from the Samoan language.
MAMOUDOU	Means "praiseworthy" and is of West African origin.
MANASSEH	Means "causing to forget" and originates from Hebrew.
MANNING	Means "son of a man" and has English origins.
MANSOUR	Means "victorious" or "one who achieves success" and has Arabic origins.
MANSUR	Means "victorious" or "one who is helped" and has Arabic origins.
MARCANT HONY	The first name MarcAnthony is derived from the combination of the names Marc and Anthony, and it originated from Latin and Greek roots, meaning "warlike" and "priceless
MARCHELLO	Means "warlike" or "belonging to Mars" and originates from the Italian variation of the name Marcello.
MARCIANO	Means "belonging to Mars" and has Latin origins.
MARCOAN TONIO	Means "warlike man" and has Italian and Spanish origins.

MARDOCHEE	The first name Mardochée is of Hebrew origin meaning "servant of Marduk," and it is derived from the Hebrew name Mordecai.
MARICIO	Spanish origin and it means "mighty warrior" or "warrior prince".
MARKEEM	American origin and it means "a modern variation of the name Mark."
MARKEITH	The name Markeith originates from the United States and means "warrior leader."
MARKOS	Means "warlike" or "dedicated to Mars" and it originates from the Latin name Marcus, derived from Mars, the Roman god of war.
MARQUAN	The first name Marquan is of American origin and means "gift of Mars" or "warrior."
MARQUAVIOUS	The first name Marquavious, of American origin, typically means "noble leader" or "distinguished ruler."
MARSDEN	Means "valley of the marsh" and has an English origin.
MARSEAN	American origin and it means "a modern variation of the name Marcellus, which is derived from the Roman god of war, Mars."
MARSHON	The first name Marshon is of American origin and it means "from the marsh or swamp."
MARTAVIOUS	The first name Martavious is of American origin and it means "dedicated to Mars," referring to the Roman god of war.
MARTAVIUS	American origin and it means "warlike, dedicated to Mars."
MARTRELL	Unknown origin and meaning, as it does not have a widely recognized or documented history.
MARVELOUS	Means extraordinary or awe-inspiring and has origins in the English language.
MARVENS	Latin origin and means "famous friend."
MARVENSKY	There is limited information available on the first name "Marvensky," suggesting that it may be a less common or possibly unique name with unknown origin and meaning.
MARWAN	Arabic origin and it means "flint stone".
MASUD	Masculine name of Arabic origin meaning "fortunate" or "lucky."
MATAIO	Means "gift of God" and has origins in the Hebrew language.
MATEUSZ	The first name Mateusz is of Polish origin and it means "gift of God."
MATHAYUS	The first name Mathayus is of unknown origin and meaning.
MATHIEU	Means "gift of God" and it originates from the Hebrew name Mattityahu.
MATHYUS	The name Mathyus has no widely recognized meaning or origin as it appears to be a unique or rare variant of the name Matthias or Matthew.
MATIJA	Means "gift of God" and originates from the Slavic languages, particularly in Croatia and Slovenia.
MATRIX	The first name Matrix has a futuristic connotation and is of Greek origin, meaning "womb" or "source of creation".
MATVIY	The first name Matviy typically originates from Ukraine and means "gift of God."
MAVERYK	The first name Maveryk originates from the word "maverick" and means an independent and unorthodox individual.
MAXAMILLION	Means "greatest" and it is derived from the Latin name Maximilianus, which was originally a Roman family name later adopted as a given name.
MAXENCE	French masculine name meaning "greatest, largest," originating from the Latin name Maxentius.
MAXIMILANO	Means "greatest" or "most excellent" and its origin can be traced back to Latin and the Roman Empire.
MAXIMINO	Spanish given name meaning "greatest" or "most excellent," derived from the Latin name Maximinus.
MAYANK	The first name Mayank is of Indian origin and means "moon" or "descended from the Moon God".
MAYCON	Variant spelling of the name Maicon, which originated as a variation of the name Michael and can be derived from various cultural and linguistic sources.
MAYJOR	The meaning of the first name Mayjor is unknown, and its origin is uncertain as well.
MAYKEL	Cuban origin and it means "gift from God" or "who is like God".
MAYNARD	The name Maynard has Germanic origins and means "brave, hardy," or "powerful, hardy."
MAZION	The first name Mazion has no definitive meaning or origin, as it does not appear to have a widely recognized cultural or linguistic background.

MAZIYON	The name Maziyon does not have a widely recognized meaning or origin as it is relatively uncommon.
MBAYE	Senegalese name meaning "father" or "leader," commonly given to sons of respected leaders in the Wolof ethnic group.
MCALLISTER	Surname of Scottish origin that means "son of Alistair" or "son of Alasdair."
MCARTHUR	Scottish origin and means "son of Arthur," denoting a descendant or son of a person named Arthur.
MCCAULEY	The meaning of the first name McCauley is "son of Cawley" and it has Irish origins.
MCCLAIN	Scottish surname that means "son of Lain," derived from the Scottish Gaelic Mac Gille Fhionntain.
MCCRAE	The first name McCrae, of Scottish origin, means "son of grace" or "graceful son".
MCKOY	The first name McKoy originated as a variation of the Scottish surname McCoy, meaning "son of Aodh," referring to a mythical Scottish figure.
MCLAREN	The first name McLaren is of Scottish origin and means "son of the follower of Saint Laurence."
MEDARDO	The first name Medardo originates from Spanish and means "brave counselor" or "powerful advisor".
MEDHANSH	Means "an intelligent and noble person" and originates from the Indian Sanskrit language.
MEHKI	The meaning of the first name Mehki is "one who is like a prince" and it has an African origin.
MEHMET	Means "praiseworthy" and originates from Turkish and Arabic cultures.
MEHTAB	Means "moonlight" and originates from Persian and Urdu languages.
MEILECH	Means "little king" and it originates from Yiddish.
MELCHIZEDEK	Means "king of righteousness" and it originates from Hebrew biblical texts.
MELESIO	Means "chosen by God" and it originates from the Greek name Meletios.
MELIODAS	Means "honeyed sorrow" and originates from Arthurian legend.
MELQUIS EDEC	Hebrew origin and it means "king of righteousness," often associated with the biblical figure seen in the Old Testament.
MENELIK	The meaning of the first name Menelik is "Son of the wise man" and it is of Ethiopian origin, derived from the Ethiopian royal lineage.
MERCURY	Means "swift messenger" and comes from Roman mythology, being the name of the Roman god of trade, communication, and travel.
MERLIN	Welsh name meaning "sea fortress" or "falcon," and is associated with the legendary sorcerer and advisor to King Arthur.
MESHACK	Means "who is like God" and it originates from the Bible, specifically from the Book of Daniel in the Old Testament.
MESHILEM	Hebrew name meaning "peaceful" or "complete" and it originated from Jewish culture and religious traditions.
MESSIYAH	Means "savior" or "anointed one" and originates from Jewish and Christian religious beliefs.
METEHAN	The first name Metehan is of Turkish origin meaning "brave ruler."
MICHAEL ANGELO	Means "angel who is like God" and originates from Italian, derived from the combination of the names Michael and Angelo.
MICTLAN	Means "place of the dead" in Nahuatl, the language of the Aztecs.
MIDAS	Means "kingly" or "fathoming" and originates from Greek mythology as the name of a legendary king known for his golden touch.
MIHRAN	Armenian origin and it means "merciful."
MIKAIL	The name Mikail originated from Hebrew and means "who is like God."
MIKAYEL	The name Mikayel originated from Hebrew and the meaning of the name is "who is like God?".
MIKING	The first name "Miking" does not have a widely recognized origin or meaning, as it is a highly uncommon or invented name.
MIKIYAS	Ethiopian origin and means "who is like God?".
MIKLO	Unique and modern name of uncertain origin, possibly a variation or combination of other names.

MIKOLAJ	Means "who is like God?" and originates from the Slavic language.
MILOH	Means "merciful" or "gift from God" and has origins in both Hebrew and Slavic languages.
MIQDAD	Miqdad is an Arabic name that means "strong and respected" and is derived from an Arabic word meaning "to support or strengthen."
MIQUEAS	Means "who is like God" and has Hebrew origins.
MISTER	Modern, unique name derived from the English word "mister" used as a term of respect or address for a man.
MITHRAN	Means "friend" or "companion" and originates from the Sanskrit language.
MODESTO	Means "modest" or "humble" and its origin can be traced back to Latin.
MODIBO	The first name Modibo originates from the Malian language and means "one who comes with dignity."
MODOU	Gambian given name of West African origin meaning "born after a loss" or "one who replaces."
MOHAMMA DNABI	Mohammadnabi is an Arabic name meaning "the praised prophet", originating from Islamic culture and beliefs.
MOHAMMA DOMAR	The first name Mohammadomar is of Arabic origin and typically given to children with Muslim background, combining the names "Mohammad" and "Omar" to form a composite name.
MOHAMMA DTAHA	Arabic origin and means "praised one" (Muhammad) and "pure" or "virtuous" (Taha).
MOHAMME DALI	Arabic origin and means "praised one" or "chosen one" and is commonly used as a combination of the names Mohammed and Ali.
MOHSEN	Male Arabic name meaning "charitable" or "beneficent," originating from Islamic culture.
MOKSH	Means "liberation" and originates from Sanskrit, an ancient Indic language of India.
MOKSHITH	Means "liberator" or "one who attains salvation" and originates from Sanskrit.
MOMODOU	Means "I am directed by God" and it originates from the Gambia in West Africa.
MONACO	Means "from Monaco" and is of Italian origin.
MONTAGUE	Means "pointed mountain" and originated from the Old French surname Montagu, derived from the Latin words "mons" (mountain) and "acutus" (pointed).
MONTEGO	Means "mountainous" and it has Jamaican origins.
MONTEZUMA	Spanish name meaning "one who frowns like a lord" and is derived from the Aztec ruler of the same name.
MONTRELL	American origin and means "monarch-like" or "royal ruler".
MORDCHE	Means "Warrior" and it originates from Hebrew.
MOROCCO	The first name "Morocco" does not have a widely recognized origin, but it is likely inspired by the country of Morocco located in North Africa.
MORPHEUS	Greek origin, means "shaper of forms" and refers to the Greek god of dreams and sleep.
MORTIMER	Means "dead sea" or "still water" and has English origins derived from the Old French name Mortemer.
MOSESE	Variant of Moses, which originated from the Hebrew name Moshe, meaning "drawn out" or "born of."
MOUHAMA DOU	Arabic origin and it means "praiseworthy" or "the praised one."
MOUHAMED	Arabic origin, meaning "praiseworthy" or "highly praised".
MOUNIR	Means "illuminated" or "enlightened" and originates from Arabic.
MOURYA	The first name "MOURYA" is of Indian origin and typically means "descendant of Moray" or "belonging to the Maurya dynasty."
MOUSSA	The first name Moussa, of Arabic origin, means "drawn out of the water" and is commonly used to refer to the biblical figure Moses.
MOUSTAFA	Means "chosen one" and has Arabic origin.
MOUSTAPHA	Means "the chosen one" and has its origin in Arabic.
MOXON	The first name MOXON is of English origin and it means "son of Mogg," a diminutive form of the personal name Margaret.
MOZIAH	The first name MOZIAH is of Hebrew origin and means "God is my strength."
MUAD	The first name "Muad" is of Arabic origin and it means "restorer" or "one who brings back life."

MUBARAK	Means "blessed" or "fortunate" and has Arabic origin.
MUBASHIR	Arabic origin and means "one who brings good news."
MUCHEN	Means "magnificent" and has origins in Chinese language and culture.
MUDASIR	Means "gathering" or "assembled" and it originated from Arabic language.
MUGISHA	Means "one who brings luck" and originates from the Rukiga language spoken in Uganda.
MUHAMMA DADAM	The first name Muhammadadam is of Arabic origin and combines the names Muhammad and Adam, potentially representing a fusion of Islamic and Biblical significance.
MUHAMMA DALI	The name Muhammad Ali means "praiseworthy and noble" and its origin is Arabic.
MUHAMMA DHAMZA	Combination of two Arabic names - "Muhammad" meaning praised or praiseworthy, and "Hamza" meaning lion or strong.
MUHAMMA DHASSAN	Means "praiseworthy and beautiful" and originates from Arabic.
MUHAMMA DIBRAHIM	Combination of two commonly used Arabic names, Muhammad (meaning "praised" or "praiseworthy") and Ibrahim (meaning "father of nations" or "friend of God").
MUHAMMA DISA	Unique name of Arabic origin, meaning "praiseworthy" or "one who is praised".
MUHAMMA DJON	Combination of the Arabic name "Muhammad" meaning "praised" and the Persian name "Jon" meaning "dear" or "beloved," and it is commonly used as a given name in Central Asia, particularly in countries like Uzbekistan and Tajikistan.
MUHAMMA DMUSA	The first name MuhammadMusa is of Arabic origin and commonly used amongst Muslims, combining the names Muhammad (meaning "praiseworthy") and Musa (meaning "Moses") to create a compound name.
MUHAMMA DMUSTAFA	The name Muhammamustafa is of Arabic origin and it means "the chosen one praised and highly esteemed."
MUHAMMA DUMAR	The name Muhammadumar, predominantly used in Uzbekistan, combines the Arabic name "Muhammad" (meaning "praised") and the Uzbek name "Umar" (derived from the Arabic name "Umar," meaning "prospering, flourishing").
MUHAMMA DYASIN	Means "praiseworthy" and has Arabic origins.
MUHAMMA DYUNUS	Means "praiseworthy companion" and is of Arabic origin.
MUHAMMA DYUSUF	The first name Muhammad Yusuf is of Arabic origin and it means "praised one" or "worthy of praise".
MUHAMMA DZAYD	Means "praiseworthy and abundant" and is of Arabic origin.
MUHAYMIN	Means "the guardian" or "the watchful one" and has Arabic origins.
MUHSIN	Masculine Arabic name meaning "beneficent" or "kind," originating from Islamic traditions.
MUIZ	Means "one who is blessed with knowledge" and has Arabic origins.
MUJAHID	The name "Mujahid" has Arabic origins and its meaning is "one who strives or struggles in the way of God."
MUJTABA	Means "chosen" or "selected" and originates from Arabic language and Islamic tradition.
MUKHAMM AD	Means "praiseworthy" and originates from Arabic.
MUKHAMM ADALI	Traditional Uzbek name meaning "chosen one of Ali" and is commonly used in Central Asia and Islamic cultures.
MUKHTAR	Means "chosen" or "selected" and has Arabic origins.
MUNASAR	Arabic origin and it means "guide" or "leader."
MUNEEB	Means "one who turns to God in repentance" and it is of Arabic origin.
MUNTASIR	Means "one who seeks help or victory" and has Arabic origins.
MURDOCK	Means "sea warrior" and has Scottish origins.
MURILO	The first name Murilo has Brazilian origins and its meaning is "small ripe fruit" or "little ripe one."

MURTAZA	Means "chosen" or "selected" and is of Arabic origin.
MUSAWIR	Means "one who forms or creates" and it originates from Arabic.
MUSCAB	Arabic origin and its meaning refers to a "praiseworthy" or "commendable" person.
MUSTAPHA	Means "chosen one" and originates from Arabic.
MUTASIM	Means "seeker of refuge" and has Arabic origins.
MUZAMMIL	Means "veiled, wrapped" and it originates from Arabic.
MYEIR	The first name Myeir has no widely recognized meaning or origin as it is a rare and uncommon name.
MYERS	English origin and means "son of the mayor."
MYHEIR	The meaning and origin of the first name Myheir is unknown as it does not have a widely recognized origin or meaning.
MYLEN	Variant of the name Mileena, which is of Greek origin and means "gracious" or "kind-hearted."
MYNOR	English origin and its meaning is "from the lake with the small island; renowned warrior."
NABIL	Arabic origin, meaning "noble" or "highborn."
NACHMAN	Means "comfort" or "consolation" in Hebrew, and it originated from the Old Testament.
NACHUM	Means "comforted" in Hebrew and it is of biblical origin.
NAETOCH UKWU	Means "God's own portion" and originates from the Igbo ethnic group in Nigeria.
NAFTULA	Means "small napkin" and it has Hebrew origins.
NAHSHON	Means "divinely inspired" and it has Hebrew origins.
NAHUEL	Means "jaguar" or "tiger" in the Mapuche language of indigenous people in Chile and Argentina.
NAHZIR	Means "messenger" and has Arabic origins.
NAJEE	Arabic origin meaning "safe" or "secure".
NAKUL	Means "person of sound mind" and originates from Sanskrit.
NAMISH	Indian origin and its meaning is "one who is calm and composed".
NANAYAW	Means "born on a Thursday" and originates from the Akan people of Ghana.
NAPHTALI	Means "my struggle" and has Hebrew origins.
NAPOLEON	The first name Napoleon, of French origin, means "lion of the new city" or "lion of Naples."
NARUTO	The meaning of the first name Naruto is "maelstrom" or "whirlpool" in Japanese, and it originates from the popular manga and anime series created by Masashi Kishimoto.
NASAIAH	Hebrew origin and means "God has healed."
NASHVILLE	Means "from the city of Nashville" and it is of English origin.
NASHWAN	The name Nashwan originates from Arabic and it means "cheerful" or "happy."
NASIER	Arabic origin and means "victorious" or "helper."
NASRATU LLAH	Muslim name meaning "Help of God" in Arabic, commonly used in Iran.
NATANEL	The first name Natanel is of Hebrew origin and means "gift of God" or "given by God."
NATHANEAL	Means "gift of God" and originates from the Hebrew language.
NATION	Means a group of people united by a common bond or shared characteristics, and its origin can be traced back to the English language.
NATNAEL	Means "gift from God" and originates from the Ethiopian and Eritrean cultures.
NATSU	Means "summer" in Japanese and is of Japanese origin.
NAUJOUR	The first name Naujour is of French origin and has no specific meaning as it appears to be a rare or unique name.
NAVARRO	Means "plains or treeless plateau" and has Spanish origins.
NAVRAJ	Means "new king" and has Indian origins.
NAYIB	Means "noble, generous" and originated from Arabic.
NEAMIN	Means "left-handed" and originates from Ethiopia.
NECALLI	The first name Necalli has a Native American origin and it means "battle" or "fighter".
NECHEMIA	Means "comforted by God" and it originates from the Hebrew language.
NEFTALY	Hebrew name meaning "my struggle, my wrestling" and is derived from the biblical figure Jacob.

NEIZAN	The meaning and origin of the first name Neizan is unclear.
NEKODA	Hebrew origin, meaning "marked by God" or "pointed out by God."
NEKTARIOS	Means "gift of God" and it originates from Greek.
NEOMIAH	Variant of the biblical name Nehemiah and originates from Hebrew, meaning "comforted by God."
NEPHI	Means "good, desirable" and originates from the Hebrew name Nefi, found in the Book of Mormon.
NERY	Means "noble" and it is of Irish and Welsh origin.
NESANEL	Means "gift of God" and has Hebrew origins.
NETEYAM	Native American name meaning "walking together" in the Mi'kmaq language.
NEWT	The first name "Newt" is of English origin and refers to a small salamander-like amphibian, also known as a "newt."
NEWTON	Means "new town" or "new settlement" and has English and Scottish origins.
NEYSER	Neysler is a Spanish name derived from the Latin name Nestor, meaning "traveler" or "homecoming."
NEYTHAN	Modern variant of the name Nathan, with origins in Hebrew, meaning "gift from God."
NGAWANG	Tibetan name meaning "powerful speech" and it originated in Tibetan culture.
NICANOR	Means "victorious army" and has Greek origins.
NICKLAUS	Means "victory of the people" and originated from the Greek name Nikolaos.
NICKOLAI	Means "victory of the people" and it is of Russian origin.
NICKSON	Means "son of Nicholas" and it is of English origin.
NICODEMUS	Means "victory of the people" and has origins in Greek and Hebrew.
NIEKO	Means "victory of the people" and originates from the Hawaiian language.
NIHAL	Means "contentment" or "joyful" in Arabic, and it is of Persian and Turkish origin.
NIHANSH	Means "part of the day" and it originates from Sanskrit, an ancient language of India.
NIHILUS	Nihilus means "nothing" in Latin and is believed to be derived from the word "nihil," which means "nothingness" or "void."
NIHITH	The meaning and origin of the first name Nihith is unclear as it does not have a widely recognized derivation or significance.
NIKHOLAI	Variant of the name Nicholas, which means "victory of the people" and has Greek origins.
NIKODEM	Means "victory of the people" and originates from Greek.
NIKOLOZ	Means "victory of the people" and originates from the country of Georgia.
NILS	Scandinavian variant of the name Nicholas, meaning "victory of the people," and it is derived from the Germanic name Nikolaus.
NIRVAIR	Means "without enmity or hostility" and originates from the Punjabi language in India.
NISHANT	Means "dawn" or "end of the night" and has Indian origins.
NIVEK	Variant of Kevin, which originated from the Irish surname Caoimhín, meaning "handsome" or "gentle birth."
NIXSON	The first name Nixson derives from an English surname meaning "son of Nicholas" and is of Anglo-Saxon origin.
NIYEAR	The first name Niyear does not have a widely recognized meaning or origin.
NNAEMEKA	Means "my father is kind" and it originates from the Igbo language in Nigeria.
NNAMDI	Means "my father is alive" and it originates from the Igbo language of Nigeria.
NOAHJAMES	Means "peaceful and respected" and has a Biblical origin derived from the Hebrew name Noah, meaning "rest" or "comfort."
NOAHKAI	Means "rested upon the ocean" and is a combination of the names Noah and Kai.
NOCTIS	Means "night" and it originates from Latin.
NOGIVEN NAME	The meaning of the first name NOGIVENNAME is that it is an indication that no name has been provided. This name is not a traditional given name and is likely a placeholder or error.
NOLAWI	Masculine Ethiopian name, meaning "he who is surrounded by glory" or "he who is renowned," and it has its roots in the Amharic language.
NORBERTO	Means "bright north" and has Germanic origins.
NORIEL	Spanish origin and means "golden light" or "bright light."
NOSSON	The first name "Nossen" means "miracle" and has Hebrew origins.
NOTORIOUS	Means widely and unfavorably known, and its origin can be attributed to the English language.

NOVIAN	The name "Novian" does not have a clear origin or meaning as it is uncommon and does not have a widely recognized source or etymology.
NUCHEM	Hebrew origin, means "comfort" or "consolation."
NUNZIO	Means "messenger" or "announcer" in Italian, and it originated from the Latin word "nuntius."
NURMUHA MMAD	Means "light of Muhammad" and has Arabic origins.
NYHEIM	The first name Nyheim is of Scandinavian origin and it means "new home" or "new village."
NYKO	The name Nyko originated as a modern variation of the name Nico, which is a shortened form of the Greek name Nicholas, meaning "victorious people."
NYLES	The first name Nyles is of English origin and means "champion" or "victorious."
NYSIR	The first name Nysir is of unknown origin and meaning.
NYYEAR	The name NYYEAR does not have a widely recognized meaning or origin as it appears to be a unique or unconventional name.
NYZAIAH	Modern invented name with no known origin, typically given to boys.
NYZIER	The name "Nyzier" does not have a widely recognized meaning or origin as it appears to be a unique or uncommon name.
OAK	Means "strong and enduring" and is of English origin.
OAKES	Means "dweller near the oak trees" and originated from the English surname derived from the Old English word "āc" meaning "oak".
OBAIDULLAH	Means "worshipper of Allah" and originates from Arabic.
OBALOLUWA	Means "God's royalty" and originates from the Yoruba language of Nigeria.
OBERON	Means "noble bear" and originated from Germanic mythology, later popularized by Shakespeare's play "A Midsummer Night's Dream."
OBREMPONG	The first name "Obrempong" comes from Akan origin and typically means "chief" or "king."
OBSA	Ethiopian origin and means "one who saves or rescues."
OBSIDIAN	Means "volcanic glass" and is derived from the Latin word "obsidianus" which originated from Obsis, a Roman doctor.
OCTAVIANO	Means "eighth" and has Latin origins.
OCTAVIOUS	Means "eighth" and has Latin origins, derived from the word "octavus."
ODAY	Means "awakening" and it has Arabic origins.
ODHRAN	Means "pale green" and originates from Irish Gaelic.
OGDEN	The first name Ogden originates from Old English and means "from the oak valley."
OGHENETEGA	Means "God's time" and originates from the Urhobo and Isoko ethnic groups of Nigeria.
OHAJI	The first name Ohaji has a meaning and origin that are unclear as it does not appear to have a widely recognized definition or historical background.
OJAS	The name "Ojas" originates from Sanskrit and means "vigor, energy, brilliance" or "divine glow."
OLADAYO	Means "wealth brings joy" and originates from the Yoruba language in Nigeria.
OLAF	Means "ancestor's relic" or "ancestor's descendant" and originated from Old Norse.
OLAJUWON	Means "God is worthy to be praised" and originates from the Yoruba culture in Nigeria.
OLAMIDE	Means "my wealth has come" and is of Yoruba origin in Nigeria.
OLAOLUWA	Means "God's wealth" or "God's honor" and originates from the Yoruba people of Nigeria.
OLEGARIO	Means "defender of heritage" and originates from Latin.
OLEK	The first name OLEK is of Slavic origin and it means "defender of mankind."
OLIVERIO	Masculine given name of Spanish origin meaning "olive tree."
OLLIVANDER	Means "powerful defender of elves" and has origins in Old English and Nordic languages.
OLUWADA MILARE	Means "God has rewarded me" and it has Yoruba origin.
OLUWADA MILOLA	Yoruba name meaning "God has rewarded me with wealth" and is of Nigerian origin.
OLUWADE MILADE	Means "God has crowned me" in Yoruba and is of Nigerian origin.

OLUWAFEMI	Means "God loves me" in Yoruba and has its origin in Nigeria.
OLUWAFE RANMI	Means "God loves me" and originated from Yoruba, a Nigerian language.
OLUWAFI KAYOMI	Yoruba name meaning "God has given me joy" in Nigeria.
OLUWAJO MILOJU	Means "God has blessed me abundantly" and originates from the Yoruba language in Nigeria.
OLUWATOBI	Oluwatobi means "God is great" in Yoruba and is of Nigerian origin.
OLUWATO BILOBA	Means "God is great" and it originates from the Yoruba culture in Nigeria.
OLYMPUS	Means "mountain of the gods" and is derived from Greek mythology, specifically the home of the Olympian gods.
OMEGA	Greek name meaning "the end" or "the last," often used symbolically to denote the last in a series or the ultimate.
OMERE	Means "one who is a leader" and its origin is uncertain.
OMID	The first name Omid, of Persian origin, means "hope" or "expectation."
OMRI	Means "my sheaf of grain" and originates from Hebrew.
ONEAL	Irish origin and it means "champion or descendant of Niall."
ONESIMO	Means "profitable" or "useful" and it is of Greek origin.
ONUR	Means "honor" in Turkish and it originates from the Turkish language.
ORACLE	Means "a person or thing regarded as an infallible authority or guide" and has its origin in Greek mythology, referring to the priestess at Delphi who communicated with the gods.
ORBELIN	Spanish first name that possibly originates from the combination of Orbe, meaning "world" in Basque, and -lin, a diminutive suffix.
OREL	Means "light" or "eagle" and originated from Hebrew.
ORHAN	Means "ruler" or "leader" and originates from the Turkish language.
ORVILLE	Means "golden city" and originates from Old French.
OSAZE	Means "God chooses or God favors" and it originates from the Edo-speaking people of Nigeria.
OSBORNE	The first name Osborn means "divine bear" and has Old English origins.
OSBOURNE	Means "divine bear" and originated from medieval English.
OSEAS	Means "salvation" and has biblical origins.
OSEIAS	Means "salvation" and originates from the Hebrew Bible.
OSHAE	Means "God's gift" and has origins in the African-American community.
OSINACHI	Unisex Igbo name of Nigerian origin that means "from God I have received."
OSLO	Means "God and sunshine" and originates from Old Norse.
OSTIN	Variant of the name Austin, which originated from the Latin name "Augustinus" meaning "great" or "magnificent".
OTAVIO	Means "noble" or "of the emperor" and has its origin in ancient Rome.
OTHELLO	Means "prosperous" in Greek and has Shakespearean origins, derived from the tragic protagonist of Shakespeare's play "Othello."
OTHMAN	Means "one who is blessed or successful" and has Arabic origins.
OTHNIEL	Means "God is my strength" and originates from the Hebrew language.
OUMAR	Arabic origin, means "life" or "long-lived" and is commonly used in Islamic cultures.
OUSMANE	Means "young camel" and has origins in Arabic and African cultures.
OVIDIO	Means "sheep herder" and originates from Latin.
OVIYAN	South Indian name meaning "artist" or "poet", derived from the Tamil language.
OWAIS	Means "little wolf" and has Arabic origins.
OZWALD	Means "divine power" or "ruling power" and has Teutonic origins.
OZYMANDIAS	Means "powerful ruler" and originates from an Ancient Egyptian poem written by Percy Bysshe Shelley in 1818.
PABLITO	Means "little Paul" and originates from Spanish.
PADRAIG	Means "noble" or "patrician" and originates from Ireland as the Irish variant of the name Patrick.
PANAGIOTIS	Means "all-holy" or "blessed" in Greek, and it originates from the Greek Orthodox tradition.

PARAM	The name PARAM has a Sanskrit origin and it means "supreme" or "highest."
PARTH	Means "warrior" or "son of Pritha" and has originated from ancient Sanskrit texts and Hindu mythology.
PASCAL	Means "Easter" and originates from Latin.
PASCUAL	Means "passover" or "Easter" and is of Spanish and Portuguese origin.
PATTERSON	The first name Patterson is of English origin and it means "son of Patrick".
PEARSON	Means "son of Piers/Peter" and has English origins.
PEDRITO	Means "little Peter" and has Spanish origin.
PEDROHE NRIQUE	The first name "PedroHenrique" is a combination of the names "Pedro" and "Henrique," which is of Portuguese origin and means "rock" and "ruler of the home" respectively.
PERCIVAL	Means "pierce the valley" and it is of Old French origin.
PEREGRINE	Meaning "traveler" or "pilgrim," Peregrine is of Latin origin and has historically been a popular name among Christians due to its association with Saint Peregrine, the patron saint of cancer patients.
PERNELL	The first name Pernell, of English origin, means "little rock" or "rocky."
PERRIN	Means "rock" or "wanderer" and is of French origin.
PHAROAH	Means "great house" and originates from Ancient Egypt.
PHARRELL	Means "revelation" or "God's love" and is of American origin.
PHEONIX	The name Phoenix means "dark red" and its origin is Greek.
PHIL	Means "lover of horses" and it is of Greek origin.
PHILEMON	Means "affectionate" or "loving" and is of Greek origin.
PHILOPATER	Means "lover of the father" and originates from Ancient Greek.
PHINEHAS	Means "oracle" or "serpent's mouth" and originates from the Hebrew language.
PHINLEY	Variation of the name Finley, which means "fair warrior" and originates from Gaelic or Irish roots.
PHONG	Means "wind" or "distinguish" and originates from Vietnamese and Chinese cultures.
PIETRO	Means "rock" and has its origin in Italian and Latin.
PILOT	Means "navigator" and has origins in both English and Greek.
PINCHAS	Means "dark-skinned" or "dark eyes" and it originates from Hebrew.
PIUS	Means "pious" or "devout" and originated from Latin.
PLATON	Means "broad-shouldered" and has its origin in Greek mythology, deriving from the name of the philosopher Plato.
PORFIRIO	Means "purple" in Greek and is of Spanish origin.
POSEIDON	Means "god of the sea" and originates from Greek mythology.
POWER	The name "Power" is a modern English word name that conveys a sense of strength, authority, and influence, likely originating from the concept of having control or
POYRAZ	Means "north wind" and originates from Turkish.
PRADYUMNA	Sanskrit name meaning "exceedingly intelligent" and is often associated with the Hindu deity Krishna's son.
PRAHAN	Means "beloved" and is of Sanskrit origin.
PRANEEL	The first name Praneel originated from Sanskrit and means "full of life or energy."
PRANISH	The meaning and origin of the first name "Pranish" is unclear as it does not appear to have a widely recognized meaning or specific origin.
PRATHAM	The name Pratham originates from Sanskrit and means "first" or "foremost."
PRATYUSH	The name Pratyush originates from Sanskrit and means "dawn" or "first light of the day."
PRAYUSH	Meaning: Ancient Indian name meaning "full of life and energy."
PREMIER	Means "first" or "leading" in French, and it originated from the use of the term to denote the head of government or a person of importance.
PRENTICE	Means "apprentice" or "learner" and originates from Old French or Latin.
PRESCOTT	Means "priest's cottage" and originates from Old English.
PRICE	Means "son of Rhys" and originated from Wales.
PRIEST	Means "religious minister" and has English origins.
PRIMUS	Means "first" or "leader" and originates from Latin.
PRINCEAMIR	Means "royal leader" and has origins rooted in Arabic and English cultures.
PRINCESTON	The name Princeton means "town of princes" and originated from Old English as a locational surname.

PRINSTON	Means "town of princes" and has English origin.
PRITHVI	Means "earth" and has its origins in Sanskrit, an ancient Indo-Aryan language.
PRODIGY	Means "an exceptionally talented or gifted person" and originated from the English language.
PROMETHEUS	Means "forethought" or "forethinker" and originates from Greek mythology, where Prometheus was a Titan who stole fire from the gods to benefit humanity.
PROPHET	Means "one who predicts or foretells future events" and has its origin in English from the word "prophēt" derived from Latin and Greek.
PROSPER	Means "successful" or "fortunate" and has Latin origins.
PRUITT	The first name Pruitt is of Irish origin and means "gallant, brave".
PRYOR	Means "caretaker of the meadow" and it is of English origin.
PSALM	Means a sacred song or hymn and its origin is from the Hebrew word "mizmor" meaning song.
PTOLEMY	Means "warlike" and originates from the Greek name "Ptolemaios."
QADIR	Means "capable" or "powerful" in Arabic, derived from the Arabic word "qadir" which translates to "able" or "competent."
QUAID	Means "leader" or "guide" and has Irish and Scottish origins.
QUALYN	Contemporary, invented name with no widely recognized meaning or origin.
QUAMARI	The first name Quamari is of African origin and means "moonlight" or "bright as the moon."
QUASHAWN	Modern, invented name of American origin, likely derived from combining elements of the names Quay and Shawn.
QUAVON	Means "a modern invented name with unknown origins"
QUILLAN	Means "descendant of Cuiléin" and has Irish Gaelic origins.
QUINLAN	Unisex name of Irish origin meaning "fit and strong."
QUINTAVIOUS	Means "fifth" and is of Latin origin.
QUINTAVIUS	Means "fifth-born" and has Latin origins.
QUINTRELL	Means "from the fifth estate" and has origins in the English language.
QUINTUS	The first name Quintus, of Latin origin, means "fifth" and was historically given to the fifth-born child in a Roman family.
QURAN	Means "the holy book of Islam" and originates from Arabic.
RACHID	Means "rightly guided" and originates from Arabic.
RADAMES	The first name Radames originated from ancient Egypt and means "child of Ra," referring to the Egyptian sun god.
RADEK	Means "famous ruler" and it originates from the Slavic language.
RAEF	Means "compassionate" and has Arabic origins.
RAEKWON	Means "born in wealth" or "enlightened leader" and has its origin in American modern naming trends.
RAFFERTY	The first name Rafferty likely originates from Ireland and means "flood tide" or "prosperity bringer."
RAFIQ	Means "kind, compassionate" and originates from Arabic.
RAGHAV	The first name Raghav originates from Sanskrit and means "one who is born in the Raghu dynasty" or "descendant of King Raghu."
RAHMATULLAH	Means "mercy of God" and has Arabic and Persian origins.
RAHUL	Means "efficient" or "conqueror of all miseries" and originates from Sanskrit, an ancient language of India.
RAIDON	Means "thunder god" in Japanese and is derived from the Japanese word "rai" meaning thunder and "don" meaning deity or god.
RAIJIN	Means "thunder god" and originates from Japanese mythology.
RAINER	German origin and means "warrior" or "advice-giver."
RAINIER	Means "wise warrior" and has Germanic origins.
RAJAH	Means "king" in Hindi and has origins in Sanskrit.
RAJVIR	Means "brave king" and has Punjabi origins.

RAKAN	Means "friend" or "companion" in Arabic and is of Arabic origin.
RAKIM	Means "one who is elevated" and originates from Arabic.
RALPHAEL	Means "God has healed" and is of Hebrew origin.
RAMADAN	Ramadan is an Arabic name that refers to the holy month of fasting in Islam, with its origin in Arabic and Islamic culture.
RAMADHANI	Means "born during the month of Ramadhan" and has Swahili origins.
RAMESSES	The first name Rameses means "son of Ra" and originates from Ancient Egypt.
RAMSAY	Means "garlic island" and is of Old English origin.
RAMY	The first name Ramy is of Arabic origin and means "loving" or "compassionate."
RAMZEY	Means "symbol" or "mystery" and originates from Arabic.
RANBIR	Means "the warrior who delights in battles" and originates from Sanskrit.
RANDOLPH	Means "shield-wolf" and originates from Old English, specifically a combination of "rand" (shield) and "wulf" (wolf).
RANVEER	Means "brave and courageous" and originates from the Indian subcontinent.
RAPHEAL	The name Raphael means "God has healed" and has Biblical origins.
RASHEEN	Means "wise" or "counselor" and originated from the Arabic and Hebrew language.
RASMUS	Means "beloved" and it originated from the Scandinavian countries.
RAWLEY	The first name Rawley is of English origin and means "from the rough meadow."
RAWLIN	The first name Rawlin is of English origin and it means "ravine" or "little red-haired one".
RAYBURN	Means "stream of robins" and has an English origin.
RAYDEL	Modern invented name of uncertain origin and meaning.
RAYHAN	Derived from the Arabic name "Rayhan," the first name Rayhan means "fragrant herb" and is commonly used in Muslim cultures.
RAYMEIR	The first name Raymeir is of American origin and means "counselor with a bright and noble personality."
RAYMIR	Arabic origin and means "one who is blessed with noble and illustrious status."
RAYNOR	The meaning of the first name Raynor is "mighty warrior" and it has Old Norse origins.
RAYSHAWN	Contemporary American name, often used within the African American community, which combines the names Ray and Shawn to form a unique and individualized name.
RAYSHON	Modern American name, likely derived from the combination of the names Ray and Shawn or a variation of the name Rashawn.
REACHER	The first name "Reacher" is a modern English name of uncertain origin, often associated with the character Jack Reacher in Lee Child's novels.
REASON	The name Reason originated from the English vocabulary word, meaning logical thinking or the capacity for sound judgment.
REAVES	English origin and it means "son of Reeve," referring to a bailiff or high-ranking official in medieval times.
RECORD	The meaning and origin of the first name RECORD are unknown, as it is an uncommon and rare name.
REDDING	Means "a place of reeds" and has an English origin.
REDMOND	Means "wise protector" and originates from Old English.
REFOEL	Means "healed by God" and originates from Hebrew.
REFUGIO	Means "refuge" or "shelter" and has Spanish origin.
REGULUS	Masculine given name meaning "prince" or "little king" that originates from ancient Rome.
REIKER	Modern American invention and does not have a specific meaning or origin.
REINHARDT	Means "strong counselor" and originates from Germanic origins.
REMIEL	Means "mercy of God" and it originates from Hebrew.
REMIGIO	Means "one who is peaceful" and has Latin origins.
RENALDO	Means "ruler's advisor" and has Spanish and Portuguese origins.
RENEGADE	The first name Renegade, of English origin, means a rebellious or unconventional person who defies societal norms.
RENLY	Modern invented name, derived from the English word "ren" meaning "clean, pure" combined with the suffix "-ly."
RENNICK	The meaning of the first name RENNICK is "ruler with counsel," and it originates from the Scottish and Irish surnames, derived from Mac Rannall or Mac Raghnail.

REXFORD	Means "king's ford" and is of Old English origin.
REXTON	Means "king's town" and originates from English and Old English.
REYMUNDO	Means "wise protector" and has Spanish origin.
REYNOLDS	The first name Reynolds is of Old English origin and means "son of Reynold," with the element "Reyn-" possibly derived from the Old Germanic name Raginwald, meaning "counsel-power."
REZWAN	Means "one who is content" and originates from Arabic.
RHETTLEE	Modern and unique American name, likely derived from the name Rhett combined with the suffix -lee.
RHONIN	Masculine given name of uncertain origin, often associated with fantasy literature and derived from the character "Rhonin Redhair" in the Warcraft series.
RHYDIAN	Welsh origin and means "brave warrior."
RHYLAN	Modern, invented name possibly derived from the Welsh name Rhylan, meaning "valley" or "stream."
RHYSON	Means "rhythmic son" and it has a modern origin as a variant of the name Ryson.
RHYZEN	Modern and unique name of uncertain origin, possibly a variation of the name Rhyse or a made-up name with no known meaning.
RICHARDSON	Means "son of Richard" and has an English origin.
RICHARLISON	Brazilian origin and means "powerful ruler."
RICHMOND	Means "powerful protector" and originates from the Old English words "ric" (meaning "ruler") and "mond" (meaning "protector").
RICHTER	Means "judge" or "ruler" and has German origins.
RIDDICK	Means "powerful ruler" and has English origins.
RIDGELY	The name Ridgely originated as an English surname derived from the Old English words "rydge" meaning "ridge" and "leah" meaning "clearing," and it refers to someone who lived near a ridge or hill clearing.
RIDHARV	Unique Indian name meaning "one who is blessed with goodness" and its origin comes from the Sanskrit language.
RIDWAN	Means "satisfaction" or "contentment" and originates from Arabic.
RIFTYN	The first name RIFTYN does not have an established meaning or origin as it is a relatively rare and unique name.
RIGBY	Means "from the ridge farm" and is of English origin.
RIGDON	Means "ridge hill" and has an English origin.
RIGGSLEY	Modern English name of uncertain origin, likely a combination of the surnames Riggs and Lee.
RIGHTEOUS	Means morally upright or just, and it originated from Old English as a virtue name reflecting the qualities of righteousness or uprightness.
RIGSBY	The first name Rigsby likely originated as a surname meaning "farm by the rye" in English.
RIKU	Means "land" or "land of strength" and is of Finnish origin.
RINGO	Means "apple, round object" and is of Japanese origin.
RIORDAN	Means "royal poet" and has Irish Gaelic origin.
RIPKEN	The first name "Ripken" is of English origin and means "from the rippling brook."
RISHABH	Means "bull" or "morality" and has its origin in Sanskrit.
RISHIKESH	Means "lord of the senses" and originates from Sanskrit.
RITCHIE	Means "powerful ruler" and has English and Scottish origins.
RITHAV	Rithav is an Indian name meaning "a person who is brave and intelligent" and is of Sanskrit origin.
RITHVIK	Means "sacred fire or priest" and originates from the Sanskrit language, commonly found in Indian culture.
RITVIK	The first name "Ritvik" is of Sanskrit origin and means "one who performs Vedic rituals."
RIVERTON	The first name Riverton is of English origin and means "town near the river."
ROAM	The first name Roam derives from Latin origin and it means "to wander or explore freely."
ROANIN	Modern variant of the Irish name Ronan, meaning "little seal" or "wise."
ROBINSON	The first name Robinson, of English origin, means "son of Robin" or "son of Robert."
ROBSAN	The name ROBSAN does not have a widely recognized meaning or origin as it appears to be a rare or uncommon name.

ROCKFORD	Masculine given name of English origin meaning "ford where rock grows."
ROCKLAND	Masculine name of English origin meaning "land of rocks" or "rocky land."
ROCZEN	The first name Roczen has a German origin and it means "rocky" or "strong like a rock".
RODARIUS	The first name Rodarius, of uncertain origin, carries the meaning of a unique and distinctive individual.
RODION	Means "warrior" or "hero" and originates from Russian and Greek languages.
RODRICK	Means "famous ruler" and has Scottish and Germanic origins.
RODRIQUEZ	The first name Rodriguez originated from Spain and means "son of Rodrigo."
ROLDAN	Means "famous throughout the land" and is of Spanish origin.
ROMAINE	Means "from Rome" and originates from the Latin name "Romanus."
ROMANCE	The name Romance originates from the Latin word "romanticus" meaning "of the Roman style."
ROMULUS	Means "founder" and originates from Roman mythology, as Romulus was the legendary founder and first king of Rome.
RONAV	The first name Ronav has no known meaning or origin as it is a very rare and uncommon name.
RONDELL	The first name Ronde ll is of French origin and means "round-shaped" or "round hill."
ROODENSLEY	Haitian Creole name that means "famous ruler" or "renowned leader."
ROOSEVELT	Means "field of roses" and originates from the Dutch language.
RORONOA	The first name Roronoa is of Japanese origin and its meaning is unclear or unknown.
ROSENDO	Means "famous rose" and has Spanish and Portuguese origins.
ROSHAWN	Modern American name, likely a blend of the names Roscoe and Shawn, meaning "graceful and God is gracious."
ROSTAM	Means "strong and brave" and has Persian origins.
ROURKE	Means "red-haired" and has Irish origins.
ROWLAND	Means "famous land" or "fame of the country" and it originates from Old Germanic, deriving from the elements "hrod" meaning fame and "land" meaning land or territory.
ROXAS	Means "roses" and is of Spanish origin.
ROYSTON	The first name Royston originated from Old English and means "royal stone" or "regal town".
ROZAY	Modern American name derived from the nickname of rapper Rick Ross and popularized further by the brand "Belaire Rosé" of sparkling wine.
RUAIRI	Means "red king" and originates from Ireland.
RUDHRA	Means "roaring or howling" and originates from Sanskrit, a sacred language of Hinduism.
RUDHVIK	Sanskrit name meaning "one who is strong and powerful."
RUDOLPH	Means "famous wolf" and originates from Germanic roots.
RUDRANSH	Means "a part of Lord Shiva" and originates from Hindu mythology.
RUEBEN	The name Reuben means "behold, a son" and originates from Hebrew.
RUFINO	Masculine given name of Latin origin meaning "red-haired" or "red complexioned," derived from the Latin word "rufus."
RUFUS	Means "red-haired" and has Latin origins.
RUSLAN	Means "lion" and originates from various cultures, including Persian, Russian, and Turkish.
RUSTON	Means "from the town of rust" and has English origins.
RUTHERFORD	Means "ford where cattle cross the river" and is of Old English origin.
RUTLEDGE	Means "red ledge" and originates from Old English.
RYELAND	The meaning and origin of the first name RYELAND is uncertain and it is likely a modern invented name.
RYERSON	Means "son of Ryer" and has Dutch origin.
RYOMA	Means "dragon horse" in Japanese and its origin can be traced back to Japanese culture and mythology.
RYZEN	American origin and means "rising," symbolizing growth and progression.
SABAS	Hebrew origin, means "old man" or "elder" and is derived from the biblical figure Saint Sabas, an influential monk and saint in the Eastern Orthodox Church.
SABATINO	Means "born on the Sabbath" and comes from the Italian and Spanish language, derived from the Latin word "sabbatum" referring to the holy day of rest, Saturday.

SACHIN	Means "pure" or "essence" and has its origin in Sanskrit language and Hindu mythology.
SACRED	Means holy or deserving of reverence, and it is of English origin.
SAEID	Means "happy" or "fortunate" and originates from Persian/Iranian culture.
SAFAREE	Means "companion for a journey" and is of African origin.
SAFWAN	Arabic origin and means "rock" or "pebble," symbolizing strength and solidity.
SAIDOU	The first name Saidou originated from West Africa and its meaning is "happiness" or "joyful."
SAIFULLAH	Means "sword of Allah" and originates from Arabic.
SAKONI	Means "bird" in the Native American Choctaw language and is of Native American origin.
SALAHUDDIN	Salahuddin is an Arabic name meaning "the righteousness of the religion", and it originates from Islamic tradition as a significant historical figure.
SALIOU	The first name Saliou is of African origin and it means "he who makes prayers."
SAMARPAN	The name Samdarpan means "reflection" or "mirror" in Hindi and is of Indian origin.
SAMARVEER	Hindu name meaning "brave in battle" and is of Indian origin.
SAMEIR	Means "pleasant companion" and has an Arabic origin.
SAMIULLAH	Muslim boy's name meaning "elevated by God" that originates from Arabic and is commonly used in in South Asia and the Middle East.
SAMPSON	Means "sun child" in Hebrew and its origin can be traced back to biblical times.
SAMRATH	Indian origin and means "supreme ruler" or "emperor".
SAMVED	Means "knowledge of the chants" and originates from Sanskrit.
SAMWISE	The meaning of the first name Samwise is "half-wise" and it originated from J.R.R. Tolkien's fictional universe in the book "The Lord of the Rings."
SAMYAR	Persian origin, and it means "bearer of beauty."
SAMYOG	Nepali origin, meaning "connection" or "union."
SANAD	Means "support" or "foundation" and has Arabic origins.
SANCHEZ	The first name Sanchez originates from Spanish and it means "son of Sancho."
SANDLER	The first name "Sandler" has a Jewish origin and means "one who works with sand."
SANFORD	Means "sandy ford" and originated from the Old English words "sand" (meaning sand) and "ford" (meaning a shallow place in a river that can be crossed).
SANJAY	Means "triumphant" or "victorious" and it originates from Sanskrit.
SANKALP	Means "determination" or "resolution" in Sanskrit and originates from India.
SANTHIAGO	Means "Saint James" and originates from the combination of the Spanish name Santiago, meaning "Saint James," with the Portuguese variation San Tiago.
SANTIEL	Spanish origin and means "holy angel of God."
SARANSH	The first name Saransh is of Indian origin and means "summary" or "essence" in Hindi.
SARIM	The first name Sarim likely has Arabic origins and refers to someone who is a leader or noble.
SARKIS	Means "one who is brave and victorious" and it has Armenian origin.
SARTAJ	Means "crown of honor" and originates from Persian or Arabic languages.
SARTHAK	Means "fulfilled" or "successful" and originates from Sanskrit, an ancient language of India.
SARVESH	Means "lord of all" or "ruler of everything" and originates from Sanskrit, an ancient language of India.
SASCHA	Unisex name of Russian origin meaning "defender of mankind."
SASUKE	Means "helper" or "assistant" and originates from Japanese culture, popularized by the fictional character Sasuke Uchiha from the manga and anime series, Naruto.
SATHVIK	Hindi name meaning "pure" or "virtuous," originating from Sanskrit.
SATOSHI	Means "wise" or "quick-thinking" and originates from Japanese culture.
SATURNINO	Spanish and Italian name of Latin origin; its meaning is derived from the Latin word "Saturnus," referring to the Roman god of agriculture and time.
SAVAGE	The first name "Savage" derives from the Middle English word "sauvage," which means wild, untamed, or feral.
SAVELIY	Means "rescue" or "savior" and has Russian origins.
SAVERIO	Means "savior" and originates from Italian.
SAVIOR	Means "one who saves" and it originated from Latin.
SAYVIOR	Meaning "savior" in English, SAYVIOR is a modern variant of the name Savior which is derived from the Latin word "salvator".

SCHAEFER	German origin and means "shepherd," referring to someone who herds and tends to sheep.
SCHNEIDER	Means "tailor" in German, and it has a occupational origin as a surname given to individuals who worked as tailors.
SCHNEUR	The first name "Schneur" is of Hebrew origin and means "luminous" or "bright."
SCHUYLER	Means "scholar" or "scholarly" and originated from the Dutch surname Schuyler.
SCION	Means a descendant or heir, and it has Latin and French origins.
SEAGER	Means "victory" or "conqueror" and originates from Old English as a variant of the name Seger.
SEBASHTIAN	The first name Sebashtian is derived from the Latin name Sebastianus, meaning "man from Sebastia" or "from the city of Sebaste" in ancient Greece.
SEBASTAIN	The name Sebastian means "venerable" and it originated from the Latin name Sebastianus, derived from the Greek word sebastos meaning "revered" or "honored."
SEBASTHIAN	Variant spelling of the name Sebastian, which originated from Latin and means "venerable" or "revered."
SEBATIAN	The name Sebastian means "venerable" or "respected" and has Latin origins.
SEELEY	Means "blessed and happy" and originated from Old English.
SEHRAJ	Punjabi name meaning "king of the dawn" or "dawn king" and originates from India.
SEIF	Means "sword" in Arabic and has origins in Middle Eastern cultures.
SEKHANI	Means "one who is brave and fearless" and has its origin in the African Zulu language.
SEKOU	Means "man born to serve" and it originates from the Mandinka language in West Africa.
SEMISI	Tongan male given name meaning "James" or "Jacob" and it originates from the Semitic name Shamshiyu, meaning "sun-like."
SENSEI	Means "teacher" or "master" in Japanese and is traditionally used to address a person of high expertise or rank in martial arts or other disciples.
SERAPH	Hebrew name meaning "fiery ones" and is derived from the biblical creature known as the Seraphim.
SERGEY	Means "protector" or "guardian" and it originated from Russia.
SERIGNE	Senegalese origin and it means "spiritual leader" or "holy person."
SERVANDO	Means "to serve" and it has Spanish and Portuguese origins.
SEVERIN	Means "stern" or "severe" and originates from Latin.
SEVERUS	Means "stern" or "serious" and it originates from Latin.
SEVRYN	Modern variation of the name Séverin with origin in Latin, meaning "serious" or "stern."
SEYDINA	The first name Seydina derives from Arabic origin and it means "master" or "lord."
SEYMOUR	Means "from the saint's hill" and it originated from an English surname derived from the Norman French word "seigneur," meaning "lord" or "master."
SEYVEN	Modern variant of the name Sven, which means "young man" in Old Norse.
SHABAZZ	Means "royal" or "noble" and originates from Arabic and African cultures.
SHADOW	Means "dark silhouette cast by an object blocking light" and originated as a modern English word name.
SHADRACH	The first name Shadrach is of biblical origin and means "command of Aku," referring to the Babylonian god of the moon.
SHAHMIR	Means "mighty king" and has Persian origins.
SHAHVEER	The first name "Shahveer" originates from Persian and means "royal hero" or "brave king."
SHAHZAIN	The first name Shahzain is of Persian origin and means "crown of beauty" or "pride of a king."
SHAIDEN	Uncertain origin and meaning, as it is a modern, invented name with no widely recognized heritage or etymology.
SHAKUR	Means "thankful" or "grateful" and it originated from Arabic and Swahili.
SHAQUAN	Means "handsome" or "well-formed" and is of African-American origin.
SHAQUILLE	Means "handsome" and it is of African-American origin.
SHARIF	Means "noble" or "honorable" and has Arabic origins.
SHARVIL	The first name Sharvil is of Indian origin and means "divinely handsome" or "charming."
SHASHWAT	Indian origin and means "eternal" or "everlasting."
SHEAMUS	Means "supplanter" and has Irish origins.
SHEDEUR	Modern name of uncertain origin and meaning.

SHEDRICK	The first name Shedrick is of Hebrew origin, meaning "God is gracious."
SHEHBAAZ	The first name Shehbaaz is of Persian origin and means "beautiful falcon."
SHEHZAD	Persian-origin name meaning "son of a prince" or "son of a king."
SHEMUEL	Means "heard by God" and it has Hebrew origins.
SHERMAN	Means "shearer of woolen cloth" and originated as an English occupational surname.
SHERROD	Variant of the English surname Sherwood, derived from the Old English words "scir" meaning "bright" and "wudu" meaning "wood," referring to someone who lived near a bright or clear wood.
SHERWIN	The first name Sherwin is of English origin and means "swift friend" or "quick-witted friend".
SHERWOOD	Means "from the bright forest" and originates from Old English.
SHIHAB	Means "shooting star" or "meteor" and has Arabic origin.
SHIMSHON	Means "sun" or "sunshine" and originates from Hebrew.
SHIVAY	Means "auspicious" or "benevolent" and it has Indian origin.
SHIVEN	Means "auspicious" and originates from Sanskrit, an ancient Indo-Aryan language.
SHLOIMY	Yiddish diminutive form of the Hebrew name Shlomo, meaning "peaceful" or "peaceful one," and it is commonly used in Jewish communities.
SHMEIL	The first name Shmeil is of Yiddish origin meaning "Samuel" or "His name is God" and it is commonly used among Jewish communities.
SHMIEL	Means "heard by God" and has Hebrew origins.
SHNEUR	Means "illumination" or "bright" and originates from Hebrew.
SHOHEI	Means "shining, excellent" in Japanese and it originates from Japan.
SHOOTER	The name "Shooter" is a modern English name derived from the word "shooter," typically associated with someone skilled in shooting or a person passionately engaged in shooting sports or activities.
SHRAGA	The first name Shraga is of Hebrew origin and means "bright" or "radiant."
SHREYANSH	Means "part of a divine glory" and originated from the Sanskrit language.
SHRIHAN	Modern Indian name derived from two Sanskrit words, "shri" meaning prosperity or wealth, and "han" meaning the one who possesses or acquires.
SHRITHIK	The first name "Shrithik" is of Indian origin and typically means "one who is blessed with wealth or prosperity."
SHUAIB	Means "prophet" and originates from Arabic Islamic culture.
SHUBH	The name Shubh is derived from Sanskrit, meaning "auspicious" or "fortunate."
SHUBHAM	Means "auspicious" or "goodness" and originates from Sanskrit, an ancient language of India.
SHUBHDEEP	Means "auspicious light" and originates from Indian and Punjabi cultures.
SHURAIM	Means "radiant" and originates from Arabic.
SIAIRE	Means "excellent" or "supreme" and has an African origin.
SIAOSI	Means "George" in the Polynesian language and is of Tongan origin.
SID	Means "wide valley" and originated as a nickname for individuals with the given name Sydney or Sidney.
SIDDIQ	Means "truthful" or "one who is honest" and originates from Arabic.
SIEGFRIED	Means "victory" and originates from Germanic and Norse mythology.
SIGURD	Means "victory guardian" and originates from Old Norse.
SIKANDAR	Means "conqueror" in Persian and is of Middle Eastern origin.
SILVANUS	Means "of the forest" and has its origin in ancient Roman mythology.
SILVERIO	The first name Silverio originates from Latin and means "silver," often associated with wealth or strength.
SILVESTRE	Means "of the forest" or "wild" and has its origin in Latin.
SILVIANO	The first name Silviano originates from Latin and means "from the forest" or "of the woods".
SIMBA	Means "lion" in Swahili and is commonly used in East Africa.
SIRIUS	Means "brightest star" and originates from the Latin word for "dog."
SIRMICHAEL	The first name SIRMICHAEL is of English origin and its meaning is derived from combining the titles "Sir" (a term of respect) and "Michael" (meaning "who is like God"), resulting in a name that conveys an honorable, divine likeness.

SIRROYAL	The first name Sirroyal is of modern origin and likely signifies someone who is regarded or treated as royalty.
SIRUS	Persian-origin name meaning "shining one" or "bright star."
SITKA	Native American origin, derived from the Tlingit word "Sheet'ká," meaning "people on the outside of Shee."
SIXTO	Means "sixth" and it originates from Spanish and Latin cultures.
SIYERE	Yoruba name of African origin meaning "blessing" or "gift from God."
SKANDA	Means "spurting" or "he who leaps" and it originates from Hindu mythology, referring to the god of war and victory.
SKIP	The first name Skip is of English origin and it is a nickname or shortened form of "skipper", referring to the captain or leader of a ship.
SLAYDE	Means "valley dweller" and it originated as an English surname.
SMAYAN	The meaning and origin of the first name Smayan are not clear as it does not appear to have a widely recognized meaning or background.
SNEIJDER	Means "son of Schneider" and has Dutch origin.
SNEYDER	The first name SNEYDER is of Dutch origin and means "tailor," referring to someone skilled in sewing and making clothes.
SNYDER	Means "tailor" and originates from the German occupational surname "Schneider."
SOHAM	The name Soham originates from Sanskrit and means "I am He" or "I am that."
SOHRAB	Means "shining like the sun" and it originates from Persian/Iranian mythology.
SOLACE	Solace means comfort or consolation, and it is of Latin origin.
SOLAIRE	Unique French name meaning "sunny" or "of the sun," derived from the Latin word for sun, "sol."
SOMTOCH UKWU	Unisex Igbo name from Nigeria that means "praise God" or "worship God" in English.
SONDER	Means "to realize that each random passerby is living a life as vivid and complex as your own," and it originates from the English word "sonder" popularized in 2012 by the Dictionary of Obscure Sorrows.
SOSAIA	Means "precious gift of God" and originates from the Polynesian culture.
SOTIRIOS	Means "savior" and has Greek origins.
SOULEYMANE	Means "peaceful, blessed" and is of Arabic origin.
SOUTHERN	Means relating to or characteristic of the southern part of a region, and likely originated as a geographical surname.
SPIROS	Greek name meaning "man of the spirit" or "man of the breath," derived from the Greek word "spiritos."
SRIANSH	Means "part of Lord Vishnu" and it originates from Indian Hindu mythology.
SRIHAN	The meaning and origin of the first name Srihan is currently unknown.
STAFFORD	Means "ford by a landing-place" and it originated from Old English.
STANFORD	Means "stone ford" and it originates from Old English.
STANISLAW	Means "glorious government" and has Slavic origins.
STANTON	Means "from the stony town" and has English origins.
STATLER	The first name Statler originated as a German surname meaning "state ruler" or "official" and became a popular given name influenced by the Muppet character Statler.
STAVROS	Means "cross" in Greek and it originates from the Greek word for "cross" or "crucifix."
STEVENSON	Means "son of Steven" and it originated as a patronymic surname in Scotland and England.
STEWART	Means "steward" or "guardian" and originates from Old English and Scottish Gaelic.
STILES	The first name "Stiles" is of English origin and means "one who lives by a steep path or hillside."
STOCKTON	Means "from the tree-stump settlement" and has an English origin.
STOIC	Means "someone who is impassive and unwavering in their demeanor" and originates from the ancient Greek philosophy of Stoicism.
STOKELY	Means "from the oak tree meadow" and has English origins.
STRIDER	Means "one who walks or moves swiftly" and originates from English.
STURGILL	The first name Sturgill is of Scottish origin and means "strong child."

STYLEZ   The first name Stylez is of modern origin and carries a stylish and trendy connotation.

SUBHAN   Means "praiseworthy, glorified" and originates from Arabic.

SUDAIS   Means "fortunate, blessed" and it has Arabic origins.

SUFIYAN   Arabic origin and it means "one who follows a mystical Islamic tradition."

SUFYAN   Means "rock" or "hardness" and has Arabic origins.

SUHAYB   Means "small star" and has Arabic origins.

SULEYMAN   Means "man of peace" and originates from Arabic and Turkish.

SUMNER   Meaning "summit dweller" or "summit of the hill," Sumner is of English origin.

SUPREME   Means highest or greatest, and its origin is English.

SURYANSH   Means "part of the sun" and originates from Sanskrit, an ancient language of India.

SVIATOSLAV   Means "glory" and "intent" and it originates from Slavic roots.

SYHIR   Unique and modern male given name with an uncertain origin and meaning.

SYIRE   The meaning and origin of the first name Syire are unknown as it is a rare and uncommon name with no widely recognized origins or meanings.

SYLAR   Means "powerful leader" and is of unknown origin.

SYLIAS   The first name Sylias does not have a clear meaning or origin as it appears to be a rare or fictional name.

SYLVAN   Name of Latin origin meaning "of the forest" or "woodsy," referencing the mythical woodland deity Sylvanus.

SZYMON   Means "hearkening" and originates from the Hebrew name Shim'on.

TABOR   Hebrew name meaning "drum" or "small musical instrument," originating from the biblical Mount Tabor in Israel.

TADASHI   Means "loyalty" or "correctness" in Japanese and has its origin in the Japanese culture and language.

TADEUSZ   Means "praise-worthy" or "gift of God" and originated from the Greek name Thaddaios, which was later adapted in various languages.

TADGH   Means "poet" or "philosopher" and originates from Irish Gaelic.

TADHG   Means "poet" or "philosopher" and originates from Irish and Gaelic languages.

TAEVEON   The name Taeveon does not have a widely recognized meaning or origin as it is a creative and unique name likely derived from combining various elements or sounds.

TAEVON   American origin and it means "God is good."

TAFARI   Male name of Ethiopian origin meaning "he who inspires awe and respect."

TAHJAE   Modern name of American origin, likely a phonetic variation or combination of the names Tahj and Jae.

TAIKA   Means "magic" or "wizardry" and originates from the Maori language in New Zealand.

TAIMUR   Means "iron" or "strong" and originates from the Turkic-Mongol Empire.

TAISEI   Means "great star" or "great achievement" and it originated in Japan.

TAIYO   Means "sun" in Japanese and it is of Japanese origin.

TAKESHI   Means "warrior" and it has Japanese origin.

TAKODA   Means "friend to everyone" and is of Native American Lakota Sioux origin.

TAKRIM   Arabic origin and means "honor" or "respect."

TALAL   Means "dew" or "moisture" and originates from Arabic.

TALIESIN   Means "shining brow" and originates from Welsh mythology, associated with a renowned poet and bard.

TALMADGE   Means "one who lives near the elm tree" and has English and Scottish origins.

TALMAGE   Means "one who brings comfort" and originates from the English language.

TAMATOA   Means "brave warrior" in Maori language and originates from Polynesia.

TAMIM   Means "complete" or "perfect" and is of Arabic origin.

TANAY   Means "son" in Sanskrit and is of Indian origin.

TANJIRO   Means "many second sons" in Japanese and originates from Japanese literature.

TAOS   The first name "Taos" originated from the Native American Taos Pueblo tribe and means "place of red willows" or "place of the red willow trees."

TAREK   Tarek is an Arabic name meaning "one who knocks at the gate" and it originates from the Arabic language.

TASHFIN   Means "one who recognizes his faith" and it originates from Arabic.

TASRIF   Muslim name of Arabic origin meaning "refinement" or "polishing."

TATEN   The first name "Taten" is of German origin and means "deeds" or "actions."

TAUREAN   Means "pertaining to Taurus" and it originated from the zodiac sign Taurus, which is represented by a bull.

TAURUS   Means "bull" and originates from Latin mythology.

TAVARES   Means "from a Spanish and Portuguese surname meaning 'farm' or 'estate'."

TAWHEED   Means "the belief in the oneness of Allah" and has Arabic origin.

TAYM   The first name TAYM is of Arabic origin and means "strong" or "brave".

TAYSHAUN   Means "God's gift" and has African origins.

TAYTON   English origin and its meaning is "town by the river."

TAYVIN   The first name Tayvin is of American origin and is a modern variant of the name "Kevin," meaning "handsome" or "gentle birth."

TEAGUE   Gender-neutral name of Irish origin, meaning "bard" or "poet."

TECUANI   Tecuani means "brave one" in Nahuatl, the language of the Aztecs.

TEGH   Means "sharp" or "mighty" and originates from Punjabi and Sikh cultures.

TEMESGEN   Means "one who brings hope" and it has Ethiopian origin.

TEMIDAYO   The first name Temidayo is of Yoruba origin and means "my happiness has come" or "mine is happiness."

TEMUJIN   The first name Temujin, of Mongolian origin, means "iron worker" or "blacksmith" and was the birth name of the Mongol ruler Genghis Khan.

TENNYSON   The meaning of the first name Tennyson is "son of Dennis" and it originates from the Irish surname Ó Tanaiste, meaning "the descendant of the champion".

TENUUN   The first name Tenuun is of Mongolian origin and it means "eternal" or "unending."

TEODORO   Masculine name of Greek origin meaning "gift of God".

TEOFILO   Greek given name meaning "loved by god" that originated from the Greek word "theos" meaning "god" and "philein" meaning "to love".

TEOMAN   Turkish origin, means "brave man" or "leader" and is typically given to boys.

TERRIAN   Means "from the Earth" or "of the earth" and has uncertain origins, possibly derived from the English name Terri or a combination of Tera and Ryan.

TERRYON   Means "ruler of the people" and has an American origin.

TEVITA   Means "beloved" or "dear one" and originates from the Hebrew name David.

TEWODROS   Means "gift of God" and originates from the Amharic language in Ethiopia.

THABIT   Means "firm, resolute" and has Arabic origins.

THADDAEUS   Masculine given name of Aramaic origin meaning "courageous heart," often associated with the apostle Thaddeus in the Bible.

THAILAND   The first name "Thailand" does not have a historical origin or a specific meaning as it is primarily associated with the country in Southeast Asia.

THAISON   Vietnamese origin and it means "brave warrior."

THANG   Vietnamese name generally given to males which means "victory" or "win."

THAXTON   Means "from the enclosure town" and has English origins.

THAYER   Means "one who lives by the river" and originates from the Old English word "þæger" meaning "watercourse" or "rivulet."

THAYLOR   Modern variant of the name Taylor, originating from Old French and meaning "tailor".

THAYNE   Means "follower of Christ" and is of English origin.

THELONIOUS   Means "like Thelonius" and originates from the combination of the English name Theodore and the Greek name Athelstan or Anselm.

THEODEN   Means "ruler of the people" and it originated from Old English.

THEODOR   Means "God's gift of protection" and it is a combination of the Greek name Theodore and
EJAMES   the English name James.

THEOPHIL   Means "lover of God" and has biblical origins.

THEOPHILUS   Means "loved by God" and it originates from the Greek words "theos" meaning "God" and "philos" meaning "loved, dear."

THEORDORE   The name Theodore means "gift of God" and originates from the Greek name Theodoros.

THESEUS   Means "glory of God" and originates from Greek mythology.

THIELEN   Means "son of Thiel" and has Dutch and German origins.

THIERRY	Means "ruler of the people" and originated from Germanic and French roots.
THOEDORE	The first name Theodore means "gift of God" and originated from the Greek name Theodoros.
THOMASJ AMES	Means "twin-born supplanter" and is a combination of the names Thomas, derived from Aramaic, meaning "twin," and James, derived from Hebrew, meaning "supplanter."
THOMPSON	Means "son of Tom" and originates from Scotland and England.
THORFINN	Means "fins of Thor" in Old Norse and is of Norse origin.
THORNE	Means "thorn bush" and has English origins.
THORNTON	Means "thorn enclosure" and its origin can be traced back to the Old English language.
THORSON	Means "son of Thor" and has Nordic origins.
THORSTEN	Means "Thor's stone" and has its origins in Old Norse and Germanic language.
THUNDER	Means a loud, powerful sound and has origins from the English vocabulary word.
THURMAN	Means "servant of Thor" and has English and Old Norse origins.
THURSTON	Thurston is an English name meaning "town of thorns" and has origins in Old Norse and Old English.
TIERNAN	Tiernan is an Irish name meaning "lord of the household," derived from the Gaelic word "tighearna" meaning lord or master.
TIFEOLUWA	Gender-neutral Nigerian name derived from the Yoruba language, meaning "enjoyment of God's grace" or "God's grace is enough."
TIGER	Means a large, carnivorous feline animal and originated from the Old English word "tigras".
TIGRAN	Masculine Armenian given name meaning "tiger" and derived from the Armenian word for "tiger."
TILAK	Sanskrit name meaning "mark" or "ornament" and it originates from India.
TILDEN	The name Tilden originated from a surname, signifying "valley of wild garlic," and refers to an individual with a connection to nature and tranquility.
TILLMAN	The first name Tillman is of German origin and it means "strong-willed man" or "ruler of the people".
TIMOFEY	Means "honoring God" and it originates from the Greek name Timotheos, meaning "honoring God" or "God's honor."
TIMOTEO	Means "honoring God" and it is of Greek origin.
TIMUR	Means "iron" or "strong" and originates from Turkic and Mongolian languages.
TIRSO	Means "arrow" and has Spanish and Greek origins.
TIRTH	Means "sacred place" and originates from Sanskrit.
TIZIANO	Means "from ancient Roman times" and originates from Italian.
TLALOC	Means "he who makes things sprout" and originates from the Aztec culture in Mesoamerica.
TOBECHI	Means "praise God" and has its origin in the Igbo language of Nigeria.
TOBECHU KWU	Means "praise God" and originates from the Igbo language of Nigeria.
TOBENNA	Igbo origin and means "the father's love" or "father's love is with me" in the Igbo language of Nigeria.
TOMMASO	Tommaso is an Italian given name meaning "twin," derived from the Aramaic name □ □ □ □ □ (Ta'oma).
TONATIUH	Means "sun" in Nahuatl and originates from Aztec mythology.
TOPHER	Shortened form of Christopher, meaning "bearer of Christ," and it originates from the Greek name Khristophoros.
TOPRAK	Means "earth" or "soil" in Turkish, and it originates from Turkish and other Turkic languages.
TORETTO	The first name Toretto likely has no specific meaning or origin as it appears to be a fictional name created for the character Dominic Toretto in the Fast and Furious film
TORIBIO	Means "victorious" and it has Spanish origins.
TORRENCE	The meaning of the first name Torrence is "from the hills or rocky grounds," and it has English and Scottish origin.

TORSTEN	Means "thunderstone" and originates from Old Norse, combining the elements "Thor" referring to the Norse god of thunder, and "sten" meaning stone.
TOSHIRO	Means "talented and intelligent" and it originated in Japan.
TOUSSAINT	Means "all saints" or "all saints' day," and it originates from French and Haitian Creole languages, commonly used in countries influenced by Catholicism.
TOWNSEND	The first name Townsend is of English origin and it means "settlement near the town."
TRAEGER	The first name Traeger is of German origin and means "maker of wooden objects or works with wood."
TRAIL	Means "route or path" and has an English origin.
TRAJAN	Latin origin, means "from Trajan's town" and is derived from the Roman emperor Trajan.
TRAMARI	The first name Tramari is of American origin and its meaning is currently unknown.
TRAMEL	English origin and means "from the meadow of the elder trees."
TRAPPER	Means a person skilled in trapping animals, and it originates from the occupation of trapping, particularly in North America.
TRAVEON	Modern invented name of uncertain origin, likely created by combining elements from various existing names.
TRAYCE	Variant of the name Tracey, derived from an English surname ultimately from a place name meaning "crossroads" in Old French.
TRAYVEON	Modern invented name with no specific meaning or origin.
TREMIR	The first name Tremir is of English origin and it means "faithful or trustworthy."
TREMON	Means "town on a hill" and has an American origin.
TRESHAWN	Modern and unique American name primarily used for boys, possibly originating as a combination of the names Trey and Shawn.
TREVION	The first name Trevion, of American origin, means "a modern variation of the name Trevor, derived from a Welsh surname."
TREVONTE	The name Trevonte has an American origin and means "inventive" or "innovative."
TREVYN	Means "fair town" or "homestead" and is of Welsh origin.
TREYDEN	Means "from the valley with three hills" and has an American origin.
TREYLIN	The first name Treylind is of American origin and has no specific meaning.
TREYVION	American origin, means "combination of Trey, referring to 'third' and Vion, of unknown meaning."
TRIGGER	Means "a device or action that causes a particular reaction or event" and has its origin as a word in Old English, later evolving as a term for the part of a gun that releases the shot.
TRILLION	Means "a very large number" and is of modern English origin.
TRINIDAD	Means "Trinity" and is of Spanish origin.
TRIUMPH	Means a significant victory or achievement, and it originates from the English language.
TROPHY	Means a prize or award given as a symbol of victory, and it is of English origin.
TRUCE	Means "a state of peace or cessation of hostilities" and originated as a variant of the word "truce," ultimately derived from Old English and Old French.
TRUSTIN	Means "having confidence or faith" and its origin is uncertain, potentially a modern variant of biblical name 'Justin'.
TRYGVE	Norwegian name that means "trustworthy" and originates from Old Norse.
TRYSTEN	Modern spelling variant of the name Tristan, which originates from Celtic legend and means "sorrowful" or "sad."
TUFF	The first name Tuff is of English origin and means "strong-willed or tough".
TYCHO	Means "luck" or "fortunate" and it has its origin in Greek and Danish cultures.
TYDUS	Means "god-like" or "giant-killer" and originates from Greek mythology, referring to the mythical figure Tydeus who was known for his bravery and strength.
TYJAI	Means "little king" and has an American origin.
TYKEEM	Means "a graceful and noble person" and is of African American origin.
TYLERJAMES	Modern composite name combining the given name Tyler, derived from an English surname meaning "tiler of roofs", and the given name James, originating from the Hebrew name Yaakov meaning "supplanter".

TYMARI	Uncertain origin, but it is believed to be a modern name possibly a variation of Tamari or a combination of Tyler and Mari.
TYMOTEUSZ	Means "honoring God" and is of Greek origin.
TYQUAN	Modern American name of uncertain origin, possibly a variant of the name Taquan or a combination of Tyler and Quan.
TYRAEL	Means "God's herald" and is of Hebrew origin, derived from the combination of the elements "el" meaning "God" and "tyr" meaning "herald."
TYRION	Welsh origin and its meaning is "king of the land of the trees."
TYRIQUE	The first name Tyrique is of African American origin and means "a unique and powerful individual."
TYSEAN	American origin and means "a combination of Tyler and Sean."
TYSHUN	American origin and its meaning is unclear.
TYTAN	The first name Tytan likely originated from the English word "Titan," meaning a person or thing of great strength or significance.
TYUS	Means "chieftain, leader" and originates from Arabic or African cultures.
TYZIR	The first name TYZIR does not have a clear meaning or origin as it is not a commonly used name.
UBALDO	Germanic origin and it means "bold and intelligent; ruler of all."
UCHECHU KWU	UCHECHUKWU means "God's will" and it is of Nigerian Igbo origin.
UCHENNA	Means "God's plan" in Igbo and is of Nigerian origin.
UDAYVEER	Udayveer is an Indian name meaning "brave as the rising sun" and is of Sanskrit origin.
UGOCHUKWU	Means "God's glory" and it originates from the Igbo language of Nigeria.
UHTRED	Means "prosperity of glory" and originated from Old English.
ULRICH	The first name Ulrich originated from Germanic origins and means "prosperity and power of the wolf."
UMARBEK	Masculine given name of Turkic origin, meaning "ruling prince" or "noble ruler".
UMAYR	Arabic origin, means "young lion" or "little noble."
UMUT	Turkish name meaning "hope" and it is of Turkic origin.
UNNAMED	Means without a given name or identity, and its origin is English.
USAYD	Means "lion cub" and originates from Arabic.
USMON	The name Usmon originates from Arabic and means "faithful" or "loyal."
UZAIR	Means "helper" in Arabic and is derived from the Hebrew name Ezra, referencing a biblical figure.
VADHIR	The first name Vadhir is of Irish origin and it means "boldness" or "courage."
VAIBHAV	Means "prosperity" or "glory" and originates from the Indian subcontinent, particularly from Hindi and Sanskrit.
VALENTE	Means "brave" or "valiant" in Italian and Spanish, and it is derived from the Latin word "valens" which has the same meaning.
VALTTERI	Finnish name meaning "ruler of the army" and is derived from the name Walter.
VANSH	The name Vansh originates from the Indian Sanskrit word "vansh" which means "lineage" or "descendant."
VARDHAN	Means "giver of wealth" or "one who bestows prosperity" and it originates from the Sanskrit language.
VARIAN	The first name Varian is of Latin origin and means "versatile" or "changeable."
VASCO	Means "crow" and originates from the Latin word "vassus."
VASILEIOS	Means "royal" or "kingly" and it is of Greek origin.
VASILIJE	Means "king" and it originated from the Slavic form of the Greek name Basileios.
VASILIOS	Means "royal" and it is of Greek origin.
VEDANSH REDDY	Indian origin and it means "part of the divine, sun ray, and warrior-like."
VEDH	Indian origin and it means "knowledge" or "sacred scripture" in Sanskrit.
VENANCIO	Means "hunter" or "desire" and it originates from Latin.
VENIAMIN	Means "blessed" or "loved by God" and has its origins in Hebrew and Russian languages.
VENTURE	The name Ventura means "adventure" and originates from Latin.
VERSAI	The first name Versai is of unknown origin and meaning.

VETRI	Means "victory" and has origins in the Tamil language of India.
VIAANSH	The first name "Viaansh" is of Indian origin and means "part of the universe" or "divine".
VICTORIANO	The first name Victorian originates from the Latin name Victorius, meaning "victory" and "conqueror," and it denotes a person who is victorious and successful in their endeavors.
VICTORIOUS	Means "triumphant" and is of Latin origin.
VIDHART HREDDY	Compound Indian name meaning "possessor of knowledge" with roots in Hindu mythology.
VIDYUTH	Hindu boy's name of Sanskrit origin meaning "electricity" or "brilliance".
VIET	The first name "Viet" is of Vietnamese origin and it means "victorious" or "successful."
VIHAANR EDDY	Hindu name of Indian origin, meaning "brave and victorious," which combines the elements Vihaan, meaning "morning" or "dawn," and Reddy, a surname commonly associated with the Telugu-speaking people of India.
VIKRAM	Sanskrit origin and means "brave, powerful, or victorious."
VIKRAMA DITYA	Sanskrit origin, means "sun of valor" or "mighty warrior king" and is associated with legendary Hindu emperor King Vikramaditya from ancient times.
VIKRANTH	Indian origin and it means "brave, victorious."
VIKYATH	Means "famous or renowned" and originates from the Sanskrit language.
VINICIUS	Means "conqueror" or "victorious" and has Latin origins.
VINSON	Means "son of Vincent" and has English origins.
VIRAJREDDY	The meaning and origin of the first name Virajreddy is not readily available as it is a relatively uncommon name.
VIRANSH	Means "part of a brave warrior" and it originates from Sanskrit, an ancient Indo-Aryan language.
VIREN	Means "brave" or "heroic" and has Indian origins.
VIRGILIO	Means "flourishing" or "lively" and originates from Latin.
VIRLAN	The name Virlan originated as a modern invented name with no specific meaning.
VISERYS	Means "beloved king" and it is of Valyrian origin, popularized by the character Viserys Targaryen in the book and TV series Game of Thrones.
VISHAGAN	Traditional Indian name meaning "lord of the universe" and is of Hindu origin.
VISHNU	Means "all-pervading" or "the preserver" and it originates from Hindu mythology.
VISHRUTH	Means "celebrated" or "famous" and originates from Sanskrit.
VISHWAK	Indian origin and means "universal" or "of the whole world."
VISION	Means a clear mental image or foresight and is of English origin.
VLADISLAV	Slavic origin and means "ruler of glory" or "one who brings glory."
VOLODYMYR	Ukrainian name meaning "ruler of peace" and is of Slavic origin.
VOLVY	The meaning and origin of the first name Volvy is currently unclear as it does not appear to have a widely recognized meaning or origin.
VRAJ	Indian origin and means "divine place" or "sacred abode."
VUKAN	Means "wolf" and originates from Serbian and Croatian languages.
VYAS	The first name Vyas is of Indian origin and means "sage" or "learned person."
WAIKS	The first name "Waiks" does not have a widely recognized meaning or origin as it is uncommon and may not be of specific cultural or linguistic origin.
WAKINYAN	Means "thunder" and originates from the Lakota Sioux Native American tribe.
WALDEN	Means "valley of the Britons" and originated from Old English.
WALT	Means "ruler of the army" and originated as a short form of the name Walter, which in turn came from the Old Germanic elements "wald" meaning rule and "heri" meaning
WARRICK	Means "fortress" or "strong leader" and is of Old English origin.
WASEEM	Arabic name meaning "handsome" or "graceful," commonly given to baby boys.
WASHING TON	Means "from the settlement of Wassa" and originates from Old English.
WASIF	The name Wasif is derived from Arabic origin and means "describing someone who is capable, knowledgeable, or eloquent."
WEBSTER	The first name Webster is of English origin and means "a weaver of cloth" or "one who lives near a web or marsh."

WELDON	Means "hill near a well" and it originates from the Old English word "waella" (well) and "dūn" (hill).
WEYLIN	The first name Weylin is of Old English origin and means "from a reasonable place."
WHALEN	Surname derived from the Irish Gaelic name Ó Faoileáin, meaning "descendant of Faoileán," which itself means "seagull" or "plunderer."
WHEELER	The first name "Wheeler" originated from an occupational surname meaning "one who constructs or repairs wheels" and is of English origin.
WHIT	Means "white" and originated as a nickname or surname referring to a person with fair or light-colored hair or complexion.
WHITAKER	Means "white field" and is of English origin.
WHITFIELD	Whitfield is an English surname-derived first name, meaning "white field," likely referring to a location with white-colored soil or a peaceful, open field.
WHITMAN	Surname-derived first name of English origin, meaning "white man" or "fair-haired man".
WHITTEN	Modern English name likely derived from the Old English word "hwita," meaning white or fair, with a variety of possible meanings such as "white town" or "fair hill."
WHYATT	Variant of the name Wyatt, which has Old English origins and means "brave in battle."
WILBUR	Means "bright will" and originated from an Old English surname.
WILFORD	Means "willow tree ford" and has an English origin.
WILFREDO	Means "desires peace" and it is of Germanic origin.
WILHELM	Means "resolute protector" and has Germanic origins.
WILKES	Means "from the settlement of Will's estate" and has an English origin.
WILKIN	The first name Wilkin is of English origin and means "son of William" or "descendant of William."
WILLARD	Means "strong-willed" and has English origins.
WILLIAMSON	Means "son of William" and originated from English patronymic surnames, typically derived from male given names.
WILMAR	Means "famous will" and is of Germanic origin.
WILONDJA	The first name Wilondja is of African origin and its meaning is currently unknown.
WINCHESTER	The name Winchester originates from England and signifies a settlement or fortification by a Roman fort called Venta, later becoming the name of a historic city and a surname.
WINDELL	The name WindeLL originates from Old English, meaning "wanderer" or someone who lives near a winding stream or hill.
WINFIELD	Means "field of victory" and has an Old English origin.
WINTHROP	Means "friendly village" and has English roots.
WINTON	Means "from the friend's settlement" and it originated from Old English.
WISDOM	Virtue and quality of having good judgment and knowledge, of Old English origin.
WOLFRAM	Means "wolf raven" or "famous wolf" and originates from Germanic languages.
WOODENSKY	The meaning and origin of the first name Woodensky are unclear as it is a rare and unique name with no specific information available.
WOODFORD	Means "from the wooded ford" and has English origins.
WOODLAND	Means "dweller of the forest" and originates from the English language.
WOODLEY	The first name Woodley derives from an English surname meaning "clearing in the woods," and it is of Anglo-Saxon origin.
WOODS	Means "dweller near the woods" and has English origins.
WOODSON	Means "son of the woods" and originated as an English surname that was derived from a place name.
WORTH	Means "valuable" or "worthy" and it has an Old English origin.
WRANGLER	Means a person who herds and manages horses or cattle and is of English origin.
WRIGHT	Means "craftsman" or "builder" and has its origin in Old English.
WRIGLEY	Wrigley is an English surname turned first name, meaning "dragon clearing" or "sheep meadow," derived from Old English elements.
WULFRIC	Means "wolf power" and it originates from Old English.
WYNDHAM	Means "from the windy village" and has English origins.
XAIVER	Means "bright, new house" and originates from the Basque language.
XAVIUS	Means "new house" and has Latin origins.
XERXES	Means "ruler over heroes" and originates from ancient Persian/Iranian culture.

XZANDER	Modern American name derived from the name Alexander, meaning "defender of mankind" in Greek.
XZAVION	Modern variation of the name Xavier, originating from the Basque language meaning "new house" or "bright."
YACOUB	Masculine given name of Arabic origin, meaning "Jacob" or "supplanter."
YADER	Means "river" or "stream" and has Spanish and Hebrew origins.
YAHSHUA	Means "Yahweh is salvation" and it originates from ancient Hebrew.
YAHWEH	The first name YAHWEH, of Hebrew origin, means "He is" or "I am who I am," and it is the personal name of God in the Hebrew Bible.
YAJAT	Means "sacrificed" or "offered" and has origins in the Sanskrit language.
YAMIN	Means "right hand" or "blessed" and it has Arabic origins.
YANCARLOS	The first name "Yancarlos" is of Spanish origin and it is a combination of the names "Yan" and "Carlos", meaning "God is gracious" and "free man" respectively.
YANDIEL	The meaning and origin of the first name Yandiel is not available in the current database.
YANDRIEL	Means "God is my judge" and has its origin in Hebrew.
YANIS	French variant of the name Yannis, which is a form of John and means "God is gracious" in Hebrew.
YANKY	Hebrew-derived nickname for the given name Yehoshua, meaning "God is salvation," traditionally used in Jewish communities.
YAQUB	Arabic origin and means "supplanter" or "one who replaces."
YARDEN	Means "river of judgment" in Hebrew and is of biblical origin.
YAROSLAV	Means "fierce and glorious" and it originates from Slavic languages, with "yar" meaning fierce and "slav" referring to glory or fame.
YASHVEER	Means "brave and victorious" and originates from Indian/Sanskrit roots.
YASHWIN	Indian origin and means "glorious" or "filled with fame."
YASUO	Means "peaceful man" or "calm man" and has Japanese origin.
YATHARTH	Unisex Indian name meaning "truth" or "reality," derived from the Sanskrit language.
YAXIEL	Means "gift of God" and its origin can be traced back to the Hebrew language.
YAZHAN	Means "hero" and has Indian origins.
YAZID	Masculine Arabic name meaning "increasing" or "growing" and it originated from Islamic culture.
YEAB	The first name Yeab has origins in the Ethiopian Amharic language and means "he who is powerful".
YECHEZKEL	Means "God will strengthen" and it originated from the Hebrew language.
YEDIDYA	Means "beloved of God" in Hebrew and has biblical origins, as it is the given name of King Solomon in the Old Testament.
YEFRY	Spanish boys' name that is likely a variant of the name Jeffrey, which originated from the Germanic name Geofrey, meaning "peaceful ruler."
YEHIA	The first name Yehia is of Arabic origin and means "to be alive" or "to live."
YEICOB	Variant of the Hebrew name Jacob, meaning "supplanter" or "holder of the heel," and originates from the Old Testament.
YEIDEN	Hebrew origin and means "gift of God."
YEILER	Spanish name that is of uncertain origin and meaning.
YEISON	Variant of the name Jason, which is of Greek origin and means "healer" or "to heal."
YELTSIN	The first name Yeltsin originated as a patronymic surname in Russia and means "son of Yeltsy."
YERACHMIEL	Means "God will have compassion" and it has Hebrew origins.
YEREMI	Means "may God uplift" and it is of Hebrew origin.
YESHAYA	Means "God is salvation" and originates from Hebrew.
YETZAEL	The first name Yetzael is of Hebrew origin and it means "God's arrow" or "divine arrow."
YEZEN	The name Yezan means "to prosper" or "increase" and is of Arabic origin.
YEZIEL	Means "God exists" and its origin is Hebrew.
YICHEN	Chinese name meaning "artistic morning" or "elegant morning."
YIRMEYAH	Means "God will uplift" in Hebrew and it originates from the biblical prophet Jeremiah.
YISSOCHOR	Hebrew origin and means "gifted" or "rewarded," referring to someone who is blessed or fortunate.

YITZHAK Means "he will laugh" in Hebrew and it originated from the Bible, where it was the given name of Isaac, the biblical patriarch.

YIYANG The first name Yiyang is of Chinese origin and means "bright sun."

YOAKIN Hebrew name meaning "God increases" or "God will establish," and is a variant of the name Joachim.

YOANDRI Means "God is gracious" and has Spanish origins.

YOAV Means "the Lord is Father" and has Hebrew origins.

YOBANI The first name Yobani originated from the Hebrew name "Yehovah" meaning "God is gracious" and is of biblical origin.

YOCHANAN Means "God is gracious" and its origin is Hebrew.

YOHANCE Means "God is gracious" and originates from Hebrew.

YOHANNES Male given name of Ethiopian and Eritrean origin, meaning "God is gracious" or "God is merciful."

YONAEL Means "God answers" and originated from Hebrew.

YORDIN The given name Yordin is of Bulgarian origin and its meaning is not available.

YORICK Male given name of Danish origin meaning "long farm" or "yew farm," most famously associated with the Shakespearean character in Hamlet.

YORIDAN Irish origin and means "little dark-haired one."

YORK Means "yew tree estate" and it originated from Old English, derived from the city of York in northern England.

YOSHI The first name Yoshi is of Japanese origin and means "good, respectful, or joyful."

YOSHMEL Hebrew origin and means "God hears."

YOSOHN The first name Yosohn is of Hebrew origin and means "God is gracious."

YOUNIS Means "Jonah" and originates from Hebrew and Arabic cultures.

YOUSSOUF Means "God will increase" and originates from the Arabic language.

YOVANY Spanish name meaning "gift from God" and is a variant of the name Yohanni, which is of Hebrew origin.

YSMAEL Variant of Ishmael, derived from Hebrew origins, meaning "God hears."

YUNUEN Female Spanish name of Nahuatl origin meaning "beautiful".

YUVANSH Means "part of the youth" and is of Indian origin.

YUVEN Means "youthful" or "eternally young" and is of Tamil origin.

YUVINREDDY Means "young prince" and is of Indian origin.

YUXUAN Means "jade spring" in Chinese, and it has Chinese origins.

ZACARI Modern variation of the Hebrew name Zechariah, meaning "God remembers."

ZACARIAS Means "remembered by God" and it has Hebrew origins.

ZACCHAEUS Means "pure" or "righteous" and its origin can be traced back to Hebrew.

ZADKIEL Means "righteousness of God" and is of Hebrew origin.

ZADOK The name Zadok originates from Hebrew and means "righteous" or "just".

ZADQUIEL The first name Zadquiel has a Hebrew origin and means "righteousness of God" or "one who is just in the sight of God."

ZAGREUS Means "hunter" and originates from Greek mythology, referring to a divine figure associated with hunting and rebirth.

ZAHEEN Means "intelligent" or "clever" in Arabic and it originates from the Middle East.

ZAHKARI Hebrew origin and it means "remembered by God."

ZAHKI African origin and means "bright and intelligent."

ZAHMERE Means "gift of beauty" and its origin is uncertain.

ZAKARIAH Means "God has remembered" and it has origins in the Hebrew language.

ZAKHAI Hebrew name meaning "remembered by God" and has roots in biblical and Hebrew traditions.

ZAKIAH Means "pure" or "innocent" in Arabic and has origins in Islamic culture.

ZAKIUS The first name Zakius is derived from the Hebrew name Zacchaeus, meaning "pure" or "innocent," and it has biblical origins as a name mentioned in the Gospel of Luke.

ZAKIYUS Means "intelligent" or "pure" and has Arabic origins.

ZAKYE Modern variant of the Hebrew name Zechariah, meaning "God remembers" or "Yahweh remembers," and it is of biblical origin.

ZAKYIUS Modern American name of uncertain origin, possibly a creative variation of the name Zachary.

ZAKYRIE American origin and its meaning is currently unknown or not widely documented.

ZALMEN Yiddish name meaning "peaceful" or "man of peace", originating from the Hebrew name Solomon.

ZAMIEN Means "one who has been observed" and its origin is uncertain.

ZANDEN The first name Zanden has a modern and unique sound, with an unknown origin, which may be a variant or derivative of other names.

ZAQUEO Means "God remembers" and it originates from the Hebrew name Zaccheus found in the Bible.

ZAREH Means "golden" or "shining" and is of Armenian origin.

ZAVEON The meaning of the name Zaveon is "light of God" and it is of American origin.

ZAVIYAR The meaning and origin of the first name Zaviyar are unknown as it does not have a widely recognized history or background.

ZAYDON Unknown origin and meaning, as it does not have a widely recognized source or established significance.

ZAYDRIAN Means "unique gift from God" and has the origin of blending the names Zayden and Adrian.

ZAYLAND The name Zayland originated as a modern American name and its meaning is currently uncertain.

ZAYVIER Means "bright, splendid" and it is a modern variant of the name Xavier, derived from the Basque place name "Etcheberria," meaning "the new house."

ZEAL Means passionate enthusiasm or fervor, and has its origin in the English language.

ZEBADIAH Means "gift of God" and it originates from Hebrew.

ZEBEDEE Means "gift of God" and originated from Hebrew.

ZEBULON Means "dwelling" or "habitation" and originates from the Hebrew name Zebulun found in the Bible.

ZEDEKIAH Means "Yahweh is righteous" and it has Hebrew origins.

ZEESHAN Means "dignified" or "respected" and it originates from Persian and Arabic languages.

ZEFERINO Means "triumphant" and originates from the Spanish and Portuguese languages.

ZEIN Means "beauty" or "ornament" and originates from Arabic and Greek.

ZEKARI Means "God will remember" and it has African origins.

ZELDRIS Means "powerful ruler" and originates from the Hebrew language.

ZELIG Means "blessed" or "fortunate" and has Hebrew origins.

ZENITH Means the highest point or culmination; it is of Arabic and English origin.

ZENON Means "gift of Zeus" and is of Greek origin.

ZEPHYRUS The first name Zephyrus, of Greek origin, means "west wind" and is derived from the Greek god of the west wind in Greek mythology.

ZEPPLIN Means "a strong and powerful airship" and it originates from the German surname Zeppelin, which was named after the inventor of the airship, Ferdinand von Zeppelin.

ZHYEIR Modern and unique American name of uncertain origin, potentially derived from a combination of elements or made-up sounds.

ZIARE Means "river" in Arabic and is of Swahili origin.

ZIDANE The first name Zidane originates from Arabic and means "increaser" or "abundance."

ZIGMUND Means "victorious protector" and is of Slavic origin.

ZIMRI Means "my music" or "my praise" and originates from Hebrew and biblical sources.

ZIYAIR Modern American name of uncertain origin, likely a variant spelling of the Arabic name Zayir, meaning "visitor" or "one who visits."

ZIYON Hebrew origin and means "God's own nation" or "the highest point."

ZOHAIB Means "radiant" or "luminous" and has Arabic origins.

ZOLTAN Means "life" or "sultan" in Hungarian, and it originates from the Hungarian language.

ZORAIZ Means "rays of light" and it originates from the Arabic language.

ZORAWAR Punjabi name meaning "brave and powerful" that originated in northern India.

ZUBAYR Means "strong and courageous" and originates from Arabic.

ZUKO The first name Zuko is of African origin and means "esteem, respect" in Zulu.

ZULQARNAIN Means "possessor of two horns" and has its origin in Arabic and Islamic history.

ZYAHIR	Means "shining" or "bright" and it originates from Arabic.
ZYDEN	Means "from the valley of olive trees" and has a modern American origin.
ZYERE	American origin and its meaning is currently unknown.
ZYGMUNT	Means "victorious protector" and originates from Old High German and Polish.
ZYHAIRE	Modern, invented name with no established meaning or origin.
ZYIER	Uncertain origin and meaning, possibly a modern variation or phonetic spelling of existing names.
ZYKING	The name Zyking does not have a widely recognized meaning or origin as it appears to be a unique and uncommon name.
ZYMARION	The first name Zymarion is of modern origin and does not have a universally recognized meaning.
ZYMEIR	Means "one who is noble" and it has an uncertain origin.
ZYMIER	Modern American creation and its meaning is unclear.

Printed in Dunstable, United Kingdom